BOXING
ENCYCLOPEDIA

Nigel Benn

BOXING
ENCYCLOPEDIA

Barry J. Hugman & Peter Arnold

TW

First published in 1993 by
TW Publications
24a Queen Square
North Curry
Taunton
Somerset TA3 6LE

TW Publications is an imprint of Football Directories

This book is a product of FORSTER Books

Designed by Bob Bickerton

Typeset by Tradespools Limited

Printed in Great Britain by Ian Allan Printing Ltd,
Coombelands House, Addlestone, Surrey KT15 1HY

ISBN: 1-86983300-7

PICTURE CREDITS

The authors personally wish
to thank the following
photographers and
photographic agencies –
Action Images (4), Allsport
(5), Chris Bevan (1), Tom
Casino (4), Les Clark (3),
Chris Farina (11), Peter
Goldfield (6), Harry
Goodwin (2), Professional
Sport (1), Derek Rowe (2),
Sporting Pictures (1) – for
helping to illustrate the
Boxing Encyclopedia. Our
thanks also go to Derek
O'Dell and George Zeleny
for making their exclusive
photographic libraries
available to us in time of
need.

Marvin Hagler v Tony Sibson

INTRODUCTION

Boxing has had its practitioners and its followers for centuries, and modern champions have been documented since James Figg in 1719. In recent times it has frequently been said to be enjoying its swansong on the grounds that such a barbaric practice – two men trying to knock each other senseless – has no place in 'civilisation'.

However civilisation's inventions, particularly television, ensure that boxing has more followers each year, and the big fights are watched by millions. Indeed, what makes boxing so fascinating is, in fact, its primitiveness. The boxer enters the ring not with a safe career path mapped out for him but facing the prospect of real pain and oblivion. He is alone with only his skill and courage to help him – indeed boxers sometimes say that the only friend they have at that time is the opponent, even though each man's task is to separate the other from his senses. The boxer is the modern gladiator. 'Pressure' and 'courage' – words used so frequently in sports like tennis, golf, even snooker, have completely different meanings when applied to boxing.

Boxing is unlike these other sports also in that it does not lend itself to precise records. There is not even agreement, for example, about whether certain fights were for world titles or not. And not only are there still great champions whose records are incomplete, there are even some, like Archie Moore and Sonny Liston, whose dates of birth are far from certain.

However, none of this matters too much because bare records do not tell the complete story of a boxer. These days, with so many self-appointed bodies sanctioning world title bouts, it is possible for a boxer like Tommy Hearns to win six 'world' titles, which does not, of course, give him a better record than Henry Armstrong who, in other days, won only three and was beaten 20 times in his career. Nor does Armstrong's 20 defeats make him a lesser champion than Rocky Marciano, who was never beaten. Armstrong, after all, fought 49 times – Marciano's career total – in less than 2½ years in the middle of his long career.

A boxer achieves greatness not through records or figures but through performance: the demonstration of his skill, toughness, bravery and spirit in the ring. He might be at his best for only three or four years, and it is the contests he has in this period which establish his reputation. Occasionally a great boxer finds an opponent of similar charisma, and an outstanding contest emerges.

In this encyclopedia, therefore, the entries are mainly for the boxers and the battles. Some 136 of the greatest boxers in history have their stories told, and there are descriptions of 31 of the contests which, over the years, have stirred the fans. Miscellaneous entries cover such things as Rules, Medicine v Boxing, Prize Fighting, Upsets etc. It is hoped the result is worthy of all those – champions, near-champions and 'opponents' – who have climbed through the ropes for our enjoyment.

Mike Tyson v Razor Ruddock

AGE

Oldest

The oldest boxer to have fought in a bona fide contest is believed to be the American Walter Edgerton, who was 63 when he fought John Henry Johnson on 4 December 1916.

Jem Mace, the 'Swaffham Gypsy', fought Charley Mitchell on 7 February 1890 aged 58 years 10 months.

The oldest boxers to win world titles for the first time at the eight traditional weights are:

Heavyweight Jersey Joe Walcott (1951) 37 years 6 months

Light-heavyweight Bob Fitzsimmons (1903) 40 years 6 months

Middleweight Joey Giardello (1963) 33 years 5 months

Welterweight Jack Britton (1915) 29 years 8 months

Lightweight Claude Noel (1981, WBA) 30 years 11 months

Featherweight Jackie Wilson (1941) 32 years 6 months

Bantamweight Johnny Buff (1921) 33 years 3 months

Flyweight Dado Marino (1950) 33 years 11 months

Note: In some cases a champion moving up a weight, or winning a title for the second (or in the case of Sugar Ray Robinson, fifth) time might be older than the examples given.

The oldest man to hold a world championship at any weight was Archie Moore, who was 48 years 3 months when stripped by the NYSAC and EBU of his light-heavyweight championship in 1962.

The oldest boxer to make his debut as a professional was Dr Herbert Odom, who was 46 when he fought Eddie Partee (19) in 1979.

The oldest boxer who was formerly a world champion was Bob Fitzsimmons, who was 50 years 9 months when he retired in 1914.

Youngest

The youngest boxer to have fought as a professional is believed to be Len Harvey, who was 12 years 6 months when he made his debut on 2 January 1920.

The youngest boxers to win world titles at the eight traditional weights are:

Heavyweight Mike Tyson (1986, WBC) 20 years 5 months

Light-heavyweight John Henry Lewis (1935) 21 years 5 months

Middleweight Al McCoy (1914, USA version) 19 years 6 months

Welterweight Pipino Cuevas (1976, WBA) 18 years 7 months

Lightweight Mando Ramos (1969) 20 years 3 months

Featherweight Tony Canzoneri (1927, New York version) 19 years

Bantamweight Pedlar Palmer (1895) 19 years

Flyweight Fighting Harada (1962) 19 years 6 months

Georges Carpentier was only 15 years 11 months when he won the French lightweight title on 22 December 1909. He was also the youngest holder of a European title when he won the European welterweight title on 23 October 1911. He was aged 17 years 9 months.

Wilfred Benitez is the youngest world champion when the 'in-between' weights are included. He was 17 years 6 months old when winning the WBA light-welterweight title on 6 March 1976.

MUHAMMAD ALI

born: (Cassius Clay) 17 January 1942, Louisville, Kentucky, USA

Muhammad Ali, who was then Cassius Marcellus Clay, took up boxing when he was 12 and his new $60 bicycle was stolen. The patrolman to whom he reported it, Joe Martin, persuaded him to attend his local gym. Cassius won his first bout six weeks later, progressed impressively through his teens, and in 1960 proudly won an Olympic gold medal in Rome in the light-heavyweight class. The exuberant, garrulous 18-year-old wore the medal at all times until, back in the States, he was insulted and refused service by whites in a restaurant. He and his friends were followed and taunted, and Clay in disgust threw his much-prized medal in the Ohio River, calling it 'phoney gold'. The deeply patriotic Clay never forgot this example of where blacks stood in the USA.

He had previously accepted the sponsorship of a group of white Louisville millionaires who signed Angelo Dundee to manage him. On 29 October 1960 he outpointed Tunney Hunsaker over six rounds at Louisville and was launched on his professional career. Always self-confident to the point of being a braggart, Clay made a box-office virtue of this when he adopted the publicity technique of a wrestler whom he met on a TV show, Gorgeous George. He began to predict in very poor poetry how he would beat his opponents, and in which round.

After 15 impressive victories in two years, Clay met his most formidable foe yet, Archie Moore, in November 1962, predicting 'Moore would go in four'. Moore was an all-time great ex-light-heavyweight champion, but was now at least 46. 'Ancient' Archie did, indeed, fall in four. In June 1963 Clay had his first overseas contest, facing Henry Cooper in London, winning on cuts after being all but knocked out himself. His next fight, 25 November 1964, was against Sonny Liston for the world title. He hyped himself up for this encounter, and shook the boxing world by beating the man he called 'the Ugly Bear'. Liston retired with a damaged shoulder and a severely baffled ego after six rounds (Clay had predicted eight).

Although he had just failed to fulfil his prediction that he would become the youngest-ever heavyweight champion (Patterson was 12 months younger), Clay was now utterly his own man. He renounced his name, a slave name dating back to the family's 19th century 'owner', joined the Black Muslim movement and became 'Muhammad Ali'. He beat Liston in a mysterious return fight when Liston went down after a punch many didn't see, and was counted out in farcical circumstances. He then tormented for 12 rounds Floyd Patterson, a former champion whose demeanour towards whites he didn't

RIGHT: Muhammad Ali in real aggressive mood, punishing Floyd Patterson.

BELOW: In typical playful pose.

like, overcame four challengers in Canada and Europe, including Henry Cooper, and knocked out Cleveland Williams, a fight in which he demonstrated his greatness. He showed another side of himself when battering Ernie Terrell, whom the WBA had installed as champion because they disapproved of Ali's return clause for the Liston fight. The unfortunate Terrell refused to use Ali's new name and Ali continually asked him 'What's my name?' as he punished him for 15 rounds while declining to effect the knock-out.

Ali's most dangerous opponent hereabouts was the US Army. Ali refused to join them in Vietnam, claiming he was a minister of the cloth and that he had no quarrels with the Viet Cong. Sentenced to five years imprisonment, he found his licence withdrawn by state after state, and his knockout of Zora Folley in March 1967 proved his last contest for over 3½ years.

Ali won his appeal, opinion over Vietnam changed, and he was granted a licence to fight Jerry Quarry in Atlanta in October 1970. Five months later he challenged Joe Frazier, who had succeeded to the crown he still regarded as his own. It was a unique fight between two unbeaten world heavyweight champions. Ali, who not surprisingly had lost some snap during his lay-off, lost a decision – his first defeat.

In his great days Ali's style had been described: he 'floats like a butterfly and stings like a bee'. For a very big man (6ft 3in, 230lb) Ali was amazingly light on his feet. He was brilliant defensively, but would take a punch if one got through. Because of his fast style he rarely knocked out opponents with a single punch, but he was not a light puncher and stopped many of his title challengers. After his enforced retirement, he was more static in style but built up a list of impressive victims on his come-back

trail. He suffered a setback in March 1973 when he lost to Ken Norton, who broke his jaw but couldn't stop him. He avenged this defeat six months later and outpointed his other conqueror, Joe Frazier, who had meanwhile lost the world title to George Foreman.

On 30 October 1974 Ali challenged Foreman in Kinshasa, and once again surprised the boxing world by taking his old title back with an eighth-round knockout.

Ali took on allcomers, dominating the division as before. In 3½ years he defended ten times, beating once again challengers Frazier and Norton, the only men to have beaten him. In February 1978 the 36-year-old came up against Leon Spinks, 11 years his junior, and was outspeeded, but he easily won the title back again seven months later. He retired as the first man to win the heavyweight title three times, but in 1980 he was persuaded to challenge Larry Holmes, the WBC champion.

With hindsight, it is possible to suspect that the Parkinson's Disease which became obvious soon after he retired, had already begun to affect him. He withdrew after ten rounds, his only stoppage, and after one more contest, a fifth career defeat, he retired.

Muhammad Ali is most people's choice as the greatest of all heavyweights. He was certainly the most famous boxer of all time. **Overall record: 61 contests, 56 wins, 5 defeats**

See also: Ali v Cooper, Ali v Foreman, Ali v Frazier, Ali v Liston

MUHAMMAD ALI V HENRY COOPER

**18 June 1963, London
21 May 1966, London**

Ali was still Cassius Clay when he arrived in London to meet British champion Henry Cooper in June 1963. He was one fight away from meeting Sonny Liston for the world title. His publicity

antics were already well-known to the British, and he was regarded as an amiable eccentric. While Clay was hated in his native country, the British were happy to laugh at him.

Henry Cooper was the British and Empire champion, and half-way to becoming the most popular of British boxers. He had been boxing professionally for nine years, and had another eight to come. But it was a punch he was to throw the night he met Clay at Wembley that most helped along his reputation as Uncle 'Enry, the national figure.

Clay forfeited a lot of the goodwill the public felt for him by calling Cooper a 'bum'. He said he would go in five. Fans told Henry that he must shut that big mouth. When Clay entered the ring wearing a crown and flowing robes as if he were the king of England the numbers who wanted to see him dethroned increased.

Clay boxed well in the first four rounds and managed to get enough slashing blows to Cooper's face to start the blood flowing copiously from a gash above his left eye, the sort of cut he suffered frequently in his career. Indeed it seemed that, in the third and fourth rounds, Clay was just concentrating on keeping the blood flowing nicely preparatory to finishing the fight in the forecast fifth.

All the plans nearly came to grief near the end of the fourth. Cooper managed to get Clay with his back to the ropes. A favourite defensive technique of Clay was to drop his hands and lean back before skipping away. This time, as Cooper led with a jab, Clay moved to avoid the expected right cross. The ropes hampered him and Cooper surprised him with a long left hook, his favourite punch. It was the punch known by his Cockney friends as 'Enery's 'Ammer. It landed on Clay's chin, and Clay subsided down the ropes, his right arm hooked over the middle rope. His eyes were glazed. At the count of 'four' the bell rang to rescue him.

Clay rose on wobbly legs and his manager Angelo Dundee had to run round the apron of the ring to guide him back to his corner. Clay looked as if he would not recover as he sat slumped on his stool, with Dundee trying to revive him with smelling salts and water poured over his head. It was a small split in Clay's glove which saved him. It had been there for most of the contest, but now Dundee stuck his finger in it and started to make it longer. When it was big enough, Dundee began to shout at the referee and officials, pointing to the glove and insisting on a new pair. While everybody examined the glove, precious minutes were lost to Cooper. In the end, it was decided that the glove was OK, despite Dundee's handiwork (although Dundee thinks there were no spare ones anyway). The fight continued, but by now Clay had recovered his senses.

Clay's prophecy was fulfilled, because Cooper's corner had not been able to staunch the blood from his cut, and soon his face was such a gory mess that the referee had to stop it.

Clay beat Liston in his next fight and became champion, continuing one of the greatest careers in boxing history. It might have been slightly different if his manager hadn't saved him from a probable knockout by Cooper. At least Clay withdrew his remark about Cooper being a 'bum' and gave him a title shot on the Arsenal football ground at Highbury in May 1966. By then he had repaired his image with the British public, who never lost the affection they had for him. Cooper fought well, and always thought he had the style to beat Ali, as by then the champion was called, but the cuts defeated him again, this time in the sixth round.

MUHAMMAD ALI V GEORGE FOREMAN

30 October 1974, Kinshasa, Zaire

George Foreman, the world heavyweight champion, seemed unbeatable. Since turning professional after winning the Olympic gold medal he had had 40 contests, and only three men had gone the distance with him, all in his first year. He had won the championship by knocking Joe Frazier clean off his feet on the way to a second round victory that saw Frazier down six times. His first challenger, Joe Roman, did not last the first round, and the second, Ken Norton, was despatched in the second. Foreman at 6ft 3in and over 15 stone, was regarded as possibly the hardest hitting boxer in history. There were many who thought that Ali, in his 33rd year, was in danger of being seriously hurt. He was a former champion who had been forced to give up the title for refusing to join the US Army and who had been four years on the comeback trail after over three years inactivity.

Ali's strengths were speed and ringcraft, defensive boxing of the highest calibre interspersed with damaging blows: 'floating like a butterfly and stinging like a bee'.

The fight was the first fight of such stature to be staged in Africa. It was

backed by the government, and a 60,000 crowd as well as the television millions watched it. A cut eye suffered by Foreman in training postponed it for a few days, during which time Ali's flair for publicity had built him a great following among the locals. Nevertheless Foreman was a long odds-on favourite with the betting men.

Ali was actually the same height as Foreman and four pounds heavier, but Foreman looked the more powerful as he marched into Ali from the opening bell, always attempting to throw his big right. Ali, to everybody's surprise including Foreman's, did not dance. Instead he backed off, even to the ropes, and either grabbed Foreman, denying him the space to measure his blows, or slid along the ropes to take the impetus from them. It was what he later described as his 'rope-a-dope' technique.

Ali deliberately took many blows to his ribs, and there were times when it seemed Foreman must overpower him. But at the critical times Ali, from his flat-footed stance, would flick out a fast counter punch, then cover up, all the time just frustrating Foreman from getting set enough to deliver the blow which would signal the beginning of the end.

From the fifth it was noticeable that a subtle change was coming over the bout, and for the first time the ringside experts thought Ali could win. His blows began to have authority while Foreman looked as if he were tiring from the many ineffectual punches he was throwing. By the eighth the champion was obviously bereft of ideas, and was lumbering after Ali, still trying to land the big punch which would settle it. Suddenly Ali switched to offence and a succession of hooks stopped Foreman in his tracks. A left followed by a downward chopping right sent the by now exhausted and demoralised Foreman to

ALI sways back to avoid a Foreman left in the 'Rumble in the Jungle'.

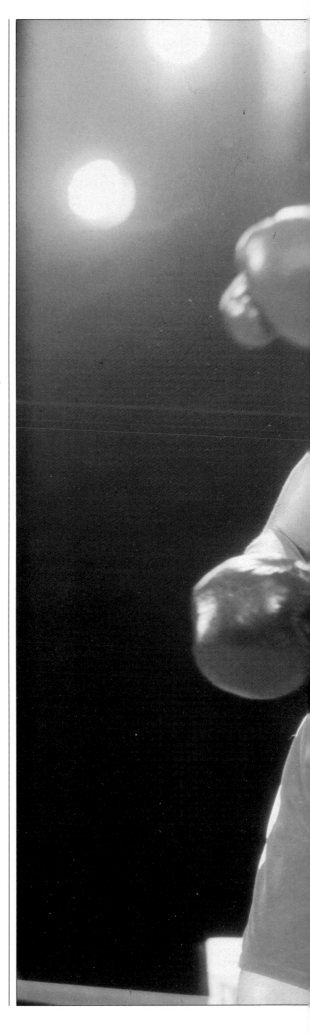

the canvas face down. He rolled on his back and heard his corner telling him to rise, but he could not beat the count.

Ali was champion for the second time, winning the title more than ten years after winning it for the first time. On both occasions he had beaten a man thought to be unbeatable. This time, when it was expected he could not last the pace, it was his six-years-younger opponent who had wilted. It was a triumph of boxing intelligence over youth and strength.

MUHAMMAD ALI V JOE FRAZIER

**8 March 1971, New York
28 January 1974, New York
1 October 1975, Manila**

Muhammad Ali and Joe Frazier had three great fights. Their styles complemented each other. Frazier, short with thick legs, advanced all the time like a tank, throwing powerful hooks at Ali, Ali danced and dodged and grabbed and countered, and occasionally stopped the tank's advance with barrages of fast punches.

Their first meeting was described, naturally, as the Fight of the Century. Both were unbeaten heavyweight champions, an unprecedented encounter. Ali was on his third contest since the three-year break forced on him by the authorities for his anti-Vietnam War stance. Frazier was the WBC champion. Only 20,455 fans could get inside Madison Square Garden to see it live, but 1.3 million others watched on closed-circuit television.

Frazier, 3½ inches shorter and with a five-inch disadvantage in reach, flailed in from the start, and while for most of the time his fists swept the air, occasionally he caught Ali on the ropes, getting under his guard and battering him with hooks. Ali survived this onslaught and in the eighth round fought back to wobble Frazier. The fight was settled in the 11th when Frazier caught Ali with a hook to the chin and Ali just managed to survive the round. Ali fought off Frazier for the next three rounds but

was dropped by a left hook in the last. Again he fought back bravely, but at the end went off to hospital with a badly swollen jaw. The almost equally disfigured Frazier won a unanimous points verdict.

The two met again nearly three years later. Frazier had, in the meantime, been relieved of the title by George Foreman, his only defeat. Ali had been much the busier boxer and had won the title of a new body, the North American Boxing Federation. He had suffered a second defeat, by Ken Norton who broke his jaw, but had avenged it in his next contest. The two provided another huge success for Madison Square Garden, Frazier challenging for the NABF title. The fight followed a similar pattern to the first but this time Ali was sharper and managed to dominate the early and late rounds, Frazier's mid-fight rally not being enough to prevent Ali winning a unanimous decision.

By 1975 Ali was champion again, and a challenge from Frazier was a natural. This time they went to Manila, in the Philippines, for the 'Thrilla in Manila'. Although they were both veterans, each had still lost only once, discounting their losses to each other.

Ali confidently expected to win easily this time, and stood his ground from the beginning. He hit Frazier at will, buckled him in the first round and almost stopped him in the third. But Frazier kept boxing and, in the sixth, shook Ali with two tremendous hooks to the face causing Ali to change tactics and revert to defence. By the tenth the fight was even, with Ali showing the more distress. In the 11th round, however, Ali's long shots began to change the shape of Frazier's face as, at last, Frazier began to show the effects of his earlier punishment and slow down. By the 14th only Frazier's courage kept him upright, as Ali tried his hardest to finish the fight. But Frazier could no longer see and his manager, Eddie Futch, would not allow him to go out for the 15th round.

Ali, who himself sank to the canvas exhausted at the

end, said his state was as close to dying as he could imagine. Frazier fought only twice more and, though the amazing Ali continued for six more years, he did not reach these heights again.

MUHAMMAD ALI V SONNY LISTON

**25 February 1964, Miami
25 May 1965, Lewiston, Maine**

Sonny Liston had had two heavyweight title fights and won them both in a grand total of four minutes 16 seconds. Probably Floyd Patterson had already lost those fights when Liston first stared balefully into his eyes. Liston was a master of psychology, who sometimes stuffed towels under his robe to make himself look even bigger and more malevolent than he was. His well known underworld connections helped his air of menace. He had few supporters among the fans, yet when the 22-year-old Muhammad Ali (then known as Cassius Clay) challenged him for the title, the majority probably wanted him to win. The upstart Clay, who bragged about himself at every opportunity, was disliked even more.

Clay had taunted Liston in the weeks before the fight to the extent that Liston (with his bodyguards handy) had slapped his face. Clay's act was seen as bravado arising from fear, and this seemed to be confirmed at the weigh-in where he caused bedlam, screaming at Liston and prancing around in a hyper-active state. Clay had to be restrained and forced to sit down and the boxing commission's doctor found his blood-pressure so abnormal that he wanted to postpone the contest. Most critics put the performance down to fear, but Clay later claimed that it was carefully calculated to upset Liston. If so, it no doubt worked. Liston, who was 7-1 favourite in the betting, expected his opponents to be cowed before the bout – he now had to face one who was a maniac. Clay even called Liston a 'chump' when Liston went into his eyeball-to-eyeball act while the

referee gave instructions.

Liston began the fight as he always did, aiming his blows as if expecting that the first to land would start his opponent on the way to oblivion, as usual. But Clay, who was only seven pounds lighter than Liston and much faster than anyone Liston had met before, danced away. It was not until the second round that Liston landed a good left, but Clay was landing good jabs, too, one of which nicked a small cut on Liston's cheek. At the end of the third round, Liston sat on his stool for the first time.

Clay kept out of trouble in the fourth but, back in his corner, he complained of a substance that was troubling his eyes. When manager Angelo Dundee wiped his face Clay began screaming that he wanted to quit. Suddenly he could hardly see and demanded that the gloves be cut off. Dundee pushed him out for the fifth.

There has been a lot of speculation about the substance which near-blinded Clay and it was always assumed that it was liniment from Liston's corner which had got onto his gloves. However years later information from an ex-corner man suggested that there might well have been a substance that the corner kept in reserve for emergencies, and had even used before. In any event Clay spent the fifth round keeping Liston at bay, sometimes keeping his long left on Liston's forehead as he danced around him. As Clay's eyes gradually cleared the ponderous champion realised his chance was disappearing. A doctor checked Clay's eyes in the interval before the sixth round, in which Clay went on the offensive, pouring punches into Liston's face and taking the occasional reply without problems.

At the end of the round, Liston sat on his stool and told his corner he'd had enough. The corner men still prepared him for action but, at the bell, Liston repeated that he had had enough. He retired. He claimed his shoulder was injured, and a doctor later corroborated the fact, but it seems more likely that Liston realised before anybody else in boxing just

how good the man before him was. He knew his title had gone.

Clay acted as if the weigh-in hysteria was not play-acting at all. He pranced round the ring, shouting at the press who had underrated him, telling everybody that he was the greatest.

The return fight had even more mystery about it than the first. Liston's personality was such that he was again installed as the betting favourite, but only at about 7-5 this time. There was trouble in getting a licence to hold the contest in the more usual fight towns because of Liston's criminal record, and the fight was held in St Dominic's Hall at Lewiston, Maine, before only 2,434 spectators – the fewest ever for a heavyweight title fight.

After a little feeling out, Ali (he had changed his name directly after becoming champion) landed a right to Liston's head. Many never saw the blow, although the television replay showed one had landed. But was it hard enough to fell Liston? Few critics since have thought so, but Liston went down. Ali stood over him telling him to get up, which suggests that Ali, whatever he might have said afterwards, was surprised that Liston sank to the canvas. Ex-champion Jersey Joe Walcott, the referee, rightly did not begin the count until Ali had retired to a neutral corner. Eventually Liston rose before ten was reached, and he and Ali boxed on.

However, the time-keeper's count had reached something like 22, and the editor of *The Ring*, Nat Fleischer, called to Walcott that the fight was over. To his shame Walcott stopped it, saying that Liston had been knocked out. The contest had at that stage run for two minutes 12 seconds. The official time was given as one minute of the first round. Timing the television action shows that it actually lasted one minute 42 seconds.

Did Liston deliberately throw the fight? Most observers think so, though Liston's premature and mysterious death less than six years later means nobody can be sure he did or, if he did throw it, why. Perhaps his underground friends had ordered him to, perhaps it was a final gesture towards the public who refused to accept him, or perhaps he was much older than his official 33 and, knowing he couldn't win, decided to get it over as soon as possible.

LOU AMBERS

born: (Luigi Guiseppe d'Ambrosio) 8 November 1913, Herkimer, New York, USA

Ambers, one of ten children of an Italian immigrant, loved to fight. When the Wall Street crash came in 1929 and his father's saloon went bust, Lou began fighting in 'bootleg' fights for ten dollars a time. In 1932 he began appearing in licensed shows, building up a fine record. After one defeat in 48 fights he fought Tony Canzoneri for the world lightweight title. He had been a sparring partner for Canzoneri, his idol, and was overawed. Floored three times, he lost on points.

In his next fight, Fritzie Zivic, a future welterweight champion, broke his jaw in the seventh round, but Lou carried on to win on points. This meant a break in his programme of a contest every three or four weeks. His unhappiest fight was with Tony Scarpati in 1936. Scarpati died three days after being knocked out. Less than six months and six fights later Ambers outpointed Canzoneri to win the lightweight crown.

Ambers was a non-stop attacker, an instinctive fighter with at first no claims to skill. He was called the 'Herkimer Hurricane'. Before outpointing Canzoneri again, Ambers lost three decisions, one to Pedro Montanez, who then challenged him for the title. This time Ambers won, but he lost his next defence, against Henry Armstrong, the featherweight and welterweight champion. It was a great fight and Ambers thought he'd won. He did win a year and five days later, when Armstrong was penalised several points for

low blows.

Ambers was stopped for the first time in his career in the first defence of his second spell as champion. Lew Jenkins stopped him in the third round. Nine months later Jenkins stopped him again in the seventh, and Ambers called it a day.
Record: 102 contests; 88 wins; 6 draws; 8 defeats

LOU AMBERS, the 'Herkimer Hurricane', had two great fights with Henry Armstrong.

DENNIS ANDRIES

born: 5 November 1953, Georgetown, Guyana

Dennis Andries, born in Guyana but bought up in Hackney, London, is a great example of determination triumphing over a lack of natural talent. Andries was awful in his early fights, showing nothing more than an ability to brawl and take punishment. In 1980, in his 14th contest, he challenged for the British light-heavyweight title, and was outpointed by Bunny Johnson. The same thing happened when he challenged Tom Collins two years later, but in 1984 he outpointed Collins for the title. He drew with Alex Blanchard for the European title and then, in 1986, surprised the world by outpointing J.B. Williamson for the WBC title. In 1987 he lost the title to Tommy Hearns in Detroit, bravely taking a bad beating before the referee stepped in in the tenth round.

At 33, Andries then began a second career. He joined Hearns' famous Kronk gymnasium and, after a victory over former IBF

champion Bobby Czyz, he stopped Tony Willis in 1989 for the vacant WBC title. This title was soon lost when Australia's Jeff Harding proved too strong at Atlantic City, but Andries stunned the boxing world again by reclaiming it when he knocked out the unbeaten Harding in Melbourne in July 1990. Andries poured everything into a seventh round that ended with the man believed to have the strongest chin in boxing on his back.

LEFT: Dennis Andries with Kronk cutman Ralph Citro in the corner.

BELOW: Two world champions, Iran Barkley and Alexis Arguello.

Andries was 36, but made two successful defences before coming up against Harding again in Hammersmith, London, in September 1991. After a superb fight in which both boxers took heavy punishment, Harding got a narrow verdict from two judges while the third made it a draw.

But the man with no skills had created a record by becoming the first Briton to win a world title at the same weight three times. He switched to cruiserweight but in February 1992 failed to win the vacant European title when outpointed by Akim Tafer in France.
Record: 53 contests; 41 wins; 2 draws; 10 defeats

See also: Harding v Andries

ALEXIS ARGUELLO

born: 19 April 1952, Managua, Nicaragua

The first 33 of Alexis Arguello's professional contests were in his home city, Managua, the capital of Nicaragua. Two of them he lost, but most he won by knock-outs. He had started professional boxing at 16, and grew into a 5ft 10in featherweight. He was thin and wiry, with arms that looked like drinking straws. He also had a finely chiselled face, a clear olive skin, and a polite and smiling demeanour which all added up to something more like a juvenile lead than a boxer. Yet in the 1970s and early 1980s his skill and his sharp punching carved out a career equal to the best of the day.

In 1974 he first challenged for the WBA featherweight title, and was outpointed by Ernesto Marcel in Panama City. Later that year, however, he knocked out Marcel's successor, Ruben Olivares, to take the crown.

Arguello, having won the title abroad, now proceeded to travel anywhere for his bouts. After defences in Caracas, Granada, Tokyo and Inglewood, he relinquished the title to campaign as a super-featherweight, and in January 1978 he stopped Alfredo Escalera in Puerto Rico to win the WBC title. After eight defences of this in various towns, he relinquished it to chase a lightweight crown. In June 1981 at Wembley he outpointed Scotland's Jim

Watt to take the WBC title. In his first defence he stopped Ray Mancini in Atlantic City and as Mancini won the WBA title, Arguello could legitimately claim to be the world's best lightweight.

For the third time he relinquished his title to move up a weight, but finally he met his match. Although betting favourite, he was stopped in the 14th in his challenge for Aaron Pryor's light-welterweight title. He was knocked out in the return and called it a day. He had won three world titles in opponents' territory and relinquished them all unbeaten after a total of 16 successful defences.
Record: 86 contests; 80 wins; 6 defeats

HENRY ARMSTRONG

born: (Henry Jackson) 12 December 1912, Columbus, Mississippi, USA
died: 22 October 1988, Los Angeles, USA

Brought up as a member of a large poor family in St Louis, Armstrong boxed as an amateur before turning professional in 1931 as Melody Jackson. In 1932 he went to Los Angeles where he took the name of a friend, Harry Armstrong, to disguise his professional status. He wanted to get into the Olympic team, failed, and turned professional in earnest. At first he boxed to orders in the clubs, but in 1936, after a victory over Baby Arizmendi, his career took an upturn. Al Jolson, the famous singer, saw the fight and bought Armstrong's contract. Eddie Mead was hired as manager. Mead was associated with underworld figures like Bugsy Siegel. George Raft, a film star with gangster connections, was another of Armstrong's backers. Between them they devised an ambitious programme for Armstrong – to win three world titles.

Armstrong was a fighter of unlimited stamina. He had the slow heartbeat of a marathon runner and could come forward relentlessly for 15 rounds. With thin legs but the broad back of a welterweight he was a perpetual motion punching machine. He took a few in return, but not many opponents could withstand his non-stop aggression. He was called Homicide Hank.

In an incredible year, 1937, Armstrong fought and won 27 times – only one opponent lasting the distance. On 29 October he knocked out Petey Sarron to become world featherweight champion.

Armstrong now chased the welterweight title and, on 31 May 1938, he outpointed Barney Ross to take it. Although conceding anything up to 25 pounds he so battered Ross that Ross retired. On 17 August Armstrong challenged Lou Ambers for the 'in-between' lightweight title, and after a bloody and close fight won the decision. He was the only man in boxing history to hold three world titles simultaneously. He immediately relinquished the featherweight crown, being unable to do the weight any more.

After six successful welterweight defences, Armstrong returned the lightweight title to Ambers after another bloody battle in which he was penalised for persistent fouls. After eight more welterweight defences, Armstrong challenged Ceferino Garcia for the middleweight title. He had beaten Garcia as a welter, but in a suspected fix Armstrong was denied the title when the decision was a draw.

Finally, in October 1940 he lost his last title, the welterweight, on a decision to Fritzie Zivic, a rough boxer from Pittsburgh. He was knocked out in the return. He carried on till 1945. He hadn't been allowed to keep much money, businesses failed and he went downhill until becoming an ordained minister in 1951. He had an eye operation near the end of his boxing career and was poverty-stricken and blind when he died in 1988.

Record: 174 contests; 145 wins; 9 draws; 20 defeats

BELOW and RIGHT: The triple world champion, Henry Armstrong.

Best Wishes
From
Henry Armstrong

ABE ATTELL

born: 22 February 1884, San Francisco, USA
died: 7 February 1970, New York, USA

A clever, hard-hitting Jewish featherweight, the 5ft 4in Attell began his professional career when only 16 in 1900. In October 1901 he outpointed George Dixon and claimed the world featherweight title, aged only 17, but this claim was based on Terry McGovern, the champion, being unable to make the weight. In February 1904, in his 47th contest, he knocked out Harry Forbes, one of only two men to have beaten him, and had a more acceptable claim to the title. However even this claim was based on champion Young Corbett II losing recognition because of weight difficulties, and in fact Young Corbett retained his claim until outpointed by Jimmy Britt in March 1904. Britt was a lightweight, and Attell was recognised as featherweight champ until knocked out by Brooklyn Tommy Sullivan in October 1904. Sullivan was then inactive for nearly two years and lost recognition, Attell beginning in 1906 a 24-fight, six-year reign as champion. During this time he had three draws, two in San Francisco against Owen Moran of Birmingham. Moran was convinced he'd won the first, over 25 rounds, and there had to be a return. Attell this time wanted 20 rounds, Moran 25, so a unique compromise of 23 rounds was agreed. Again the verdict was a draw.

Attell was also helped to retain his title by no-decision bouts. The British champion, Jim Driscoll, 'beat' him easily over ten rounds in New York in 1909 but could not claim the title, and Owen Moran was also kept at bay in three further no-decision contests. Finally Britain and Europe withdrew recognition from Attell because of his refusal to face Driscoll again, and in February 1912 Attell finally lost all recognition when outpointed by Johnny Kilbane. Attell's last fight was in January 1917.

Attell was a gambler, and later claimed that many

LEFT: Abe Attell

of his close and no-decision bouts were arranged for the betting on the return. Attell was involved in the famous World Series baseball fix of 1919.

Record: 165 contests; 92 wins; 18 draws; 10 defeats; 45 no-decision

ATTENDANCES

The record attendance at any boxing match is 135,132. This was not a title fight. It was a middleweight contest at Juneau Park, Milwaukee, Wisconsin, USA between Tony Zale and Billy Prior on 18 August 1941. It was a free show organised by the Fraternal Order of Eagles.

The highest paying attendance is 120,757, at the Jack Dempsey v Gene Tunney world heavyweight championship contest at the Sesquicentennial Stadium, Philadelphia, 23 September 1926.

The highest indoor attendance is 63,350, at the Muhammad Ali v Leon Spinks world heavyweight championship contest at the Superdome, New Orleans, 15 September 1978.

The highest attendance at a non-heavyweight contest is 100,000, at the Danny Lopez v David Kotey WBC featherweight title fight at the Sports Stadium, Accra, Ghana, 5 November 1976.

The highest indoor attendance at a non-heavyweight contest is 61,437 at the Randolph Turpin v Sugar Ray Robinson world middleweight championship contest at the Polo Grounds, New York, 12 September 1951.

The highest British attendance is 82,000 at the Len Harvey v Jock McAvoy contest for the British version of the world light heavyweight championship, White City, 10 July 1939.

The highest British indoor attendance is 18,197 at the Freddie Mills v Joey Maxim world light-heavyweight championship contest at Earl's Court, London, 24 January 1950.

The smallest attendance at a world heavyweight championship contest is 2,434, at St Dominic's Hall, Lewiston, Maine for the Muhammad Ali v Sonny Liston bout on 25 May 1965.

AUTHORITIES

There are now at least four authorities sanctioning world title fights. None of them have any power beyond those they have granted themselves. Their function is to sanction world title fights and accept a sanctioning fee. Each draws up its ranking list of contenders and since these usually bear little relation to each other it is clear that they are not based on any dispassionate estimate of a boxer's ability, but on the most convenient way to make money. Promoters, of course, like the sanctioning bodies because it enables the tag 'for the world title' to be attached to far more bouts than really justify the description. For their favourite promoters, or for what is seen as an attractive contest from the point of view of the gate, the authorities are not averse to re-organising the ranking list to suit the occasion.

A particular case in point is the way the World Boxing Organisation's ratings for June 1991 featured two men at 1 and 2 in the super-middleweight rankings who disappeared from the July 1991 list altogether, to be replaced by two men, Chris Eubank and Michael Watson, who weren't ranked in the top ten the previous month. The reason was to enable the sanctioning of the fight between the two as being for the WBO world title. There was no logic to the exercise. Similarly the WBC, in order to make a contest between featherweight champion Paul Hodkinson and substitute Steve Cruz look more credible, moved Cruz up the ratings from outside the top 30 to number ten, where the original opponent stood. How can a boxer leap up the ratings just because he is signed for a fight?

These authorities are all known by their initials and their weird machinations have led many to call them collectively and contemptuously the 'alphabet boys'. In the records at the back of this book only the current world champions recognised by the World Boxing Association (WBA), the World Boxing Council (WBC), the

International Boxing Federation (IBF) and the World Boxing Organisation (WBO) are listed.

World Boxing Association This body succeeded the National Boxing Association (NBA) in 1962. The NBA was formed in 1920 following a meeting in New York called by an Englishman, William A. Gavin, who wanted to set up an International Sporting Club along the lines of the National Sporting Club in London. It didn't materialise, but the WBA did. Its object was to challenge the Boxing Department of the New York State Athletic Commission which, till then, proclaimed the world champions and sanctioned the title bouts. Other states perceived a preference granted to New York boxers and were only too pleased to form a rival body. At first 13 states formed the Association but this number grew until the Association became the WBA in 1962. From 1927 the NBA began to differ from the New York authority on the contenders when a world title fell vacant, and from then on it was common for there to be two world champions at one weight. Later the two bodies differed on challengers to the champion and one body or other might declare a title vacant if the champion did not meet its own contender.

At a convention in 1962 the NBA reformed itself into the World Boxing Association. It had 51 state and city boxing authorities as the core of its membership and now includes authorities from outside the United States.

World Boxing Council This body was formed in 1963 in answer to the formation of the WBA to prevent this body becoming the predominant arbiter of world champions. In fact the WBC is far more internationally based. The British Boxing Board of Control and other national bodies and federations from South America, Europe, South Africa, the Far East and other countries joined with those American States not in the WBA to form a body covering much more territory than the WBA. The WBC also receives strong

support from the Boxing Department of the New York State Athletic Commission, whose constitution does not permit it to amalgamate with other bodies. It can be seen that the WBA and WBC are enlarged representatives of the old NBA and NYSAC.

International Boxing Federation This body was formed as a breakaway unit from the WBA in New Jersey in 1983, and is supported especially by authorities in Australia and the Far East. Despite the lack of appeal many felt for the WBA and WBC, it was difficult to see how a third body could gain the influence which the IBF has. Their first champions were Joo-do Chun and Dodie Penalosa in the light-bantamweight and light-flyweight classes, and the IBF has led the way in an attempt to introduce yet lighter classes, with particular appeal to the Far Eastern countries. In 1987 the IBF were first to introduce a 105-lb class, which they called strawweight. Their best known champion in the heavier classes was at first Marvin Camel, who won their inaugural cruiserweight title in 1983, but they really put themselves in a position which couldn't be ignored in 1984 when Larry Holmes, the best heavyweight in the world, relinquished the WBC title to become the first IBF heavyweight champion.

World Boxing Organisation This organisation was formed in the late 1980s with the support of a few boxing delegations around the world. Despite recognition by the British Boxing Board of Control and interest in Britain when boxers like Chris Eubank and Colin McMillan win a WBO title, it has not yet achieved the credibility of the other bodies.

British Boxing Board of Control This body was formed in 1929, with many of its initial board members being from the old National Sporting Club which, from its formation in 1891, had greatly influenced British Boxing. Indeed the NSC formalised the eight weight classes and established the possibility of there being universally accepted British champions by instituting the Lonsdale Belt scheme in 1909. The NSC had a permanent seat on the BBBC until it ceased to function as a club in 1937. The NSC formed in 1947 is a separate body. The BBBC exercises control over all aspects of boxing in Britain and has been particularly occupied in ensuring the safety of boxers.

European Boxing Union This body was founded in 1948 with 17 countries affiliated, including Great Britain. It is a descendant of the International Boxing Union, formed mainly by the French in 1911 to amalgamate the interests of European boxing authorities. Its main function is to administer European championships. The IBU and subsequently the EBU have occasionally recognised world champions independently of the other bodies.

BACKROOM

Boxing has more colourful characters and hangers-on than any other sport. Behind the boxer is the trainer who gets him into shape, and the manager who gets him his fights. Before a fight can take place it needs a promoter. Some of the roles merge, and a trainer can become the manager, too. Often the manager is the promoter, or is in association with the promoter, a state of affairs which is not in the boxer's interest and which the authorities have tried unsuccessfully to stop.

Some of the men who have been in the corner or behind the box office in Britain and America are:

Ray Arcel was born at the turn of the century and became the greatest trainer of boxers there has been. It is estimated that in 60 years he trained around 2,000 of whom 20 became world champions. The first was Charley Phil Rosenberg who beat Eddie Martin for the bantamweight title in 1925. Rosenberg had to lose 37 pounds in three months to make the weight and Arcel joined him on his diet –

Arcel was a physical wreck but his fighter won the title. Benny Leonard engaged Arcel when he was forced by circumstances to make a comeback. Arcel never trained Joe Louis, but he trained 14 of the men beaten by him and, because he always seemed to be carting them out of the ring, he was nicknamed the 'Meat Wagon'. Arcel trained Ezzard Charles, who took over from Louis, and more recently the great Roberto Duran. He retired in 1982, having helped Larry Holmes defend his title against Gerry Cooney.

Johnny Best took over the Liverpool Stadium in 1929 and promoted there and at the stadium built three years later with the same name. For major shows he used the Anfield Soccer stadium, where Nat Tarleton challenged Freddie Miller for the world featherweight title. As well as Tarleton, Peter Kane and Ernie Roderick often fought on Best's shows.

William A. Brady was a theatrical impresario who took over the managership of James J. Corbett, the heavyweight champion of the world, in the 1890s. Corbett appeared on the stage in Brady's shows as well as in the ring. When Corbett lost the title, Brady managed his sparring partner, James J. Jeffries, and guided him to the world title.

Ted Broadribb, who fought as Young Snowball and was the only Englishman to knock out Georges Carpentier, became a successful manager who could claim that boxers under his managership won every British title from flyweight to heavyweight. He managed Tommy Farr when Farr challenged Joe Louis for the heavyweight title in New York in 1937, and had his biggest success with his protégé, Freddie Mills, won the world light-heavyweight title in 1948.

Charles B. Cochran, famous as a theatrical impresario, staged the world lightweight championship match at Olympia, London when Freddie Welsh won the title from Willie Ritchie in 1914. After the First World War he shocked fans by charging 25 guineas (£26.25)

for a ringside seat for the Georges Carpentier – Joe Beckett match, which lasted 74 seconds. Cochran popularised the Albert Hall as a venue and brought Mickey Walker to London to defend his middleweight title against Tommy Milligan at Olympia in 1927.

Jim Coffroth was known as 'Sunny Jim' because of his luck with the weather for his outside promotions. He promoted at San Francisco and in the outdoor arena at Colma nearby, and because of the 'no-decision' law in New York staged many important fights as the boxers flocked to the west. Two of his favourite boxers were Stanley Ketchel, the great middleweight who fought Jack Johnson at Colma, and Battling Nelson, who won the lightweight championship there.

Cus d'Amato was not a prepossessing individual. Small, virtually blind in one eye through street fighting, he nevertheless loved the fight game and, with a colleague, formed the Empire Sporting Club to develop young boxers. In the 1950s he found himself coaching an ex-delinquent named Floyd Patterson. D'Amato shrewdly built Patterson up into the world heavyweight champion and, as his manager, carefully kept him at the top by skilful choice of opponents. He resisted the International Boxing Club in New York which had most of the leading contenders under its control and was proved right when that body fell foul of the anti-trust laws. Soon d'Amato had another world champion in his stable in Jose Torres. Things didn't go to well later and in 1971 he was made bankrupt. His next big chance came when another delinquent, the 13-year-old Mike Tyson, was sent to him. D'Amato spotted the potential in Tyson and carefully groomed him to become the world heavyweight champion, a peak he forecast for him from the beginning. Alas he died just before Tyson won the title.

Angelo Dundee began managing boxers on the road for his brother Chris, a promoter. He made himself an expert cut man and training shaded into

management. He had a fantastic night on 21 March 1963 when two of his boxers, Luis Rodriguez and Sugar Ramos, won world title fights one after the other at the Dodger Stadium, Los Angeles. He had already worked the corner for Carmen Basilio, and other champions like Ralph Dupas, Jose Napoles, Jimmy Ellis and Pinklon Thomas followed. But his biggest success followed his appointment as Muhammad Ali's trainer at the beginning of Ali's career. Dundee was in Ali's corner throughout his reign as champion, later on becoming his manager. Nobody could replace Ali, of course, but Dundee went on to the next best thing by training Sugar Ray Leonard to his glittering collection of world titles.

Lou Duva was a welterweight boxer who became a trainer, then a manager, then the chief of a boxing empire. He built a trucking business in Paterson, New Jersey, soon after the Second World War, and dabbled in boxing, operating a gym and promoting local fight cards. Soon he began managing boxers as a sideline. In the 1980s he joined Shelly Finkel, a concert promoter with whom he had staged occasional amateur shows. Soon he managed his first champions: Leo Randolph, Johnny Bumphus and Rocky Lockridge. He worked with others like Pernell Whitaker, Meldrick Taylor, Livingstone Bramble, Mike McCallum. But his biggest claim to glory is as co-trainer and general guide for Evander Holyfield, heavyweight champion of the world. Meanwhile his lawyer son Dan is the promoter, and it seems his whole family work in the office: Main Events Inc.

Harry Jacobs was a showman from the East End of London who put on those shows which packed plenty of action in long nights which gave the customers their moneysworth. He was the promoter at Wonderland in the Whitechapel Road, putting on twice-weekly shows at bargain prices. When this famous arena burned down in 1911, Jacobs turned a warehouse into

Premierland and continued the good work. He also staged shows at the Albert Hall.

Joe Jacobs was an American-Jewish manager who looked after Max Schmeling when he won the world heavyweight championship in 1930 on a foul, the only boxer ever to

do so. Jacobs played his part by climbing into the ring and causing a fuss. Schmeling later didn't have the best of luck, especially when he lost a controversial decision to Sharkey in 1932. Jacobs coined the managerial complaint of the ages: 'We wuz robbed'. His broken language was a trademark and, in disgust at another decision, he uttered the memorable: 'We should of stood in bed'.

Mike Jacobs began as a ticket tout. In 1933 he formed an alliance with three members of the powerful Hearst press (Damon Runyon, the author of 'Guys and Dolls' was one) and formed the 20th Century Sporting Club. The three attacked the Madison Square Garden promotions in their papers, while Jacobs managed to persuade the rising Joe Louis to appoint him his sole promoter. When Louis won the world heavyweight championship in Chicago, the Garden management was forced to invite Jacobs to take over the promotion of boxing in the arena. Jacobs found a way to ditch his three partners and built up a virtual monopoly of world championship promotion. At the Polo Grounds on 23 September 1937 he staged four world title fights Fred Apostoli v Marcel Thil (middleweight), Barney Ross v Ceferino Garcia (welterweight), Lou Ambers v Pedro Montanez (lightweight) and Harry Jeffra v Sixto Escobar (bantamweight).

Jack Kearns, always known as 'Doc', had his lucky day when he met a slugger named Jack Dempsey who was getting disheartened in trying to forge a professional career. The business-like Kearns and Dempsey formed a manager/fighter team that, with promoter Rickard, cashed in on the boxing boom of the 1920s. They were involved in earning the first $1 million gate when Dempsey beat Carpentier in 1921. 'Doc' helped ruin many citizens in the town of Shelby when he signed a contract for $300,000 for Dempsey to fight Tom Gibbons, but the fight flopped and the local big-wigs and banks who had paid most of the money in advance went bust. Towards the end of Dempsey's career he fell out with Kearns, principally over Dempsey's marriage to filmstar Estelle Taylor, but Kearns later managed world champions in Mickey Walker and Joey Maxim.

Don King became the first black promoter to become the most important in the world. A one-time big noise in the numbers racket (he is known to have killed two men and served a four-year sentence for manslaughter) he got himself into the Muhammad Ali camp and obtained the sponsorship of President Mobuto of Zaire for the Foreman-Ali heavyweight bout in Kinshasa. The Zaire government lost $6 million on the deal and King never looked back. By return clauses in fights, a close association with the

LEFT: Don King, shock-haired man of many boxing parts.

sanctioning bodies, and the device of granting challengers title fights in return for a share of their management, he managed to bring many world champions under his control. From Ali he moved to Holmes, but his biggest success was to become the manager of Mike Tyson, and virtually control the heavyweight championship. His son Carl became the promoter and other members of his family took cuts from the fights but Don King controlled just about everything including where all the money went. When Tyson was beaten by Buster Douglas in Tokyo and King could see his dominance disappearing for a while, he tried to get the result of the fight 'suspended' on the ludicrous grounds of a 'long count' given to Douglas. In a Senate investigation into corruption in boxing in August 1992, King frequently took the Fifth Amendment, declining to answer questions which might incriminate him.

Harry Levene was a manager who, in 1957, turned promoter to challenge Jack Solomons and eventually take over from him as the leading promoter in Britain. In 1966 he staged the world heavyweight championship match between Muhammad Ali and Henry Cooper at the Arsenal football ground at Highbury, London.

Hugh D. McIntosh was an Australian caterer who staged the world heavyweight championship fight at Rushcutters Bay, Sydney on Boxing Day 1908, in which Jack Johnson won the title from Tommy Burns. Although he was forced to pay Burns an amazing £6,000 he made a fortune on the match. The black Johnson became a hated man in boxing and McIntosh joined others in searching for a 'White Hope' to beat him. Developing the black and white theme, McIntosh later opened a well-known chain of 'Black and White' milk bars in London.

Jim Norris was one of a string of promoters who, by signing a contract with the heavyweight champion of the day, was able to control boxing and build up an

B

empire. Norris created the International Boxing Club and had Rocky Marciano under contract, which forced Madison Square Garden to hand over its promotional activities to Norris. With television contracts and the Garden, Norris built up a near monopoly of title fights which ended in 1957 when he and the IBC were found guilty of violating anti-trust laws.

Tex Rickard was the greatest promoter of all. He began his career by staging a lightweight championship bout between Joe Gans and Battling Nelson in Goldfield, Nevada, in 1906. This was designed to put Goldfield on the map and bring trade to the town. Rickard paid over $30,000 to the principals, an unheard of sum for lightweights, but for publicity he put the money in coins in his window and invited the press to look at it. He ended up making a big profit. When offers were invited for the Johnson-Jeffries fight he went to New York and bid $101,000 which won the auction. Rickard had another big success at Reno. He latched on to Dempsey and, with more skilful publicity, drew the world's first $1 million gate for his match with Carpentier. Rickard promoted the first five bouts to draw over $1 million, ending with a gate of $2,658,660 for the second Dempsey-Tunney contest in 1927. He died in 1929.

Jack Solomons was the leading promoter in Britain after the Second World War, running weekly shows at the Albert Hall and big events at the Harringay Arena and White City. His biggest promotion was the world middleweight title fight at Earl's Court in 1951 when a capacity 18,000 audience saw Randolph Turpin beat Sugar Ray Robinson.

LEFT: Jack Solomons, one of Britain's most colourful promoters, who had a near-monopoly of big British fights in the 1950s.

MAX BAER

born: 11 February 1909, Omaha, Nebraska, USA
died: 21 November 1959, Hollywood, California, USA

The son of a cattle-dealer, Max Baer developed through a boyhood on the range a magnificent physique of 6ft 2in and 210lb. With the strongest right-hand punch in the business, he was equipped to become a great champion. Although he won the world heavyweight title, his achievement stayed below his potential.

The Livermore Larruper, as he was called, built up a big string of victories after turning professional in May 1929, halted by a four-month layoff in 1930 after an opponent, Frankie Campbell, died after a bad beating. A knockout of ex-champion Max Schmeling in June 1933 meant that after 46 contests in four years he had earned a chance at Primo Carnera's world title. Baer, a quick-witted lively personality, established a strong psychological advantage over the slow Carnera during a film they made together, and in the ring he clowned as he demolished the champion, who was put down 11 times in 11 rounds. Twice the impetus of Baer's blows took them both to the canvas together, when Baer said: 'Last one up is a cissy'.

After becoming champion, playboy Baer boxed exhibitions for a year and devoted himself to his radio show. He then took on challenger James J. Braddock, a has-been rated at 10-1 to win, but Baer so underrated him that he was beaten on points. In an effort to re-establish himself he fought the new sensation Joe Louis, but was badly beaten in four rounds. He carried on successfully for six more years without justifying another title shot.
Record: 83 contests; 70 wins; 13 defeats

RIGHT: Max Baer, one of the hardest punchers boxing has seen.

BELOW: Baer (right) boxing Tommy Farr.

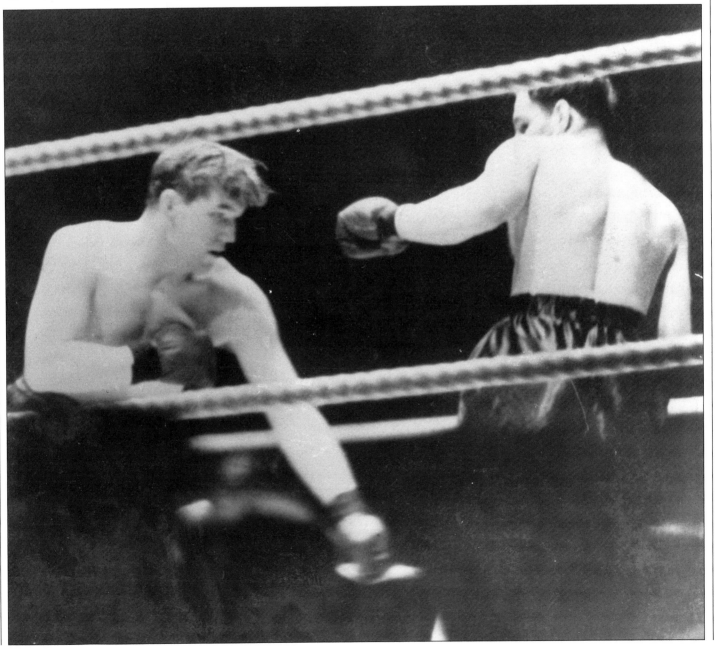

BELTS

The practice of awarding belts to champions dates back to prize ring days. Tom Cribb was given a belt when he beat the American challenger for his title, Tom Molineaux, in 1810. It was presented by George III.

Belts were presented to champions by their admirers but, in 1841, a belt was paid for by public subscription to be awarded to the winner of the contest between Nick Ward and Ben Caunt for the championship of England. It contained shields inscribed with the names of previous champions and was to be held by future champions.

A special belt was made for each of Tom Sayers and his American challenger John C. Heenan after they had fought a draw in 1860.

A handsome belt was made for the world heavyweight champion by Richard K. Fox, the proprietor of the American journal *Police Gazette*, which reported the American prize ring. This belt was awarded to Jake Kilrain, who lost it in battle in 1889 with John L. Sullivan who refused to accept it because he and Fox had a personal feud bubbling. Sullivan was given a belt by his Boston fans. It contained gold ring posts and ropes, various shields, portraits of Sullivan and his manager, and a centre-piece which proclaimed Sullivan the 'Champion of Champions'. Sullivan's name was spelt out by 291 of the 351 diamonds the belt contained. Sullivan kept his belt, of course, and the *Police Gazette* belt was put back into circulation when James J. Corbett beat Sullivan for the title, but it was stolen from a jewellers while in Corbett's possession and disappeared forever.

A belt was at stake when Sullivan met the British fighter Charley Mitchell at the Rothschild racing stables near Chantilly in 1887. The match was a draw but, as the belt was paid for by Mitchell's friends, it was awarded to him. Many years later it was bought by Nat Fleischer, the famous editor of *The Ring* magazine.

The most famous boxing belts are the Lonsdale Belts. These were inaugurated by the National Sporting Club in 1909, when they first stipulated the eight weight classes in which a boxer could become champion. A belt was to be awarded to each of the British champions, as decided by the NSC. The name arose from the President of the club, Lord Lonsdale. A champion was to hold the belt while champion, and it became his property once he had won three title fights at the same weight. The British Boxing Board of Control took over the manufacture and distribution of the Lonsdale Belts from the NSC, and they are as prized today as they were then, except that they now contain less gold.

A few boxers won two Lonsdale Belts outright (for six championship victories) but Henry Cooper is the only boxer to win three. The rules were changed in 1978 to allow a boxer only one belt in each weight class.

The Ring magazine began issuing belts upon their launch in 1922 to all world champions. But these ceased with the death of the original proprietor and editor, Nat Fleischer, in 1972. Emile Griffith won six of these belts.

Nowadays all the sanctioning authorities issue belts which are the symbol of that body's championship at any particular weight. They are generally not nearly as valuable or elegant as the old belts. They are large, cheap and gaudy, which perhaps reflects the status of the bodies themselves.

WILFRED BENITEZ

born: 12 September 1958, Bronx, New York

Benitez had just turned 15 when he turned professional in November 1973, and 24 straight wins, 18 inside the distance, saw him get a chance to take the WBA light-welterweight title from Antonio Cervantes in March 1976. Benitez won on points in San Juan and at under 17 years 6 months became the youngest ever world champion. After two defences the WBA stripped him for not granting Cervantes a return. In any case Benitez moved up to welter and in January 1979 outpointed Carlos Palomino in San Juan to become WBC champion. A fast, clever, skilful boxer, Benitez suffered his first defeat when challenged by Sugar Ray Leonard in November 1979. After a terrific battle of great skill Benitez was stopped six seconds from the end of the 15th round with the fight in the balance.

Benitez then took the WBC light-middleweight crown by knocking out Maurice Hope in Las Vegas and defended successfully twice, including a points win over Roberto Duran. However in another great battle in 1982 he was outscored by Tommy Hearns. In July 1985 he lost his third bout when outpointed by Mustafa Hamsho in Las Vegas. He was never as good again and, through bad management – largely by his father – rapidly lost all the money he had made in the ring.
Record: 61 contests; 52 wins; 1 draw; 8 defeats

NIGEL BENN

born: 22 January 1964, Ilford, Essex

Nigel Benn was a fast and furious amateur boxer who won the ABA middleweight title in 1986. Turning professional in January 1987 he quickly disposed of a number of opponents, only one of the 22 opponents he stopped in his first 26 months managing to get beyond the fourth round. During this time he won the vacant Commonwealth middleweight title and because many of his contests were shown on a regular television fight programme he became the best-known prospect in the country. In May 1989 he suffered his first defeat and lost his title when Michael Watson knocked him out in the sixth round of one of the best fights of the year. It demonstrated that Benn was brilliantly destructive on attack but that he was vulnerable to the counters of a top-class boxer.

NIGEL BENN (right) in his one-round dismantling of Iran Barkley in 1990.

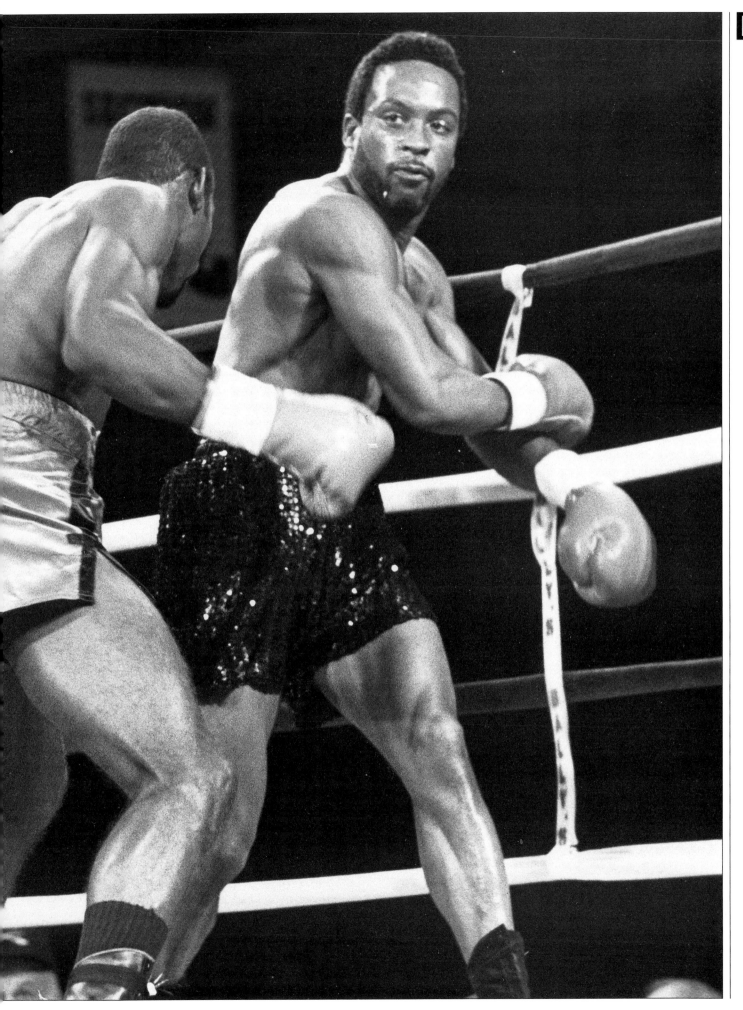

Benn's brave answer was to campaign in the States, and after three wins he challenged Doug de Witt for his WBO middleweight title at Atlantic City. The tough de Witt was stopped in the eighth round. Benn had his best win yet in August 1990 when in Las Vegas he demolished challenger Iran Barkley, the former WBC champion, in the first round. Three months later, however, back in England, Benn lost his title to fellow-Briton Chris Eubank, when after a tremendous battle the referee stepped in to save Benn in the ninth.

Benn remodelled his style to become a more patient boxer, trying to throw off the 'Dark Destroyer' nickname he had fostered. He continued to win and became so anxious to get a return with Eubank that, when Eubank moved up to super-middleweight, Benn followed. He began impressively at his new weight but his points win over Thulane Malinga in May 1992 caused controversy.
Record: 35 contests; 33 wins; 2 defeats

See also: Eubank v Benn

NINO BENVENUTI

born: 26 April 1938, Trieste, Italy

The son of a fisherman, Benvenuti was one of four brothers who were good amateur boxers. Nino was so good he won the welterweight gold medal at the 1960 Olympics in Rome. A handsome, stylish boxer of great skill and with a powerful left hook, he turned professional in 1961 and soon won the Italian middleweight title. After 56 straight victories he took the world light-middleweight crown in June 1965, knocking out fellow-countryman Sandro Mazzinghi. After winning the European middleweight title he challenged Emile Griffith for the world title in April 1967. Nino won impressively on points in New York. Griffith took the return but Benvenuti won the rubber match in 1968 on the opening of a new Madison

Square Garden in New York. He made four successful defences before Carlos Monzon surprised his army of fans by knocking him out in the twelfth round in Rome in 1970. Monzon was better than anybody thought, and stopped Nino in three in the return in Monte Carlo. It was time to hang up the gloves.
Record: 90 contests; 82 wins; 1 draw; 7 defeats

JACK 'KID' BERG

born: (Judah Bergman) 28 June 1909, London
died: 21 April 1991, London

Berg was born in the East End of London, his parents being Jewish immigrants from Russia. All he wanted to do was fight, and he made his professional debut on 8 June 1924, not quite 15 years old. His idol was the Jewish world champion Ted 'Kid' Lewis, which influenced Berg's choice of ring name. He fought in the Premierland ring and his all-action non-stop style earned him the nickname of 'The Whitechapel Whirlwind'. In 1928, with a record of 59 fights (53 wins to 3 losses) he went to America. He was still not 19.

After a successful two years in which he beat Tony Canzoneri and Mushy Callahan, he returned to London to challenge Mushy Callahan for his newly created light-welterweight title, the announcement of which brought Lord Lonsdale from his ringside seat to declare: 'There's no such thing.' Berg won it though, when Callahan retired after ten rounds. He returned to the States, and defended a number of times, avenging a previous loss to Billy Petrolle and beating Kid Chocolate, before he challenged Tony Canzoneri for his lightweight title in 1931. Canzoneri knocked him out in the third, and claimed Berg's title, too, a claim which Berg would not countenance. However a points defeat by Canzoneri later in the year seemed to settle the matter.

JACK 'KID' BERG, the 'Whitechapel Whirlwind'.

Berg continued to campaign equally in Britain and America, meeting and usually beating the best in both countries and winning British and Empire lightweight titles before he retired after 21 years and 192 contests in May 1945.
Record: 192 contests; 157 wins; 9 draws; 26 defeats

BLACK BOXERS

The first black boxers to make an impression in the history of the sport were Bill Richmond and Tom Molineaux, American slaves who came over to fight the British champions in the early days of the 19th century. They did not win the championship but they brought interest and excitement to the scene.

In the United States in the days before the First World War, black boxers found it very difficult to get chances at world titles. Although some were tolerated in the lightest divisions, there was no chance that a heavyweight champion would be allowed. In the end Jack Johnson went to Australia to challenge and beat the heavyweight champion, Tommy Burns, a Canadian. Johnson was a bitter pill for white Americans to swallow, and they never did digest it properly. There were widespread race riots when Johnson beat Jeffries in 1910. There was universal white relief and rejoicing when Johnson was relieved of the title, and care was taken that a black boxer did not get another chance until Joe Louis was allowed to become champion in 1937.

There were several outstanding black heavyweights in the Johnson era and before. Peter Jackson, a West Indian who was dodged by John L. Sullivan but fought a draw with James J. Corbett before Corbett won the world title, is generally considered to be the best heavyweight around in the late 19th century. Sam Langford, who was really only a middleweight but fought heavies in a career from 1902 to 1923, is sometimes regarded as the best boxer for his weight ever, but he never got a title

shot. Joe Jeannette and Sam McVey were heavyweights who fought each other and Johnson in numerous bouts, usually 'no-decision', because white fighters wouldn't fight them.

A popular entertainment around the turn of the century was the 'battle royal', where black boxers entered the ring together, maybe six at a time, and fought each other simultaneously, the winner being the last man standing.

The best black heavyweight in the 1920s was Harry Wills, whom many thought in his prime could well have beaten Jack Dempsey, the world champion, but Dempsey, or his handlers, wouldn't fight him. At one time the Boxing

Commission ordered the two to meet, and a contract was signed and tickets printed, but Dempsey's manager made sure the contest didn't take place.

The first black boxers to win world titles were:

Heavyweight Jack Johnson (USA) (1908 in Australia)
Light-heavyweight Battling Siki (Senegal) (1933 in Paris)
Middleweight Tiger Flowers (USA) (1926 in New York)
Welterweight Joe Walcott (Barbados) (1901 in Fort Erie, Canada)
Lightweight Joe Gans (USA) (1902 in Fort Erie, Canada)
Featherweight George Dixon (Canada) (1891 in London)
Bantamweight George

Dixon (Canada) (1890 in New York)

The first heavyweight title fight between two black boxers took place in Paris on 19 December 1913 when Jack Johnson drew with Jim Johnson. However this is sometimes regarded as not a serious contest, but one arranged in more ways than one by Jack Johnson to get some revenue. Some historians therefore prefer to regard the contest between Joe Louis and John Henry Lewis in New York City on 25 January 1939 as the first.

The first black fighter to win a British title was Andrew Jephtha, a South African, who knocked out Robert 'Curley' Watson in London on 25 March 1907 to win the welterweight title.

JOE LOUIS (left) became only the second black heavyweight champion in 1937. Jersey Joe Walcott (right) was champion in 1951.

However this was before the NSC 'governed' British title fights, and their successors, the BBBC, sanctioned a colour bar. When this was dropped after the Second World War the first black champion was Dick Turpin, who outpointed Vince Hawkins for the middleweight title at Birmingham on 28 June 1948.

JAMES J. BRADDOCK

born: 7 June 1906, New York City
died: 29 November 1974, North Bergen, NJ, USA

Braddock's is one of the most extraordinary of boxing stories. He began professionally as a middleweight when nearly 20 and was successful for a couple of years, but increasing weight forced him into the light-heavyweight class. Despite three defeats in his previous nine contests he was given a chance at the world title in July 1929 but was outpointed by Tommy Loughran. From then on his career was poor, until in September 1933 he and his opponent were thrown out for not trying by a referee in a match declared 'no contest'. He had won 11 of 31 contests since his title challenge. With no matches offered, he worked as a dockhand and then, with a wife and three children to support, went on 'welfare'.

In June 1934, his manager, Joe Gould, persuaded a promoter to put him in as a 'safe' opponent against an up-and-coming prospect, Corn Griffin. Braddock won by a knock-out in the third. He then outpointed two more boxers, one of whom had also been earmarked as a 'safe' opponent, but as a safe opponent for new heavyweight champion Max Baer. Braddock faced Baer instead, in June 1934. It is said that an ambulance was discreetly in attendance waiting to take Braddock away. But Baer clowned and tired while Braddock, always a skilful boxer, jabbed him to pieces and took the crown. Damon Runyan gave him his nickname, 'The Cinderella Man'.

He did not defend for over two years, and then dodged rightful challenger Max Schmeling to take on Joe Louis, the two managers

having worked out a secret deal which was to pay Braddock, in the event of Louis winning, ten per cent of all Mike Jacobs' future promotions featuring Louis.

Braddock did not lie down, and dropped Louis in the first round, but subsequently took a brave beating before being knocked out in the eighth. The deal, if he got his dues, would have made him a very rich man. He had one more contest, a points win.

Record: 86 contests; 46 wins; 4 draws; 23 defeats; 11 no-decision; 2 no-contest

JAMES J. BRADDOCK (left) outpointing Tommy Farr in his last fight, in 1938.

JACK BRITTON

born: (William J. Breslin) 14 October 1885, Clinton, New York
died: 27 March 1962, Miami, USA

Britton was a brilliant boxer who relied on skill and counter-punching rather than a knockout blow. In a long career he had over 300 recorded bouts. He moved via New Britain to Chicago as a teenager where he became known as 'Britain', a name which stuck when he had his first professional contest in 1905.

By 1915 he was one of the best welterweights around, and claimed the world title after outpointing Mike Glover in Boston. Ted 'Kid' Lewis immediately took it from him, and the two had a series of 20 contests over six years in which they swapped the title. They met 20 times: Britton won four and Lewis three, with one drawn and 14 no-decision. Britton ended with the title, and continued to hold it till November 1922, when Mickey Walker outpointed him.

It was the last of Britton as a champion, but he continued boxing until 1930, and then began teaching his skills to others.

Record: 327 contests; 100 wins; 20 draws; 29 defeats; 177 no-decision; 1 no-contest

JACK BRITTON, standing between Jack Harding and Syd Walker, had 327 contests, 20 with his great welterweight world championship rival Ted 'Kid' Lewis.

BROADCASTING

The first fight result broadcast on the radio was the world heavyweight championship fight in which Jack Dempsey took the title from Jess Willard at Toledo, Ohio, on 4 July 1919.

The first radio commentary of a boxing match was from Jersey City, on 2 July 1921 and was of the Jack Dempsey v Georges Carpentier world heavyweight title bout. In fact the broadcast began during the last round of a preliminary bout, a no-decision contest between Packey O'Gatty and Frankie Burns.

The first radio commentary in Great Britain was on Station 2LO from Olympia, London, on 11 May 1922 and was of the Ted 'Kid' Lewis v Georges Carpentier world light-heavyweight title fight.

The first televised

boxing match was an exhibition staged in Broadcasting House, London, on 22 August 1933 between Archie Sexton and Lauri Raiteri.

The first match televised for closed-circuit purposes was at Harringay Arena, London, on 7 April 1938 between Len Harvey and Jock McAvoy for the British light-heavyweight championship.

The first match televised for public screening was from the Harringay Arena, London, on 23 February 1939 between Eric Boon and Arthur Danahar for the British lightweight championship.

The first world title fight to be televised was from Madison Square Garden, New York, on 29 September 1944 between Willie Pep and Chalky Wright for the New York version of the featherweight title.

The first world heavyweight title fight to be televised was from Madison Square Garden, New York, on 5 December 1947 between Joe Louis and Jersey Joe Walcott.

The first match to be televised in colour was from Madison Square Garden, New York, on 26 March 1954. It was a bout between Gustav Scholz and Al Andrews.

The first world title fight to be televised in colour was from Madison Square Garden, New York, on 10 December 1965 between Emile Griffith and Manuel Gonzalez for the undisputed welterweight title.

JACK BROUGHTON

**born: 1704, Cirencester
died: 8 January 1789, Lambeth, London**

Jack Broughton was called 'The Father of Boxing'. He ran away from an unhappy home when 12, and growing into a big strong youth who liked to fight, was spotted by James Figg, the champion of England, and fought in his amphitheatre. Figg nominated George Taylor as his successor, but Broughton beat him and other claimants to become champion. Broughton opened his own amphitheatre in the Haymarket and taught

boxing, which then allowed all sorts of throws. Broughton concentrated on the delivery of punches, thus refining the sport, and to save his aristocratic patrons the inconvenience of black eyes and bleeding noses he introduced boxing gloves, or mufflers as they were known.

When George Stevenson, a Yorkshire coachman, died after challenging Broughton, Broughton was so upset that he drew up his rules to prevent such tragedies in future. Broughton's Rules became accepted and were current for 100 years. Eventually, aged 46, he was beaten by Jack Slack who, after taking a beating, managed temporarily to blind Broughton with his blows. As Broughton groped at his opponent, the Duke of Cumberland, his backer, cried: 'What are you about, Broughton? You're beat, we shall lose our money.' Broughton replied: 'I am blind but not beat, Your Highness. Place me before him and we will yet win the day.' He didn't, and it was his last fight. He died at 85, a rich man. He was appointed a Yeoman of the Guard, and a stone on the floor of Westminster Abbey commemorates him.

PANAMA AL BROWN

**born: (Alphonse Theodore Brown) 5 July 1902, Colon, Panama
died: 11 April 1951, New York**

Brown was a remarkable boxer – a black bantamweight from Panama who stood 5ft 11in. He was, of course, very thin and had long, skinny arms. However, they could deliver a punch and 57 of his opponents did not last the distance. He began his professional career in 1919 but his record is unknown until 1922 when he won the Isthmus flyweight title.

In 1929 he outpointed Vidal Gregorio at Madison Square Garden for the vacant world bantamweight championship and then campaigned equally in America and Europe, particularly Paris, where he eventually decided to live. He defended his title in

Copenhagen, New York, Paris, Montreal, Marseille, Toronto, Milan, Manchester, Tunis and Valencia. It was in Valencia that he eventually surrendered his crown in 1935, being outpointed by Baltazar Sangchili.

From a poor family – his mother washed clothes for a living even when he was a champion – he learned English and French and struck up a friendship with the famous writer Jean Cocteau. Rich, black and homosexual, he led a fashionable life in Paris until Hitler threatened, when he fled to the States, leaving property behind. He retired after his only knockout (to future featherweight champion Harry Jeffra in 1939) but fought again in 1941 and 1942 before his licence was taken when he was 40. He died penniless in New York of tuberculosis nine years later.

Record: 152 contests, 120 wins; 11 draws; 19 defeats; 2 no-decision

FRANK BRUNO

born: 16 November 1961, Hammersmith, London

A magnificently muscled 6ft 3½ in, Bruno was a strong man in the amateur ranks, winning the ABA heavyweight title in 1980 with the closest of split decisions over Rudi Pika. After a minor eye operation he made his professional debut in March 1981 with a one-round knockout. Most of his early opponents were stopped in the first two rounds, but Floyd Cummings lasted seven and shook Bruno in the second. His first ranked opponent was James 'Bonecrusher' Smith in May 1984. Bruno built up a big points lead but in the last round Smith launched an all-out assault and knocked Bruno out. It seemed Bruno had a punch capable of knocking out anybody but lacked the skill to keep out the top heavyweights.

Bruno fought back by winning the European title in October 1985, flattening Anders Eklund, and five months later he knocked out former WBA champion Gerrie Coetzee in the first. It earned a WBA title shot in July 1986, and he fought evenly with Tim Witherspoon

until Witherspoon suddenly got on top and exposed again Bruno's slowness of thought when cornered. The referee stepped in in the 11th. Bruno's handlers, however,

carefully picked opponents until in February 1989 Bruno received his big payday in a challenge to Mike Tyson for the WBC crown at Las Vegas.

Down in the first half-minute, Bruno recovered to hurt Tyson momentarily later in the round – the first sign that Tyson was no longer invincible. Bruno was

rescued by the referee in the fifth when again helpless on the ropes.

Bruno then devoted himself to pantomime work and groomed his celebrity

status while having a retina operation. This did not prevent the BBBC granting him a licence to make a comeback in 1991 – against the advice of their doctor.

Two quick knockouts put Bruno in line for more rewards.

Record: 37 contests; 34 wins; 3 defeats

FRANK BRUNO, Britain's hard-punching heavyweight contender.

KEN BUCHANAN

born: 28 July 1945, Edinburgh

Ken Buchanan received a pair of boxing gloves for Christmas when he was eight and joined a local club. He became one of the most skilful lightweights ever seen, but he was also tough, could take a punch and had a powerful jab and right cross himself. Turning professional at 20, he took the British title in February 1968, but in the summer of 1969 announced his retirement after 32 unbeaten contests because he alleged he was being mismanaged. The argument was resolved, but he suffered his first reverse when outpointed by Miguel Velasquez in Madrid for the European title in January 1970. Nevertheless in September that year he went to San Juan and took the undisputed world title from Ismael Laguna on points. He defended successfully twice in America before meeting the rough up-and-coming Roberto Duran in Madison Square Garden. Duran got away with street-fighting tactics which culminated in a low blow after the bell to end the 13th round. The referee stopped the contest in Duran's favour when Buchanan could not come out for the 14th, the only time Buchanan was ever stopped. Duran said it was his hardest fight and would never give Buchanan a return.

Buchanan resumed by knocking out Carlos Ortiz in New York and later regained the British title from Jim Watt and took the European title from Antonio Puddu. In 1975 he had a crack at the WBC title but was outpointed in Tokyo by Ishimatsu Suzuki (who later became Guts Ishimatsu). Buchanan retired in 1975, but came back for monetary reasons in 1979, continuing for nearly three years, latterly as a light-welter. Unfortunately five defeats in this spell disfigured what was otherwise an outstanding record.

Record: 69 contests; 61 wins; 8 defeats

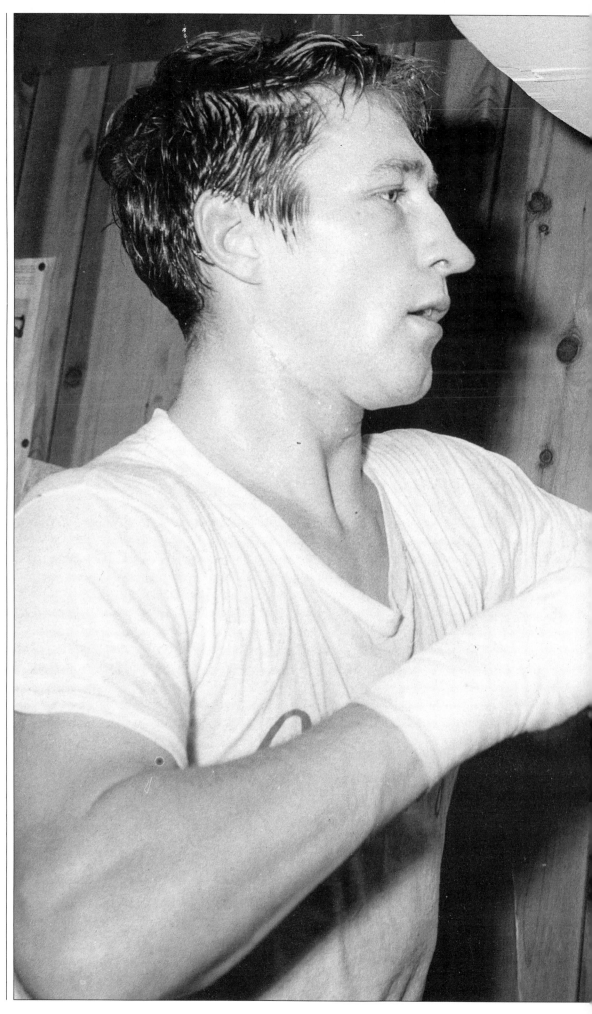

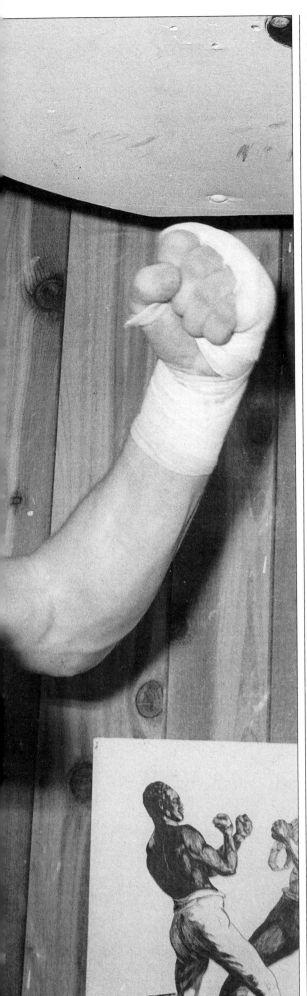

LEFT: One of Britain's most skilful boxers, world lightweight champion Ken Buchanan, in the gym with two bare-knuckle fighters.

BELOW: Tommy Burns had a busy reign as world heavyweight champion, despite being only 5ft 7in.

TOMMY BURNS

born: (Noah Brusso) 17 June 1881, Chesley, Ontario, Canada
died: 10 May 1955, Vancouver, Canada

Burns enjoyed many sports as a youngster, finally choosing to turn professional as a boxer in 1900. He began as a middleweight and never weighed more than about 184lb. Yet in February 1906, and coming off a loss, he outpointed Marvin Hart to win the vacant heavyweight championship of the world. He was only 5ft 7in, and remains the shortest-ever heavyweight champion.

Nevertheless Burns had a long reach and was a skilful boxer, and defended 11 times. He was also his own astute manager.

Unfortunately for him, in the wings was Jack Johnson. Burns went to Europe and Johnson followed – then to Australia. Promoter Hugh D. McIntosh offered him £6,000, then a great sum, to defend against Johnson in Sydney. Burns put up a brave show but was stopped in the 14th round. Burns fought six more times in the next 12 years, retiring after being knocked out by Joe Beckett in London in 1920.

Record: 60 contests; 46 wins; 8 draws; 5 defeats; 1 no-decision

C

TONY CANZONERI

born: 6 November 1908, Slidell, Louisiana, USA
died: 9 December 1959, New York

Born of Italian parents, Canzoneri was brought up in New York where be became an amateur champion before turning pro in June 1925. His all-action punch-swapping style made him a great favourite of the Italian fans. In his third year he drew with Bud Taylor for the vacant NBA bantamweight title but was outpointed in the return. In 1928, however, he took the undisputed world featherweight title by outpointing Benny Bass. It was a title he held for only seven months, losing a decision to Frenchman Andre Routis. Undeterred, the busy Canzoneri challenged Sammy Mandell for the lightweight crown in 1929, being outpointed, but again he persevered and won the title in November 1930, knocking out Al Singer in a record for the division of 66 seconds.

Canzoneri had lost earlier in the year to Jack 'Kid' Berg, the light-welterweight champion, and was immediately challenged by Berg, whom he knocked out in the third round, claiming Berg's title as well. This was lost in January 1932, however, on points to Johnny Jadick, who confirmed the decision in July. In 1933 Canzoneri lost the lightweight title in two great battles with Barney Ross, but he continued in the top flight, and in May 1935 he won the lightweight crown for a second time, the first man to do so, when he outpointed Lou Ambers. Ambers retrieved the title in 1936 and beat Canzoneri again in 1937. Canzoneri remained as busy as ever, giving value for money, winning 11 of 17 contests in his last year, 1939. His first stoppage, by Al Davis, caused him to retire and become a restaurant owner and cabaret actor. He died of a heart attack when only 51.

Record: 176 contests; 139 wins; 10 draws; 24 defeats; 3 no-decision

PRIMO CARNERA

born: 26 October 1906, Sequals, Italy
died: 29 June 1967, Sequals, Italy

Carnera was a giant of 6ft 5¾ in and 270lb, the biggest of all heavyweight champions. He worked in a quarry, which developed his muscles, and then in a circus, where he was a wrestler and strong man as well as principal labourer in erecting the big top. An ex-boxer recommended him to Leon See, his former manager, and Carnera was taught basic skills and built up an impressive record from his debut in 1928. In 1930 they went to America, where the much-hyped giant's management was taken over by gangsters. Many of his subsequent contests were fixed.

Carnera's progress was halted by Jack Sharkey, who floored him before winning on points. However, he carefully built up another string of successes. In 1933 Ernie Schaaf did not recover consciousness after being knocked out by Carnera, an event which had a profound effect on the amiable giant, especially when a boxing commissioner claimed that Carnera was too big for ordinary heavyweights. In fact, Schaaf's death was more due to an earlier beating by Max Baer.

Carnera challenged Jack Sharkey for the heavyweight title four months later and knocked him out in the sixth round to become champion. Even this fight was tinged with suspicion, although Sharkey has always maintained it was legitimate. After two defences, one against light-heavyweight champion Tommy Loughran, who conceded 86lb, Carnera lost his crown when knocked out by Max Baer in June 1934. Next year Joe Louis beat him badly in six rounds. He retired in 1937 but had five contests in Italy in 1945–46. Having been cheated out of his ring earnings, he returned to the States and made enough money at his first love, wrestling, to open a liquor store in Los Angeles, before returning finally to the place of his birth, Sequals.

Record: 103 contests; 88 wins; 14 defeats; 1 no-contest

BELOW: The huge Primo Carnera.

GEORGES CARPENTIER

born: 12 January 1894, Lens, France
died: 28 October 1975, Paris

France's most famous boxer had a film-star profile which brought many female fans to boxing. He also had great boxing skill and a lightning right-hand punch which despatched over half of his opponents before the final bell. The son of a miner he practised *savate*, French boxing, as a boy, and impressed François Descamp, a one-man touring show. They teamed up, took a fancy to *la boxe Anglais* and Carpentier had his first contest at 14. The still growing Carpentier rose in the weights until, in 1911 when 17, he became welterweight champion of France. He was a veteran of 54 contests. The same month he won the European title in London, the youngest-ever champion. In 1912 he won and defended the European middleweight crown. In February and June 1913 he knocked out Bandsman Rice and Bombardier Billy Wells to win the European light-heavy and heavyweight titles. He was still only 19, a boxing phenomenon.

In 1914 Georges, known as 'The Orchid Man', beat Gunboat Smith on a foul, becoming the last man to hold the 'white heavyweight championship of the world' while Jack Johnson was the true champ. The war then interrupted the 20-year-old's career. Georges became an officer in the air force and was twice decorated for gallantry. Resuming his career after five years he twice successfully defended his European heavyweight crown.

In 1920 Tex Rickard matched the war hero against the heavyweight champion, Jack Dempsey, who was considered a wartime 'slacker'. First Carpentier took the world light-heavyweight title from Battling Levinsky with a fourth-round knockout.

The Dempsey fight in 1921 was the first million-dollar contest. Unfortunately Carpentier conceded too much weight (about 24lb) to Dempsey and although he hit him with his famous right in the second round the blow did most damage to his hand, and he was stopped in the fourth. Fourteen months later he lost his light-heavyweight title in a shock defeat by Battling Siki. In 1924 he went to New York but did not come out for the last round against future heavyweight champion Gene Tunney, claiming a low blow in the 14th.

Four more bouts and Carpentier retired, opened a bar in Paris, went on the halls and remained a much loved celebrity till his death.
Record: 109 contests; 88 wins; 6 draws; 14 defeats; 1 no-decision

GEORGES CARPENTIER near the end of a long and distinguished career which took in the world light-heavyweight title.

MARCEL CERDAN

born: 22 July 1916, Sidi Bel-Abbes, Algeria
died: 27 October 1949, Azores

Marcel Cerdan followed his elder brothers into the boxing business, turning professional in November 1934. He began as a welterweight, and many of his early contests were in Casablanca, where he proved

so outstanding that by 1937 he had been persuaded to switch his centre of operations to Paris. He returned to Casablanca in 1938 to win the French welterweight title, and in 1939 he went to Milan for the European title. Unfortunately war broke out when he was at his peak, but he kept active as the star of Inter-Allied boxing shows in North Africa, Italy and France.

Several Americans who saw Cerdan in these years raved about him and in 1946 he made a successful trip to the States. By now he was an outstanding middleweight, with the French and European titles. Cerdan had everything: skill, strength, stamina, determination and a terrific punch with either hand. His only two defeats in his first 100 fights were through disqualifications, but in May 1948 Cyrille

Delannoit, a Belgian, outpointed him in Brussels for the European title. In July Cerdan reversed the verdict.

Marcel's next contest was for the world title in Jersey City, where after injuring his right hand in the third round he outpunched Tony Zale with his left only, causing the champion to retire after 11 rounds. In June 1949 Cerdan was in Detroit to defend against Jake LaMotta. He pulled a muscle

in his shoulder when he was wrestled to the canvas in the first round, but again he held his own with one hand for nine rounds, when his seconds retired him. In September he was in New York for the return, confident of victory, when LaMotta withdrew with a sprained shoulder. Cerdan returned to France, taking off again for New York for the rescheduled bout in October. The plane crashed in the

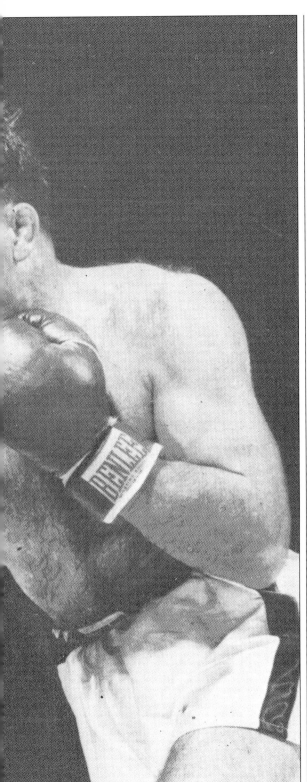

EZZARD CHARLES

born: 7 July 1921, Lawrenceville, Georgia, USA
died: 27 May 1975, Chicago, Illinois, USA

Ezzard Charles was one of the most under-rated of boxers, perhaps because of a cautious style. His skill was unquestioned. He won every domestic honour in an unbeaten amateur career and built up a string of victories after turning professional in 1940. He recorded wins over future light-heavyweight world champions Joey Maxim and Archie Moore, three times each. But Charles never got a shot at this title.

He moved up to heavyweight, and after Joe Louis retired was matched with Jersey Joe Walcott for the vacant title, winning on points in June 1949. He was not universally recognised because Louis made a comeback but in September 1950, after three defences, he beat Louis to end the arguments. He made three more defences before Jersey Joe Walcott took the title from him in 1951.

Charles was nearly 31 but continued boxing and two years later earned a crack at new unbeaten champion Rocky Marciano. A late rally earned Marciano a decision in a bloody bout that denied Charles'

reputation as an unexciting fighter. He lost an even bloodier return three months later by a knockout, but the damage he inflicted on Marciano helped Marciano's decision to retire after two more defences.

Charles carried on for five years until he was 38 but lost 13 out of 23 more fights, which disfigured an otherwise brilliant record. He spent his last years in a wheelchair and died at 54 without the recognition he deserved.

Record: 122 contests; 96 wins; 1 draw; 25 defeats

See also: Marciano v Charles

Azores, and Marcel and manager Jo Longman were killed.

Cerdan and his long-time friend, the singer Edith Piaf, were worshipped in France, and there was national mourning over the loss of one of the all-time great middleweights.
Record: 115 contests; 111 wins; 4 defeats

ABOVE: Marcel Cerdan (right), on his way to winning the world title from Tony Zale.

RIGHT: Ezzard Charles taking the vacant heavyweight championship.

JULIO CESAR CHAVEZ

born: 12 July 1962, Ciudad Obregon, Sonora, Mexico

When Chavez was three, his parents moved to Culiacan, where he had a few amateur bouts before following his brother (he was the fourth of ten children) into the pro ranks in 1980. He began as a bantam and his early record is a little unclear. An early loss by disqualification is a possibility but in May 1983 he took a record of 35 straight wins to San Juan and Los Angeles, before in September 1984 winning the vacant WBC super-featherweight title by stopping Mario Martinez in Los Angeles.

A superb boxer with a strong punch in both hands and unlimited stamina, Chavez began to dominate his weight class with victories in the USA, Europe and Mexico. Strong contenders like Roger Mayweather, Refugio Rojas, Rocky Lockridge and Juan Laporte were among the nine challengers he beat up to August 1987. In November 1987 he stopped Edwin Rosario to take the WBA lightweight crown and in October 1988, after one defence, he added the WBC version when he won a technical decision over his former stablemate Jose Luis Ramirez after a clash of heads in the 11th, Chavez having fought with a rib injury.

Chavez moved up another weight in May 1989, stopping Roger Mayweather in the tenth round to win the WBC light-welter title. He again amalgamated titles on 17 March 1990 by stopping IBF champion Meldrick Taylor to add this crown to his collection. This was a controversial decision, Taylor being ahead on points when the referee stopped the bout with two seconds to go in the last round. However Chavez kept defending successfully. When Lonnie Smith went the distance with him on 14 September 1991 he was the first to do so for over four years.

Idolised in Mexico, the good-looking Chavez has been handicapped in his quest for superstardom in the States by a lack of English, but his unbeaten record and collection of titles mounts up.

Record: 80 contests; 80 wins

See also: Chavez v Taylor

ONE of the 1990s greats, Julio Cesar Chavez.

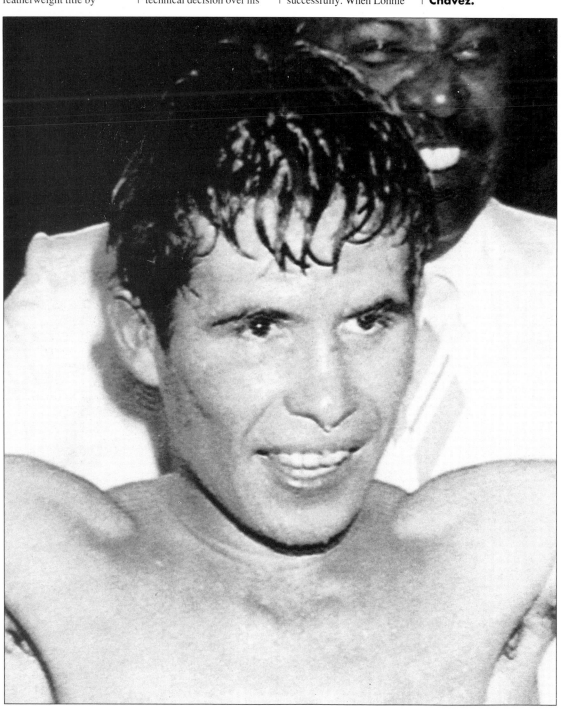

JULIO CESAR CHAVEZ V MELDRICK TAYLOR

17 March 1990, Las Vegas

Julio Cesar Chavez was spoken of as the 1990s opened as a candidate for the best pound-for-pound fighter in the world. He had moved up the divisions from super-featherweight through lightweight and into light-welterweight. In each he had been a world champion. A total of 68 unbeaten contests spoke for his ability. Meldrick Taylor, four years younger, had turned professional four years later than Chavez and was also unbeaten in 25 contests. Less of a puncher than Chavez, he was nevertheless a very smooth boxer, who had taken the IBF light-welterweight title with an impressive win over James 'Buddy' McGirt. There were plenty to say that Taylor would give WBC champion Chavez plenty of trouble when they met in the Las Vegas Hilton to unify the two titles.

Taylor's plan was to use his speed to score points and escape without allowing the heavy punching of Chavez to catch him. However Taylor took a punch to the eye in the first round which blurred his vision, upset his judgement of distance and forced him to change his plans. The injury was later described as a blow-out fracture of the left eye. He decided to keep in close to the puncher Chavez. To the surprise of the fans, who did not know why Taylor was fighting as he was, Taylor proved at least the equal of Chavez inside, where his hand speed and his combination punching continually piled up the points and kept Chavez off balance. Chavez, however, being a class boxer, was scoring with heavy punches himself, and throughout had the ability, if he could get set, to hurt Taylor more than Taylor could hurt him.

In the tenth round, Taylor at last seemed to stagger Chavez with a flurry of shots to the head but, as he piled in to take advantage, Chavez pulled him up short with some punishing blows which nearly put Taylor down.

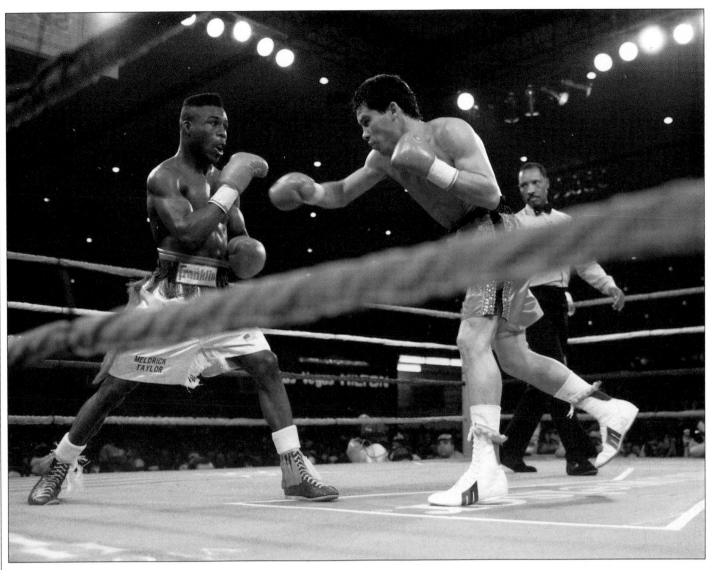

CHAVEZ, Meldrick Taylor and referee Richard Steele in their controversial encounter.

Coming out for the last round, Taylor's corner advised him that he needed it to be sure of the verdict – a mistaken view – and the weary Taylor went all out in a big finish. This was a bad mistake as, half-way through the round, he ran out of steam. The unbeaten Chavez, a three-time world champion, was punching as strongly as at the first bell, and a series of rights to Taylor's head finally sent him crashing down. Taylor rose at five in command of his senses but, as referee Richard Steele peered into his eyes to ensure he had recovered, so Taylor's corner made a second mistake. Trainer and manager Lou Duva climbed onto the apron of the ring and Taylor stared in puzzlement beyond Steele

towards Duva. Taylor assumed the fight was over and was not responsive to the referee's question 'Are you OK?' It seemed to Steele as Taylor looked past him that the boxer was trying to focus and he consequently stopped the bout. Chavez had won. There were only two seconds of the last round remaining.

There was uproar when the judges' score-cards were revealed. After 11 rounds Taylor was so far ahead on the cards of two judges (by seven and five points) that, had the contest not been stopped, he was the clear winner. There was not time for Chavez to knock him out, or even to get in another punch. The third judge had Chavez ahead by one point, and the majority press opinion had the contest very close, with Taylor just ahead.

Despite the fact that Taylor was ahead on points, there was no doubt that he suffered the worse injuries. Apart from his eye injury, he

had been swallowing blood for ten rounds and had been bleeding in his kidneys. He was kept in hospital overnight. The contest posed that question which makes a classic fight: will the outstanding ringcraft of one man foil the punching power of the other? But the brilliance of the bout was overshadowed by the controversy of the stoppage.

Those who thought the referee's decision premature pointed to the fact that Taylor was near a neutral corner where a red light blinks during the last ten seconds of a round. So Steele should have known that the fight was practically over and there was no need to stop it. Also, Steele did not go through the usual procedure to test if a boxer has recovered of holding up fingers for the boxer to count. Just doing this would have exhausted the two seconds remaining, and Taylor would have won.

Those who thought Steele was right claimed that when a fighter, at the end of a mandatory eight count, does not raise his gloves in readiness to continue or answer the referee's repeated question as to his condition, the referee has no option but to end the contest.

Two other points were made. The WBC had decreed title fights would be over 12 rounds rather than the old 15. It is probable that Chavez would have won on a genuine knockout had the fight gone to 15 rounds although, of course, Taylor might well have paced a 15-rounder differently. And the excitable Lou Duva, loudest in his objections after the contest, by deciding to climb into the ring before the bell rang to end the fight, possibly cost Taylor the decision and, in any case, risked his disqualification. All in all it was a contest which had almost everything.

KID CHOCOLATE

born: (Eligio Sardinias) 6 January 1910, Cerro, Cuba
died: 8 August 1988, Havana, Cuba

Kid Chocolate was a supremely proportioned 'exquisitely handsome' (Damon Runyon) featherweight, who could box silkily but at the same time deliver a knockout punch. He was known in New York as the Havana Bon Bon, or the Kandy Kid. In or out of the ring, with his cars, suits and nightclubbing, he had style.

He began professionally in 1928, after over 100 amateur victories, and soon moved his centre of operations from Havana to New York. He cried when in his 53rd fight he lost for the first time, to light-welter Jack 'Kid' Berg. This famous meeting of the Kids was at lightweight. Soon afterwards he challenged Battling

C

Battalino for the world featherweight crown, but was outpointed. However, seven months later the 21-year-old won the super-featherweight title by stopping Benny Bass in Philadelphia, and in the same year he challenged Tony Canzoneri for both the light and light-welterweight titles which Canzoneri held, but

was outpointed. But the Kid did win a second world title when he knocked out Lew Feldman for the New York version of the featherweight championship in October 1932.

Kid Chocolate successfully defended his titles in four contests, but his life-style got to him on 26 December 1935 when he lost

his super-featherweight title to Frankie Klick on a stoppage. He relinquished the lighter title because he could not make the weight any more. He continued to box regularly till 1938, having 24 contests in 1937 alone (without being beaten).
Record: 148 contests; 132 wins; 6 draws; 10 defeats

BILLY CONN

born: 8 October 1917, East Liberty, Pennsylvania, USA

Billy Conn, of Irish descent, was a scrapaper as a kid. He walked into a gym at 11 and his courage so impressed trainer Johnny Ray that he was allowed to stick around. As he grew up he sparred with the likes of Mickey Walker and in 1935 at 17 he made his pro debut, never having fought as an amateur. He won a few and lost a few, and then gradully began winning more, but he grew into an awkward size, just too big for a middleweight. This earned a tilt at the vacant light-heavyweight championship, and on 13 July he outpointed Melia Bettina to claim the crown.

Billy, a charming, handsome man who liked to brag and to live in the fast lane was never a big puncher but he had fast handspeed and was a brilliant boxer, quick moving and well-balanced. He and his managers realised that to cash in on his great appeal to the fans he had to tackle the heavyweights, and he got his weight up to around 180lb. Surprisingly, he beat rated heavies Lee Savold, Bob Pastor and Buddy Knox, actually stopping the last two. With his charisma and big Irish following it was natural to put him in with champion Joe Louis. In a famous contest in 1941 he led until caught by a Louis knockout in the 13th round. After the war he fought Louis again, but was a shadow of his former self and fought only twice more.
Record: 75 contests; 63 wins; 1 draw; 11 defeats

See also: Louis v Conn

JOHN CONTEH

born: 27 May 1951, Liverpool

Conteh was an excellent amateur boxer who won ABA titles at middle and light-heavyweight before turning professional in October 1971. A handsome,

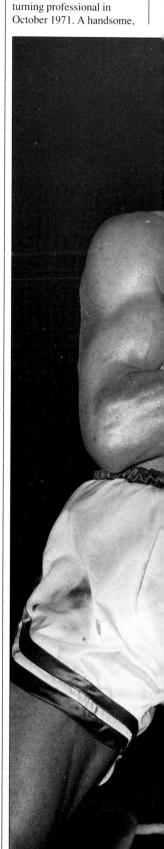

LEFT: Billy Conn, most remembered for his epic 1941 battle with Joe Louis.

RIGHT: John Conteh (left) who proved himself Britain's best with his victory over Chris Finnegan.

superbly proportioned 6ft fighter, he excited the fans with his ruthless combination punching which brought him 15 knockouts in his first 18 contests. He then knocked out Rudiger Schmidtke for the European light-heavyweight title, and in his next bout added the British and Commonwealth titles after a superb contest with Chris Finnegan, whom he beat on points. His successful run continued until in October 1974 he outpointed Jorge Ahumada to win the WBC belt.

Conteh made three successful defences but began having trouble with his right hand, twice suffering a break. A strong-willed character who managed himself, he upset the WBC when he pulled out of a defence against Miguel Cuello in Monte Carlo in 1977 and was stripped of his title. He beat Joe Cokes and challenged new champion Mate Parlov in Belgrade in 1978 but was controversially adjudged a loser on a split decision. He was not quite as good after that, and two challenges to Matthew Saad Muhammad, in Atlantic City in 1979 and 1980, ended in a points defeat and his only stoppage. He soon retired to run one of the clubs he was fond of.

Record: 39 contests; 34 wins; 1 draw; 4 defeats

CONTESTS

Boxers fought more often in the old days than they do now (even as late as the 1930s Henry Armstrong fought 27 times in 1937 and had 12 world title fights in 1939). Especially from days before the First World War many fighters records are incomplete. In assessing who had most contests there is also the problem of exhibition matches, which were commonplace even beyond the Second World War, and matches fought in boxing booths, where the best, such as Jim Driscoll, had hundreds of contests.

The boxer generally credited with most contests is Abe Hollandersky, who fought as Abe the Newsboy between 1905 and 1918 and is reputed to have had 1,309 contests. However many of these were exhibitions.

Bobby Dobbs, a black American born in Knoxville, Tennessee, 1858, is said to have had 1,204 bouts between 1875 and 1914. He was nicknamed the 'Master Teacher', but the records are sketchy and the exact number of genuine contests he had will never be known.

The great world flyweight champion, Jimmy Wilde, who developed his skills in boxing booths, claimed a total of 864 contests in his career, of which he claimed to have lost four. His total of recorded fights is 153.

Other boxers whose 'complete' records would exceed 600 or so contests are Sam Langford, who fought from around 1898 to 1926, Jeff Smith, a New Yorker, who was known as the 'Globe Trotter', who boxed from around 1909 to 1927 and Frank Parkes, a bantamweight from Dundee, who claimed around 700 contests, most in booths, between the two world wars.

Among world champions, Ted 'Kid' Lewis and Jack Britton, who fought each other 20 times with the world welterweight title at stake, both claimed to have had over 350 contests in all. Britton's recorded total is 327, while that of Lewis is 281.

The most recorded bouts between the same two men is 23 between Sam Langford of Canada and Harry Wills of the USA between 1914 and 1922. Both men might have been a world champion had they not been black. Langford also met Sam McVey (USA) 15 times and Joe Jeannette (USA) 14 times.

See also Wins and defeats; Knockouts

JIMMY WILDE claimed to have fought 864 times, including the many challenges he faced in boxing booths.

HENRY COOPER

born: 3 May 1934, Bellingham, Kent

Henry Cooper was one of identical twins, his brother George also fighting professionally (as Jim). Henry was the better, twice winning the ABA light-heavyweight title before turning pro in 1954. He was successful enough as a fast, slim heavyweight with a devastating left hook until a two-year spell from September 1956, when he won only one fight in seven, including knockout defeats by Joe Bygraves for the British Empire title and Ingemar Johansson for the European. A battle on 3 September 1958 turned the tables. Cut in the first and down in the fifth against future European champion Dick Richardson, Cooper got up off the canvas to knock Richardson off his feet and clean out with his famous left hook.

Henry immediately outpointed tough American Zora Folley and in his next fight took the British and Empire titles from Brian London. Cooper made eight successful defences over the next ten years, uniquely becoming the only boxer to win three Lonsdale belts outright. During this time he added the European title and fought the then Cassius Clay. In June 1963 Clay was groggy at the end of the fourth round, but enjoyed a long rest (and illegal smelling salts) when a split in his glove suddenly worsened. He returned to cut Cooper so badly in the fifth that it was stopped. It was perhaps the closest Clay came to defeat in his prime.

Prominent bones and thin skin above the eyes was Cooper's greatest handicap. Many of his defeats came when his eyebrows spurted blood. They were the problem when he challenged Ali for his world title in 1966. He was holding his own until stopped in the sixth.

RIGHT: One of Britain's most popular boxers, Henry Cooper.

HENRY COOPER with one of his three Lonsdale belts.

When Ali was side-lined in 1969 Cooper was matched with Jimmy Ellis for the WBA title, but the BBBC, who supported the WBC but not the WBA, refused to recognise the contest as for the title. In disgust Cooper resigned his British and Empire titles, and gave up the European after a cartilage operation. He came back and in two contests in 1970 immediately won all three titles back. However when Joe Bugner took them all from him in 1971 with a decision that few agreed with, the 37-year-old finally gave up. His down-to-earth Cockney commonsense soon made him a long-lasting favourite on the celebrity circuit.

Record: 55 contests; 40 wins: 1 draw; 14 defeats

See also: Ali v Cooper

JAMES J. CORBETT

born: 1 September 1866, San Francisco, California, USA
died: 18 February 1933, Bayside, New York

Corbett was a bank clerk by profession but was so successful as an amateur boxer that at 19 he decided to turn professional. His good looks, stylish dress and educated manners (not common among the pros) earned him the nickname of Gentleman Jim. His main rival on his way up was the local Joe Choynski, whom he fought four times, finally disposing of him with a 27th round knockout in a battle fought on a barge in 1889. Two years later he fought a tremendous 61-round draw with Peter Jackson, an outstanding West Indian heavyweight whom champion Sullivan refused to fight because of his colour. Corbett met Sullivan in an exhibition bout and, convinced he could beat him, challenged him for the title. They met at the Olympic Club in New Orleans in September 1892, the first heavyweight title fight under Queensberry Rules.

At 6ft 1in and 178lb Corbett was outweighed by 34lb, but was eight years the younger. He was also a much more scientific boxer than the 4-1 favourite. After outboxing Sullivan for 20 rounds, Corbett knocked him out in the next. Corbett defended against Englishman Charley Mitchell, who weighed only 158lb, and then in 1897 was knocked out by another Englishman, Bob Fitzsimmons, the former middleweight champion, who weighed only 167lb. Corbett was on top until Fitz produced a famous blow to the solar plexus. Corbett was conscious but too winded to defend his crown further.

Corbett challenged new champion James J. Jeffries in May 1900, but after outclassing him for 23 rounds was caught by a

punch and knocked out. Another try in 1903 ended in the tenth.

Because he introduced science to heavyweight boxing and because he beat the fans' favourite, the roistering John L. Sullivan, Corbett was never accorded the recognition he deserved as the first heavyweight champion.

Record: 19 contests; 11 wins; 2 draws; 4 defeats; 2 no-contest

See also: Corbett v Sullivan

JAMES J. CORBETT V JOHN L. SULLIVAN

7 September 1892, New Orleans

Some claim John L. Sullivan was the first heavyweight champion on the grounds that a match between him and Dominick McCaffrey in Cincinatti on 29 August 1885 was billed as 'The Marquess of Queensberry glove contest for the championship of the world'. But as the referee of this six-rounder did not declare a winner until asked for one two days later, it seems a skimpy claim, and it was not made before 1936 when somebody discovered the old record of the fight.

Better to let John L. remain the last bare-knuckle champion and recognise the match at New Orleans in 1892 as the first for the heavyweight championship. Sullivan arrived in majestic style in New Orleans, his train full of champagne-quaffing well-wishers. Having worked hard to remove the traces of whisky drinking from his body, he weighed 16 stone, most of it muscle. Everybody wanted to shake the hand of the great man. Corbett, a 'California Dandy', was eight years younger, and a sleek 12 stone ten pounds. He, too, had trained hard and was fit. New Orleans was packed with fans and hangers-on, including pickpockets and gamblers. Sullivan, despite his known roistering, was four to one favourite with the gamblers. Few thought the Boston Strong Boy, who had seen off all-comers by sheer strength and punching power, could be beaten by an ex-bank clerk, and it was said even Corbett's father had bet on Sullivan.

Corbett entered the ring in the 'star spot' of second place after Sullivan had arrived alone, thus establishing a clever psychological advantage. The contest soon developed a pattern. Sullivan began as he always did, rushing at his opponent in order to land his heavy artillery. But Corbett sidestepped, slipped punches, moved out of range. Occasionally he countered, picking off the lumbering Sullivan or stepping in with hooks when the big man missed. No doubt to Sullivan this all seemed somewhat unmanly. He had met a slippery customer who wouldn't stand toe-to-toe before in the Briton, Charley Mitchell, who had foiled him in a draw in Paris. But he had not met an opponent who retaliated like Corbett. Sullivan still had his punch, but not only did Corbett refuse to stand still while he delivered it, he hit back.

As the match went on, Sullivan's face began to show the results of Corbett's punches. Eventually his own efforts began to wear him out. In the 21st round Corbett put him down, and Sullivan could not get his great bulk upright in time to continue. The crowd didn't like Corbett's tactics. They were used to big punchers slugging it out. The 'noble art of self defence' was not appreciated at all. Corbett never overcame the unpopularity caused by this display.

Sullivan, on the other hand, made a tearful speech in which he said he was pleased the championship had stayed in America, and left more popular than ever.

BELOW: Corbett and Sullivan.

TOM CRIBB

born: 8 July 1781, Hanham, Gloucestershire
died: 11 May 1848, London

Tom Cribb left his home for London aged 14 and lived with relations. He worked on the docks, then joined the navy, where he won enough skirmishes to persuade him to become a prizefighter. At 5ft 10in and nearly 200lb he was a formidable scrapper, who nevertheless tasted hls only defeat in his fourth fight – by George Nicholls after 52 rounds in 1805. But he easily beat Bill Richmond, a black former slave from America, and after wins over champion Jem Belcher and claimant Bob Gregson was acclaimed champion.

Cribb wanted to retire then, but another former slave, Tom Molineaux, came from America claiming to be American champion, and after some good wins he challenged Cribb. The Fancy reacted with horror at the idea of an American – and a black one at that – being champion of the world, and Cribb was persuaded to fight him.

On a cold rainy December day in 1810, which was greatly to his disadvantage, Molineaux fought so well that after 28 rounds Cribb could not come up to the mark, and by the rules should have lost. But his quick-thinking second caused a diversion by accusing Molineaux of carrying weights in his hands. The referee's investigation and the uproar gave Cribb time to recover, and five rounds later it was Molineaux who was carried away the loser. Cribb became a hero and retired, but again Molineaux claimed the title by default, so Cribb was forced to fight him again. This time he trained hard and won more easily. There is a large memorial to Cribb in Woolwich churchyard, London.

LES DARCY

born: 31 October 1895, Woodville,NSW, Australia
died: 24 May 1917,

Memphis, Tennessee, USA

Les Darcy was possibly the best boxer Australia produced. His story is also possibly the most tragic. The family breadwinner from a young age because his father was a semi-invalid, he became a blacksmith's apprentice. With his strong build he became a pro boxer at 15 and was only just 18 when outpointed for the Australian welterweight title by Bob Whitelaw. However, he knocked out Whitelaw the following year, and challenged American Jeff Smith, who was in Australia, for the world middleweight title which Smith claimed. Smith struck Darcy low, and was awarded the fight when Darcy couldn't continue. The same thing happened in a return four months later, but this time Darcy was given the decision on a disqualification.

Darcy defended his world title six times in 1915, twice beating an American, Eddie McGoorty, who also claimed the title after losing controversially to Smith. By September 1916 Darcy had also twice beaten another ranked American, George Clabby, and on the last day of that month he knocked out George Chip, another American and former middleweight champion.

The strong, hard-punching Australian, whose only defeats were the two mentioned and two disqualifications, looked the world's best middleweight, but of course Americans would not allow the title to stay in Australia, so promoter Tex Rickard invited him to the States to meet Al McCoy, the US claimant. Alas Australia had now entered the war and being over 18 Darcy was forbidden to leave the country. Seeing his chances to settle matters and make a fortune disappearing, Darcy fled to America anyway. By the time he arrived, the US were in the war, too, and Darcy was denied a licence, and called a slacker. He went on the stage and kept in trim, but after losing a tooth sparring with a heavyweight he developed pneumonia and died, dispirited, still only 21.
Record: 50 contests; 46 wins; 4 defeats

JACK DEMPSEY

born: (John Kelly) 15 December 1862, County Kildare, Ireland
died: 2 November 1895, Portland, Oregon, USA

The original Jack Dempsey was taken to New York as a boy and became a cooper. He volunteered his services at a boxing booth in 1883 and at 150lb proved without equal at his weight, and was called 'The Nonpareil'. In 1884 he knocked out George Fulljames in New York and claimed to be the world's first middleweight champion. A Canadian, George LaBlanche, knocked him out in 32 rounds in 1889 but was not recognised as champion because he used a pivot punch, which was immediately banned. However the heavily gambled-on Dempsey lost the title in an upset in 1891 to Bob Fitzsimmons, putting up a tremendously brave display before being knocked out in the 13th round.

Dempsey died in 1895 and his neglected grave, found in 1899, is the subject of a famous poem.
Record: 68 contests; 48 wins; 7 draws; 3 defeats; 7 no-decision; 3 no-contest

JACK DEMPSEY

born: 24 June 1895, Manassa, Colorado, USA
died: 31 May 1983, New York City

Dempsey's forenames were William Harrison, and when he followed his brother Bernie into boxing, he boxed as 'Young Dempsey' or 'Kid Blackie', his brother having called himself Jack after the old middleweight. When Bernie gave up Dempsey became 'Jack'. He worked in mining and timber camps while fighting but nearly gave up as he was getting nowhere. It was meeting manager Jack 'Doc' Kearns that transformed his career.

Dempsey was a tough slugger with no pretensions to defence. His sole object was to take out his opponent as quickly as possible, and from 1917 many were despatched in the first round. Kearns persuaded promoter Tex Rickard to put Dempsey in with the giant Jess Willard for the heavyweight title, and

bet Dempsey's purse on a first-round win. Willard was down seven times and Dempsey thought he'd won the bet, but in the excitement nobody had heard the timekeeper end the round. Dempsey won in the third.

After two defences in 1920, Rickard matched Dempsey with the light-heavyweight champion, Frenchman Georges Carpentier. Dempsey was very unpopular because he had dodged serving in the war, and Rickard shrewdly selected the decorated hero Carpentier for the 'Fight of the Century'. It resulted in boxing's first million-dollar gate in Jersey City, but Carpentier had little chance of conceding the weight and was stopped in the fourth. After numerous exhibitions, Dempsey defended twice in 1923, ruining banks in Shelby, Montana, who forked out more than the customers would pay to see him outpoint Tommy Gibbons, and then, back with Rickard, knocking out Luis Firpo in the second round after himself being knocked out of the ring in the first. It was the most action-packed of all heavyweight title fights, and grossed another $1 million.

Dempsey then fell out with his manager Kearns over Dempsey's marriage with a Hollywood starlet, Estelle Taylor. He lived the soft life in Hollywood, had his nose remodelled and made films. Estelle objected to Kearns' cut of Dempsey's earnings, and Dempsey put his trust in Rickard. It was three years after he beat Firpo that he fought again. Over ten rounds in Philadelphia in the rain, before boxing's highest-ever paying audience of 120,757, he was thoroughly outpointed by Gene Tunney. It was like the end of a legend, with the ultra-macho Dempsey clinically destroyed by a technician. The bruised Dempsey explained to his wife: 'Honey, I forgot to duck' and overnight became as popular as any fighter.

Dempsey fought Jack Sharkey to re-establish himself. He was getting a beating and began fouling. When Sharkey finally turned his head to appeal to the

referee Dempsey knocked him out with a hook. It set up his last great fight, the return with Tunney. It was the story as before, except that once Dempsey did catch Tunney and floor him. Unfortunately he forgot to go to a neutral corner, and gave Tunney a precious 14 seconds rest while the referee took him away. It was all Tunney needed.

Dempsey retired and his marriage broke up, but he kept a lot of his money and for many years owned a New York restaurant.
Record: 78 contests; 62 wins; 10 draws; 6 defeats

See also: Dempsey v Firpo; Tunney v Dempsey

JACK DEMPSEY V LUIS FIRPO

14 September 1923, New York

Jack Dempsey was an awesome figure in 1923, the heavyweight champion of the world with, apparently, nobody around capable of standing up to his blazing fists. In 1921 he had demolished Georges Carpentier in the first $1 million fight, but when his manager Doc Kearns tried to promote a title fight himself, against Tommy Gibbons, it was a financial flop which ruined many good citizens of Shelby, Montana, who had invested in it. Dempsey and Kearns returned to top promoter Tex Rickard for another money-spinner and Rickard discovered the perfect opponent.

He was Luis Firpo, a 6ft 3in strong man from Buenos Aires, who was the South American champion. Firpo was raw and crude, but he had a record of quick knockout wins, and had stopped Gunboat Smith in 1921. He did not think he was ready for Dempsey, but Rickard waved his cheque-book and said it was now or never and Firpo, who had a

JACK DEMPSEY, posing at ramshackle training quarters, became a byword for destructive punching.

THE moment when Jack Dempsey was knocked out of the ring by Luis Firpo at the end of one of the most exciting rounds in boxing history. Dempsey was pushed back and won in the second round.

keen desire to make a fortune, agreed to the match. He was brought over to the States and, in 1923, beat a number of opponents to impress himself on the American public. Jess Willard, the veteran ex-champion, was one, Firpo disposing of him in the eighth round. Firpo built up his image by eating vast quantities of food with the press in attendance.

In September at New York's Polo Grounds, Firpo, nicknamed the 'Wild Bull of the Pampas', stepped into the ring against the 'Manassa Mauler'. Firpo was nearly three inches taller and a little heavier than Dempsey, and looked much more of a physical threat than the previous two challengers Carpentier and Gibbons. Celebrities packed the front rows and Rickard said to Dempsey: 'We've got another million-dollar gate. Give them their moneysworth and don't knock him out with the first punch.' Dempsey looked at Firpo and realised he couldn't risk being caught by this slugger.

At the bell both boxers advanced in a crouching stance and the challenger threw the first punch, a clumsy blow that nevertheless caught Dempsey on the chin. Down went the champion. This knockdown heralded the most savage round in boxing history.

Dempsey rose and clinched. The referee said 'break' and as Firpo dropped his hands Dempsey swung a left hook and Firpo was on the deck. Firpo rose and landed another blow but it was he who went down as Dempsey's countering uppercut caught him on the chin. Both men continued to swing punches at each other, but Dempsey was the quicker puncher and usually got his in first. He had another advantage – whenever Firpo was down Dempsey stood over him and resumed the initiative as soon as Firpo was upright, sometimes being not too squeamish to put the challenger down again while he was still groggily rising. In all Firpo was down seven times in the first round and looked almost out on the last occasion. But somehow he rose and threw desperate punches at Dempsey as he at last forced him back across the ring. A thunderous left stunned Dempsey by the ropes, and a crashing right sent the champion clean through them.

It should have been the end of the fight, but Dempsey landed on the sports writers in the front row. While the blackness was clearing from his head, the reporters pushed him back onto the apron of the ring. Dempsey claimed he never remembered climbing back into the ring. Luckily for him the bell rang before Firpo could do any more damage.

In the interval Dempsey came round and learned he was still in the fight. At the start of the second round he took another punch from Firpo, but clinched, and landed a flurry on the break which put Firpo down for the eighth time. He got up, but Dempsey crashed a left to his jaw and that was that.

The rules were infringed during this fight. Dempsey illegally received help in getting back into the ring, but this can hardly be legislated against. However, the way he stood over Firpo when he was down led to referees insisting that the boxer who achieves a knockdown retires to a neutral corner. It was to have an effect on Dempsey in a future fight (*see* Tunney v Dempsey). For the meantime, the fans who had paid $1 million to see three minutes 57 seconds of boxing did not feel cheated in the least.

GEORGE DIXON

born: 29 July 1870, Halifax, Nova Scotia, Canada
died: 6 January 1909, New York City

George Dixon was a black Canadian, who was called 'Little Chocolate' because of his height (5ft 3½ in) and colour. He was an exquisite boxer with a good punch, who began pro boxing in 1886. In the days when weight divisions were less defined than they are now, his 18th round stoppage of Nunc Wallace in London in June 1890 made him bantamweight champion of the world. Difficulty in making the weight, however, caused him to move to featherweight in 1891, when his stoppage of Cal McCarthy in 22 rounds in Troy, New York made him champion. Dixon defended this title 14 times up to October 1897, but was then outpointed by Solly Smith in San Francisco. However, in November 1898 he regained the title when champion Dave Sullivan was disqualified, and Dixon defended it eight more times. He was finally stopped in January 1900 by Terry McGovern. Dixon had taken part in 29 world title fights, losing only three.

His overall record suffers because as a black boxer he was often forced to lose fights to get work. After losing his title he fought 58 more times, winning only nine and losing 20. He died two years after retiring.
Record: 130 contests; 50 wins; 42 draws; 26 defeats; 7 no-decision; 5 no-contest

JAMES 'BUSTER' DOUGLAS V MIKE TYSON

10 February 1990, Tokyo, Japan

Of all the upsets in boxing history, the one that took place in Tokyo in 1990 would probably win a vote as the biggest. Mike Tyson was the unbeaten, undisputed heavyweight champion. He had swept aside the world's best in 36 unbeaten contests, ten of them title fights. Only three men had managed to go the distance with him. His punching power and speed, particularly his hand-speed, and his ruthlessness when on top gave him an air of destructive invincibility. He was the youngest-ever heavyweight champion and, when he announced his intention of being the oldest, too, there were none who thought it impossible.

James 'Buster' Douglas, on the other hand, was a no-hoper, an opponent filling in until Evander Holyfield was ready to challenge. Douglas had lost four times in his 34 bouts, including a stoppage by Tony Tucker for the vacant IBF title. For amusement more than serious betting, one bookmaker offered odds of 40-1 against Douglas winning.

Douglas had advantages of 11lb (at 16st 7½lb) and 5½ inches (at 6ft 4½in). He looked fit and trained, which was not always the case in his previous bouts. Two weeks before the fight his mother died of hypertension and at the time of the fight the mother of his son was seriously ill. These emotional upsets he was able to put aside when he climbed into the ring, and he boxed beautifully to his plan – moving and jabbing to frustrate Tyson's attempts to bully his way inside in his usual manner. Douglas kept his concentration, and his jabs mixed with an occasional uppercut began to jolt the sluggish Tyson. He grabbed when necessary and did not come off the worse when there was an exchange of punches to end the fourth. All the time his confidence seemed to be increasing.

In the fifth round Douglas began to put together combination punches and shook Tyson. Tyson seemed to be out of ideas as, almost for the first time, he found an opponent systematically attacking him. Douglas did not get carried away by his success and did little in the sixth and seventh, being content to consolidate and use his jab to keep Tyson at a distance and his bulk to wrestle him when he did get close. Tyson's left eye was closing.

The eighth round was crucial. With about a minute to go Douglas shook Tyson with a right to the mouth but, as Douglas came in again after the referee had separated them, Tyson launched a right uppercut that knocked Douglas backwards onto the canvas. Douglas slapped the canvas with disgust at his slackening of concentration, but began to rise at 'seven' and was up at 'eight'. He was groggy, and groggy boxers did not usually last long with Tyson, but luckily for him the bell came to end the round.

Tyson had not enough strength left to mount the decisive attack in the ninth round. Douglas survived the little pressure that Tyson applied as he tried to find the one punch to finish it, and by the end of the round was shaking Tyson with more lefts and rights. Douglas resumed on top in the tenth and his heavy jabs set up the opportunity for a right uppercut which jerked Tyson's head back. Rapid follow-up punches dropped Tyson to the floor where he showed no signs of rising, scrabbling around for his lost gumshield as the referee completed the count. Douglas wept, as a man is entitled to do who pulls off the impossible.

However, Douglas couldn't yet call himself champion. The WBA and WBC, prompted by Tyson's promoter Don King, who saw millions of dollars disappearing with the title, announced that they were 'suspending the result' on the grounds that referee Octavio Meyran had not taken up the timekeeper's count when Douglas was down in the eighth but had started one of his own, thus granting Douglas a rest of more than ten seconds. Luckily the whole sordid manoeuvre was laughed to scorn by public opinion and came to nothing. It is as well that Douglas won the title in such a decisive manner because, although the American judge had Douglas ahead by six points at the end of the ninth round,

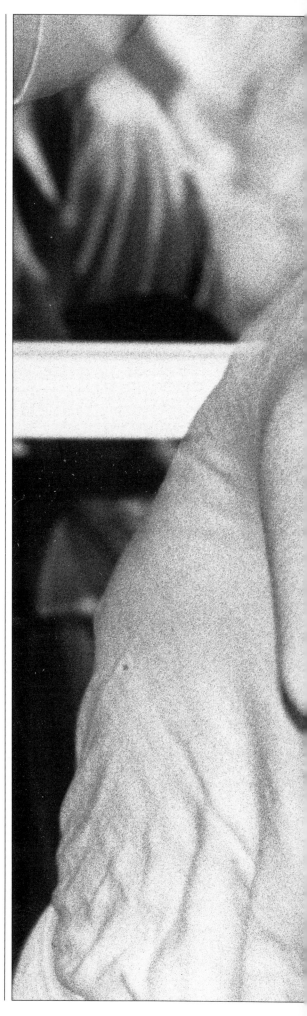

MIKE TYSON looked invincible before tackling James 'Buster' Douglas in Tokyo.

a reasonable margin in the estimation of most critics, the two Japanese judges had Tyson level on one card and a point ahead on the other.

Unfortunately, this fight was a one-off for Douglas. He weighed a flabby 17st 8lb when facing his first challenge against Evander Holyfield (38lb lighter) and hardly put up a fight, being knocked out in the third.

TERRY DOWNES

born: 9 May 1936, Paddington, London

Downes boxed as an amateur until, when he was 15, his parents took him to the United States, where his sister had been in an accident. He joined the US Marines, continued boxing, and won the US All-Services title. Back in London, he began his professional career in April 1957. He had an all-action windmill style and scorned defence which meant that few of his fights went the distance. Occasionally he was stopped through cuts and suffered particularly with what he called his 'bleeding hooter', a nose which bled copiously. He won the British middleweight title in 1958 and in 1961 challenged Paul Pender for the world title in Boston, but was stopped by cuts. Back in London six months later he took the title from Pender, only to surrender it back in Boston in 1962. He beat an ageing Sugar Ray Robinson, then challenged for the world light-heavyweight title. He was well ahead into the 11th round at Manchester in November 1964, but champion Willie Pastrano dropped him with one punch and the referee stopped it to Downes' disgust. He retired immediately, bought a demolition business and then owned a chain of betting shops.
Record: 44 contests; 35 wins; 9 defeats

TERRY DOWNES protects his 'hooter' while taking the vacant British title against Phil Edwards.

JIM DRISCOLL

born: 15 December 1880, Cardiff, Wales
died: 31 January 1925, Cardiff, Wales

Driscoll, a Welshman of Irish ancestry, learned to box when an apprentice in a newspaper office. Soon he was boxing in the booths, where hundreds of fights perfected his skills. A handsome youth, he was a great favourite around Cardiff. He turned professional in 1901, winning the Welsh featherweight title before the end of the year.

'Peerless' Jim Driscoll was an artistic boxer. His defence was perfect, his punching textbook. Although he did not possess a conventional knockout punch, half his opponents were stopped. In 1907 he knocked out Joe Bowker in the 17th round to win the British title and in 1908 he added the British Empire title. Driscoll then went to the United States to seek the world title, and all his ten contests there are in the record books as wins, although some decisions rest on the newspaper vote, as they were no-decision bouts. The last was against champion Abe Attell, whom Driscoll outclassed, but could not knock out in the scheduled ten rounds and so could not claim the title.

Back in Cardiff in 1910 he was persuaded to box Freddie Welsh, the future world lightweight champion, and in a dirty fight was disqualified for butting. It was only his second defeat.

In 1912 the 32-year-old Driscoll won the vacant European title when knocking out Frenchman Jean Posey. He was recognised in Europe as world champion because of Attell's refusal to face him again. He defended once but war broke out and he was inactive for nearly five years, being forced to relinquish all his titles.

After the war he was persuaded to make a comeback at 38, and had his last three contests. In the last he suffered his third defeat when facing future European champion Charles Ledoux. His seconds threw in the towel in the 16th to save him unnecessary punishment. It is possible he was already suffering from the consumption from which he died five years later.

Record: 69 contests; 60 wins; 6 draws; 3 defeats

ROBERTO DURAN

born: 16 June 1951, Guarare, Panama

Duran was just under 16 when he made his professional debut in Colon in March 1967. He won on points but only one of his next eight opponents reached the second round, when he, like the rest, was knocked out. It was obvious that the aggressive Duran was going to be good. His countrymen called him 'Manos de Piedra' (Hands of Stone).

After 28 straight wins Duran challenged Ken Buchanan for the WBA lightweight title in New York in June 1972. After a tremendous battle the classy Buchanan failed to come out for the 14th. Duran defended 11 times in 5½ years and then unified the title by knocking out WBC champion Estaban de Jesus in Las Vegas. Duran, unbeaten as a lightweight, moved up to welterweight.

The macho-man Duran was a merciless destroyer of opponents, never letting them get off the hook. But he was more than an outstanding puncher. He was a clever mover, who knew how to minimise the effects of punches and to keep his opponent off-balance. In June 1980 Duran challenged Sugar Ray Leonard for the WBC welterweight title in Montreal, and to the surprise of boxing fans crowded the smooth Leonard so effectively that he inflicted his first defeat on him and took his crown. However, the idol of Panama blotted his copybook in the return five months later when he became demoralised by Leonard's boxing and turned his back on him in the eighth round, saying: 'No mas' (no more).

For the macho-man this was disgrace, and Duran set about retrieving his reputation. He moved up to light middleweight and challenged Wilfred Benitez for the WBC title but was outpointed. He was then outpointed by Kirkland Laing, but in June 1983 he was given a chance at Davey Moore's WBA title and was much too experienced for the young champion, who was stopped in the eighth. Duran now audaciously challenged the outstanding middleweight champion, Marvin Hagler, and surprised fans again by going the distance.

However in June 1984 Duran was knocked out in the second round by Thomas Hearns, and appeared to be at the end of the road. He was outpointed by Robbie Sims, and between fights his weight ballooned. But five more wins and he challenged Iran Barklay for the WBC middleweight title and after a great battle won on points. He was nearly 38, and it was a world title at a fourth weight. Trouble with the taxman kept him going, and in December 1989 he challenged Sugar Ray Leonard for his WBC super-middleweight crown, losing on points after a tame fight.

Record: 93 contests; 85 wins; 8 defeats

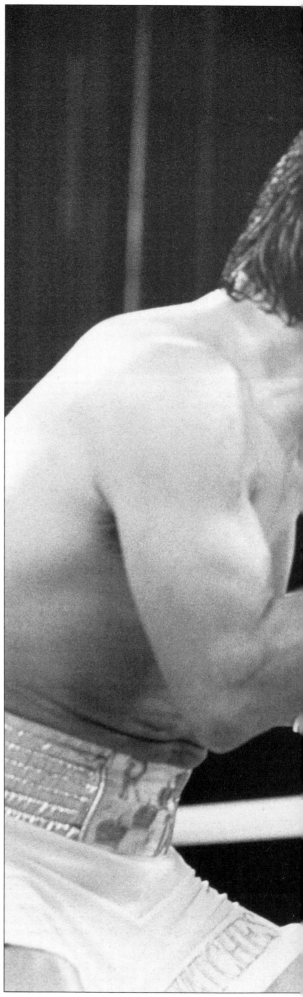

RIGHT: Roberto Duran (left) on the attack against an apprehensive Sugar Ray Leonard. Duran's first two battles with Leonard produced the highest and lowest points of his career.

BELOW: Duran's loss to Marvin Hagler was no disgrace for the ageing warrior.

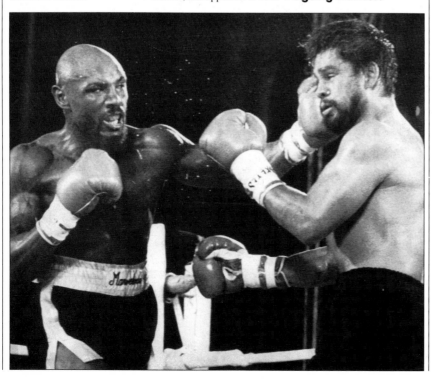

CHRIS EUBANK

born: 8 August 1966, Dulwich, London

Eubank boxed as an amateur for clubs in Peckham and the Bronx, New York, where he had been taken in 1982. He had 19 wins in 26 amateur contests there before beginning his professional career in Atlantic City in 1985, where he had five points victories. He returned to England and built up a good record of 20 straight wins and then won the WBC international middleweight title. He built up a reputation as an arrogant boxer by antics like leaping into the ring over the top rope and statuesque posing. The public wanted to see him beaten, and he was also treated with suspicion by the boxing world because of his carefully enunciated distaste of the sport, which he practised, he claimed, solely for the money.

In September 1990 he challenged Nigel Benn for the WBO middleweight title, and in a superb battle won on a ninth-round stoppage. He returned to Brighton, where he now lived, to win a technical decision over Canadian Dan Sherry, who could not continue after Eubank had butted him in the tenth round as they were separated by the referee from a clinch. Eubank had two points deducted but was given a very controversial technical decision. His third defence was against Michael Watson in June 1991, and Eubank won on points in another controversial decision.

Managed and promoted by Barry Hearn, Eubank faced Watson again in September in a much-hyped return. This was for the vacant WBO super-middleweight title, the two having moved up in weight and the WBO having cynically revised their ratings to allow the contest to be for the title. After looking a loser and being put down in the 11th round, Eubank rose to fell Watson immediately with a right uppercut. Although Watson beat the count, the referee stepped in early in the 12th when it was seen that he was badly injured. Watson, who had hit his head on the bottom rope as he fell, needed brain surgery and began a long period in hospital.

CHRIS EUBANK with WBO championship belt.

Eubank decided to fight on and in February 1992 outpointed Thulane Malinga. But then tragedy struck again when his car was involved in an accident which killed a roadside worker. In April 1992 he made a second defence when knocking out John Jarvis in the third round.

Record: 31 contests; 31 wins

See also: Eubank v Benn

CHRIS EUBANK V NIGEL BENN

18 November 1990, Birmingham

One of the most eagerly anticipated British fights in recent years was the WBO middleweight championship between Chris Eubank and Nigel Benn, not because the title was worth much, and not because the two men were even the best middleweights in England (Herol Graham was champion and Benn had lost to Michael Watson) but for the personalities of the two in what was something of a needle match.

Benn was the crowd-pleasing knockout specialist whose fights were rarely dull. He had won the WBO title in Atlantic City in April 1990 with a hard-hitting stoppage of the tough Doug de Witt, who had put Benn down during the fight. And he had destroyed Iran Barkley in one round in August. Eubank was unbeaten in 24 contests and was the boxer the fans loved to hate. He had the habit of entering the ring by vaulting the ropes and then strutting arrogantly around posing like a bodybuilder displaying his muscles. He also did a lot of talking, much of it to the detriment of boxing, which he implied was a barbaric sport which he practised purely for the money it brought him. He tended to do no more than was necessary to win, and half of the boxing world thought he was only a poseur with little talent behind his posturing. Benn was the opposite, fully exposed as an honest and enthusiastic destroyer who was nevertheless vulnerable to a punch. The fight would answer basic questions about Eubank and reveal whether or not Benn was capable of going further.

After they entered the ring at the National Exhibition Centre and Eubank had performed his trance-like pose, the battle commenced with Eubank moving and jabbing and Benn swinging and missing. Eubank edged the first and then stalked round the ring showing the fans his torso before returning to his corner. Eubank took a right smack in the face in the second but had Benn reeling at the end of the round with a barrage of punches which reddened Benn's eye.

The fight had warmed up quickly, and Benn took the third with punches which ripped into Eubank's body. Eubank replied with an uppercut but at the end of the round had blood coming from a cut on his cheek.

Benn also scored with lefts and rights in the fourth, but Benn's eye was closing from the punches taken in the second round.

Eubank now took the initiative, jabbing Benn relentlessly and accurately to the face. In the sixth the frustrated Benn dug a low blow into Eubank's groin, forcing Eubank to drop on one knee. Eubank was given a 30-second rest to recover from the foul. However the punch seemed to give Benn the advantage, and he mounted a body attack for a couple of rounds that troubled Eubank, especially when another blow seemed low.

In the eighth Benn caught Eubank to the head as Eubank slipped and the referee, Richard Steele of Las Vegas, ruled a knockdown and gave a mandatory eight count, to Eubank's obvious disgust. Two judges had Benn ahead after eight rounds, although both men had taken and given plenty of punishment, and Benn was in the worse position as his eye was now completely closed.

Eubank capitalised in the ninth by keeping the fight at long range and prodded Benn to the face, and Benn was reduced to rushing in to try to get in close, on one occasion bundling Eubank to the floor. Suddenly two rights from Eubank wobbled Benn and Eubank was on him in a flash, pouring in punches as Benn tried to take evasive action on the ropes. He momentarily got free but Eubank's assault was not to be stopped and the referee stepped in as Eubank ripped into Benn in a neutral corner. Eubank dropped to his knees in relief and joy.

It had been a tremendous encounter in which both men had given everything and answered the questions: Benn was not yet finished and Eubank was a prospect, not just a poseur.

CHRIS EUBANK on the point of finishing off Nigel Benn in 1990.

FAMILIES

Six sets of brothers have won world titles. They are:
Orlando Canizales (IBF bantamweight) and Gaby Canizales (WBA bantamweight)
Prudencio Cardona (WBC flyweight) and Ricardo Cardona (WBC light-featherweight)
Bruce Curry (WBC light-welterweight) and Don Curry (world welterweight and light-middleweight)
Joe Dundee (world welterweight) and Vince Dundee (world middleweight)
Kaosai Galaxy (WBA light-bantamweight) and Kaokor Galaxy (WBA bantamweight)
Leon Spinks (world heavyweight) and Michael Spinks (world light-heavyweight and IBF heavyweight)
(The Spinks brothers also won Olympic gold medals)

Other brothers who won titles are:
Dick and Harry Corbett (British champions)
Brian and Cliff Curvis (British champions). Ken Curvis also boxed.
Ray Famechon (European champion), Andre and Emile (both French champions)
George and John Feeney (British champions)
Chris and Kevin Finnegan (British champions)
Kirkland and Tony Laing (British champions)
John and Pat McCormack (British champions)
Duke McKenzie (IBF flyweight champion and WBO bantamweight champion) and Clinton McKenzie (British champion). Dudley McKenzie also boxed.
Vic Toweel (world bantamweight champion) and Willie Toweel (Commonwealth champion). Jimmy and Fraser Toweel were also boxers.
Randolph Turpin (world middleweight champion) and Dick Turpin (British champion). Jackie Turpin also boxed.

ON this spread are five men from boxing families. From bottom left, clockwise, they are Duke McKenzie, Marvin Hagler, Michael Spinks, Abe Attell and Dick Turpin.

Among other famous brothers are:

Abe Attell (world featherweight champion) and Monte

Max Baer (world heavyweight champion) and Buddy (heavyweight contender)

Alex Buxton (British champion) and Alan, Joe, Lawrie

Marvin Hagler (world middleweight champion) and Robbie Sims (half-brother)

Benny Leonard (world lightweight champion), Charlie and Joey

Terry Norris (WBA light-middleweight champion) and Orlin

Fritzie Zivic (world welterweight champion), Pete, Joe, Jack and Eddie

Twins:

Mike Sullivan (world welterweight champion) and Jack Sullivan (heavyweight contender). They boxed as Mike (Twin) Sullivan and Jack (Twin) Sullivan.

Henry Cooper (European champion) and George (who boxed as Jim Cooper)

Among fathers and sons who boxed are:

Marcel Cerdan (world middleweight champion) and Marcel junior

Andre Famechon and Johnny (world featherweight champion) *see also* Brothers (above)

Joe Frazier (world heavyweight champion) and Marvis and Hector

Jacob Hyer and Tom (both bare-knuckle champions of America)

Jack London (British champion) and sons Brian (British champion) and Jack junior

Phil Johnson and Harold (world light-heavyweight champion)

Jim 'Spider' Kelly and Billy 'Spider' Kelly (both British champions)

Wally Swift and son Wally (both British champions)

A unique family are the Pattersons. Floyd Patterson was world heavyweight champion and his adopted son Tracy Harris Patterson was WBC light-featherweight champion.

Jersey Joe Walcott, the world heavyweight champion, had the odd experience of knocking out Phil Johnson in Philadelphia in three rounds in 1936, and knocking out his son, Harold Johnson, also in Philadelphia and also in three rounds, in 1950.

TOMMY FARR

born: 12 March 1913, Tonypandy, Wales
died: 1 March 1986, Brighton, Sussex

Tommy Farr worked down the mines as a boy and began boxing in the booths in Wales when 13. He went to London, mostly on foot, but suffered a defeat, returning to Wales to win the Welsh light-heavyweight title when 19. He tried to win the British title in London but lost to Eddie Phillips.

Farr became a heavyweight, won the Welsh title, and surprised everybody by outpointing Ben Foord for the British and Empire title in 1937. His tough apprenticeship had led to an awkward, crouching style, but he was a cagey boxer with a good straight left. All he lacked to be world champion was a knockout punch.

Farr really captured the imagination of the public later in 1937 when he easily outpointed former world champion Max Baer and knocked out the German Walter Neusel. He was immediately matched with Max Schmeling who had shamefully been manoeuvred out of a world title shot, in a bout advertised as for the world title, but Mike Jacobs stepped in and offered him a fight with Joe Louis, the real champion. Farr again shocked the boxing world by taking Louis the distance before losing narrowly to the heavier puncher. He relinquished his title and fought four more times in the USA, losing them all, although partly because of differences in scoring methods between the US and Britain.

Farr retired soon after the Second World War began, but, needing cash, he made a comeback in 1950 when 36. Even after this layoff, he won 11 of 16 fights, although he suffered the only knockout of his career. He retired in 1953.
Record: 125 contests; 80 wins; 13 draws; 30 defeats; 2 no-decision

See also: Louis v Farr

F

60

ABOVE: Tommy Farr in training.

LEFT: Farr, hair flying, misses with a right swing while outpointing USA's 'Red' Burman in 1939, two years after his famous fight with Louis.

JEFF FENECH

born: 28 May 1964, Sydney, NSW, Australia

Jeff Fenech, the son of Maltese parents, was somewhat wild as a boy, but when he walked into a gym in Sydney he found a way to channel his aggression. He began boxing and in 1984 went to the Los Angeles Olympics with great hopes. He cried when, after being given a decision over a Yugoslavian which would have guaranteed him at least a bronze medal, the verdict was reversed. He turned professional in October 1984, and became a rough, tough, two-fisted brawler who won the Australian light-bantamweight title in his third contest. In his seventh contest he stopped Satoshi Shingaki in Sydney to win the IBF bantamweight title. After three defences he took the Australian featherweight title and in June 1987 won the WBC light-featherweight title from Samart Payakarun. After two defences, he moved up again, to featherweight, and won the vacant WBC title from Victor Callejas.

Fenech, with his colourful all-action style, became a hero in Australia, where gates for boxing rocketed to 15,000 or more. He defended his new title five times up to November 1989, his last opponent being Mario Martinez. Fenech damaged his hands in that fight – his only weakness throughout his career had been fragile hands.

Fenech did not box at all in 1990, and then came back as a super-featherweight, winning a non-title bout in Adelaide. Then in June 1991 he returned to America for the first time since the ill-fated Olympics to challenge Azumah Nelson for the WBC title at Caesars Palace, Las Vegas. It was an outstanding battle, with one judge scoring for each and the third for a draw. Nelson kept the title, but majority press opinion was that Fenech was unlucky. He wept again in frustration. It was the first minor blot on his record – but a second major one came in the return in Melbourne on 1 March 1992. Fenech was this time a firm favourite, and 30,000 fans cheered him on, but the old champion Nelson was inspired, and stopped him in the eighth round. Fenech failed to win a world title at a fourth weight, but had the remarkable record that 15 of his 27 bouts had been for world titles.

Record: 27 contests; 25 wins; 1 draw; 1 defeat

JAMES FIGG

born: 1695, Thame, Oxfordshire
died: 8 December 1734, London

Figg was the first acknowledged boxing champion, partly due to his being featured in William Hogarth's picture of Southwark Fair, and because Hogarth drew him a business card. He claimed the championship in 1719 when he opened his amphitheatre. Figg taught the noble science of defence, the small backsword and the quarterstaff, and was patronised by royalty. Among those he beat with fists and sometimes with cudgels were Tim Buck, Tom Stokes and Bill Flanders. When Ned Sutton, the pipe-maker from Gravesend, challenged him in 1727, Figg beat him with both fists and cudgels. Figg gave up the championship in 1730, passing it on to his pupil George Taylor.

FILMS

The first fight films were made at the Edison Laboratory at Orange, New Jersey, in 1894. The first fight actually filmed was an exhibition, by nature of a trial, between Mike Leonard and Jack Cushing. But the first fight filmed for 'real' took place on 8 September 1894, between the heavyweight champion, James J. Corbett, and Peter Courtney. The studio, or Kinetographic Theatre, to give it its grander name, was not much more than a sort of shed, 15 feet wide. It swivelled on a circular track, so that it could follow the sun, which had to be focused onto the ring. The inside of the shed was padded up to about six feet. The 'ring' actually needed ropes only at the front and back, as the walls themselves were the limits of the ring at the sides.

The reel of film lasted about 90 seconds, so each round lasted this time. Intervals were at least two minutes, as this was the time needed to re-set the camera. In fact, as a report of the event related that the shed, known as 'Black Maria', was occasionally moved between rounds, it is likely that the intervals were considerably longer. Corbett was paid $5,000 for his trouble, and Courtney $1,000. Corbett won with a sixth-round knockout, and the fight was reported as legitimate, but it is suspected that it was arranged.

The first attempt to film a genuine match was made on 21 February 1896 at Langtry, Texas. The contest was Bob Fitzsimmons v Peter Maher in an eliminator for Corbett's crown. Fitzsimmons felt he had been double-crossed over the financial arrangements for the film and took delight in winning by a first-round knockout before the camera crew could get set up.

The first contest to be filmed for public display was the heavyweight title fight on 17 March 1897 at Carson City, Nevada, in which Bob Fitzsimmons knocked out James J. Corbett.

The first contest filmed under artificial lights was between James J. Jeffries and Tom Sharkey for the

heavyweight title on 3 November 1899 at Coney Island, New York. it was one of the most brutal contests ever, over 25 hard-fought rounds, in which Sharkey suffered two broken ribs. The heat of the day plus the 400 arc lights of 200 candlepower each which were above the ring to allow the filming, meant an

exhausting time for Sharkey, who nearly didn't recover.

The first fight believed to be filmed in England featured Jack Johnson, who was in England before going off to Australia to take the heavyweight championship. In his last contest before becoming champion he knocked out Ben Taylor in the eighth round at the

Cosmopolitan Club, Plymouth on 31 July 1908 before the cameras.

Although an introduction with sound was added to a film of the Mickey Walker – Tommy Milligan middleweight title fight at the NSC, London, on 30 June 1927, the first 'talkie' film of a boxing match was made at the heavyweight title fight

MAX SCHMELING (right), seen with Mike Tyson in 1989, took part in the first 'talkie' fight film.

between Max Schmeling and Jack Sharkey on 12 June 1930 in New York, when Schmeling won on a foul.

BOB FITZSIMMONS

born: 26 May 1863, Helston, Cornwall
died: 22 October 1917, Chicago, USA

Fitzsimmons was taken from Cornwall to New Zealand as a child, where he worked in his father's forge, becoming expert at making horseshoes. The work built up tremendous back and shoulder muscles, and Bob began bare-fist fighting at 15. Jem Mace, the world champion, visited New Zealand and in 1880 and 1881 Bob won his novice competitions and set out on a boxing career in Australia. He was then a middleweight, and fought for seven years with mixed fortunes in Sydney before in April 1890 he sailed for San Francisco.

After three impressive wins, Bob challenged Jack Dempsey the Nonpareil for the middleweight championship of the world, and won impressively with a 13th round knockout. Fitzsimmons defended once and then went after the more lucrative heavyweight title. Fitzsimmons never weighed more than 172lb, most of it in his torso, for he had spindly legs. He was called Ruby Robert and with his freckles and sparse carroty hair, he looked unlike a boxer, much less a heavyweight. But a 95-second demolition of contender Peter Maher earned him a shot at Jim Corbett's crown in 1897. Giving away 20lb Fitz took a lot of punishment early on and was down for a long count in the sixth. But he was a wily campaigner and in the 14th he switched to southpaw and delivered a tremendous left to Corbett's solar plexus, knocking him out.

Fitzsimmons held the title for two years, but on his first defence, just past his 36th birthday, he was knocked out in the 11th round by the 12-years younger Jim Jeffries, who outweighed him by around 60lb. Fitz was not finished, and defeats of Gus Ruhlin and Tom Sharkey, who both fought for the title, led to another chance. He was 39 when Jeffries knocked him out in the eighth, after Fitzsimmons had broken his right hand in giving the champion plenty of trouble.

Still Fitzsimmons did not retire and, in November 1903, outpointed George Gardner over 20 rounds to become light-heavyweight champion. He was 40, and the first of only two boxers ever to be undisputed world champion at three of the classic weights. Fitz retired in the 13th round when defending against Philadelphia Jack O'Brien in December 1905.

Fitz returned to Sydney in 1909 to challenge for the Australian heavyweight title, but was knocked out in the 12th. His last contest was in the States in 1914, when he was 51.

Record: 62 contests; 40 wins; 11 defeats; 10 no-decision; 1 no contest

BOB FITZSIMMONS (left) and James J. Corbett in their 1897 fight, in which Fitzsimmons won the world title.

F

GEORGE FOREMAN

born: 22 January 1948, Marshall, Texas, USA

Foreman was the fifth of seven children born to a railroad construction worker, and was often in trouble as a boy. He tried to learn bricklaying and carpentry but was persuaded to try boxing. At his size (he grew to 6ft 3in and 220lb) he had a terrific punch and was instantly successful. In the 1968 Olympic Games he won the heavyweight gold medal and in June 1969 he turned professional. In three years he had 36 contests and 36 wins, only three men lasting the distance with him. In January 1972 he challenged Joe Frazier for the heavyweight championship of the world, and the champion went the way of many others, knocked out in two rounds after six knockdowns. Foreman looked unbeatable.

Jose Roman and Ken Norton lasted three rounds between them in challenges and then Foreman faced Muhammad Ali in Kinshasa in October 1974. Ali surprised everybody by absorbing Foreman's blows and knocking him out in the eighth round. Foreman fought exhibitions in 1975, but in 1976 came back with five more knockout wins, including Ron Lyle and Joe Frazier among his victims. But after being outpointed by Jimmy Young in 1976, Foreman retired.

Foreman became a minister of religion and his weight ballooned to over 300lb. And then, on 9 March 1987, he appeared in the ring again, a 'trim' 260lb, winning by another knockout in Sacramento. With his head shaved and his waist wide, Foreman began a comeback career at 39, over ten years after his last fight, so different in appearance from his previous self that he was like a completely new boxer. Foreman had not followed boxing in the interim, and said his comeback was to pay for expansion of his youth centre.

At first the comeback was regarded by the boxing reporters as a big joke, but as carefully chosen opponents were knocked out one by one, it became a curiosity and finally half believable. At last, on 19 April 1991, the unbelievable happened and Foreman stepped into the ring at Atlantic City to face Evander Holyfield for the heavyweight title, over 18 years since he first won it. In his comeback he had disposed of 24 opponents, 23 by knockout. Foreman did not win the title, but he put up a good show in the 12 bruising rounds before losing on points. And with Tyson sidelined, the 43-year-old grandfather decided he might hang around a bit longer.

Record: 74 contests; 71 wins; 3 defeats

See also: Ali v Foreman

RIGHT: Perspiration flies from Foreman's shaven head in his 1988 fight with Dwight Muhammad Qawi.

BELOW: George Foreman in his second incarnation as a boxer.

BOB FOSTER

born: 15 December 1938, Albuquerque, New Mexico, USA

Foster was 6ft 3in, but without the corresponding bulk to be a heavyweight. But he was a skilful boxer and he had a punch. He began well as a pro in March 1961, but in October 1962 was knocked out by Doug Jones, a heavyweight. Foster was only a light-heavy, but was knocked out again by a bigger man, Ernie Terrell, in 1964. A defeat by another big man, Zora Folley, in 1965, persuaded Foster boxing was not for him, despite his 21 wins. He took work in a munitions factory, and moved his wife and four children to Washington.

In December 1966, he began again, and in May 1968 challenged Dick Tiger for the light-heavyweight championship of the world. Foster was out of pocket on the fight, but a fourth-round knockout won him the title.

Foster made three successful defences and then again tangled with the heavyweights, challenging champion Joe Frazier. He was knocked out in the second round. He made seven more light-heavy defences, the last against Olympic gold medalist Chris Finnegan in London, whom he knocked out in the 14th round of a stirring battle. He then fought Muhammad Ali, who was on his comeback trail in 1972, and was stopped in the eighth round.

In June 1974 Foster got a home-town draw in his 13th successful light-heavyweight defence and decided to retire. A year later he came back

with five wins, but two knockout defeats in 1978 persuaded him to stop for good.
Record: 65 contests; 56 wins; 1 draw; 8 defeats

BOB FOSTER dumps Chris Finnegan on his bottom in 1972.

JOE FRAZIER

born: 12 January 1944, Beaufort, South Carolina, USA

The seventh son and youngest child in a family of 13 children, Frazier was raised on a poor vegetable plantation, and determined to be a boxer like his idol Joe Louis. He got married at 15, moved to Philadelphia, worked in a slaughterhouse and began amateur boxing. He lost to Buster Mathis in the Olympic trials for 1964, but Mathis broke his finger boxing Frazier in an exhibition and Joe fought in Tokyo instead. He returned with the heavyweight gold medal (and a broken thumb of his own). Joe turned professional and by 1968 had won his first 19 contests; 17 by the short route. With Ali sidelined because of his Vietnam stance, Frazier fought Buster Mathis for the vacant WBC version of the world heavyweight title, and won with an 11th round stoppage. Meanwhile Jimmy Ellis won a WBA elimination contest to become their champion. After Frazier had made four successful defences he easily beat Ellis, who could not appear for the fifth round, and was undisputed champion (not counting Ali). Frazier then disposed of Bob Foster, and in March 1971 met the come-backing Ali in Madison Square Garden, both men unbeaten. It was described as the fight of the Century, watched by 300 million on television. Smokin' Joe, as he was called, sealed a points win with a knockdown of Ali in the 15th round.

Frazier was short for a modern heavyweight at 5ft 11½in. At 205lb he was heavy enough, but much of the weight was in his legs, which gave him the ability to keep coming forward like a tank, throwing hooks. At his best he looked indestructible. He made two more defences but in January 1973 met the man who succeeded him as Olympic champion, George Foreman. Foreman was much bigger, but even so it was a surprise when he blasted Joe off his feet and out in the second round.

Frazier kept going but in 1974 lost to Ali when both

were on a comeback trail. When Ali reclaimed the world title from Foreman, Frazier fought him again in Manila. After a see-saw battle he could not come out for the last round. In 1976 Joe was again knocked out by Foreman. He retired and devoted himself to a band, but five years later, in 1981, returned for one fight, a draw, and retired finally. His name will always be coupled with Ali for their three great battles. Of his 37 contests, 13 were for world titles and only Ali and Foreman beat him.
Record: 37 contests; 32 wins; 1 draw; 4 defeats

See also: Ali v Frazier

SMOKIN' JOE FRAZIER was only beaten by two men – both world champions. He was the first to beat Muhammad Ali, with whom he had three outstanding battles.

GENE FULLMER

born: 21 July 1931, West Jordan, Utah, USA

Fullmer was given his forename because his mother admired Gene Tunney. He built up his physique as a welder in the mines and turned professional in June 1951. He proved a tough, solid-punching middleweight. He had no science, was easily hit, yet ran up 17 wins, 14 by the quick route, before entering the US Army in 1952. Resuming in 1954, he carried on in his rugged fashion until in January 1957 he surprised the fans by taking the world middleweight title from Sugar Ray Robinson. In May Robinson took it back on a fifth-round knockout, but when the WBA deposed Robinson for not defending, Fullmer won it again in 1959 by stopping Carmen Basilio.

Fullmer, a Mormon who gave ten per cent of his earnings to the church, fought at times by rote, delivering the combinations his manager called to him. This time Fullmer made seven defences, including two over Robinson, one a draw and one a points win. He also gave a tremendous beating to welterweight champion Benny Paret which it was thought contributed to Paret's death when he took another bad beating in his next fight with Emile Griffith.

In 1962 Fullmer lost his title when outpointed by Dick Tiger in San Francisco. He drew the return in Las Vegas in 1963, but later in the year suffered his second career knockout when losing to Tiger in Ibadan. He announced his retirement.
Record: 64 contests; 55 wins; 3 draws; 6 defeats

KHAOSAI GALAXY

born: 15 May 1959, Petchaboon, Thailand

Galaxy made his professional debut in December 1980 in Bangkok. He lost his seventh contest, a challenge for the Thailand bantamweight title, but he avenged the defeat, by Sakda Saksuree, with a knockout and in January 1982 he won the title. All but one of his first 32 bouts were in Bangkok, only four going the distance. In the 29th Galaxy won the vacant WBA super flyweight title with a sixth-round knockout of Eusebio Espinal.

This was in November 1984 and in the next seven years Galaxy made 19 defences. Most were in Bangkok, but he did knock out Israel Contreras in Curacao, Elly Pical in Jakarta and Chang-Ho Choi in Seoul. He also beat two Japanese challengers in their own land.

Galaxy's twin brother Khaokor was also a world champion, winning the WBA bantamweight crown in 1988 and 1989 but he was forced to retire through injuries caused when the brothers' car crashed returning from a charity event. Khaosai escaped injury.

Galaxy announced his retirement with two defences still to make. Before the last he was presented to the king, and received gifts and acclaim from 11,000 of his countrymen for 35 minutes before the fight began. It is estimated that 25 million watched the bout from Bangkok on television. Armando Castro dropped Galaxy in the first round and the bell was opportune, but the champion recovered to win comfortably on points.
Record: 50 contests; 49 wins; 1 defeat

JOE GANS

born: (Joseph Gaines) 25 November 1874, Baltimore, Maryland, USA
died: 10 August 1910, Baltimore, Maryland, USA

Gans started boxing when he was 16, but his early record is incomplete. He was a brilliant boxer who, in his later years, was called the Old Master, but to be recognised he had to overcome racial prejudice and no doubt lose a decision occasionally. From a poor family he would wire home after a win that he was 'bringing home the bacon', a luxury meal for them. He was so good that in March 1900 he was allowed to challenge Frank Erne for the world lightweight title, but he mysteriously retired in the 12th round when on top. He had a cut eye. Later he 'threw' a fight with Terry McGovern. Given a second chance at Erne in 1902, he knocked out the champion in about 90 seconds. Although he was now in his 28th year, he lost only once in the next six years: a 15-round decision to Sam Langford – a man who usually fought heavyweights. Gans so

JOE GANS, the 'Old Master'.

dominated the lightweights that in 1904 he temporarily lost recognition while Jimmy Britt, a white boxer, was named champion.

Gans later beat Britt, and also Battling Nelson, who had taken Britt's title, and was undisputed again. In all Gans defended successfully 16 times up to 1908. Between times he fought many heavier men, and drew over 20 rounds in an attempt on Joe Walcott's welterweight title.

Gans eventually lost his title in July 1908 to the primitive Battling Nelson, whom he had beaten memorably over 42 rounds two years earlier. He was knocked out in the 17th, and was knocked out again in the 21st in a return two months later. But by then the Old Master had probably contracted the consumption from which he was dead within two years. In his prime he was unbeatable.
Record: 156 contests; 120 wins; 10 draws, 8 defeats; 18 no-decision
See also: Gans v Nelson

JOE GANS V BATTLING NELSON

3 September 1906, Goldfield, Nevada
4 July 1908, San Francisco
9 September 1908, San Francisco

George 'Tex' Rickard owned a small gambling saloon in the desert town of Goldfield, Nevada. Rickard was himself a gambler. The citizens of Goldfield decided that it would be a good idea to publicise their prosperous mining town with a view to attracting investment from the east. They formed a committee to discuss. Rickard, the chairman, decided to take matters into his own hands. His idea was to stage a great fight.

The heavyweight scene in 1906 was uninspiring. Jeffries had retired two years earlier and Tommy Burns was challenging Marvin Hart for the title – two boxers with little charisma in the States. The lightweights presented a much better picture. One of the outstanding champions of that or any era was Joe Gans. He had defended the title ten times in 16 months after

winning it in 1902, the last occasion being on a foul when Jimmy Britt deliberately hit him low after taking a bad beating. However when Britt beat Battling Nelson soon afterwards Britt claimed the title on the grounds that Gans couldn't make the weight. The weight divisions were less rigid in those days, and Britt gained recognition, if only for being the 'white champion', only to lose it in 1905 when Nelson stopped him in the 18th round.

Rickard realised that there was needle among the lightweights, and that there were two claimants to the title, the black Gans and the white Nelson. He offered a purse of $30,000 to the two to decide the true champion at Goldfield. This was an unprecedented amount in those days for lightweights and many thought Rickard was mad.

Nelson insisted on taking $20,000 for his share, and even then took another $2,000 as a signing fee. Gans took half what Nelson received and, as Rickard had to pay the boxer's expenses, it actually cost him $34,000 to stage the fight.

Rickard was a superb salesman. He put the $30,000 in his window at Goldfield, and the press was invited to photograph it. Rickard played up the black v white aspect of the clash, and the press took the hint. He built an open-air arena to hold 8,000 spectators, and had a sell-out. His gate receipts totalled $69,715, outstanding for the time, and Goldfield became a boom town.

The contest was scheduled for 45 rounds. Nelson insisted on the weight being 9st 7lb, two pounds less than Gans wanted, the current lightweight limit. Gans boxed superbly under a hot sun and completely outclassed Nelson for 32 rounds, by when he was well ahead. He then broke his hand, but was still good enough to hold off Nelson one-handed. Nelson was a crude fighter not too concerned with rules. He concentrated on Gans' body and delivered many punches to the liver and kidneys. At one point Gans was sick over the ropes. But Nelson could make no real impression and,

in the 42nd round, got so frustrated that he deliberately fouled Gans and was disqualified. The 'Old Master' had proved he was still the best.

Gans made four more defences before meeting Nelson again in 1908. He was now 33, and the privations of making the weight, the blows he'd taken to his body and the consumption which had probably already begun its course meant he could not hold off the eight-years-younger Nelson and was knocked out in the 17th round. Later in the year he outboxed Nelson again for 20 rounds but was knocked out in the 21st. He died less than two years later.

KID GAVILAN (left) had two fights with Peter Waterman in 1956, losing and winning.

KID GAVILAN

born: (Geraldo Gonzalez) 6 January 1926, Camaguey, Cuba

Gavilan worked in the sugar plantations before turning professional aged 17 in June 1943. Most of his early contests were in Havana but he finally switched his headquarters to America in 1947.

He was outpointed twice by Sugar Ray Robinson, the second time in July 1949 in a challenge for Robinson's welterweight title. Both contests were close. Competition was good, and Gavilan beat Ike Williams, Beau Jack and Billy Graham before he won the vacant welterweight title by outpointing Johnny Bratton in New York in May 1951.

Gavilan was an aggressive, all-action crowd-pleaser, who gained fame for his use of a 'bolo' punch, a

wide swing brought from near the floor in a similar way that the bolo knife is used on sugar plantations. Many thought he was lucky to retain his title in his first defence against Billy Graham but he beat the same opponent a year later. Future champion Carmen Basilio was another to be beaten in his seven defences.

In 1954 Gavilan challenged Carl Bobo Olson for the world middleweight title but was outpointed and, in his next contest, he was outpointed by Johnny Saxton to lose his welterweight crown. Gavilan subsided after that and lost a number of decisions in his final four years, but he had the remarkable record of never losing inside the distance in 143 contests.
Record: 143 contests; 106 wins; 6 draws; 30 defeats; 1 no-contest

HEROL GRAHAM

born: 13 September 1959, Nottingham

Herol Graham won amateur titles at all levels from schoolboy to ABA, and when he began his professional career in November 1978 he was already an accomplished technician. Graham is outstanding as a defensive boxer, making even the classiest opponents look clumsy. Although lacking a knockout punch, he stopped many opponents by the overwhelming number of his blows.

In May 1981 he won the British light-middleweight title, and added in November the Commonwealth title. In May 1983 the European title was gathered in.

BELOW: The outstanding boxer, Herol Graham.

RIGHT: Graham (right) in his unsuccessful world title challenge against Mike McCallum.

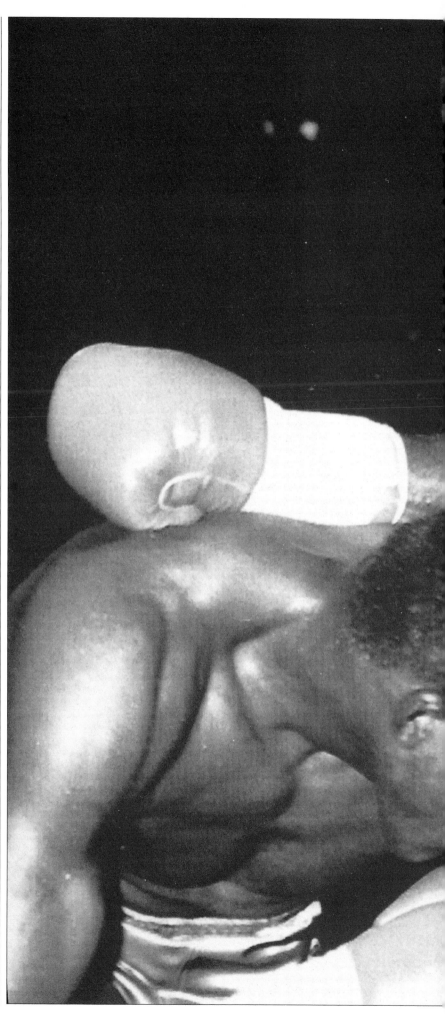

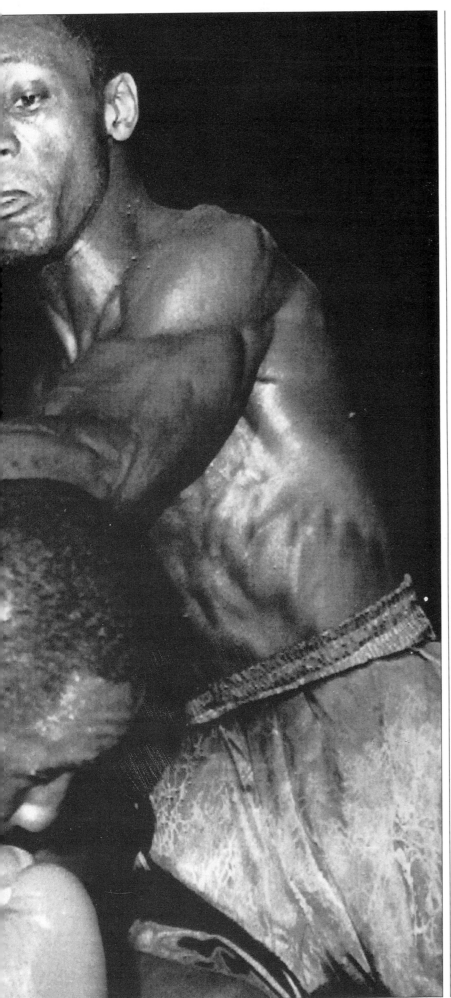

Graham moved up to middleweight to take the British title with a first-round knockout of Jimmy Price in 1985, and again added the European title. It came as a shock when Graham suffered his first defeat and lost the European title to Sumbu Kalambay in May 1987. He won back the British title and was then outpointed in May 1989 by Mike McCallum in a bid for the WBA title. The luckless Graham lost on a split decision, a deducted point for an attempt to throw McCallum being crucial.

Graham had a second chance at a world title when challenging WBC champion Julian Jackson in November 1990. Graham outboxed Jackson for three rounds, cutting his eye and being completely on top, but in the fourth walked on to a right hook which knocked him out completely. In 1992 Graham challenged Sumbu Kalambay for the European title, and again had two points deducted for his habit of turning his opponent. He lost a controversial decision.
Record: 48 contests; 44 wins; 4 defeats

ROCKY GRAZIANO

**born: (Thomas Rocco Barbella), 1 January 1922, New York City
died: 21 May 1990, New York City**

Rocky Graziano, from a Brooklyn tenement, was wild as a youngster and ended up in prison, where he assaulted a warder. In the army in 1942 he struck an officer and deserted. While free he passed an arena and decided to earn some money boxing, and had his first eight contests in 55 days before the military police found him. He was discharged from the army and his boxing career took off. An all-action swinger and swiper, Graziano piled into opponents savagely and mercilessly, not caring much for the niceties of rules. A shock third-round knockout of rated Billy Arnold announced his arrival. A middleweight, he twice beat welterweight champion Freddie Cochrane and then forced new welterweight king Marto Servo to retire after breaking his nose.

In 1946, 1947 and 1948 Graziano had the three middleweight title fights with Tony Zale by which he will always be remembered. He won the second, and for 11 months was champion of the world. In 1948 he was suspended for a year by the New York authorities for not reporting an attempted bribe before a fight which was later called off. In 1952 he challenged Sugar Ray Robinson for the middleweight title but was knocked out in the third.

Graziano retired soon after and with his down-to-earth philosophy became a TV celebrity for a while and opened a New York restaurant. His autobiography *Somebody Up There Likes Me* was filmed with Paul Newman playing Graziano.
Record: 83 contests; 67 wins; 6 draws; 10 defeats

See also: Zale v Graziano

GREATEST FIGHTS

The following fights are covered within the body of the text, in their relevant alphabetic position.

Ali v Cooper
Ali v Foreman
Ali v Frazier
Ali v Liston
Chavez v Taylor
Corbett v Sullivan
Dempsey v Firpo
Douglas v Tyson
Eubank v Benn
Gans v Nelson
Harding v Andries
Hagler v Hearns
Honeyghan v Curry
Johnson v Jeffries
Lamotta v Dauthuille
Leonard v Hagler
Leonard v Hearns
Louis v Conn
Louis v Farr
Louis v Schmeling
McGuigan v Pedroza
Marciano v Charles
Marciano v Walcott
Moore v Durelle
Patterson v Johansson
Saddler v Pep
Sayers v Heenan
Tunney v Dempsey
Turpin v Robinson
Wolgast v Rivers
Zale v Graziano

HARRY GREB

born; 6 June 1894, Pittsburgh, Pennsylvania, USA
died: 22 October 1926, Atlantic City, New Jersey, USA

Greb wasn't good enough to be a baseball player, so he began fighting as a profession. Most of his fights were no-decision contests, though he usually won the newspaper verdict. In his first year, 1913, he suffered a knockout, but the only other time he was stopped in 294 contests was when he broke a bone in his arm.

Greb was a natural middleweight and a fighting phenomenon. Though not a knockout puncher, he swarmed all over his opponents, putting in blows from all angles. He was called the Human Windmill. If he couldn't win fairly he had no hesitation in winning by fouls, and did not mind being called the dirtiest fighter of all time. The thumb in the eye was a particular trademark, but it rebounded on Greb when an opponent retaliated and blinded him permanently in one eye. That Greb subsequently became world champion is a measure of how good he was.

Greb had had around 70 fights before the US joined the First World War in 1917, and he enlisted for the navy. His only two fights outside America were at the Albert Hall in London in December 1918 in a services tournament, where the fans showed disapproval of his tactics. After the war he took on heavyweights like Billy Miske, Bill Brennan and Tommy Gibbons, all of whom fought Dempsey for the title. He knocked out in one round Gunboat Smith, one-time 'white heavyweight champion'. In 1919 Greb had 44 contests.

In 1922 Greb beat Gene Tunney for the vacant American light-heavyweight championship, breaking Tunney's nose and inflicting terrible punishment. It was the only defeat in Tunney's career. Greb defended successfully against Tommy Loughran, later the world champion, in a dirty fight, before losing the title to Tunney, later world heavyweight champion, in a very close one. Greb conceded 14lb to Tunney.

In 1925 Greb won the world middleweight title by outpointing Johnny Wilson. It is said Greb faked bouts of drunkenness when he should have been training to convince Wilson that he was safe to take on. Greb was not a great believer in training in any case, but averaging 21 contests a year he hardly needed to be. Greb held the title for 2½ years, defending it six times – notably against Mickey Walker – before surrendering it in 1926 to Tiger Flowers. He also lost the return. Two months later Greb, a lifelong ladies' man, went to hospital for minor plastic surgery on his nose. There was a haemorrhage and he died.

Record: 294 contests; 112 wins; 3 draws; 8 defeats; 170 no-decision; 1 no-contest

LEFT: Harry Greb, a natural fighter.

EMILE GRIFFITH

born: 3 February 1938, St Thomas, Virgin Islands

Griffith left the Virgin Islands for New York when 11 and worked in a ladies' hat factory, where the owner got him interested in boxing. He won many amateur tournaments and became a professional in 1958.

Griffith began as a welterweight and was a

smooth mover and crisp puncher with both hands. Despite a couple of early losses, he earned a title fight with Benny Paret in 1961 and won with a 13th-round knockout. After one successful defence he was deposed on points by Paret. Griffith regained the title in March 1962 in a tragic fight. There was needle between the boxers, and in retrospect the referee allowed the contest to go on too long with Griffith pummelling the helpless Paret in the 12th round. Paret sank into a coma and did not recover. It was a fight seen on nationwide television in the US and proved strong ammunition for the anti-boxing lobby. Griffith never again was such a destructive puncher.

Griffith outpointed Ted Wright in Vienna in October 1962 in a contest advertised as for the light-middleweight title, and defended it in 1963, but these contests did not gain general recognition. He lost and regained his welterweight title in bouts with Luis Rodriguez in 1963 and then in 1966, after further defences, outpointed Dick Tiger for the world middleweight championship, giving up his lighter title. After two defences of his new crown, Griffith lost, regained and lost it again in three contests with Nino Benvenuti.

Griffith was able to fight equally at welter or middleweight and now challenged Jose Napoles for the welter title, but was outpointed. Twice he tried to regain the middleweight title from Carlos Monzon without success, then challenged Eckhart Dagge in Berlin for the light-middleweight title, being outpointed. After three straight defeats in 1977 Griffith retired. Griffith took part in 22 world title fights in a 19-year career.

Record: 112 contests; 85 wins; 2 draws: 24 defeats; 1 no-contest

EMILE GRIFFITH (left) in a world defence against Brian Curvis.

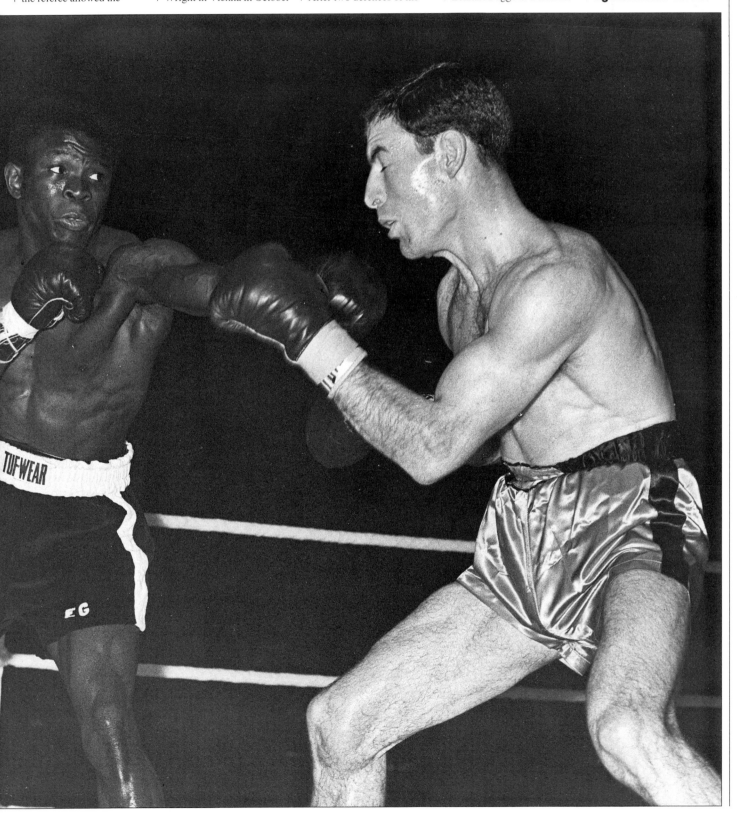

MARVIN HAGLER

born 23 May 1954, Newark, New Jersey, USA

After an outstanding amateur career, Marvin Hagler turned professional five days before his 19th birthday and began a series of quick victories. With his shaven head, muscled physique and threatening eyes he was an imposing figure, and with his dedication and two-fisted controlled destructive punching he became one of the outstanding champions of the 1980s.

It took Hagler over six years to get a shot at the world title, however, and even then he could manage only a draw with Vito Antuofermo. It might have been a misjudgement, because Hagler boxed defensively in the later stages, thinking he was well ahead. In his next challenge, in 1980 against Alan Minter in London, he was the betting underdog, but put on an awesome display, stopping Minter in the third. Hagler was undisputed champion and began to dominate the division, adding by deed poll 'Marvelous' before his name. Fulgencio Obelmejias, Mustafa Hamsho and Tony Sibson were among victims stopped in his first seven defences, before in 1983 Roberto Duran managed to go the distance, Hagler treating the former lightweight with great respect. In 1985 Marvelous Marvin stopped Thomas Hearns in one of the most explosive battles seen for years, but in 1987 he lost a controversial decision and his title to Sugar Ray Leonard when opinion seemed evenly divided as to the winner. Hagler, who thought he'd won, retired. He had been undisputed champion for nearly seven years.

Record: 67 contests; 62 wins; 2 draws; 3 defeats

See also: Hagler v Hearns; Leonard v Hagler

LEFT: Marvin Hagler.

MARVIN HAGLER V TOMMY HEARNS

15 April 1985, Las Vegas

In 1985 there appeared no middleweights in the world capable of beating Marvelous Marvin Hagler who, in his fifth year as undisputed champion, had seen off ten challengers, only one of which had taken him the scheduled distance. But there was one man among the light-middleweights who was considered able to give him a good fight. He was the WBC champion, Thomas 'Hit Man' Hearns. Hearns had knocked out Roberto Duran in two rounds the previous year while, in 1983, Duran had been the man who had gone all the way with Hagler.

Both men had outstanding records. Hagler had not lost for over ten years. Hearns had lost only once in his career, to Sugar Ray Leonard. Both men were destructive punchers. Those who favoured Hagler to win pointed to the fact that he was, and always had been, a natural middleweight, comfortable at the weight, whereas Hearns had been welterweight champion only four years before and had come up two divisions. He was tall and slim and did not resemble a middleweight. Those who favoured Hearns, claimed he had always hit with the power of a middleweight and was not called the 'Hit Man' for nothing. At 6ft 1in he was 3½ inches taller than Hagler, as well as four years younger and, it was felt, his reach and speed would be too much for the champion. Opinions were fairly evenly divided.

There was consensus on the way the fight would start, however. Hagler was a notoriously slow starter while Hearns was usually at ease from the bell, and everybody expected that Hearns would pressurise Hagler and try to take him out of his stride from the beginning. Few of the 15,000 packed into Caesars Palace expected to see one of the greatest opening rounds in boxing history.

Hagler began as never before, putting all the ferocity of a champion at bay into an assault calculated at battering Hearns into instant submission. Hearns, too, began throwing bombs and both of their heads were jolted back by full-blooded punches. Neither fighter had time to collect their thoughts. Hagler kept coming forward relentlessly throwing punches while Hearns tried to keep his distance and step in with counters. At the end of a round in which 30 full-blooded shots had thundered in, both men went a little unsteadily back to their corners, Hagler's face red with blood from the attentions of Hearns' right.

It was too late for either to change tactics now. In the second round Hagler stood in front of Hearns and threw his great hooks while Hearns desperately tried to box him off. He could not stop Hagler coming forward, but he kept up his tattoo on Hagler's face, which soon had blood streaming down it from a gash between his eyes. Hearns went back to his corner unsteadily, and those who had backed the strength of the natural middleweight to prevail looked to be right. But Hagler had his problems too, particularly with his cut. It was still anybody's fight after six minutes of mayhem.

Both boxers resumed as before in the third round, and halfway through the round Hearns opened another cut on Hagler's bloody face, this time under his right eye. The doctor was called to examine the cuts and said Hagler could continue. But with Hearns repeatedly catching Hagler as Hagler continued his single-minded battering of the challenger, the doctor was called again. 'Can you see all right?' he asked Hagler. 'I ain't missing him, am I?' replied Hagler from his mask of blood. He was sent back in.

Hagler was now desperate and, after getting in a tremendous right which shook Hearns, he leapt in with another that sent Hearns reeling across the ring,

TOMMY HEARNS, who shared an outstanding fight with Marvin Hagler in 1985.

looking with his long limbs like a flamingo picking his way through water. Hagler chased him and pumped in two more rights which sent Hearns sliding to the canvas. Incredibly he rose, but his legs wouldn't obey him, and referee Richard Steele kindly said he'd taken enough.

It had been a great battle between two of the great champions of the 1980s, both of whom enhanced their reputations.

JEFF HARDING V DENNIS ANDRIES

24 June 1989, Atlantic City
28 July 1990, Melbourne
11 September 1991,
London

Dennis Andries was a tough fighter who always seemed a little unco-ordinated and clumsy. But his strength and tenacity were enough for him to win the WBC light-heavyweight championship. In June 1989, having lost it and regained it, he defended the title against a man after his own heart. Jeff Harding was the OPBF champion, unbeaten in 14 contests. He, like Andries, was a man who took plenty of punishment in order to get his own blows in. His big advantage over Andries was that he was over 11 years younger, but Andries was expected to outlast him in an old-fashioned scrap.

Heading's inexperience was evident in the first five rounds at the Atlantic City Convention Centre. Repeatedly nailed by Andries, he was down in the fifth and it looked over. But Harding continued in the only way he knew how, walking in to deliver body punches. Both his eyes were cut and still he came forward. In the tenth round Andries broke Harding's nose. But the pace was getting to the 35-year-old, and Harding's efforts began to take effect. In the 12th and last round, he got through, and an exhausted Andries was stopped.

Although Andries claimed his defeat was because he misjudged his weight and starved himself unnecessarily for three days before the fight, most thought that his long career was finally over. However in the following year Andries registered two victories and, in July 1990, found himself fighting for the title again – this time as a challenger. Harding had also won twice in the interim, each time defending his title, once

against British champion Tom Collins. He now boasted 17 wins and no losses and, as he was defending this time in Melbourne, he was a 2-1 favourite – odds which did not seem generous to him.

Harding began as if he had learned how to box and was determined to baffle Andries with science.

Andries, doing what he always did, jabbed, hooked and crossed and got in enough blows to take the first round clearly. It was the same thing in the second with a swelling appearing near Harding's eye. In the third Andries rocked Harding with a left hook and piled in the rights. It looked like the first fight over again. This

time, however, the fight turned round earlier. In the fourth Harding, forgetting about boxing, began to get punches home at last. In the fifth, Andries began to look tired. He took punishment in the sixth and it seemed as if his strength had gone.

Andries gambled in the seventh after landing a right which shook the champion.

He drove Harding to the ropes and poured in punches. Many missed, but two more rocked Harding again. As the round progressed, it looked as if Andries had punched himself out. He looked weary. He hurled himself at Harding again, though, and a long right worsened the cut over the champion's eye. Finally, an overhand right at

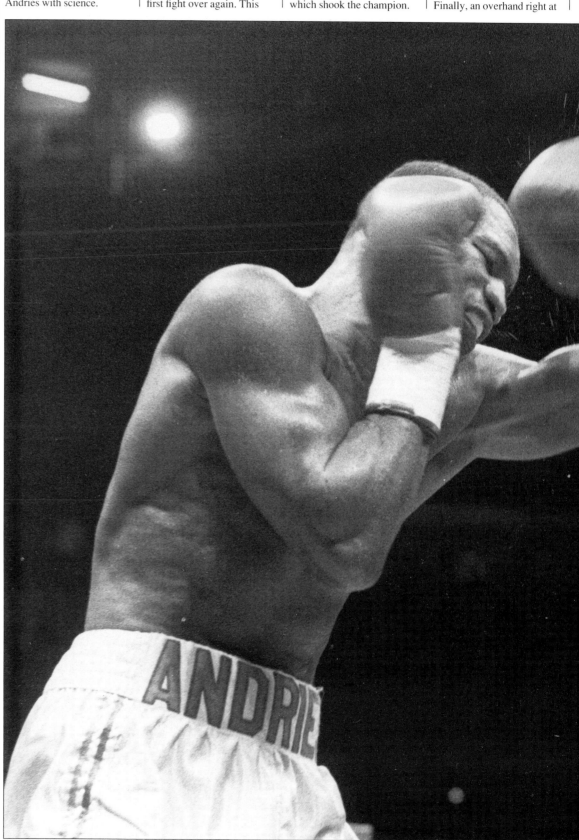

**DENNIS ANDRIES:
(left) and Jeff Harding
in the second of their
three great battles, in
Melbourne.**

last put Harding on the canvas. He managed to straighten up as referee Arthur Mercante spread his arms indicating the knockout. Andries, at 36, became the first Briton to win a world title three times.

There had to be a decider. Andries had defended his title twice by September 1991 while Harding had re-established himself with three wins. They met at the Hammersmith Odeon.

Andries attacked and opened a small cut by Harding's eye in the first round. Andries had the better of it early, as in their other fights, but Harding kept in the contest with blows to the body. Harding was rocked in the fifth and Andries was on top at this point. Andries had no difficulty in hitting Harding and it was amazing that the challenger stood up. No only that, he was not even deterred and kept plugging forward to open a cut by Andries' eye in the seventh. Andries was tiring in the eighth, and Harding's punches looked to be better directed. In the tenth Harding began to get on top. In the 11th Andries made a big effort with lefts and rights but could not put Harding down and he seemed exhausted by his efforts at the end of the round. Harding took the last round and, at the bell, both men had given everything. The decision could have gone either way, but two judges gave it to Harding, by two points and one point, while the third had it a draw.

The 37-year-old ex-champion was magnificent in defeat and Harding, who just refused to be denied, could not expect many harder fights during the rest of his career than the three he had with Andries.

MARVIN HART

born: 16 September 1876, Jefferson County, Kentucky, USA
died: 17 September 1931, Fern Creek, Kentucky, USA

Marvin Hart is the world heavyweight champion most easily overlooked by historians. He began fighting professionally as a middleweight in 1899. At 5ft 11¼ in his weight rose to 190lb and he took on the heavyweights, scorning science to march in with both hands. His feminine-like features were soon battered, as he often took two punches to score one.

On 3 July 1905 he fought Jack Root for the vacant world heavyweight title. Jeffries had retired and fancied Root as his successor. Before then Hart had had 34 contests, losing only three, one of which was a points loss to Root. However, three months before the title fight he had outpointed the great Jack Johnson over 20 rounds, easily his best result. He surprised Jeffries, who refereed the championship contest, by knocking out Root in the 12th. He held the title for only seven months, being outpointed by Tommy Burns, but he continued fighting top heavyweights for four more years.

Record: 47 contests; 28 wins; 4 draws; 7 defeats; 8 no-decision

MARVIN HART, heavyweight champion for seven months in a slack period for heavies.

LEN HARVEY

born: 11 July 1907, Stoke Climsland, Cornwall
died: 20 November, 1976, Holloway, London

Harvey's father was a boxing trainer in Plymouth, where his boys learned boxing. Len was best, becoming a highly skilful defensive boxer. He began professionally in January 1920 as a 12-year-old flyweight and when he retired in 1942 had boxed in every division up to heavyweight, uniquely winning British titles in three of them. His first title fight was in 1926 when he challenged Harry Mason for the welterweight crown and drew over 20 rounds. In 1929 he won the British and Empire middleweight titles from Alex Ireland. After six defences he challenged Marcel Thil for the European version of the world title but was narrowly outpointed. He lost his middleweight titles to Jack McAvoy in 1933, but won the vacant British light-heavyweight title by outpointing Eddie Phillips. In one of his best performances five months later he conceded Jack Petersen 28lb and outpointed him for the heavyweight title, having had title fights at middle, light-heavy and heavy in just over seven months. Harvey added the Empire title by outpointing Larry Gains but lost both his heavyweight titles to Petersen in 1934 when retiring with a cut eye, and failed to regain them in 1936, being outpointed.

Harvey became matchmaker at Wembley Stadium, and his first match was himself against John Henry Lewis for the American's world light-heavyweight title. Harvey was narrowly outpointed. Having given up his British light-heavyweight title in 1933, he now took it from McAvoy, then won the vacant heavyweight title by beating Eddie Phillips and the vacant Empire heavyweight title by beating Larry Gains.

John Henry Lewis was due to meet Harvey in a return for the world light-heavyweight championship, but was forced to retire with failing eyesight. The BBBC recognised Harvey's contest with Jock McAvoy in July 1939 as for the vacant world title, and Harvey won on points. War came two months later and Harvey joined the RAF. He had only one more contest when, after a three-year lay-off, he fought the young Freddie Mills and lost all his light-heavyweight titles. He suffered his first knockout in 134 contests when Mills knocked him through some slack ropes in the second round. He retired soon afterwards, relinquishing his British and Empire heavyweight titles. In nearly 23 years he had never seriously been hurt.

Record: 134 contests; 112 wins; 9 draws; 13 defeats

RIGHT: Harvey (left) in action against Jock McAvoy at the White City in 1939, when 82,000 saw him win the British version of the world light-heavyweight championship.

BELOW: Len Harvey in training for a points win over Dave Shade of the USA in 1930.

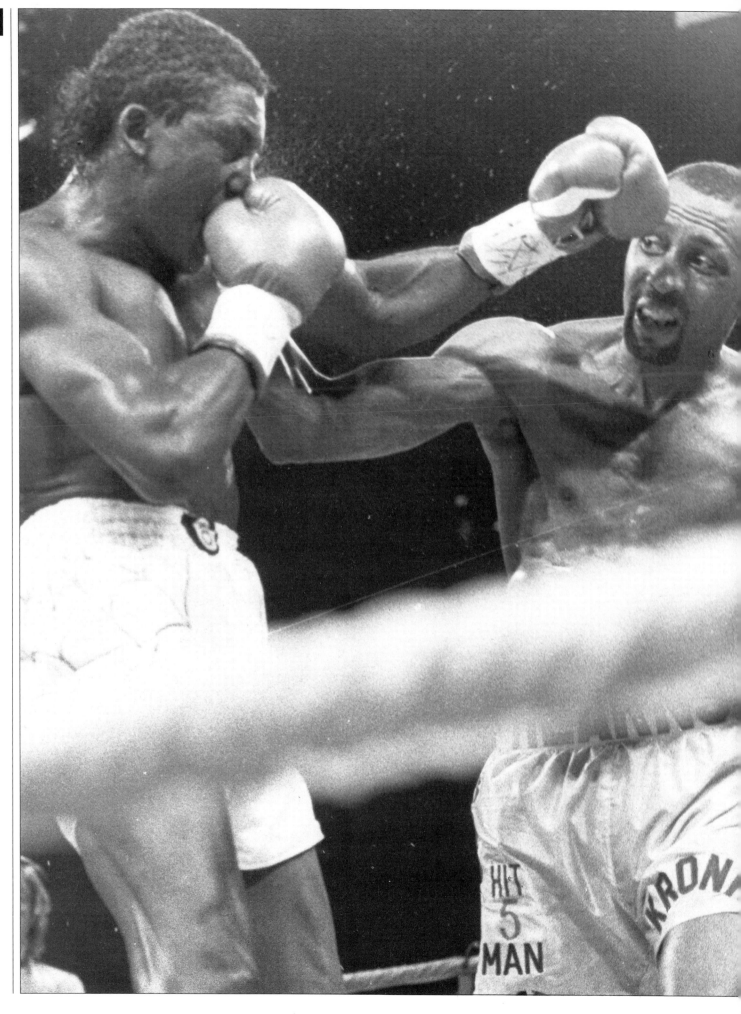

THOMAS HEARNS

born: 18 October 1958, Memphis, Tennessee, USA

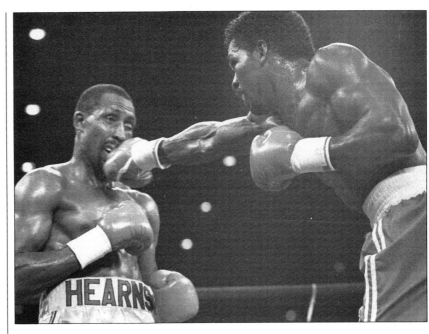

One of a family of nine children brought up on the rough East Side of Detroit, Hearns began boxing with gloves at the age of ten in the basement of the King Solomon Baptist Church. He was national Golden Gloves welterweight champion at 19 and turned professional in November 1977. Hearns' opponents tended to be stopped early, and only two of the first 26 went the distance, by which time Hearns was US welterweight champion. Three fights later he met Pipino Cuevas for the WBA title and, in the battle of the knockout specialists, it was Cuevas who was stopped in the second round.

Hearns, at 6ft 1in with long thin arms and legs, did not look the type to have a heavy punch, but so devastating was he that he was called the 'Hit Man'. He was also an astute boxer, who became one of the outstanding attractions of the 1980s. Another was Sugar Ray Leonard, the holder of the WBC title, and the meeting between them was explosive. Hearns took an early lead but Leonard lasted better, and inflicted a first defeat on the Hitman with a 14th-round stoppage.

Hearns moved up to light-middleweight and, in 1982, beat another outstanding fighter, Wilfred Benitez, to take that crown. After three defences, including one against Roberto Duran, Hearns issued an audacious challenge to middleweight champion Marvin Hagler. It was three rounds of mayhem, with Hearns suffering his second defeat on a third-round stoppage, but he had staggered Hagler in one of boxing's most exciting bouts.

ON this spread, three of Tommy Hearns' victories. From left, clockwise: over Michael Olajide in 1989, James Kinchen in 1988 and, surprisingly, against Virgil Hill in 1991.

Hearns continued to defend his light-middleweight title, to which he added the North American middleweight crown, and then went for a world title at a third weight by challenging Dennis Andries, the WBC light-heavyweight champion. Andries put up a brave show in Tommy's home town of Detroit, but Hearns' punches were too much for him and he was finally stopped in the tenth. Hearns now set about collecting world titles at as many weights as possible, and when the WBC middleweight title became vacant in 1987 after one of the retirements of Sugar Ray Leonard, Hearns knocked out Juan Domingo Roldan to make his score four, thus passing the record of Bob Fitzsimmons and Henry Armstrong, although of course the achievements are not comparable.

A new 'authorising body', the WBO, gave Hearns the opportunity in 1988 to outpoint James Kinchen to become their super-middleweight champion, and his score was five. Hearns suffered a shock defeat when Iran Barkley came from behind and stopped him with one punch to take this latest title but, in June 1988, he had the chance to put right one of the setbacks which rankled most when he challenged Leonard for the WBC super-middleweight title. The verdict was a controversial draw, with many thinking that Hearns, who had Leonard down twice, unlucky not to get the decision.

Hearns continued his career and in June 1991 provided a big upset with a unanimous points decision over the five-years younger unbeaten WBA light-heavyweight champion Virgil Hill. It was the sixth time Hearns had won a world title. But in March 1992 Hearns was himself surprisingly outpointed by Iran Barkley in a bruising contest to lose this title. **Record: 55 contests; 50 wins; 1 draw; 4 defeats**

See also: Hagler v Hearns, Leonard v Hearns

PAUL HODKINSON

born: 14 September 1965, Liverpool

Hodkinson was a hard-hitting amateur who began early by winning an ABA junior title in 1982 and who won the ABA featherweight title in 1986. He turned professional soon afterwards and, although he could manage only a draw with Tomas Arguelles when he made a trip to Panama City in July 1987, he immediately avenged this with a knockout in Belfast, and in May 1988 he was British featherweight champion with a stoppage of Peter Harris. In April 1989 he became European champion by stopping Raymond Armand. He won a Lonsdale Belt outright and then relinquished the British title to concentrate on the world scene.

In March 1990 Hodkinson, known as 'Hoko', stopped Eduardo Montoya in an IBF title eliminator then, in June, fought Marcos Villasana for the vacant WBC title. Hodkinson battered Villasana early on but could not put him down and was stopped with badly cut eyes in the eighth round. It was his first defeat. After a long rest Hodkinson returned in October 1990 to knock out Gary Bellehigne in the third round to keep his European title.

Hodkinson got his second chance at a world title in November 1991 with a return with Villasana in Belfast. In another terrific battle which lasted the 12 rounds Hodkinson was adjudged a winner by a wide margin. Hodkinson made an easy first defence of his title with a third-round stoppage of Steve Cruz in Belfast in April 1992.

Record: 22 contests; 20 wins; 1 draw; 1 defeat

A PAUL HODKINSON left catches Marcus Villasana, from whom Hoko won the world title in 1991.

LARRY HOLMES

born: 3 November 1949, Cuthbert, Georgia, USA

Holmes was one of 11 children. He boxed as an amateur without being outstanding and turned professional in March 1973. He sparred with Ali and Frazier, which is perhaps why he found it hard to get a shot at the title, despite running up an unbeaten record of 27 fights in five years. Then, because Leon Spinks, the undisputed heavyweight champion, declined to meet the WBC contender, Ken Norton, preferring a return with Ali instead, the WBC stripped Spinks and announced Norton as the champion. At the same time Norton was told to 'defend' against Holmes. In June 1978 Holmes outpointed Norton at Las Vegas and became champ.

Holmes, a good strong all-round boxer with stamina, a punch and the ability to take one, was not the popular choice as champion while Ali was still around, but Ali retired, and Holmes, with six defences in little more than two years, became the people's champion. When Ali made a comeback and Holmes stopped him in the tenth, Holmes was accepted as the world's best heavyweight, although he still suffered from the handicap of succeeding the great Ali. He rose from the canvas to beat Trevor Berbick, quickly stopped Leon Spinks and not so quickly Gerry Cooney, a much-hyped 'white hope'.

After 17 defences, the last a one-round stoppage of Marvis Frazier, son of ex-champ Joe, Holmes relinquished the WBC title to accept recognition by a new body, the IBF. After three defences of this title, Holmes' record stood at 48 contests, 48 wins, just one short of the career record of Rocky Marciano, the only heavyweight to retire unbeaten. Holmes, in view of his lack of perceived charisma, particularly wanted to equal or pass Marciano's total and, although he was by now nearly 36, thought he could handle a challenge from the light-heavyweight champion,

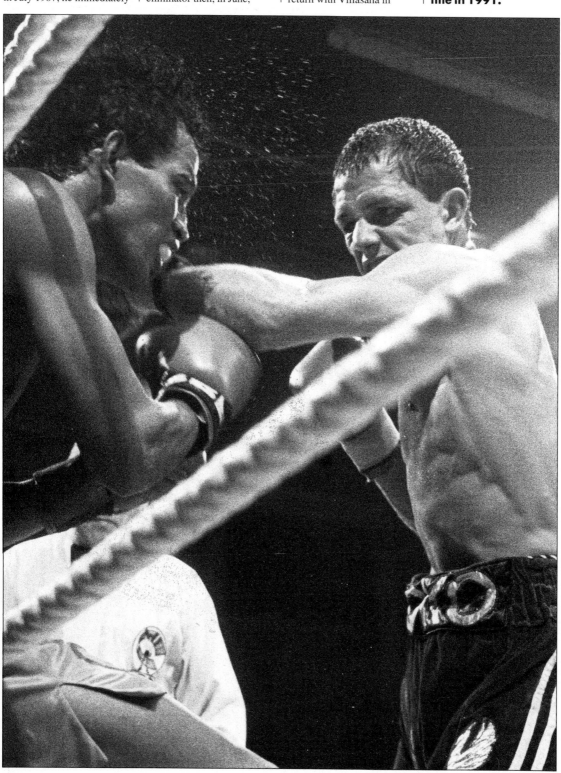

Michael Spinks, even though Spinks too, was unbeaten. However in September 1985 Larry's older legs could not catch up with the dancing Spinks and he was outpointed.

Holmes thought he had won and, in 1986, could not resist a second shot at Spinks. This time he lost a split decision, and many fans agreed with his claim that he'd won. An angry Holmes filed protests to all the authorities concerned and retired, rich but aggrieved. However in January 1988 with Mike Tyson, a new young and undisputed heavyweight champion on the throne, Holmes added to his money if not lessening his grievances, by challenging Tyson. The result was a predictable loss by a fourth-round stoppage. Holmes retired again.

However, the age was one of big purses for veterans and in April 1991 Holmes, who had allegedly made bad investments with the several million dollars he had won, came back again. Five unimpressive wins against no-hopers earned a match with the up-and-coming undefeated Ray Mercer, an Olympic gold medalist. The fight, in Atlantic City in 1992, was billed as 'The Last Stand' but amazingly the 42-year-old Holmes befuddled the hard-hitting Mercer and won a points victory. This, in turn, led to a challenge for Evander Holyfield's undisputed world title. In June 1992 in Las Vegas Holmes went the distance and, although well outpointed, he joined Louis and Ali as the only men to take part in heavyweight title fights in three separate decades.

Record: 58 contests; 54 wins; 4 defeats

RIGHT and BELOW: Larry Holmes punishes 'white hope' Gerry Cooney.

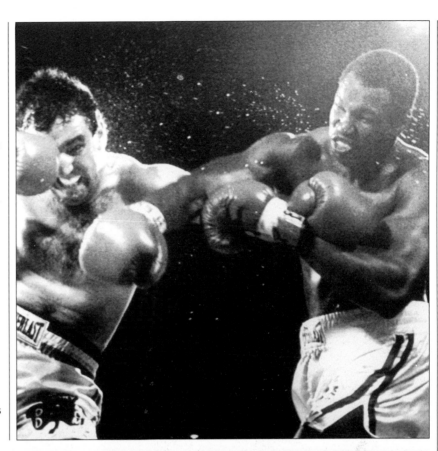

EVANDER HOLYFIELD

born: 19 October 1962, Atmore, Alabama, USA

A Golden Gloves winner, Holyfield was an outstanding amateur who won 160 of 174 contests, and was a hot favourite to take the light-heavyweight gold medal at the 1984 Olympics, but he was disqualified in the semi-final for throwing a punch after the referee called 'break'. He straightaway turned professional and directed his attention to the cruiserweight division. In his 12th contest, in July 1986, he outpointed Dwight Muhammad Qawi to take the WBA title. In his first defence he stopped Henry Tillman, the Olympic heavyweight champion, and went on to stop Rickey Parkey to add the IBF title to the WBA.

Holyfield unified the cruiserweight division by stopping the WBC champion Carlos de Leon, in April 1988. He then relinquished all the titles to campaign as a heavyweight, beating by the short route six opponents including ex-champions Pinklon Thomas and Michael Dokes. He had hoped for a big payday with Mike Tyson, but had to be content instead to challenge Tyson's surprise conqueror, Buster Douglas, for the undisputed

heavyweight crown.

Holyfield is a fine upstanding boxer with good speed and ringcraft, a good punch and a good chin. He was obviously not a big heavyweight, even at 6ft 1in, having been able to make 190lb, but he scientifically increased his weight to 208lb. He proved too good for an overweight Douglas, 38lb heavier, and knocked him out in the third round at Las Vegas in October 1990.

The first opponent for the new champion was the 42-year-old former champion George Foreman. Holyfield won but was far from impressive and could not put the veteran down. He should then have fought Tyson, but Tyson had problems elsewhere and Holyfield fought a second substitute in Bert Cooper, who had no pretensions to the title, but who inflicted on Holyfield the first count of his career in the third round. Holyfield came back to stop Cooper in the seventh round, and then played safe again by accepting the challenge of another 42-year-old ex-champion in Larry Holmes. Holyfield won on points, but none of his first three defences created the impression of true heavyweight power and his place among the heavies in boxing history remained unsure.

Record: 28 contests; 28 wins

BELOW LEFT: Evander Holyfield lands a left on Buster Douglas' head in winning the world title in 1990.

BELOW RIGHT: Evander 'The Real Deal' Holyfield.

LLOYD HONEYGHAN

born: 22 April 1960, Jamaica

Honeyghan was brought up in Bermondsey, London. A good amateur he represented England as a junior and senior. He turned professional in 1980 and in April 1983 won the vacant British welterweight title with a points victory over Cliff Gilpin. In January 1985 he showed his punching power with a third round knockout of Gianfranco Rosi in Italy to take the European title, relinquishing the British title, but in November 1985 he won back the British and added the Commonwealth title by stopping Sylvester Mittee in the eighth round.

Honeyghan's style was flashy, as he swarmed over his opponents and overpowered them. He always attacked with great confidence and, possessing a powerful punch in both hands, he never allowed an opponent to recover when he was on top. He gave up all his titles in September 1986 when he challenged Don Curry for the undisputed world title in Atlantic City. Both boxers were unbeaten and Curry was being described as the best world champion of the day. But Honeyghan put up one of the

best performances ever of a British boxer overseas by completely dominating the champion, who was forced to retire in the sixth round.

Honeyghan immediately relinquished the WBA version of the title to avoid meeting South African Harold Volbrecht – his objection was on grounds of *apartheid* – but he defended his other titles successfully three times in 1987. He then lost the WBC title in strange circumstances to Jorge Vaca at Wembley in October 1987. An accidental clash of heads in the eighth ended the contest with Vaca cut over the eye. The referee ordered the judges to render a decision on the scores at the end of the previous round, but deducting a point from Honeyghan as he was held responsible for the incident. This was enough to give Vaca the title on a split decision. But Honeyghan, reacting to recent hand injuries and publicity over domestic and managerial differences, had fought listlessly anyway, an indication that his emotional state was an important aspect of his power. The IBF also withdrew recognition from him after this defeat. Honeyghan fought back well

BELOW: Lloyd Honeyghan.

to regain the WBC title from Vaca five months later, and defend it in Atlantic City in 1988, but in February 1989 he was well beaten by Marlon Starling in Las Vegas.

A comeback stoppage by Mark Breland in a WBA challenge in March 1990 probably marked the end of Honeyghan as a world title force. He resumed his career as a light-middleweight and racked up victories in his first six contests at this level.
Record: 43 contests; 40 wins; 3 defeats

See also Honeyghan v Curry

LLOYD HONEYGHAN V DONALD CURRY

27 September 1986, Atlantic City

Donald Curry, the 'Lone Star Cobra', was regarded in 1986 as possibly the best of the world champions. Only he and Marvin Hagler were undisputed champions, and the younger Curry, having cleaned up the welterweight division, looked set to reign for years. His talents were well known in Britain for, in 1985, he had appeared at Birmingham and stopped the British champion, Colin Jones, in four rounds, severely damaging Jones' nose. He later knocked out Milton McCrory in two rounds to unify the title.

One Briton who was not frightened to meet him, however, was Lloyd Honeyghan, the British, European and Commonwealth champion. They met at Caesars Hotel, Atlantic City. Both men were unbeaten, Curry in 25 contests, Honeyghan in 27. But such was the awe in which Curry was held that he was a 6-1 favourite. Curry was two inches taller than Honeyghan, and possessed a long reach. His usual style was to box with his arms well up, presenting a difficult target for the opponent, and he was brilliant defensively. He stalked his man with great concentration, and his fast hands did the rest. He was also a good brawler, and not slow to use his elbows. In short, he seemed equipped to deal with anything an opponent could tackle him with.

Honeyghan, however, was one of the most confident boxers in the world, who usually started with a rush and tried to overwhelm his opponent from the first bell. It was not a practice he felt he ought to change just because he was facing Curry. Any plans of campaign Curry had, soon

went out of the window. Lloyd began with hard left leads to the head. A hard right had Curry's knees wobbling and the champion staggering backwards. Curry weathered the storm but was too occupied to fight back. With only one round gone the writing was on the wall.

Honeyghan gave Curry

no chance to get back into the fight. He constantly beat Curry to the punch and bullied him around the ring. Curry was not given the chance to do anything. Having got on top, Honeyghan outboxed the champion. He was faster, hit harder and inflicted more and more punishment on Curry each round. It was a complete beating. Curry was cut around the eyes and had his nose broken. While Honeyghan bounced from his corner at the start of a round and walked purposefully back at the end, Curry appeared more and more sad and apprehensive. At the end of the sixth round, Curry walked back to his corner shaking his head. He could not come out for the seventh. Honeyghan had achieved a feat which Britons have always found difficult – to take a world title from an American on his own patch. But to do it against such an outstanding champion in such a decisive manner was an all-time great performance. American magazines described the result as the shock of the year. It was probably the best British world title performance since Turpin beat Sugar Ray Robinson 35 years earlier.

ONE of the best overseas performances by a British boxer was the demolition of Donald Curry by Lloyd Honeyghan (right) in 1986.

JAMES J. JEFFRIES

born: 15 April 1875, Carroll, Ohio, USA
died: 3 March 1953, Burbank, California, USA

Jeffries was apprenticed to a boilermaker, and the physique he developed led him into boxing, initially as a sparring partner to leading heavyweights, including champion James J. Corbett. By 1896, when he began his professional career, he stood 6ft 2½ in and weighed 216lb. He was never a scientific boxer and had no defence, but he developed a pronounced crouching style which made him more difficult to hit. And his punching, particularly his left hook, was as hard as any the game has seen.

Jeffries began with five knockouts, then had two 20-round draws with Gus Ruhlin and Joe Choynski, two of the best heavyweights of the day. He knocked out Peter Jackson and outpointed Tom Sharkey, and challenged Bob Fitzsimmons for the world crown in June 1899. He proved too big, strong and young for Fitzsimmons, knocking him out in the 11th round to become champion. Six months later he outpointed Tom Sharkey in a remarkable battle under fierce lights which burnt their heads. Sharkey ended with broken ribs but there was little in it after 25 rounds.

In all Jeffries defended seven times, beating Fitzsimmons again and twice knocking out the previous champion and his former boss, Corbett. He retired in 1905 never having been beaten, but sadly was persuaded to come back in 1910 as the white hope to beat Jack Johnson and was humiliated.
Record: 21 contests; 18 wins; 2 draws; 1 defeat

See also: Johnson v Jeffries

EDER JOFRE

born: 26 March 1936, Sao Paulo, Brazil

Eder Jofre went with his father to a slaughterhouse when a boy and was so sickened that he became a vegetarian. It did not deter him from spilling opponents' blood, however. From a boxing family, he turned professional on his 21st birthday, winning by a knockout, and carried on from there.

Only 5ft 4in, Jofre was perfectly proportioned and had the strength and skill to go with his physique. A lightning jab and a devastating hook were two of the weapons with which he despatched the best in the world for nearly 20 years. In November 1960 he knocked out Eloy Sanchez to win the vacant NBA world bantamweight title. He defended twice and in January 1962 faced Johnny Caldwell, who held the European version, in Sao Paulo. Jofre unified the championship when Caldwell's corner threw in the towel in the 10th round. Jofre made five defences of his title in three years, by when he had won 17 consecutive contests inside the distance, including nine world title fights. He then went to Nagoya and was outpointed by Fighting Harada. A year later Harada repeated the result and Jofre retired.

After three years out of the ring Jofre returned in 1969 and fought as a featherweight. His skill was undiminished. Three and a half years into his second career, he outpointed Jose Legra to win the WBC featherweight title. He defended successfully against Vicente Saldivar, but was inactive in 1974 and forfeited the title. Seven more wins and he retired with only Fighting Harada having ever beaten him.
Record: 78 contests; 72 wins; 4 draws; 2 defeats

INGEMAR JOHANSSON

born: 16 October 1932, Gothenburg, Sweden

Ingemar Johansson saw his first boxing tournament at 12, and joined a gym when 13. His ambition was to become a professional, but first he had 71 amateur bouts and reached the final of the heavyweight class in the Olympic Games. His opponent, like himself, was a counterpuncher, and for two rounds both men waited for the other to attack. Finally the exasperated referee disqualified Johansson for not trying. It took 30 years of controversy before he received his silver medal.

At 6ft 0¼ in, the 195lb Johansson had a powerful righthand punch, which after he had turned professional in December 1952 brought him many knockout victories. In only his 15th contest he stopped Francesco Cavicchi in the 13th to win the European title. It was only his 22nd fight when he challenged Floyd Patterson in New York for the world title. When he arrived in New York with his family and fiancée, and seemed to train by sitting by the swimming pool, Americans wrote him off. But in his previous contest he had knocked out in one round Eddie Machen, a man Patterson had avoided. It was poetic justice when in the third round Johansson floored Patterson seven times to win by a knockout.

A year later Johansson returned to New York for the return and, over-confident, was knocked out in the fifth. Another nine months passed and Johansson lost the decider in the sixth, after this time both men had been on the canvas. There was still time for him to retain the European title, but he retired after a win against Brian London in 1963. This victory maintained the slightly bizarre nature of his career, because when the final bell went Johansson was on the canvas from a right. There are various opinions as to how far the count had reached when the bell rang (London says 'nine') but Johansson had the verdict on points.
Record: 28 contests; 26 wins; 2 defeats

See also: Patterson v Johansson

JACK JOHNSON

born: 31 March 1878, Galveston, Texas, USA
died: 10 June 1946, Raleigh, North Carolina, USA

Johnson ran away from home at 12 to work in a racing stable. He became a sparring partner and began boxing professionally in 1897 in his home town, but opportunities for black boxers were rare. On the whole they were forced to face each other, and white boxers could 'draw the colour line' and refuse to box any black fighter. Johnson in fact continued work as a painter, as he slowly built up a formidable reputation as a fighter. At 6ft 1¼ in and 195lb he became a brilliant defensive boxer and counter-puncher, with a devastating uppercut.

He lost a few fights before in 1908 he chased Tommy Burns, the heavyweight champion, to Europe, then Australia, where Burns was persuaded by a big purse to give Johnson a chance at the title. Johnson was too big, strong and skilful for Burns and won the championship. He was the first black heavyweight champion, something that white Americans found impossible to bear. Johnson's character inflamed the situation. He was arrogant and lost no opportunity to draw attention to his supremacy. He married white women, one of whom committed suicide, and surrounded himself with white mistresses, behaviour which inflamed the white race. There was a movement to find a white boxer to beat him but none could. Even the middleweight champion, Stanley Ketchel, had a try in a fight which was arranged so that Johnson would carry the lighter man. Unfortunately Ketchel got carried away and dropped Johnson in the 12th round, whereupon Johnson rose to knock Ketchel senseless with a single uppercut.

In 1910 Jim Jeffries, the former unbeaten champion, was coaxed out of retirement to challenge Johnson, but he was out of condition and was contemptuously defeated. The result provoked bitter race riots in American. Eventually white America ignored Johnson and boxing men organised a 'white' heavyweight championship, until it was realised that Johnson could be imprisoned for infringing the Mann Act, which forbade the transportation of women across a state boundary for immoral purposes. Johnson

RIGHT: Jack Johnson.

frequently travelled with a favourite white prostitute, who was persuaded to give evidence. Johnson was sentenced to a year and a day in prison, and while on bail fled to Canada and Europe.

He defended twice in Paris and then returned to Cuba in 1915 to face giant challenger Jess Willard. Willard was not a great fighter but was immensely strong and could absorb plenty of punishment. After Johnson had outboxed Willard for 26 rounds in blazing sunshine, he was knocked out. He claimed later that the promoter had promised his prison sentence would be cancelled if he were no longer champion, and also that he lost by arrangement for money, but these assertions are now treated sceptically. After all, at the time he was 37, and was entitled to be tired after 26 rounds.

Johnson returned to Europe, then went to Mexico, but eventually returned to the States, where, in fact, he was forced to serve his sentence. He continued boxing until 1928, when he was 50, and was still giving exhibitions well into his 60s. His passion was fast cars, and he died crashing one in 1946.
Record: 113 contests; 79 wins; 12 draws; 8 defeats; 14 no-decision

See also: Johnson v Jeffries

JACK JOHNSON V JAMES J. JEFFRIES

4 July 1910, Reno, Nevada

Never again will a boxing match inflame passions like that at Reno on 4 July 1910. This was the showdown. Jack Johnson was the heavyweight champion of the world, the first black man to win the title. Never has a boxer been so unpopular, among the whites at least. He was seen as arrogant and boastful and moreover consorted with white women. There was a search to find a white man to beat him, but none could. However many Americans thought they knew of one man who could 'wipe the

smile from Johnson's face'. He was James J. Jeffries, the unbeaten champion who had retired in 1904 having run out of worthwhile challengers. Jeffries was living comfortably on his alfalfa farm and was unwilling to come back after six years, but finally he was persuaded to rescue the white man's honour.

For the week before the bout, Reno was the centre of the universe. Thousands poured into the town, many of them unsavoury characters: thieves, pickpockets and gamblers. It was said the pavements were strewn with cheap watches, stolen and discarded by the thieves, and with wallets emptied of their cash by pickpockets.

Opinion was blinded by prejudice. Jeffries was the betting favourite at 10 to 6, despite his long lay-off. At 35 he was only three years older than Johnson, but Johnson had remained active. Over 16,000 spectators packed the wooden arena in blazing heat, having first had their firearms taken at the gate. This was a precaution taken by Tex Rickard, the promoter, who was going to referee the contest. He knew he might have to render an unpopular decision. Another great crowd was locked outside.

Johnson entered the ring in a black and white bathrobe, confidently smiling with his gold fillings shining in the sun. He received a tremendous welcome as did Jeffries, whom many white supporters were claiming was the champion, on the grounds that he had never been beaten for the title. Strangely, he entered the ring in a grey business suit over purple tights, and with a golf cap on his head. Jeffries, at 16st 3lb, was 19lb heavier than Johnson.

The fight began at 2.47. Jeffries was aggressive in the first rounds, but soon it seemed as if Johnson was playing with him. The predominantly white spectators grew increasingly restless and, in the sixth round when a terrific punch from Johnson shut Jeffries' right eye, they must have known the writing was on the wall. Johnson began

laughing at Jeffries in the seventh round and then began a commentary with Jim Corbett, one of Jeffries' seconds and a man who had expected Johnson's 'yellow streak' to show once Jeffries began to attack him. Johnson even winked and grinned at friends in the audience.

Johnson began to punish Jeffries from then on and began to taunt him, asking 'How do you feel, Mr Jeff?' and: 'I can go on like this all afternoon, Mr Jeff.' Jeffries was out of breath by the 13th, when the crowd began to shout to Rickard to stop it. White Americans feared the humiliation of seeing Jeffries knocked out by a black man. But there was no respite from the referee. Johnson piled in the punches and, by the end of the 14th round, Jeffries could hardly raise his arms. In the 15th Johnson knocked Jeffries through the ropes. He got up but Johnson smashed him down again. One of Jeffries' handlers threw in the towel, but Rickard did not see it as he counted over Jeffries. Spectators were beginning to climb into the ring by the time Rickard reached ten.

Johnson was undistressed at the end. Later he was to claim that he outclassed Jeffries in every department, but praised his bravery. Jeffries admitted his pride had got the better of his good judgement and regretted that he had lost the snap of youth.

Simmering racial tension turned to violence all across America after the result. There were riots everywhere, especially with white mobs hunting down black men. On the first day there were 19 deaths, over 250 seriously injured, thousands hurt and over 5,000 arrested. Boxing and race relations would never be the same again and never in the future would a sporting event provoke such feelings.

RIGHT: Peter Kane (right) on his way to stopping French champion Pierre Louis, Paris, 1937.

RIGHT ABOVE: Kane (right) beats Baltazar Sangchili, London, 1939.

PETER KANE

born: (Peter Cain) 28 February 1918, Heywood, Lancashire
died: 23 July 1991, Wigan, Lancashire

Peter Kane's family moved to Golborne, Lancashire, when he was a baby. He began boxing for money in booths while still at school, and never had an amateur bout. On leaving school he became a blacksmith's striker which helped to build strength into his less-than-eight stone frame. His surname was spelt wrongly on his official pro debut as a flyweight in Liverpool in December 1934, and he remained 'Kane'. He was 16, but already had a knockout punch to go with his indefatigable aggression.

He was unbeaten in his first 41 fights, stopping 33 of his opponents and, while still only 19, he challenged the great Benny Lynch for the world flyweight championship. In a fierce battle in October 1927 he found Lynch too experienced, and was knocked out in the 13th round. Five months later they fought a draw in an overweight return match. Lynch forfeited his title over failure to make the weight and, in September 1938, Kane easily outpointed the American Jackie Jurich to win the vacant title. He was still only 20.

Unfortunately for Kane, the Second World War

interrupted his career. He served in the RAF but kept active. In a wartime contest in Glasgow in 1943 he was knocked out by Jackie Paterson in the first round to lose his world title.

He was famous for his staring 'Eddie Cantor' eyes, but in 1944 an injury to his right eye, caused by the lapel of a coat, led to the RAF banning him from boxing. On his discharge he resumed his career after an operation but in later life was blind in that eye.

After the war he moved up to bantamweight and, in September 1947, won the European title from Theo Medina. He lost this in 1948 and after a couple more losses he retired.
Record: 102 contests; 92 wins; 2 draws; 7 defeats; 1 no-contest

STANLEY KETCHEL

born: (Stanislaus Kiecel) 14 September 1886, Grand Rapids, Michigan, USA died: 15 October 1910, Conway, Missouri, USA

Stanley Ketchel, a 16-year-old bus boy from a saloon in Butte, Montana, who had run away from home as a child, won $10 in his first fight in 1903, a first-round knockout. The pattern was set for a career which led many to call him the greatest middleweight of all time. Ketchel had everything: skill, strength, courage, a devastating punch and an unstoppable will to win. By feigning death after being shot at he captured a murderer while in his teens and pocketed the $1000 reward. He drank hard, chased women and became a legend even before his terrific fight with Joe Thomas in 1907, with whom he had already fought a 20-round draw. In the second fight, he took the loser's purse before the contest to bet it on a knockout victory within the

45 rounds scheduled. He was smashed to the floor himself in the 29th, but knocked out Thomas in the 32nd.

The following year, when he was 21, he knocked out Jack (Twin) Sullivan in the 20th round to win the vacant world middleweight title. After two defences, he lost the title to Billy Papke by trickery. Papke ignored Ketchel's glove proffered for the usual pre-fight handshake and decked Ketchel with a left hook and right cross which half-blinded the champion. Ketchel battled on under this handicap for 12 rounds before the referee stopped it in Papke's favour.

Ketchel had his revenge 11 weeks later, punishing Papke for 11 rounds before deciding to knock him out.

Because of his ferocious style, Ketchel was called the 'Michigan Assassin'. He beat all the best middleweights around and twice took on Philadelphia Jack O'Brien, the light-heavyweight champion who two years earlier had boxed a draw in his challenge for the heavyweight title. In the first

encounter O'Brien was out on the floor when the bell ended the ten-round no-decision contest. In the second Ketchel won with a third-round knockout. After beating Papke again, Ketchel challenged the feared Jack Johnson for the world heavyweight championship. It was no doubt an arranged fight, but Ketchel had the temerity to knock down the 35lb heavier Johnson in the 12th. Johnson rose to knock out Ketchel with one terrific punch.

In 1910 Ketchel was having breakfast on the ranch of an admirer when a crippled stablehand, Walter Dipley, perhaps jealous of Ketchel's advances to his girlfriend, shot him in the back. Ketchel was still only 24, and unbeatable at middleweight.

Record: 66 contests; 53 wins; 5 draws; 4 defeats; 4 no-decision

STANLEY KETCHEL (right), Billy Papke and referee James J. Jeffries before Papke's win in 1907.

KNOCKOUTS AND KNOCKDOWNS

The number of knockouts in a boxer's career is hard to determine because in America every contest that ends before the scheduled distance is recorded as a knockout. In Britain the categories 'retired' or 'referee stopped contest' are recognised and recorded accordingly. In modern times referees are quicker to stop contests when a boxer is threatened with injury, so many more fights are halted before an actual count of 'ten' takes place.

The following are held to be the boxers who achieved over 100 knockouts during their careers. They are all American, and their records are based on the American interpretation of a knockout.

145 Archie Moore 1935–65
126 Young Stribling 1921–33
125 Billy Bird 1920–48
114 George Odwell 1930–45
109 Sugar Ray Robinson 1940–65
108 Banty Lewis 1909–22
103 Sandy Saddler 1944–56

The most knockouts in world title fights were registered by Joe Louis, 22 of whose 27 title fights were won by the short route.

The best percentage of knockouts in relation to career bouts is that of former heavyweight champion George Foreman, whose first 74 bouts resulted in 66 quick wins, a proportion of 89 per cent. Another heavyweight champion, Rocky Marciano, won 43 of 49 bouts inside the distance or 88 per cent. Mike Tyson's record of 36 knockouts in 42 bouts represents 86 per cent.

Quickest Knockouts

The quickest genuine knockout, i.e. one with a count, was registered by Al Couture, who beat Ralph Walton in 10½ seconds at Lewiston, Maine, on 26 September 1946. Obviously this record cannot in practice be beaten. Several knockouts are timed at 11 seconds, however, and contests have been stopped before ten seconds have elapsed, particularly in amateur bouts.

The quickest knockouts in the eight original classes in world title fights are as follows:

Heavyweight 56 seconds, James J. Jeffries v Jack Finnegan, Detroit, 6 April 1900
Light-heavyweight 118 seconds, Gus Lesnevich v Billy Fox, New York, 5 March 1948
Middleweight 45 seconds, Lloyd Honeyghan v Gene Hatcher, Marbella, 30 August 1987
Lightweight 66 seconds, Tony Canzoneri v Al Singer, New York, 14 November 1930
Featherweight 150 seconds, Freddie Miller v Jose Girones, Barcelona, 17 February 1935
Bantamweight 75 seconds, Terry McGovern v Pedlar Palmer, New York, 12 September 1899
Flyweight 58 seconds, Emile Pladner v Frankie Genaro, Paris, 2 March 1929

Al Singer had the odd record of having won the world lightweight championship on a first-round knockout and losing it in his next fight also on a first-round knockout, 18 weeks later.

Sonny Liston had four heavyweight title fights, winning two on first-round knockouts (both against Floyd Patterson) and losing one in similar fashion (against Muhammad Ali).

In a British title fight the record for the quickest knockout is 40 seconds, when Dave Charnley knocked out Darkie Hughes for the British, European and Empire lightweight titles at Nottingham, 20 November 1961.

Knockdowns

The most knockdowns inflicted on a boxer in a contest with gloves is probably 41, the number of times that Battling Nelson downed Christy Williams in Hot Springs, Arkansas, on 26 December 1902. Nelson was down seven times before winning by a knockout in the 17th round. There were thus 48 knockdowns in the contest.

There were 47 knockdowns when Joe Jeannette fought Sam McVey in Paris in April 1909. Jeannette was down 21 times before dropping McVey in the 39th round. Thereafter McVey was knocked down 18 more times and Jeannette six. McVey collapsed after rising from his stool for the 49th round and was counted out.

The most knockdowns in a world title fight is 16, all scored by Bill Ladbury when winning the flyweight title from Sid Smith in London on 2 June 1913, Smith being stopped in the 11th. This fight was recognised by the British and European authorities.

The most knockdowns in an undisputed world title fight is 14, all scored by Vic Toweel when defending his bantamweight title against Danny O'Sullivan on 2 December 1950 in Johannesburg. O'Sullivan retired in the tenth round.

The most knockdowns in a heavyweight title fight is 11, registered twice. Max Baer scored all 11 in taking the title on an 11th round stoppage from Primo Carnera on 14 June 1934 in New York. Jack Dempsey scored nine and Luis Firpo two when Dempsey retained his title on a second-round knockout on 14 September 1923 in New York.

The most knockdowns in a single round in a world title fight is nine. Luis Firpo was down nine times and Jack Dempsey twice in the first round of the match noted above.

Vic Toweel knocked down Danny O'Sullivan eight times in the fifth round of the Johannesburg fight noted above.

JAKE LAMOTTA

born: 10 July 1922, Bronx, New York City, USA

LaMotta's forename was Giacobe, but he was known as Jake from his early Bronx days as a juvenile delinquent – behaviour which landed him in the same reform school as Rocky Graziano. He claimed the number of his street fights and amateur bouts ran into four figures. He turned pro early in 1941 and built up a big reputation as a brave middleweight. In February 1943 he became the first man to beat Sugar Ray Robinson, whom he fought six times in all, winning once.

It took the more-or-less self-managed LaMotta years to get a championship chance, and it only came after he had appeased the mob who controlled the title by losing by arrangement to Billy Fox. LaMotta won the championship a little luckily in 1949 when Marcel Cerdan was forced to retire with a damaged shoulder. LaMotta made two successful defences in 1950 but in 1951 surrendered the title to his Nemesis, Sugar Ray Robinson, the referee stopping the contest in the 13th round, although LaMotta, after terrific punishment, was still on his feet. He was inactive in 1953 before trying a short comeback in 1954.

Record: 106 contests; 83 wins; 4 draws; 19 defeats

See also: LaMotta v Dauthuille

JAKE (left) and Joey LaMotta, his boxing brother/manager and Jim Murray.

JAKE LAMOTTA V LAURENT DAUTHUILLE

13 September 1950, Detroit

Jake LaMotta became undisputed world middleweight champion in 1949 and made his first two defences against Europeans. The second was against Laurent Dauthuille, a Frenchman. It was a brave choice. Dauthuille had outpointed LaMotta over ten savage rounds in Montreal in 1950 and had had LaMotta groggy at the final bell. He was not without backing although the champion was a 3-1 favourite. Rain was coming down when the two climbed into the ring at Detroit's Olympia. It was a good era for middleweight boxing and 11,426 fans paid to go through the turnstiles.

Dauthuille was a good boxer, while LaMotta's strength lay more in raw courage and durability. Not for nothing was he called the 'Bronx Bull'. It was surprising therefore that LaMotta began as if he expected to outpoint Dauthuille. He did have an early success when he cut the Frenchman's left eye in the third round, but the younger and stronger Dauthuille began to pile up the points. As the fight got more bruising he inflicted damage on LaMotta's left eye in the eighth and soon the eye began to puff up. LaMotta's desperation was evident when he was warned for hitting low.

With four rounds to go, Dauthuille was way ahead. It had taken LaMotta many years of hardship and a scrape with the mob to get the title, and he had to try something desperate to ensure he kept it. In the 12th he took a right under the heart, and put on his famous act. He reeled against the ropes and went bleary-eyed as if he was seriously hurt. Dauthuille leapt in and put all his strength into an assault to knock out LaMotta. LaMotta, who had carefully taken most of the blows on his arms, suddenly switched himself on and tore into a surprised Dauthuille. The challenger was in trouble as the round ended, but he had remained on his feet and was still way ahead.

LaMotta tried the same tactic in the 13th round but Dauthuille was not to be tempted and LaMotta had to try to make his openings by more conventional means.

As the last round started most of the principals and fans were sure that the title was about to change hands. The one man who seemed to think Dauthuille needed a good round was his French second. He urged his man to go after LaMotta and pile up more points in a grandstand finish. Dauthuille's American second advised caution, telling him he need only to keep out of trouble and the championship was his, but it was the excitable French voice that held sway as the round began.

Dauthuille accordingly went after LaMotta and not without success. With 30 seconds to go the title was his. But suddenly LaMotta ripped a terrific left into Dauthuille's body. He put into it his last reserves of energy. Amazement and pain mingled in the Frenchman's face. LaMotta amazingly kept cool and hurled lefts and rights at the challenger, forcing him towards a corner. Then another left came crashing to the body. Dauthuille went down, ashen faced, pinning down the bottom rope as he fought to get air into his lungs. He got to one knee. But the tearing pain in his stomach and chest would not allow him to straighten up. He was counted out. There were 13 seconds left.

The score-cards of the referee and two judges showed that LaMotta had to knock out Dauthuille to win. Even with the knockdown in the last half-minute the challenger would have won if only he could have beaten the count and stood on his feet for the last 13 seconds.

Laurent Dauthuille had been badly advised by his corner. Just a little discretion in the last round and he would be in the record books as undisputed middleweight champion of the world. He was foiled by half a minute. He never got another chance.

SAM LANGFORD, an outstanding early century fighter, perhaps the best around.

SAM LANGFORD

born: 12 February 1880, Weymouth, Nova Scotia, Canada
died 12 January 1956, Cambridge, Massachusetts, USA

Sam Langford was never given a chance to fight for a world title because he was black, but critics rated him the best fighter of his era – indeed, some say of all time. In his prime Langford, known as the 'Boston Tar Baby', was only 5ft 6½in and weighed 165lb, yet he took on all the heavyweights prepared to fight him, and put on the floor such giants as Jack Johnson, Harry Wills and Fred Fulton. He was usually matched with other black fighters – for example he fought Harry Wills 23 times, Sam McVey 15 and Joe Jeanette 14. Langford had big shoulders and long arms and was a clever tactician as well as a hard puncher. In 1909 he knocked out in the fourth round the British heavyweight champion, Iron Hague, in London. He retired with failing eyesight aged 44, and when he was discovered blind in Harlem in 1944 a trust fund was established for him to which fans contributed nearly $10,000.

Record: 252 contests; 137 wins; 31 draws; 23 defeats; 59 no-decision; 2 no-contest

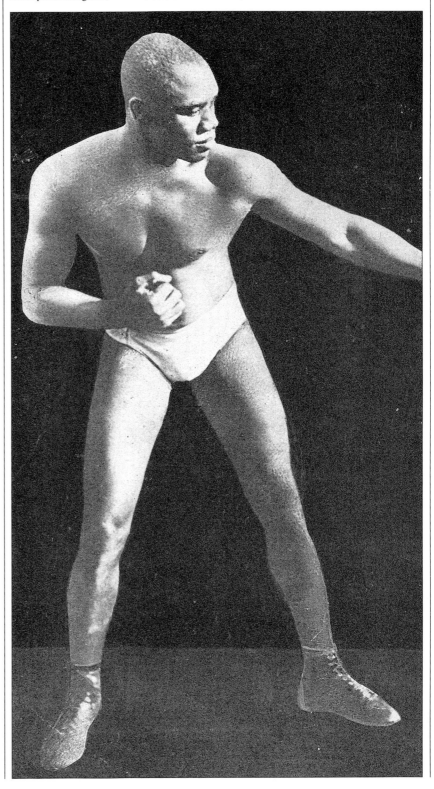

Prize fighting was always illegal in both Britain and America but, in Britain in particular, it was supported by so many influential people, from royalty downwards, that it flourished in a semi-secret world. Politicians, who made laws, and magistrates, who helped enforce them, were often seen at the big fights, as were occasionally leaders of the church, which spoke out against boxing. Thousands attended the big matches, so their venues had to be widely known, but magistrates would turn a blind eye. If police action was ordered, the organisers of the matches would get warning and could switch venues at the last minute. For this purpose, matches were often arranged in country areas near county borders, with an alternative venue lined up in the next county in case the law took action at the first venue. In the United States, where the legal situation was much the same, a favourite avoidance technique was to hold contests on barges off-shore.

Occasionally boxers and their seconds would be arrested but they were usually treated leniently. When a prize fighter died, his opponent would be charged with manslaughter but would be convicted of a lesser charge connected with fighting in public. When George Stevenson died after fighting the champion Jack Broughton in 1741, no charges were made at all. Stevenson had been backed by the Prince of Wales and Broughton by the Prince's brother, the Duke of Cumberland. Owen Swift, a great British featherweight, was involved in two ring tragedies. When Anthony Noon died in 1834 after a contest with him he was jailed for six months for manslaughter but when, four years later, Brighton Bill died he was acquitted. But he gave up boxing.

There was more effort made at stopping prize fighting in its later days, when fighting with gloves was beginning to take over from bare-knuckle fighting. The last great bareknuckle champion, John L. Sullivan, and his opponent, Charley Mitchell, were both arrested and jailed after a contest in France in 1888, despite elaborate precautions such as the venue being on the private estate of Lord Rothschild and the 'crowd' being limited to 40 or so supporters. The following year Sullivan fought Jake Kilrain in Richburg, Mississippi, in the last great bare-knuckle contest. For days the press had written of little else but the forthcoming contest. Western Union had to employ 50 extra operators to telegraph the stories of the pressmen who descended on New Orleans from all over the world. Special trains brought spectators from New York and elsewhere. Yet it was illegal. State governors swore the fight would not take place on their territory. Troops guarded the railway lines to prevent the show getting on the road, and a $1,000 award was offered for the arrest of Sullivan. Yet on the night before the fight three trains crammed with ticket holders left New Orleans and took little-used country lines to Richburg, where the fight was held on a private estate. Despite all the precautions, 5,000 spectators were there. A bribe of $250 was all that was needed to prevent the local magistrate from stepping in. There were no interruptions in a 75-round battle. However, Sullivan was arrested back in New York and extradited to Mississippi, feted at every stage of the rail journey. He was charged with and convicted of prize-fighting, the sentence for which was 12 months imprisonment. However on appeal Sullivan's sentence was quashed. Legal fees nevertheless swallowed any profit from the fight, and Sullivan thenceforth vowed to give up bare-knuckle fighting and follow the Queensberry Rules.

Not that boxing with gloves made the sport any more legal. Courts had to decide whether a match was a fight, i.e. a breach of the peace, or a sporting exhibition. In practice properly run boxing contests were allowed without harassment from the law. Again, complications arose when a contestant died. Even at London's aristocratic National Sporting Club this happened in 1897 when Jimmy Barry, the unbeaten American bantamweight champion, fought the British champion Walter Croot for what was billed as the world title. Croot died when his head struck the floor after being knocked down. The magistrate spoke of the slight distinction between a fight and a contest before ruling in favour of Barry.

A similar death occurred at the NSC in 1901, when a boxer called Murray Livingstone, who fought as Billy Smith, struck his head on the floor while boxing Jack Roberts. This time Roberts and nine members of the NSC were charged with the death of Livingstone. The prosecution stated that this was a test case aimed at determining the legality of boxing rather than a wish to punish the 'offenders'. The judge in his summing up stated he was in favour of boxing provided that it was practised under proper rules, and the jury decided that the defendants were not guilty, as the death occurred accidentally at a properly run boxing contest.

Boxing in Britain has been more or less free of interference by legal authorities since, although in 1911 a match between Jack Johnson, the black heavyweight champion of the world, and Bombadier Billy Wells, the British champion, arranged for Earls Court on 2 October, was prevented by the Home Secretary after widespread racist objections led by some churchmen.

In the United States boxing remained illegal until, in 1896, the Horton Law was passed in New York State which tentatively allowed boxing by giving the police powers to stop particular contests at their discretion. This law was superseded in 1900 by the Lewis Law, which permitted boxing only in clubs. The sport was in effect banned for the general public but clubs were permitted to stage shows for their members. In 1911 the Frawley Law was passed. This allowed public bouts of up to ten rounds only, but in order to emphasise the aspect of an exhibition, no official decisions were to be rendered. The majority of matches therefore, even those concerning world champions, were completed without a winner. In fact a champion only lost his crown in these matches if he were knocked out in the ten rounds. The 'no-decision' law was a very bad one for the fight fan, of course. Newspapers gave their views as to the winner, and the 'newspaper verdict' gained a sort of semi-official standing with the fans, especially for the purpose of settling bets. The Frawley Law was repealed in 1917, and boxing became illegal again in New York State.

Largely through the efforts of an Englishman, William Gavin, who wanted to organise a club like the National Sporting Club but effected other reforms instead, the Walker Law came into force in 1920, which allowed boxing matches of up to 15 rounds, with a decision being rendered, providing the bout was under the control of a boxing commission.

Other states and cities of the USA legalised boxing gradually. California, in fact, was the first and San Francisco became a centre of boxing activity in the early days of the century.

The 'no-decision' law was widespread in American from around 1910 until the mid-1920s. Thus most American boxers of this era have career records studded with 'no-decision' bouts.

BENNY LEONARD

born: (Benjamin Leiner) 7 April 1896, New York, USA
died: 18 April 1947, New York, USA

Leonard and his brothers boxed as amateurs at the Silver Heel Club. Leonard was persuaded to turn professional before he was 16, and suffered a couple of early knockouts. He was boxing while the Frawley Law operated in New York, meaning most of his contests were of the no-decision kind. He developed into one of the most scientific boxers in history, and could also punch.

In 1916 Leonard twice fought the brilliant world lightweight champion, Freddie Welsh, Welsh generally having the edge. In May 1917, however, Leonard surprisingly knocked out Welsh in the ninth round, thus taking the title. It was the only time Welsh was beaten inside the distance.

Leonard, a Jew, was known as the 'Ghetto Wizard'. He defended his crown successfully for eight years, retiring in 1925 as undefeated champion. During this spell he had a shot at Jack Britton's welterweight title, and seemed to be on top when he was disqualified for hitting Britton while he was down, an uncharacteristic lapse for a cool boxer.

Leonard retired partly to take care of his sick mother. He made an unsuccessful film *Flying Fists* and lost much of his fortune in the stock market crash of 1929. In 1931 he made a comeback as a welterweight. After 18 straight wins and a draw he was knocked out in October 1932 by Jimmy McLarnin, soon to become the welterweight champion. Benny retired for good. In 1943 be became a licensed New York referee but, in 1947, while refereeing the last bout of the evening at St Nick's Arena, New York, he collapsed and died. Some critics think he was the greatest of all lightweights. **Record: 210 contests; 89 wins; 1 draw; 5 defeats; 115 no-decision**

BENNY LEONARD was one of the all-time great lightweights, who had to knock out another great, Freddie Welsh, in a no-decision contest to become world champion in 1917.

SUGAR RAY LEONARD

born: 17 May 1956, Wilmington, South Carolina, USA

Sugar Ray Leonard boxed from welterweight to light-heavyweight, winning world titles on the way. He was perhaps the most outstanding boxer of the 1980s. He was groomed for stardom ever since he graduated from Golden Gloves champion to Olympic light-welterweight champion in 1976. Good-looking, charismatic, already a master ring tactician, be boxed in Montreal with pictures of his girl friend and two-year-old son on his shoes.

He turned professional in February 1977, and after 25 smooth victories, most by a knockout, he tackled Wilfred Benitez for the WBC world welterweight title. In one of the most skilful contests of modern times Leonard managed to stop Benitez with six seconds of the 15th and last round remaining. It was a shock to Leonard, and probably the biggest misjudgement of his career, when he lost the title in Montreal seven months later to Roberto Duran, the former lightweight champion. Leonard tried to beat the hustling Duran at his own game and paid the penalty on points. He rectified his error when, five months later in New Orleans, he boxed brilliantly to dishearten Duran, who famously turned his back and retired in the eighth.

In June 1981 Leonard moved up a division to take the WBA light-middleweight title with a ninth-round stoppage of Ayub Kalule. Three months later he reverted to welterweight to tackle Tommy Hearns, another 1980s great. The contest was to unify the WBC and WBA titles with Leonard receiving a record $11 million for his part. Leonard came from behind to register a 14th-round stoppage. However a legacy of this fight was eye trouble for Leonard. After an easy defence in 1982 he was forced to undergo an operation for a detached retina, and in November announced his retirement. A comeback in May 1984 resulted in a knockout victory, but when Kevin Howard decked Leonard for the first time in his career, Leonard again announced his retirement.

With his career over and his marriage failing, Leonard took to drink and cocaine, but in April 1987 his fighting heart took over again and, after a long period of training and hype he challenged the great Marvin Hagler for the WBC middleweight crown. Opinions were divided fairly evenly about the winner of this fight but the judges gave it to Leonard who, honour satisfied, retired again.

However, with his rival Thomas Hearns out to win titles at as many different weights as possible, Leonard saw a chance of raising his total to five by challenging Donny Lalonde for the WBC light-heavyweight title. By making the match at 168lb Leonard persuaded the WBC, who had never had a super-middleweight champion, to sanction the fight as for their vacant title at that weight, too. Despite being floored Leonard won on a ninth round stoppage to become a 'world champion' at five weights.

Leonard was now 32. He fought a lucrative return with Tommy Hearns, getting off the canvas to earn what most considered a fortunate draw, and then easily beat the veteran Duran in a rubber match. He was clearly fading and bit off more than he could chew with a challenge of Terry Norris for the WBC light-middleweight title on 9 February 1991. Leonard satisfied an ambition to box at Madison Square Garden, but Norris put him down twice and scored an overwhelming points victory. Leonard, fabulously rich and with a TV contract as a commentator, had no more need to fight.

Record: 39 contests; 36 wins; 1 draw; 2 defeats

See also: Leonard v Hagler; Leonard v Hearns

SUGAR RAY LEONARD V MARVIN HAGLER

6 April 1987, Las Vegas

Sugar Ray Leonard had no other reason to challenge Marvin Hagler for the middleweight championship of the world than his desire to be ranked an all-time great of boxing. He was already a double world champion, was rich, and was in retirement for the second time. He returned the first time after a detached retina, and immediately retired again on the grounds that he did not possess his old feeling for the game. But Hagler was there to be shot at – the undisputed champion for nearly seven years, unbeaten for 11. If Leonard could win, his place in history was doubly assured.

So Leonard came back again to take on Hagler after only one fight in the previous five years. Such was his charisma that he could overturn the normal rules of ratings and step straight into the big title fight. There were many who said he should not be allowed a title fight, for two reasons – its unfairness to other challengers and the danger that he might suffer serious injury. The WBA and IBF agreed with the first reason. They stripped Hagler for not facing his proper challenger Herol Graham. So the fight was for the WBC title only, at Caesars Palace.

Never has there been as much hype and speculation for a modern contest. The public interest was amazing, and the revenue broke all records, topping $100 million. The average seat cost $300, and the 15,336 were sold months in advance. The disappointed applicants, about 30,000, watched on closed circuit television. Over 300 million viewers watched later on home sets.

Hagler, as a natural middleweight, was the 3 to 1 favourite. Leonard, for all his skill, was a great welterweight who had built his weight up to Hagler's – but did his body have the same strength, especially after such a lay-off?

Those who feared the fight might not last the first round were soon proved wrong. In fact the contest developed into a fascinating battle for mastery. Leonard's plan was to win with handspeed, taking one round at a time and trying to win each, without worrying about the contest as a whole. So he retreated, blocked Hagler's blows, grabbed him round the neck when trapped on the ropes and every now and then replied in quick flurries of punches, often near the end of rounds to catch the judges' eyes.

Hagler kept pressing forward in search of Leonard, but for the first four rounds had little success. Leonard was well ahead. Hagler began to get to him in the fifth when Leonard began to slow a little. Hagler's punches were slower but carried more power than Leonard's. Hagler took rounds five to eight, so the contest was very equal as the

last third began.

The ninth was an excellent round, as Hagler began scoring with heavy punches and Leonard, momentarily in trouble, fought back. The tenth was quieter, and Leonard's little bursts of activity showed up well. Leonard put his biggest effort into the 11th, countering Hagler's punches with flashy ones of his own, at the same time beginning to clown and act as if he had everything under control. He kept it up at the start of the 12th and last round, but Hagler would not be denied and scored with some hard blows at the end.

Had Hagler's non-stop aggression and accumulation of punches outweighed Leonard's clever defensive work and stinging counters? Two judges voted 115–113, but for different men. The third made it an overwhelming 118–110 for Leonard, the new WBC champion. Oddly Hagler, or his handlers, had agreed before the other bodies withdrew recognition from him that the contest be held over the WBC distance of 12 rounds rather than 15. He might have done better over the longer distance, as he finished the stronger.

The argument will never end as to who *really* won the fight. Opinion is fairly evenly divided. There was to be no return, even though the purses would have been astronomical. Leonard didn't need the money. Hagler didn't either and, as victory over anybody else would have added nothing to his stature, he retired. So the verdict remains one of boxing's biggest talking points.

CELEBRATIONS in the Sugar Ray Leonard corner while Marvin Hagler turns away after their title fight in 1987. Leonard was awarded a much discussed split decision.

SUGAR RAY LEONARD V THOMAS HEARNS

16 September 1981, Las Vegas
12 June, 1989, Las Vegas

Two of the great boxers of the 1980s found themselves on a collision course in 1981. Thomas 'Hit Man' Hearns was the unbeaten WBA welterweight champion, while Sugar Ray Leonard was the WBC champion, having spectacularly avenged his only defeat, to Roberto Duran. Both men were at similar stages of their careers, and both were being hyped as all-time greats. A match between them was one of those naturals which doesn't always come off, but this time it did, at Caesars Palace. Hearns was a big puncher although, at 6ft 1in, he looked skinny. Leonard, three inches shorter, was a boxing artist.

Both boxers settled into a rhythm, with Hearns' crisper punching, particularly to the body, putting him in the ascendancy for the first five rounds, by which time he had built up a healthy lead and raised a welt on Leonard's left cheek which looked as if it might eventually close the eye. Leonard came back in rounds six to eight and reduced the deficit, boxing well. At this stage two judges had Hearns ahead and the other had them level, but Hearns went into a big lead by winning all the rounds from the ninth to the 12th. By now Leonard's eye was nearly closed. With three rounds to go, Leonard needed a knockdown in each to have even a chance. Realistically, he needed a knockout.

Leonard opened the 13th with a left and right to Hearns' head, but Hearns retaliated and then slipped to the canvas – it was ruled no knockdown. But Leonard suddenly got on top and drove Hearns round the ring with lefts and rights. Hearns body went back through the ropes, but again it was not a knockdown. But Hearns looked dazed as Leonard continued to punish him along the ropes. Finally, as Hearns sat on the bottom rope, referee Davey Pearl began to count. The bell rang at 'nine' and Hearns did not have to resume the fray.

Soon after the start of the 14th round, however, Leonard staggered Hearns again with a left to the head. Hearns seemed to have run out of energy and Leonard punished him with both hands. Finally four straight lefts piled into Hearns who was draped on the ropes, and the referee stepped in and gave the fight to Leonard.

Hearns was bitterly disappointed at his first defeat, and began almost immediately campaigning for a return. But their careers went different ways. After retiring twice, once with eye trouble, and coming back , Leonard picked his matches carefully to ensure he could win 'world' titles at five weights. Hearns was far busier, and three days before Leonard achieved the feat he also won a world title at a fifth weight – in fact the five weights were the same. By 1989 Hearns at last got his rematch. Leonard had not lost in the eight years interim, whereas Hearns looked the more worn: Hagler and Barkley had knocked him out. It was no doubt a discernible deterioration in Hearns which persuaded Leonard to take the return at last – he was sure he could win. For Hearns, an eight-year wait for revenge was ending. The match was at the same venue, Caesars Palace, as the first. The 'prize' was Leonard's WBC super-middleweight crown, and this time the distance was 12 rounds, at which point Hearns was ahead in the first match.

Hearns started the better, and put Leonard on the canvas in the third round. But Leonard came back in the fourth and drove Hearns round the ring in the fifth, with only Hearns' heart keeping him on his feet. He wobbled back to his corner, and many thought he was ready to go. But he fought back well to take the next two rounds. Leonard shook Hearns again in the ninth, and cut him under the eye on the tenth. It was still close going to the 11th, but then three overhead rights from Hearns put Leonard on the canvas again. Hearns threw everything when the dazed Leonard rose, but Leonard held out to the bell. Leonard needed to pull himself back and win the last round to have any chance. Unfortunately for him it began with Hearns pumping right after right at his head. But with little more than a minute to go Hearns seemed suddenly to have punched himself out and the fight ended with Leonard throwing punches at a Hearns desperately clinging on by the ropes.

The announcement was that one judge had voted for each, and the other a draw, so a draw it was. Most fans agreed with Hearns that he had won, but Hearns was not too disappointed – he had removed what he saw as a blot on his record after eight years.

BELOW and RIGHT: Two slices of action from the Leonard-Hearns drawn contest in 1989. Below, Leonard catches Hearns, and right, Hearns traps Leonard on the ropes.

LENNOX LEWIS

born: 2 September 1965, West Ham, London

Lewis went to Canada with his mother when he was 12 and began boxing at a club in Kitchener. As an amateur, he became Canadian super-heavyweight champion. In 1982 he was world junior champion, and in 1984 he lost a quarter-final in the Olympic Games to Tyrell Biggs. But he won the Commonwealth gold medal in 1986 and then, in 1988, the Olympic gold medal when he beat Riddick Bowe. He turned professional aged 23 in 1989, returning to England for his base.

The first boxer to extend the powerful 6ft 4¾in, 230lb Lewis was the veteran Ossie Ocasio, the former world cruiserweight champion who took him the eight-round distance. This was Lewis's 12th contest, and in the 14th in October 1990, he won the European heavyweight championship with a sixth-round stoppage of Jean Maurice Chanet of France. Then, in March 1991, Lewis won an eagerly awaited match with British champion Gary Mason. Both men were unbeaten but Lewis severely cut up Mason in seven rounds and forced his retirement with eye injuries.

Lewis next blasted out former WBA champion Mike Weaver in Lake Tahoe in July over six rounds and then the former IBF cruiserweight champion Glenn McCrory was stopped in two rounds at the Albert Hall in September. In November he fought on the undercard of the Holyfield-Cooper world title fight, and floored Tyrell Biggs three times on the way to a third-round stoppage. He was unimpressive in February 1992 in Las Vegas when journeyman Levi Billups just managed to stay the distance with him. In May Lewis fought Derek Williams, the Commonwealth champion, at the Albert Hall and added this title to his other two with a third-round combination which ended the fight. Lewis, in 20 contests, had put himself firmly in the queue for a shot at the world title.
Record: 20 contests; 20 wins

born: (Gershon Mendeloff)
24 October 1894, Aldgate,
London
died: 20 October 1970,
London

Lewis was a scrapper almost from the day he was born. His parents were Jews who had emigrated from Russia. Lewis was not yet 15 when he began his professional career – a loss over six rounds, for which he was paid one shilling (5p). But six days later he had his first win. Lewis was soon into his stride – in his 17th year he had 38 fights. On 6 October 1913 he won the British featherweight title. He was not quite 19 – a veteran of well over 100 contests! He soon added the European title, but in 1914 he departed for Australia, and then America, where he stayed until after the First World War, returning to Britain only near the end of 1919.

Some Americans regard Lewis as the best pound-for-pound British fighter to visit their shores. Although many of his contests were of the no-decision variety, in his 20 meetings with Jack Britton in various states the two swapped the world welterweight title back and forth. Of this series, Britton won four, Lewis three, with one draw – the rest no-decision. Lewis's two spells as champion lasted 29 months. He had 89 fights in the US, losing five.

Lewis was known as the 'Crashing, Dashing Kid' because of his all-action style, although he was by no means short on skill. Back in Britain, he took the British, British Empire and European titles at both welterweight and middleweight before challenging Georges Carpentier for the world light-heavyweight title and European heavyweight title. His object (at less than 11 stone) was to get a shot at the

LEFT: Britain's heavyweight hope of the 1990s, Lennox Lewis.

RIGHT: Ted 'Kid' Lewis, the welterweight champion of First World War days.

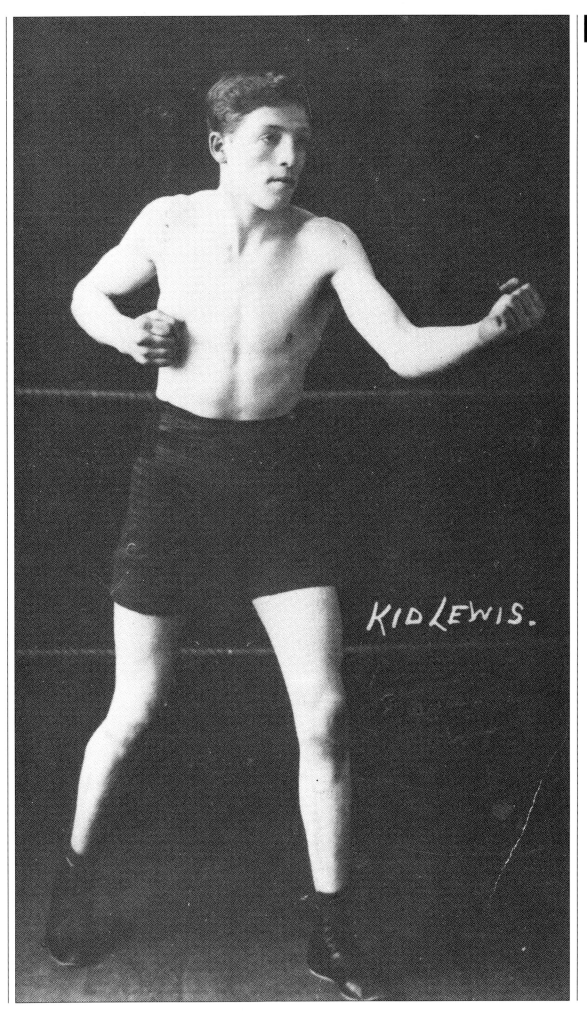

KID LEWIS.

heavyweight title held by Jack Dempsey, whom he thought he could beat. He made the mistake of turning his head to argue with the referee and Carpentier promptly knocked him out in the first round.

Gradually Lewis began to lose his various titles to younger fighters and eventually retired in 1929, appropriately with a knockout victory over Johnny Basham. Lewis had an astonishing 281 contests of which 42 were championship bouts, 29 for world titles.

Record: 281 contests; 170 wins; 13 draws; 30 defeats; 68 no-decision

SONNY LISTON

born: 8 May 1932, St Francis County, Arkansas, USA
died: 30 December 1970, Las Vegas, Nevada, USA

Liston (forename Charles) was one of 13 children born to the second wife of a cotton worker who also sired 12 children by his first wife. Poverty and lack of schooling inevitably led to teen-age crime and a sentence of five years in the Missouri State Penitentiary at Jefferson City, where the big strong Liston had his aggression channelled into boxing. He turned professional in September 1953 (with a 33-second knockout win). However his management then and often subsequently was connected with the underworld, and the 15-stone Liston, with his huge fists, dead eyes and brooding, menacing demeanour became a figure feared throughout boxing, both for his seeming invincibility and for his connections. Although he was soon clearly the logical contender for a title shot, boxing's authorities did not want the ex-con. Nat Fleischer, the influential editor of *The Ring*, hated him, and Cus d'Amato, manager of champion Floyd Patterson, avoided him. Finally, when Liston was already past 30 (and the actual year of his birth is suspected as being earlier than the 'official' one), the pride of Patterson finally granted Liston a match. Liston destroyed Patterson in

ABOVE: Liston, one of the greatest and least understood champions.

LEFT: Sonny Liston in training before winning the heavyweight title in 1962.

RIGHT: Tommy Loughran, one of the great light heavyweights.

two title fights, neither lasting more than 130 seconds. New York had refused to give Liston a licence for either fight. Earlier, when Liston moved house to Philadelphia, the police harassed him so much that he moved again. Liston was not accepted either as contender or heavyweight champion.

However on his first defence, many fans hoped he would win, because they disliked even more the loud-mouthed boasting challenger, Cassius Clay. Their two contests were

among the most controversial in boxing's history. In the first the 7-1 favourite Liston, apparently unbeatable, retired on his stool before the seventh round, claiming a shoulder injury. In the rematch, held before only 2,434 spectators in the unlikely city of Lewiston, Maine, Liston was knocked out at the first opportunity by a punch that few people saw.

The mysteries of these fights will never be solved because, after Liston had fought on for five years, he was found dead by his wife, his body having lain for six days in his kitchen while she was away over the New Year visiting relatives. Drugs were in the house. The coroner said he died from natural causes, but investigation and speculation since has suggested other verdicts: suicide, or murder by the mob, whom he is accused of double-crossing. In life and death, Liston remains a mystery.
Record: 54 contests; 50 wins; 4 defeats

See also: Ali v Liston

TOMMY LOUGHRAN

**born: 29 November 1902, Philadelphia, Pennsylvania, USA
died: 7 July 1982, Altoona, Pennsylvania**

Loughran was a skilful boxer whose disadvantage was that he was never heavy enough to challenge successfully the heavyweights. Although he tried constantly, he had to be satisfied with being an outstanding light-heavyweight. He ran away from home to join the army when he was 14 during the First World War, but was brought back. He began a professional career in 1919, interspersing knock-out victories with no-decision contests, but was outpointed when challenging Harry Greb for the American light-heavyweight title. In 1925 however, a points win over veteran Georges Carpentier, a former world champion, earned Loughran a shot for the vacant world crown and, in 1927, he outpointed Mike McTigue to become world light-heavyweight king. After seven successful defences, including one against future heavyweight champion James J. Braddock, he moved up to heavyweight, and was immediately knocked out by Jack Sharkey, another future champion. However, he had enough successes including, in 1933, revenge over Sharkey, then exchampion, with a points win, so that in 1934 he was put in as a lamb to slaughter with heavyweight champion Primo Carnera. There was an amazing 6¾ inches and 86lb between them: 270lb to 184lb. Loughran claimed his biggest handicap was Carnera's giant feet stepping on his toes. Tommy was outpointed.

He then fought in many countries on a South American tour, and in London and Paris before retiring in 1937. He became a successful businessman and after-dinner speaker. A devout Catholic, he never married, drank or smoked.
Record: 172 contests; 96 wins; 8 draws; 23 defeats; 45 no-decision

Tommy Loughran.

JOE LOUIS

born: (Joseph Louis Barrow) 13 May 1914, Lafayette, Alabama, USA
died: 12 April 1981, Las Vegas, Nevada, USA

Louis was part Cherokee Indian through his paternal grandmother. His father was admitted to a state institution after a mental breakdown when Louis was only three. When he was 13 the family (his mother married again) moved to Detroit, where Joe had boxing and violin lessons. He was better at boxing, was a successful but not outstanding amateur (43 wins in 54 bouts) and in July 1934 he turned professional. After 12 wins in his first year, he really grabbed public attention on 25 June 1935, when he knocked out recent heavyweight champion Primo Carnera before 62,000 fans at the Yankee Stadium. Three months later another exchampion, Max Baer, who had taken Carnera's title, was overwhelmed in four rounds.

Louis, at 6ft 1¼in and over 14 stone of muscle, was physically perfect as a fighter. He shuffled forward, cutting down the ring for his opponent, and punched with such power and cool accuracy that only four of his first 27 victims stayed the course. He was destined, it seemed, for greatness when, on 19 June 1936, he received a shock. The German Max Schmeling, another former champion, knocked him out in the 12th round.

Louis redeemed himself immediately by knocking out yet another former champion, Jack Sharkey, but Schmeling had prior claim to a title fight with James J. Braddock. Such a fight was actually arranged, but Braddock, in exchange for a share of Louis's future earnings, was persuaded to meet Louis instead. Louis won the title with an eighth round knockout on 22 June 1937. He was the second black heavyweight champion. Because the first, Jack Johnson, had been so unpopular with his bragging, Louis was trained not to show elation after beating white opponents. When he eventually beat Schmeling, with war with Germany

brewing, he was seen as an American hero by whites as well as blacks. His example inspired many subsequent black sportsmen to reach the top in fields where, before Louis, they were barred.

Louis defended his title successfully 25 times. He was so impressive he has his advocates as the greatest of all heavyweight champions. He knocked out Schmeling in the first round when his only previous conqueror challenged him. Of his other challengers only three went the distance, and two of

those were knocked out in return fights. Louis's reign as champion spanned the Second World War, during which he served in the army, and he retired as undefeated champion in 1949. However, severe financial difficulties with the Inland Revenue forced his comeback in 1950, which began with a world title fight against his successor, Ezzard Charles. He was outpointed. Nine fights later he fought a future champion in Rocky Marciano and at 37 suffered the second knockout of his

career. He retired again, did some wrestling, and ended as a celebrity employed to greet patrons at clubs in Las Vegas, where he died in his 67th year.

Record: 66 contests; 63 wins; 3 defeats

See also: Louis v Conn; Louis v Farr; Louis v Schmeling

JOE LOUIS, on the scales, shakes hands with Paulino Uzcudun, 1935.

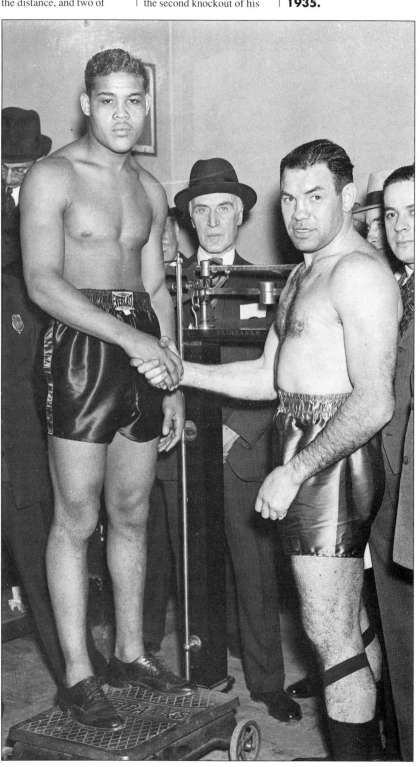

JOE LOUIS V BILLY CONN

18 June 1941, New York
19 June 1946, New York

In June 1941 Joe Louis was in the position that the heavyweight champion occasionally reaches: he seemed unbeatable. He had been champion for four years, had savagely avenged the only defeat on his record, and had defended the title 17 times. Only twice in those 17 contests had he needed to wait for a decision. At 27 he was in his prime.

His new challenger was Billy Conn, three years younger, a handsome well-dressed Irishman who had relinquished the light-heavyweight title in order to tackle Louis. He had nine defeats on his record but, on his day, was a brilliant, inspired boxer, who nearly always won his bouts on points. He predicted he would win in a drawing he made before the contest, but few thought the devil-may-care charmer could trouble the Brown Bomber, the most efficient fighting machine ever. At the weigh-in Louis was officially said to have a 25½lb advantage, Conn at 174lb being the lightest man ever to tackle Louis in a title fight. But Conn was actually lighter than the official weight, Louis heavier, and the discrepancy well over two stone.

As they climbed into the ring at the Polo Grounds, both fighters wore purple shorts, in those days the prerogative of the champion. Conn claimed he was a champion, too. Louis began the fight by stalking Conn in his usual manner, cutting down the ring, while Conn danced and cleverly avoided the attacks. Louis built up an early lead but the busy Conn began to land more blows as the fight progressed and there was nothing much in it at the tenth.

Conn began to get on top in the 11th round, however. Beating Louis to the punch he landed a barrage of hooks and crosses and suddenly Louis looked tired, hardly able to reciprocate. The crowd was now behind the smiling Conn, who waved to them like a winner as he danced back to his corner.

The 12th was even for

most of it, with both men landing good blows, but near the end Conn staggered Louis with a left hook. Louis reeled and Conn followed up with a right, forcing Louis to hold on. More hooks poured into Louis before the bell ended the round.

In the 13th round Conn tried to knock out Louis but was often pulled up short as Louis unleashed powerful counters. Conn refused to slow down and defend and kept piling into Louis. Suddenly a left from Louis to Conn's jaw followed by a right put Conn down and although he began to rise at nine he was too late and Louis had retained his title. There were two seconds of the round to go.

This fight has been acknowledged as one of the greatest, and a legend has grown up that Conn, with it won on points, succumbed to his Irish fighting blood and tried to knock Louis out. Going into that fateful 13th round Conn was three points ahead with one judge and two points ahead with the referee, while the other judge had them level. So Louis could have won on points by taking the last three rounds,

while Conn needed to win only one of them. Conn admits that, after hurting Louis in the 12th, he tried to knock him out in the 13th. It was a big mistake, and he thinks that if he'd lasted the final two seconds of the round he would have boxed till the end of the fight. Perhaps Conn got carried away by the four fights leading up to his challenge. He stopped all four opponents, never having stopped two in a row in his whole career before then. He was over-confident and, as he says, you only get one chance.

Conn did, in fact, get a second chance after the war in 1946 at the Yankee Stadium. Although he was the younger, Conn had put on much more weight than Louis, and had not kept in condition so well. It was a disappointing contest, which Louis won on an eighth-round knockout.

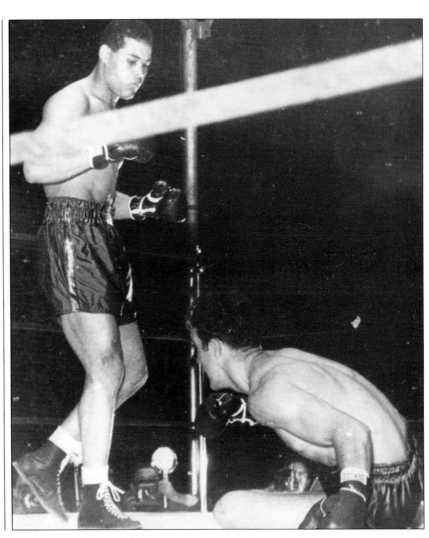

RIGHT and BELOW: Conn goes down in the 13th round to end one of the great fights of history.

JOE LOUIS V TOMMY FARR

30 August 1937, New York

When Max Schmeling knocked out Joe Louis in 1936 his manager argued for a shot at James J. Braddock, the heavyweight champion of the world. After all, Schmeling had lost the title in 1932 on a somewhat disputed decision to Jack Sharkey and, having beaten the up-and-coming Louis, saw himself as the natural contender. The New York boxing authorities agreed. Braddock was ordered to defend against Schmeling.

The promoter at Madison Square Garden, Mike Jacobs, who had Joe Louis under contract, wished to prevent this meeting at all costs. First, he thought Schmeling could win and, second, he thought that if he did the title might stay inaccessible to Louis and Jacobs in Germany. With the possibility of war in the offing, Jacobs might not be able to control the title for a long time. So Jacobs came to an arrangement with Braddock's manager, Joe Gould, by which Braddock would defy the New York commission and meet Louis in Chicago instead. For this favour – but only if Louis were to win – Braddock would receive ten per cent of Jacobs' net profits from heavyweight championship promotions for the following ten years. It was a deal that Braddock's camp could

hardly refuse, since it was probable that Braddock would lose his title whomever he faced. Max Schmeling actually had a contract and weighed in at the Madison Square Bowl for the match with Braddock which never took place – it was called the 'Phantom Fight'.

Jacobs was not the only promoter with a plot, however. Sydney Hulls, a London promoter, seeing the way things were going, planned to match Schmeling with Tommy Farr, a Welsh heavyweight who had just knocked out Walter Neusel. This would be, said Hulls, for the vacant heavyweight championship of the world. More panic for Mike Jacobs. As soon as Louis had beaten Braddock, he sent a lucrative contract to Farr's manager, Ted Broadribb, offering Farr the chance to make the first challenge to the new champion. This was a better deal for Farr, and it was accepted. Promoter Hulls ended up, like Schmeling, with nothing.

So in August 1937 Tommy Farr, given no chance by any of the boxing writers who, almost to a man, thought he would not last the distance, stepped into the ring with Joe Louis at the Yankee Stadium. Farr always claimed that the reporters who gave him no chance influenced the fans to stay away, cutting down the gate. Nevertheless 36,000 were present to witness the

supposed slaughter.

Farr, who fought from a crouch, took the fight to Louis and came in behind a long left lead to cross rights to the Brown Bomber's head. Many of Louis's right-hand counters he ducked or dodged with his footwork and Louis found him an awkward customer.

A radio commentary of the battle kept British fans up until the small hours of the morning, and conveyed an impression that Farr might actually be winning. This was quite untrue because Louis was scoring the more powerful punches with his left jab and, as the fight wore on, he began to disfigure Farr's face. In later life Farr would often point to the bumps on his head and proudly claim that Louis made them. Farr never gave up and kept coming forward with a smile on his face and terrific heart. Behind when the final round started, Farr launched a great attacking rally, and the fight ended with both men dishing out the punches.

Louis took the verdict but, in Britain, a legend arose among the uninitiated that Farr had been unlucky – a misconception that Tommy did not overbother to correct. What he did receive on that August night, however, were the cheers of the American fans when he dispelled the idea, held on the other side of the Atlantic, that British heavyweights always laid down.

JOE LOUIS V MAX SCHMELING

19 June 1936, New York
22 June 1938, New York

Max Schmeling was heavyweight champion of the world from June 1930 to June 1932. Americans weren't happy that he'd taken the title from America on a disqualification. Schmeling wasn't happy that they took it back with a highly disputed points verdict two years later.

In 1936 Schmeling was in the line of ex-champs being demolished by Joe Louis, everybody's pick as a future champion. Schmeling put a spanner in the works by spotting how he might beat Louis. He noticed Louis dropped his left after a jab, leaving the left side of his face exposed, and decided he could cross his powerful right over the jab. He did this to perfection in the fourth round, dropping Louis onto the canvas, badly hurt. After that, though he fought bravely, Louis could never get into the fight or overcome Schmeling's right hand. In the 12th round Schmeling struck again, and knocked Louis out. It was one of the biggest shocks in boxing history.

Schmeling was badly treated after this by being blatantly dodged by champion James J. Braddock, who was ordered to defend against him. Braddock accepted a profitable, if somewhat underhand, deal to fight Louis instead, and Louis became the new champion. Luckily for Schmeling (or perhaps not as it turned out) Louis had enough pride to realise he was hardly a true champion without beating Schmeling, and a title fight was fixed for 1938 at the Yankee Stadium.

War clouds were looming at the time, and the fight got hopelessly entwined with politics. Schmeling was seen as a tool of Nazism, especially when he dined

with Hitler, although he had no choice. Louis was built up as America's champion, and dined with President Roosevelt, although the black population were very much oppressed in his country. Indeed, there were plenty of Americans, like the Klu Klux Klan, who actually hoped the white Schmeling would win.

Schmeling was brave to fight in New York, and was pelted on his way to the ring, despite a police escort. The action was mayhem. Louis launched himself at Schmeling and hurt the German with the first blow he struck, which had the effect of concussing Schmeling. Schmeling seemed to realise what was about to happen to him. He looked apprehensive and after 30 seconds went down after a flurry of punches. After another trip to the canvas he was forced against the ropes, and turned with his chin resting on the upper rope. Louis piled punches into his side and back and ringsiders heard Schmeling let out a terrible scream of pain. The towel fluttered in from his corner. Schmeling eventually went down and was counted out after two minutes and four seconds. Louis's victory was acclaimed as one for good over evil, the American way of life over Hitler and Nazism. Schmeling left the ring on a stretcher and spent ten days in hospital. When he boarded the liner to return to Germany he was still on the stretcher. Four vertebrae in his back had been broken by Louis's blows.

Many years later questions were asked about this contest. Did Schmeling get a fair deal? It is suggested that Louis's chief cornerman, Jack Blackburn, had been known to boast when drunk that, in his day as a boxer, he had used plaster of Paris in his bandages. When water was splashed on it his fists became rock hard. Would he have felt justified in helping Louis to overcome the symbol of Nazism and keep the title in America by this old trick? Why take chances? The theory is based on the fact that it would be very difficult, even for a puncher like Louis, to break a man's vertebrae without some such

TOMMY FARR pokes out a left during his challenge to Louis.

assistance.

Whatever the truth, it was a significant and brutal beating, with Louis showing a clinical ferocity that he never bettered. There were no bad feelings between Louis and Schmeling, however. After the war they became firm friends.

BENNY LYNCH, facing camera, avoids a left from Small Montana during his title defence, 1937.

BENNY LYNCH

born: 2 April 1913, Clydesdale, Scotland
died: 6 August 1946, Glasgow

When Benny Lynch was 10, he and his brother trained at the St Johns Boys Guild in Glasgow, but his brother died from meningitis and Benny gave up boxing. However his parents split up and he returned to earn a little in boxing booths. His talent was spotted, and in 1931 he was persuaded to turn professional.

A newspaper boy, Lynch soon mounted the ladder and in 1934 won the Scottish flyweight championship. A draw the following year in an overweight match in Glasgow with world champion Jackie Brown earned Lynch a title shot in Brown's home town of Manchester and Lynch won by a second round knockout. For two to three years Lynch was such a brilliant boxer, with a knockout punch, that some claim he was the best-ever flyweight. But he developed a problem with alcohol, and was sometimes not at his very best. He twice lost on points to Irish champion Jim Warnock.

When he beat Small Montana, whom New York claimed as champion, it was said he had to shed 28lb in a fortnight before the fight. However there were magnificent defences in Glasgow, particularly against Peter Kane before 40,000 fans at Shawfield Park.

Lynch's world crashed in June 1938 when he was 6½lb overweight for a defence against another American, Jackie Jurich, in Paisley. He won the overweight contest but had forfeited his title. Three months later he was knocked out for the only time in his career when blatantly drunk. He lost his licence.

Although he had made a fortune, he gave much away, had tax problems and could not stop his drinking. He even had a spell in a monastery. He was unfit for service in the Second World War, and finally was reduced to begging. In 1946, down and out, he died from pneumonia brought about by his drinking. Only nine years before he had been a great world champion.

Record: 102 contests; 77 wins; 15 draws; 10 defeats

DAVE McAULEY

born: 15 June 1961, Larne, Co Antrim, Northern Ireland

McAuley was a good amateur who reached an ABA final as a 17-year-old. He turned professional as a flyweight in 1983 with a draw in Belfast. After winning two eliminators he won the vacant British title by stopping Joe Kelly in Glasgow in the ninth round.

In April 1987 McAuley challenged Fidel Bassa in Belfast for the WBA title. In a tremendous battle McAuley was down in the first, had Bassa down in the third and twice in the ninth but was knocked out in the 13th round. It was a typical McAuley contest. Tall for a flyweight at 5ft 7½in, he usually conducted wars of attrition in which stamina and willpower came into play. McAuley was never beaten just because he was down. After losing on points to Bassa in a return in Belfast he thought about retiring to concentrate on cooking, his second profession, but after a 15-month rest he outpointed Duke McKenzie at Wembley in June 1989 to win the IBF title. Dodie Penalosa and Louis Curtis were also outpointed, and then came a controversial battle with Rafael Blanco of Columbia in September 1990. In a terrific match at the King's Hall, Belfast, McAuley was down twice in the second round and also in the third

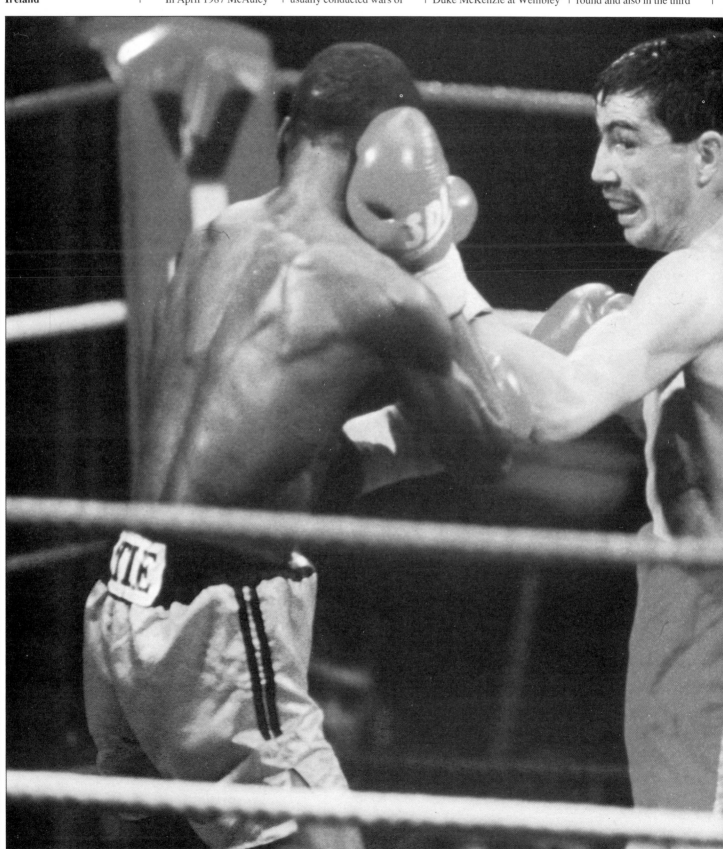

and 11th, but won a clear and unanimous points verdict. Naturally the challenger, who took only one count, disputed the decision. McAuley won two non-title fights and survived a brain-scan scare to take on Blanco again, this time in Bilbao, Spain, in June 1992. McAuley started slowly but finished with Blanco hanging on, and this time the unanimous verdict for Blanco was bitterly contested by McAuley's corner and supporters. It looked like the end for a champion who had been decked 12 times in seven world title fights but who had won four of them, always giving great value for money.

Record: 23 contests; 18 wins; 2 draws; 3 defeats

DAVE McAULEY (right) taking the flyweight title from Duke McKenzie in 1989.

JOCK McAVOY

**born: (Joe Bamford) 20 November 1908, Burnley, Lancashire
died: 20 November 1971, Rochdale, Lancashire**

McAvoy assumed his ring name because he did not want his widowed mother to know that he boxed on Sunday afternoons at an arena in Royton. He turned professional in 1927 and was a strong all-action middleweight with a hard punch.

In 1932 he challenged Len Harvey for the British title and, although knocked out of the ring in the fifth, he climbed back to lose a narrow points decision. The following year the verdict went his way, and he held the title until relinquishing it unbeaten 11 years later. In 1935 he was outpointed in Paris by Marcel Thil when trying to win the European light-heavyweight title, and then went to America, where he became popular with a string of impressive wins. In December he floored Ed 'Babe' Risko, world middleweight champion, six times before knocking him out in the first round. It was a non-title fight and Risko would not hear of a return with the title at stake. Instead McAvoy challenged John Henry Lewis in Madison Square Garden for the world light-heavyweight title and, with pain-killing injections in his hand to kill the pain from previous fights, he was outpointed. A month later, back in London, he was outpointed again when challenging Jack Petersen for the British heavyweight crown.

McAvoy added the British light-heavyweight title to his middleweight championship when he knocked out Eddie Phillips in the 14th at Wembley in 1937, but in 1938 he lost this title narrowly on points to his old adversary Len Harvey. The last of his 12 title fights, in 1939, was also against Harvey. With John Henry Lewis retired with eye trouble, this was recognised as for the British, British Empire and world light-heavyweight titles and the 80,000 fans, who crowded the White City Stadium, saw a great fight. The cool Harvey built up a points lead, but was almost knocked out in the 14th round. However, he held on to win.

After the Second World War, McAvoy, already suffering from arthritis, injured his back losing to Freddie Mills. He retired in 1944, still British middleweight champion. A three-fight, three-win comeback in 1945 petered out. For the last 20 years of his life he suffered from polio, and spent much of it on crutches.

Record: 148 contests; 134 wins; 14 defeats

JOCK McAVOY (right) had a long rivalry with Len Harvey.

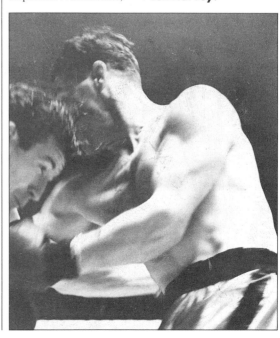

MIKE McCALLUM

born: 7 December 1956, Kingston, Jamaica

McCallum was an outstanding amateur who lost only ten or so of 250 amateur bouts. He won the Commonwealth Games gold medal in 1978 at welterweight. He was 24 when he turned professional in America in 1981, and it wasn't until his 15th contest that he was taken the distance. He stopped Ayub Kalule and in October 1984 won the vacant WBA light-middleweight title by outpointing Sean Mannion.

McCallum's strengths were in his all-round ringcraft and stalking methods. Not a quick fighter, he advanced methodically and relentlessly, wearing his opponents down with systematic body attacks. He was called the 'Body Snatcher'. One of the best defences of his title was a two-round stoppage of Julian Jackson and he was at his peak in July 1987 when he knocked out challenger Don Curry with a tremendous left hook in the fifth.

Always liable to put on weight between fights, McCallum switched to middleweight and surprisingly lost for the first time when outpointed by Sumbu Kalambay at Pesaro when challenging for the WBA title. In 1988 he based himself in Paris. In May 1989 he fought Herol Graham for the vacant WBA title at the Albert Hall and won a narrow points decision. He resisted another British challenger in April 1990 when he was too experienced for Michael Watson and knocked him out in the 11th round at the Albert Hall. In April 1991 he avenged the only blot on his record with a points defeat of Sumbu Kalambay at Monte Carlo.

In December 1991 McCallum signed to meet IBF title-holder James Toney but this attempt to unify the two titles was prevented by the WBA stripping McCallum for not meeting Steve Collins, whom he had already beaten. McCallum and Toney boxed a hard fought draw, so McCallum ended 1991 without a title for

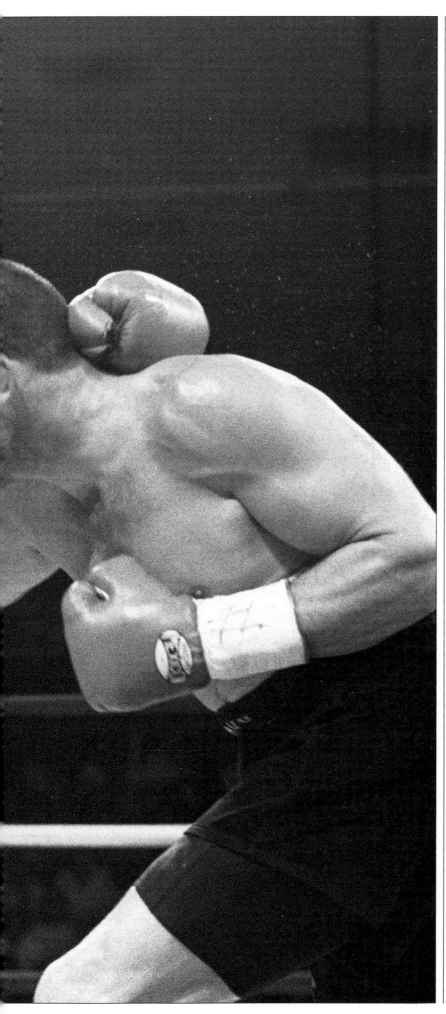

BODY SNATCHER Mike McCallum beating Nicky Walker, 1991.

only the second time since 1984.

Record: 45 contests; 43 wins; 1 draw; 1 defeat

JEM MACE

born: 15 April 1831, Beeston, Norfolk
died: 3 March 1910, Newcastle

Jem Mace began as a bare-knuckle prizefighter. He developed such skill that he revolutionised boxing, making it truly the 'Sweet Science', and becoming one of the few who have been called in retrospect the 'Father of Boxing'. In his day he was known as the 'Swaffham Gypsy' from his habit of roaming the countryside with his fiddle and his dog, giving boxing exhibitions. It is not known if he were a true Romany.

He first claimed the title of champion of England when he defeated Sam Hurst in 1861 for £200 a side. He then beat Tom King, his greatest rival, over 43 rounds in January 1862, but lost his title to him in November. Mace beat Joe Goss in 1866 to recover the title.

Mace went to South Africa, Australia, New Zealand, where he discovered future heavyweight champion Bob Fitzsimmons, and the United States. In Louisiana, be beat Tom Allen, the American champion, and drew with Joe Coburn, the fight being stopped because of the behaviour of the crowd, with Mace ahead. While in the States, Mace, who advocated boxing with gloves, influenced Jim Corbett, the first world heavyweight champion, who beat Sullivan with science.

Mace continued to give exhibitions and tuition throughout his life, sparring with the British lightweight champion, Dick Burge, when he was 64. Although he died in Newcastle, he is buried in Liverpool.

TERRY McGOVERN

born: 9 March 1880, Johnstown, Pennsylvania, USA

died: 26 February 1918, Brooklyn, New York, USA

'Terrible' Terry McGovern began boxing as an amateur aged 16, and disposed of his opponents so quickly that at 17 he turned professional. Soon he began knocking out pros, and in September 1899 he took the world bantamweight title from Pedlar Palmer in Tuckahoe, New York. The result centred on a mistake by the timekeeper, who rang his bell soon after the fight started. The referee sent both men to their corners, and then called upon them to resume boxing. Palmer offered his glove in a renewed handshake, but McGovern swung over a right and knocked out the champion – time, 75 seconds.

McGovern's next nine contests lasted fewer than 16 rounds, only one opponent reaching the third. By now he was a featherweight and he took the world title from the long-time champion George Dixon, the towel being thrown in in the eighth round, when Dixon had been down six times. McGovern was regarded as unbeatable, and registered wins over lightweights Frank Erne and Joe Gans, although this last was one of a few suspicious results in McGovern's progress. In another, he was floored for about 20 seconds in the second round in a title defence against Oscar Gardner in 1900, but his own referee began the count about ten seconds late, and managed to keep him in the fight. He won in the third.

In November 1901 McGovern seemed invincible. His terrible punching power had accounted for 25 stoppages in his previous 29 contests. The only loss in his whole career was due to a foul. But Young Corbett II, his next challenger, got him angry just before the fight started by insulting him and Ireland and knocked him out in the second round and repeated the feat in the 11th round 16 months later. His bubble burst, McGovern was never the same again. He retired in 1908 and died ten years later.

Record: 78 contests; 60 wins; 4 draws; 4 defeats; 10 no-decision

M

BARRY McGUIGAN

born: 28 February 1961, Clones, Co Monaghan, Republic of Ireland

McGuigan, born near the border between North and South Ireland, represented Northern Ireland at the 1978 Commonwealth Games in Canada, and won the gold medal at bantamweight. Two years later he represented the Republic of Ireland in the Olympic Games in Moscow but was beaten before the featherweight quarter-finals by a Zambian.

McGuigan turned professional in 1981 and was outpointed in his third contest by Peter Eubanks. However, he stopped Eubanks in a return, and began a winning streak that took the British featherweight title in 1983 and the European in 1984. There followed some exciting nights in the packed King's Hall, Belfast as the two-fisted aggressive 'Clones Cyclone', who specialised in fierce body attacks, beat world-ranked fighters in Jose Caba and Juan Laporte. It all lead to a challenge to Eusebio Pedroza, who had held the WBA title since 1978. In a sell-out at the Queen's Park Rangers football ground in London in June 1985, McGuigan took the title with an emphatic points win.

All Britain and Ireland celebrated the likeable McGuigan's success but, after two successful defences, McGuigan lost the title to a substitute, Steve Cruz, in Las Vegas on 23 June 1986. Terrific heat, to which he was less accustomed than his challenger, undermined McGuigan, and he lost narrowly on points. A bitter dispute developed between McGuigan and his manager, Barney Eastwood, which eventually was to lead to court battles, and McGuigan was inactive for nearly two years. A comeback begun in 1988 ended in defeat by Jim McDonnell, and McGuigan retired. Later he was active in the formation of a boxers' union.

Record: 35 contests; 32 wins; 3 defeats

See also: McGuigan v Pedroza

RIGHT: Triumph for Barry McGuigan, who watches from a neutral corner as Eusebio Pedroza takes a count in his world title win.

BELOW: Tragedy as McGuigan loses the crown in the heat of Las Vegas to Steve Cruz.

BARRY McGUIGAN V EUSEBIO PEDROZA

8 June 1985, London

Barry McGuigan was a two-fisted Irish featherweight who became a hero in Northern Ireland, the Republic of Ireland and Great Britain, transcending the troubles which for years have divided the population of his country. A series of exciting nights, especially at the King's Hall, Belfast, led up to the greatest of all when he challenged for the world title at the Queen's Park Rangers football club ground at Loftus Road.

The champion was Eusebio Pedroza, a superb boxer from Panama City, who had won the WBA title in April 1978 and defended it no fewer than 19 times in places as far apart as Japan, Papua New Guinea, South Korea, Venezuela, Italy and the West Indies, as well as venues in Panama and the United States. He was 32 when McGuigan challenged him. A crowd of 25,000 were there to see the fight, many over from Ireland.

The fight was even at first. Pedroza usually beat McGuigan to the punch but whenever McGuigan managed to get in close he scored good punches to the head. McGuigan found it difficult to score with his favourite body punches, but both men were boxing well and still trying each other out. In the seventh, Pedroza began darting in with quick one-twos but, on the third occasion, McGuigan replied with two jabs and followed up with a hard right to the chin.

Pedroza toppled forwards and a left hook helped him on his way to the canvas. But when he rose McGuigan couldn't trap him again and they exchanged punches, with Pedroza getting home with uppercuts and McGuigan scoring with hooks.

Pedroza fought back well in the eighth, but after that McGuigan kept pressing at close range and took control of the fight. He caught Pedroza in a corner in the tenth and fired over the right again. Pedroza was

groggy but fought back well until McGuigan caught him again with a left hook, and followed up with a right to the side of the head which sent Pedroza staggering. The excitement and noise was so intense that nobody heard the bell and Pedroza was forced to take two punches after it had rung.

Pedroza was temporarily troubled in the 13th, but fought back to catch McGuigan, who got careless, and caught him again in the 14th. But McGuigan was younger and stronger and had the best of a final round in which both gave all they had. The decision was a clear one for McGuigan.

All of Belfast turned out for a civic reception two days later, with 75,000 lining the Royal Avenue as McGuigan proceeded in an open-top bus. When McGuigan arrived home in Clones, he found the population of 3,500 had swollen to 30,000. Later there was a civic reception in Dublin. It was a great time for the Irish, for boxing and for Barry McGuigan.

DUKE McKENZIE

born: 5 May 1965, Croydon, Surrey

A younger brother of Clinton McKenzie, who was British and European lightweight champion, Duke was a good amateur who turned professional in November 1982. After two quick wins, he went to America, where he had five of his next six contests. In June 1985 he stopped Danny Flynn at the Albert Hall to win the British flyweight championship.

McKenzie was tall for a flyweight at 5ft 7in, but his long thin arms could punch and only three of his 11 contests had gone the distance. But McKenzie's strength was as a good defensive boxer who could keep his opponents at a distance while picking them off. He added the European title to the British when he ended the career of former world champion Charlie Magri with a fifth round stoppage at Wembley. He defended twice and then won the IBF flyweight title with an impressive 11th round knockout of Rolando Bohol at Wembley. On his second defence of this title, however, McKenzie was outpointed by another tall boxer, Ireland's Dave McAuley.

Having struggled to make the weight, McKenzie moved up to bantamweight and, after two wins, faced Thierry Jacob in Calais for the vacant European title. The Frenchman fought with great determination despite cuts over both eyes to wear down McKenzie for a clear win. After coming back with three wins, however, McKenzie returned to the world stage in June 1991 by easily outpointing WBO champion Gaby Canizales at Southwark. He thus became the first Briton in modern times to win world titles at two weights. McKenzie twice defended with impressive wins but then lost the title in a dramatic upset against Rafael del Valle of Puerto Rico at the Albert

DUKE McKENZIE, the new WBO bantamweight champion, 1991.

Hall in May 1992. McKenzie was caught cold and knocked out in 116 seconds, never having been down in his career before.

Record: 33 contests; 30 wins; 3 defeats

JIMMY McLARNIN

born: 17 December 1907, Inchacore, Ireland

McLarnin grew up in Canada where the family moved when he was two, and claimed to have begun boxing for money at 10 in British Columbia. He was paid one dollar, and for his last fight 20 years later he received $60,000. One of 12 children, he sold newspapers as a boy. He was fortunate to meet his manager, Pop Foster, when he was very young. Foster was a friend of his father, and the two men built a gym to teach him the basic skills.

McLarnin's official debut was in 1923, by the end of which he had moved to California. He fought in every division from flyweight to welterweight, meeting several former or future world champions early on, beating Fidel LaBarba, knocking out Jackie Fields and Louis Kaplan but losing to Bud Taylor. He beat flyweight champion Pancho Villa, who fought with infected gums and died ten days later from blood poisoning.

In 1928 McLarnin fought Sammy Mandell for the world lightweight championship and was outpointed. McLarnin, who was having difficulty making the weight, then went up to welterweight, and afterwards beat Mandell twice. He won two of three with Billy Petrolle, and ended Benny Leonard's career with a knockout. In 1933 a first-round knockout of Young Corbett III won McLarnin the world welterweight title. In 1934 and 1935 he had three contests, all with Barney Ross. Ross won two of this famous series, and ended with the title. McLarnin thought he'd won the decider.

McLarnin, who throughout his career had been known as 'Baby Face', ended in typical fashion by boxing in the top class. In

1936 he was outpointed by Tony Canzoneri, the world lightweight champion; he then beat Canzoneri in a return after Canzoneri had lost the title to Lou Ambers. McLarnin ended his career gloriously by outpointing the new champion, Ambers – all these fights being in New York. McLarnin returned to the Pacific Coast, and inherited $200,000 when his manager, Pop Foster, died in 1956. But by then McLarnin was already a happily married, wealthy and successful businessmen.

Record: 77 contests; 63 wins; 3 draws; 11 defeats

COLIN McMILLAN

born: 12 February 1966, London

McMillan was an international as an amateur, but was unlucky to be twice beaten in the ABA featherweight finals. He turned professional in November 1988, and suffered a defeat in his third fight, a third-round stoppage with a cut eye. However in May 1991, after 16 wins, he challenged Gary DeRoux for the British featherweight title and put on a dazzling display of boxing talent to stop DeRoux in the seventh. McMillan's speed, class, mobility and flair were obvious to all, the only thing lacking being a knockout punch. Nevertheless McMillan registered five knockdowns in another seventh round stoppage of Kevin Pritchard on his first defence four months later. When McMillan brilliantly outpointed Sean Murphy at the Albert Hall on 29 October, he won a Lonsdale Belt outright in record time, 160 days, one day quicker than the old record.

McMillan had his hardest task yet when in January 1992 he clearly outpointed the tall Percy Commey at Ghana to win the Commonwealth championship. McMillan's next title fight was for the WBO championship, a challenge to Maurizio Stecca, a former Olympic champion. McMillan put on his usual display to win easily on points and looked an outstanding prospect.

Record: 24 contests; 23 wins; 1 defeat

COLIN McMILLAN: (right) outpointing Percy Commey to become Commonwealth champion.

CHARLIE MAGRI

born: 20 July 1956, Tunis, Tunisia

Boxing out of Stepney, London, Magri was ABA flyweight champion three times, and turned professional in October 1977. He was a tremendous hitter for a flyweight but there were also suspicions that he was susceptible to a punch, so most of his contests were exciting. He won the vacant British flyweight title in only his third fight, all inside-the-distance wins. Only one opponent had reached the final bell when he challenged Franco Udella for the European title. Udella became the second, but lost his title on points.

Juan Diaz and Jose Torres both interrupted Magri's progress with knockout wins, but Magri avenged the Torres defeat. He then challenged for, and won, the WBC flyweight title with a stoppage of Eleoncio Mercedes at Wembley in 1983. Magri held the title for six months before being knocked out himself by Frank Cedeno at Wembley. An effort to regain the title in 1985 from Sot Chitalada ended in another knockout defeat. Magri who had, for the second time, relinquished the European title, won it for a third time with a second-round knockout of Franco Cherchi, but in 1986 he lost both his British and European titles to Duke McKenzie, and retired.

Although he had only two notches on a Lonsdale belt, the BBBC awarded it to him in recognition of his great career.
Record: 35 contests; 30 wins; 5 defeats

CHARLIE MAGRI won ABA, British, European and World flyweight championships in his career. He was an outstanding puncher for a flyweight.

ROCKY MARCIANO

born: (Rocco Francis Marchegiano) 1 September 1923, Brockton, Massachusetts, USA
died: 31 August 1969, Newton, Iowa, USA

Marciano nearly died from pneumonia as a child. His first love was baseball but he found his throwing arm was not strong enough. He started boxing when inducted into the US Army in 1943. He was not successful as an amateur, and seemed destined for a life of general labouring when he accepted $50 to fight Lee Epperson in March 1947. He used the name Rocky Mack so as not to jeopardise his amateur status. A friend, Allie Colombo, secured a trial for him with Al Weill, a New York manager, and he was taken on with Charlie Goldman as his trainer.

At 5ft 10½in, 194lb, and with absolutely no skill, Marciano had little going for him as a heavyweight except strength, courage and durability. It was not until his 13th fight that he was taken beyond the third round, and the 17th before he was forced to go the distance. At the end of 1949 he met Carmine Vingo, another promising newcomer, and won with a knockout, Vingo being seriously hurt. His next fight, against Roland LaStarza, a classy boxer, was as close as possible, Marciano winning on 'supplementary points' when the judges couldn't separate them.

In 1951 Marciano ended the comeback of the legendary Joe Louis with a knockout and, after beating Lee Savold and Harry Matthews, earned a shot at Jersey Joe Walcott's world title.

Marciano was down for the first time in his life after a minute, and was given a lesson till the 13th round, when he caught Walcott and knocked him out to win the title. Marciano's style was simple. He came in clubbing, not caring too much how many blows he took himself or where his own punches landed. He was called the 'Brockton Blockbuster' and everybody crumbled in his path. LaStarza was stopped in the 11th, but former

champion Ezzard Charles went the distance. Marciano beat Charles in a bloody return which hastened his own retirement, stopped Britain's Don Cockell in the ninth by using every dirty tactic in the book and knocked out Archie Moore in the ninth.

Marciano then retired, and remains the only heavyweight champion never to have suffered a defeat in his career. In 1967 he simulated a contest with Ali, which a computer decided he won, but two years later, on the eve of his 46th birthday, he was killed when the private plane in which he was flying to a business meeting crashed.

Record: 49 contests; 49 wins

See also: Marciano v Walcott; Marciano v Charles

UNBEATEN heavyweight champion Rocky Marciano.

ROCKY MARCIANO V EZZARD CHARLES

**17 June 1954, New York
17 September 1954, New York**

For the second defence of his heavyweight title Rocky Marciano took on former champion Ezzard Charles. Charles was not a vicious, savage fighter and was not expected to have the punch to trouble Marciano, and many regarded this as a mark-time defence. Rocky was a 19 to 5 favourite. Despite Charles' uncharismatic image, and the apparent one-sidedness of the bout, 47,585 turned up at the Yankee Stadium to see the champ.

Marciano went on the offensive from the start, but Charles controlled the fight. Powerful hooks and jabs kept the champion at bay. In the fourth he opened a deep gash by Marciano's left eye. The blood spurted out, and there were real possibilities that the contest would be stopped.

It was allowed to continue and, as if fearing his time was limited, Marciano attacked with doubled force and energy. Marciano scored with some powerful blows in the sixth, but Charles was boxing well and making the eye worse as blood poured down Marciano's cheek. Charles must have been puzzled that the cut eye seemed to be stepping up the pressure against him, especially when he received a cut himself in the eighth.

Marciano's relentless attack gave him the rounds from the ninth to the 11th, but he had thrown so many punches, and so many had missed, that he himself began to get exhausted. By the 14th his strength was gone and Charles staged a rally. But Marciano's work from the ninth onwards won him the decision in a bloody battle. It was the only time in his career Marciano went 15 rounds.

ROCKY MARCIANO and Ezzard Charles before their second world title fight.

After such a great fight, a rematch was quickly fixed for three months later. It was scheduled for 15 September at the same venue, Yankee Stadium, but two days of rain forced the date back to the 17th. This time 34,330 watched, most expecting an easy win for Marciano, the usual result of his rematches. His eye was completely healed.

Marciano began with the desire of a quick knockout. Charles boxed well but, when a right to the head shook him in the second round, Marciano pitched in with a bombardment that sent him to the canvas. But Charles bounced up at 'two' and caught the onrushing Marciano with a right that shook him. Charles defended desperately for the next three rounds and clinched to keep out the blazing Marciano.

The onslaught that Charles launched in the sixth round was therefore entirely unexpected. Marciano walked into a barrage of lefts and rights that split his left nostril in two. Blood spurted like a geyser. In the corner at the end of the round, Marciano's helpers found two pieces of flapping skin, and blood pouring down on his chest and lap. The anxious doctor was nevertheless persuaded to give Marciano another round.

Marciano charged out for the seventh knowing his title might well depend on the next three minutes. A swab in his nostril fell out and blood poured forth again. Charles fought well but it was like trying to contain a wounded animal. He survived the round, but was under great pressure. Marciano was given the all-clear to come out for another attempt.

An early right from Charles missed the nose but drew blood from Marciano's left eye. Marciano flung himself at the challenger and clubbed him down with a right. A dazed Charles mistakenly rose at 'four' instead of resting, and Marciano rained blows at him. Eventually Charles went down again. He had risen to his knees when the referee reached 'ten' with 24 seconds of the round left. Marciano, his nose still spurting blood, had got the knockout he needed just in time.

ROCKY MARCIANO V JERSEY JOE WALCOTT

23 September 1952, Philadelphia
15 May 1953, Chicago

The respective rises to heavyweight champion of Jersey Joe Walcott and Rocky Marciano could hardly have been more different. Walcott won the title at his fifth attempt after 21 years of battling. Marciano challenged him in 1952 at the Philadelphia Municipal Stadium after only four years of straightforward success. Over 40,000 fans paid to see who would win.

Walcott was 38 when he took on Marciano. All the knowledge and ringcraft were on his side, but Rocky had youth, toughness and desire as allies. Walcott had expressed his confidence in knocking out the easy-to-hit Marciano, although Marciano had never been on the canvas in his career. Only a minute of the contest had passed before Rocky had the shock of his life. Pressing forward as Walcott shuffled around, he walked straight into a perfect left hook, and discovered what it was like to hit the floor. Three seconds later, however, it was Walcott's turn to be surprised as Marciano got up and pressed forward again.

Walcott realised he would have to box his man rather than go for a quick win and it was not difficult to keep his challenger off as he picked up points with his jabs. A right in the fifth would have been enough to stop most challengers but Marciano still came on. Marciano achieved a little success in cutting Walcott's eye but Rocky himself had a deep gash on his forehead.

The seventh round could have been crucial. Bad cornerwork on Marciano's side led to some of the solution being used to stem the blood from his cut getting into his eye. The challenger carried on for several rounds with his vision impaired and Walcott continued to punish him. In the 11th he smashed a right to the body and a left to the face that brought more blood running down Marciano's features. However, still the challenger came on.

Perhaps Jersey Joe decided then that he would not knock out the challenger and that there was no point in attempting it. Marciano's attacks were getting more difficult to repulse. Walcott had only to stay on his feet to win. If Walcott decided to box cagily, it was a mistake.

After 30 seconds of the 13th round Walcott was caught on the ropes and went to throw a right, moving away to his left.

But this time Marciano beat him to the punch and Walcott walked into a terrific right swing that landed flush on his jaw. Walcott's jaw changed shape as the punch landed. He slithered down the ropes, his left arm catching the middle one and holding him up for an instant. Then he pitched forwards until his forehead was resting on the canvas and remained motionless while the referee completed the count. It was a legendary punch, one of the cleanest and most decisive knockout blows in heavyweight history. Rocky Marciano was the new champion.

The return contest eight months later at the Chicago Stadium was a formality. Walcott was in his fortieth year. Marciano just waded in and battered him until he finished it in 2 minutes 25 seconds of the first round.

TERRY MARSH

born: 7 February 1958, Stepney, London

Marsh was a London fireman with a liking for chess, two things which won him a lot of copy as he progressed to world title status without giving up his 'day job'. He turned professional in 1981 and won the British light-welterweight title when outpointing Clinton McKenzie in 1984.

Marsh's strength was a rugged non-stop style which kept him going forwards until he finally wore down his opponents. His stamina, allied to a good punch, won him the European title in 1985 when he stopped Allessandro Scapecchi in the sixth in Monte Carlo.

In 1987, in a huge marquee in his native Basildon, he won the IBF light-welterweight title by stopping Joe Manley in the tenth round. He defended this successfully against Akio Kameda in July 1987 but, with another defence lined up, he announced his retirement, admitting that he suffered from epilepsy. This caused bad feeling between him and his manager, Frank Warren. Subsequently Warren was shot by a hooded gunman; he survived and Marsh, returning from a visit to the States, was arrested and charged with attempted murder. He was acquitted and later tried unsuccessfully to regain his licence. He was unbeaten as a professional, the only 'blot' on his record being a draw with Lloyd Christie in 1982.
Record: 27 contests; 26 wins; 1 draw

BELOW: Terry Marsh.

JOEY MAXIM

born: (Guiseppe Antonio Berardinelli) 28 March 1922, Cleveland, Ohio, USA

Maxim was a Golden Gloves champion as an amateur before turning professional in 1941 under the managership of the famous 'Doc' Kearns. His manager gave him the name Maxim after an early machine gun, his left supposedly being almost as fast and effective. He was busy, and suffered a few defeats before winning the American light-heavyweight title from Gus Lesnevich in 1949. The following year he came to London and relieved Freddie Mills of the world title with a tenth-round knockout.

In 1951 Maxim challenged Ezzard Charles for the world heavyweight title, but was outpointed – in fact Charles beat him five times in his career. In 1952 the middleweight champion, Sugar Ray Robinson, challenged Maxim for his light-heavy crown, and appeared to be winning it before succumbing to a tremendous New York heatwave before the 14th round. In 1953 Archie Moore outpointed him for the title, and repeated the feat in two returns. Maxim became the only person to beat the young Floyd Patterson on his way to the heavyweight crown in 1954, but declined after this, losing eight of his last nine contests from 1955 to his retirement in 1959.
Record: 115 contests; 82 wins; 4 draws; 29 defeats

MEDICINE V BOXING

There have always been members of the medical profession who advocate the banning of professional boxing on the grounds that too many boxers suffer serious damage during their careers. Dr Edith Summerskill, the politician, campaigned for most of her life against boxing. The mere existence of the term 'punch-drunk' seems to confirm that some ex-boxers at least exhibit a slight unsteadiness in gait or slurring of speech. Whatever the medical reasons for his condition, even Muhammad Ali, the greatest boxer of modern times and a perfect physical specimen, has been unable to escape a slowing down of speech and movement.

Doctors believe that the repetitive blows to the head that a boxer cannot entirely avoid can cause gradual but serious injury to the brain by their cumulative effect. A sad confirmation came with the death of the Scottish welterweight champion Steve Watt after a bout in 1986, when the post-mortem revealed a brain already damaged after 14 professional fights and a long career as an amateur.

It is the death of a boxer that periodically brings the whole question into public debate. *The Ring Record Book* used to publish the total number of boxing deaths, amateur and professional, that occurred in each year. There was a noticeable rise in numbers after the Second World War, with the peak reached in 1953 with 22. From the mid-1960s the numbers sank back into single figures again.

Many great boxers have been involved in a match after which an opponent had died. Primo Carnera, the amiable Italian giant, fought Eddie Schaaf, who died soon afterwards. Sugar Ray Robinson and Alan Minter had to overcome the trauma of an opponent who died, as did Barry McGuigan. In his case, the boxer who died, Young Ali, was found to have an abnormally thin skull, as did Johnny Owen, the skinny Welsh bantamweight, who died after being knocked out by Lupe Pintor in Los Angeles. Of course, their having thin skulls does not change the fact that boxing was responsible for their deaths.

In the days of television, the death of a boxer in the ring makes an enormous impact on the public, and brings into the debate people who do not usually follow boxing. A dramatic example was the death of Benny Kid Paret, who did not recover after a terrific beating sustained at the fists of Emile Griffith at Madison Square Garden in 1962. This was seen by millions of television viewers, some of whom were vociferous in their attacks on boxing. The death of another popular champion, Davey Moore, after being knocked out by Sugar Ramos, renewed the attack the following year. The fact that on the same night as Moore's defeat, Griffith lost the title he'd won from Paret made an easy media link between the two deaths.

The tragedy that made the biggest impact on British television was the accident to Michael Watson in September 1991. His WBO title fight with Chris Eubank was one of the most eagerly awaited for years, partly because of the controversial decision rendered in their first match. In the 11th round of a superb contest Eubank rose from the floor to put down the oncoming Watson with an uppercut. Watson's head caught the bottom rope (it was a four-rope ring) and, although Watson rose and continued, he was stopped in the next round and later went into a coma. His life was saved, but he faced a long period in hospital as another fight began to restore his faculties.

The outcome to this contest sparked days of discussion on the merits of boxing. Ironically, Watson's lapse into a delayed coma mirrored what had happened to Davey Moore in 1963, and the injuries came about in the same way. Each boxer's head or neck had struck the bottom rope as the boxer had fallen back, causing a whiplash effect. Experts in television discussions after Watson's accident advocated moving the bottom rope back a foot or so to prevent similar accidents in future – unfortunately for Watson this wasn't done after 1963 when Moore suffered.

Defenders of boxing point out that other activities like mountaineering and motor racing (or even motoring on the roads as a pastime) are sports in which danger is as obvious as it is in boxing. Boxing's opponents point out that boxing is the only sport in which inflicting physical damage is the actual object. Defenders point to the material benefits, the fame, the self-expression and the improved life that boxing has given to many young men of a poor background, some of whom would have turned to crime without the opportunities boxing gave them. Apart from anything else, fighting with the fists is a fairly natural activity. The competitive instinct in mankind will never be subdued and will find its outlet in sports like boxing which, if banned, would go underground anyway. The only thing to do is make it safer.

The Medical Committee of the BBBC has introduced many rules and regulations to improve the safety of the sport since its foundation in the early 1950s and British boxing is as safe as boxing anywhere. Boxers are examined before being granted a licence, and before and after bouts. The Board also monitors the performances of a boxer during his career and retains the right to require a boxer to retire if his performance level slips. By this means the Board believes it prevents the brain damage which it admits was common in previous years.

If boxing is ultimately banned it is less likely to be a high-profile death on television which causes the ban than an accumulation of evidence that all or most boxers are likely to suffer brain damage in some degree.

FREDDIE MILLS

born: 26 June 1919, Parkstone, Dorset
died: 25 July 1965, London

Mills' brother was a boxer, and Mills was hooked on the game when given a pair of gloves on his birthday. Among his many jobs was milkman, where he worked with the brother of a Welsh champion, who coached him. He joined a west country boxing booth, and made his official pro debut in March 1936. Mills' main assets were his strength and courage. A light-heavyweight, his one tactic was to keep coming forward, throwing punches with both hands. Inevitably he took a lot in return, banking on wearing down his opponent by his sheer refusal to stop attacking.

Most of Mills' 52 pre-Second World War contests were in Bournemouth, but in 1940 he joined the RAF and appeared further afield. In 1940 he hitchhiked to Liverpool and outpointed Jock McAvoy, and in 1941 he stopped him in the first round in an eliminator for the British, Empire and world light-heavyweight title held by Len Harvey. In 1942 he knocked the veteran Harvey out of the ring in the second round to assume the titles.

In 1944, Mills was outpointed by Brian London for the vacant British heavyweight title. After the war, Gus Lesnevich, recognised in America as world champion, came to London and in an epic battle stopped Mills to become undisputed champion. Mills, who frequently took so much punishment in contests that he often ended fighting on instinct alone, was always willing to take on heavyweights, where his courage was not enough. He suffered losses to Bruce Woodcock and a large American, Joe Baksi. Nevertheless, in 1948 he won the vacant European light-heavyweight title, and after successfully defending it, won back the world title by clearly outpointing Gus Lesnevich. However in 1949 he challenged Bruce Woodcock for the British heavyweight title and was badly beaten before a 14th round knockout. In his next contest, in 1950, he lost his world title to Joey Maxim.

Mills retired and became a TV personality and proprietor of a Chinese restaurant, outside which in 1965 he was found shot in his car. The verdict was suicide, but there remain those who suspect something more sinister.

Record: 101 contests; 77 wins; 6 draws; 18 defeats

FREDDIE MILLS, a gallant fighter whose great spirit took him to the world light-heavyweight championship.

ALAN MINTER

born: 17 August 1951, Crawley, Sussex

Minter was a good amateur whose grunting when he threw punches earned him the nickname 'Boom boom'. A southpaw, he lost a controversial decision in the semi-final of the 1972 Munich Olympic Games light-middleweight division to the eventual German gold medalist.

He immediately turned professional and in 1975 he outpointed Kevin Finnegan to become British middleweight champion. After two defences which won him a Lonsdale belt outright, he was stripped in 1977 when he won the European title from Germano Valsecchi.

Minter was an attacking boxer with a good punch who suffered from being easily cut. He lost his European title to Gratien Tonna in Milan through a cut when seemingly well on top, but immediately reclaimed the British title and soon the European title, retaining it when stopping Tonna in the sixth. Minter then relinquished these titles to

ALAN MINTER, the world middleweight champion until beaten by Marvin Hagler.

challenge Vito Antuofermo in March 1980 for the undisputed world title. Minter won on points in Las Vegas, and stopped Antuofermo in the return at Wembley.

In his next defence Minter was stopped in the third round by Marvin Hagler at Wembley, a surprise defeat which led to ugly scenes and thrown bottles. In 1981 Hagler tried to win the European title yet again, but was knocked out by Tony Sibson and retired. **Record: 49 contests; 39 wins; 9 defeats; 1 no-contest**

CARLOS MONZON

born: 7 August 1942, San Jairer, Sante Fe, Argentina

Monzon was born into poverty, one of ten children. He entered a gymnasium as a way of alleviating a desperate existence, and became a fine boxer, with a classic stand-up pose, the coolness to use his skills under pressure, and a knockout punch. He did not turn professional until he was past 20, and his first 82 contests were all in South America. During this time, having grown into a strong middleweight with wide shoulders, he won the Argentinian and South American titles. In his first 20 contests he lost three decisions, but avenged each defeat with a win inside the distance. He was never to lose again.

Monzon's first contest outside South America came in November 1970 in Rome, where he shocked the Romans with a 12th round knockout of Nino Benvenuti to take the undisputed world title. He won the return in Monte Carlo and then disposed of all challengers, who included Emile Griffith (twice), Jean-Claude Bouttier (twice), Tom Bogs, Bennie Briscoe and welterweight champion Jose Napoles. In 1974 the WBC stripped him from their half of the world title for not meeting Rodrigo Valdez, who became their champion. In 1976 and 1977 Monzon twice outpointed Valdez to unify the titles again, and then retired as undefeated champion. He had won all his 15 world title fights, 12 of them outside his native Argentina, and 11 in Europe. Exactly half of his 102 opponents had failed to go the distance with him.

In retirement Monzon appeared a handsome haughty figure who was always expensively and fashionably dressed. It shocked boxing when in 1989 he was convicted of the murder of a former lover and the mother of his six-year-old child, after she had plunged from a second floor balcony at Mar del Plata. Monzon was imprisoned. **Record: 102 contests; 89 wins; 9 draws; 3 defeats; 1 no-contest**

ARCHIE MOORE

born: (Archibald Lee Wright) 13 December 1913, Benoit, Mississippi, USA

Archie Moore claimed his birth year as 1916, but his mother insisted it was 1913. His parents separated and Moore was brought up by his uncle Cleveland Moore, whom he admired and whose name he took. He wanted to be a musician as a boy, but was good at boxing and during a short spell in reform school at 15 decided to become a boxer. He was a good amateur and turned professional in 1935.

An independent thinker, Moore had many managers. He usually won his contests, but occasionally got a bad decision against white boxers. In 1938 he severed an artery in his wrist in a car accident, and two passing nurses not only saved his career but possibly his life. In 1941 a perforated ulcer again threatened his career but it was saved by good surgery. Peritonitis, pneumonia and appendicitis followed and the middleweight subsided to flyweight. But he built his weight up again and eventually became a light-heavyweight. Despite being a logical contender for the world title from about 1948, Moore had to wait until December 1952 before being given a chance. Even this he partly engineered himself with a vigorous campaign of challenges and letter-writing to newspapers. Moore outpointed Joey Maxim in St Louis, and then had to defeat him twice more before he could call the title completely his. He was 38 or 35, according to whom you believed.

Moore defended twice and beat top heavyweight Nino Valdes, which earned him a shot in 1955 at Rocky Marciano's heavyweight crown. In the second round Moore put Marciano down; Rocky rose at two but the referee mistakenly began a mandatory eight-count. It wasn't mandatory, and Moore insists the unsanctioned rest which Marciano received saved his title, Moore himself being knocked out in the ninth.

Moore continued defending his world title, and in November 1956 had another shot at the heavyweight title, now owned by Floyd Patterson. Patterson knocked out the 43-year-old in the fifth round. In 1958 Moore retained his title in a tremendous battle with Yvon Durelle, whom he beat again in 1959. But in 1960 the NBA withdrew their recognition of Moore as champion because of inactivity. Moore defended the New York and European version in 1961 but, in 1962, those bodies too withdrew their recognition because of his failure to defend against Harold Johnson. In 1962 Moore was knocked out by the 20-year-old Cassius Clay, and had one more fight, a knockout victory in 1963. His total of 145 knockouts is a record. In retirement Moore appeared in a number of films, the best known being *Huckleberry Finn*, opened a gym and worked with the US Office of Economic Opportunity. **Record: 234 contests; 199 wins; 8 draws; 26 defeats; 1 no-contest**

See also: Moore v Durelle

ARCHIE MOORE V YVON DURELLE

10 December 1958, Montreal
12 August 1959, Montreal

By December 1958 Archie Moore had been light-heavyweight champion of the world for six years. He had been a professional for 23 years. He was either 42 or 45, there being a disagreement about the year of his birth. Everything about him suggested longevity. He was known as 'Old Mongoose', or more simply 'Ancient Archie'. He was regarded by aficionados as one of the greats of boxing, but the general public was less convinced. What he needed was a high-profile fight to grab the headlines and make him more charismatic. That he got when he took on the challenge of Yvon Durelle in Montreal.

Durelle was a fighting fisherman with a big punch and a heart to match, but was not considered a threat to Ancient Archie. However, after one minute of the first round Durelle delivered a terrific right to the champion's chin. Moore slumped in a heap on the canvas. Referee Jack Sharkey, the old heavyweight champion, began counting. Moore came to at 'five' and when Sharkey reached 'nine' climbed unsteadily to his feet. Durelle leapt in and Moore subsided to the canvas again, half-pushed. He rose and staggered away from Durelle, who swung punches at him with both hands. Moore slid down again, rose at nine and was saved further punishment by the bell.

Moore seemed to have recovered in the second round and kept out of trouble, although Durelle edged the round. In the third Durelle got in some heavy blows while Moore at last began to throw some back. In the fourth Moore outboxed Durelle, two of whose best punches were delivered after the bell. It seemed that class might tell after all.

In the fifth round, Durelle feinted with a left and caught Moore with a right which Moore said later was harder than the punch in the first round. Moore crumpled to the canvas. He rose at six but was driven all round the ring as Durelle tried to land another finishing blow. But Moore actually got in a counter at the end. His manager at the time, Doc Kearns, said that Moore was practically out at the end of the round. But Moore came back in the sixth round with several shots to Durelle's head to take the round.

The seventh opened with Moore staggered again by yet another right, but he came back to floor Durelle with good combination punching. This was the first indication that the tide was turning. The eighth round was fairly even, with both men scoring with hard blows to the jaw. Moore got on top in the ninth, rocking Durelle with several good punches while Durelle, still attempting to knock Moore out, found most of his punches blocked by the canny champion. In the tenth, it was Durelle's turn to take a battering and, at the end of the round, he was down on one knee, the bell sounding as the count reached seven. Moore sensed he could win in the 11th and early on he sent Durelle to the canvas for a count of nine. When he rose, punches rained in on him, and he was dropped again with blood coming from his nose, mouth and a cut near his eye. He struggled to his feet, but not before the referee had reached ten …

The announcer called it the Fight of the Year, and indeed it was. Moore said that Durelle was the strongest man he'd fought except for Marciano. Moore's manager said his fighter was in a daze until the sixth round. Moore agreed. Joe Louis said it was the greatest fight he'd seen. He added that Durelle should have finished the fight in the second round. This, indeed, was Durelle's mistake. His corner had planned for Durelle to outlast Ancient Archie and were not prepared for Durelle's first-round success. They told him to hold off … and he lost the fight. Remarkably it was the 45-year-old who lasted the pace, while strong-man Durelle had exhausted himself in his efforts to knock Moore out.

Moore was greeted by a thousand fans at the airport. He was a name now, all right. He said he owed more to Durelle than anybody else he fought in 30 years. Moore won the return with a third-round knockout. But nothing can detract from their first encounter.

JOSE NAPOLES

born: 13 April 1940, Santiago de Cuba, Oriente, Cuba

An outstanding amateur, Napoles turned professional in August 1958 and his first 18 contests, to March 1961, were in Havana, two of which Napoles lost. With professional boxing banned in Cuba by Castro, Napoles switched his residence to Mexico and began building an impressive list of knockout successes which in 1969 earned him a shot at Curtis Cokes for the undisputed world welterweight title. Napoles stopped the champion in the 13th round.

Napoles was a classic boxer who delivered combinations in such a fluid style that he earned the nickname 'Mantequilla' (butter) because he moved as smoothly as if all his parts were greased. It was a great shock when Billy Backus stopped him on a cut eye in December 1970, but Napoles regained the title six months later and saw off all comers for over four more years.

In 1974 he tackled Carlos Monzon, the outstanding middleweight champion, but was stopped in the sixth round. In December 1975, in his 18th world title fight, he finally lost his welterweight crown when stopped by John H. Stracey in Mexico City, and he retired.

Record: 84 contests; 76 wins; 8 defeats

JOSE NAPOLES moved his headquarters from Cuba to Mexico and became one of the outstanding champions of the 1970s, holding the welterweight crown more or less continuously from 1969 to 1975.

AZUMAH NELSON

born: 19 July 1958, Accra, Ghana

Nelson is one of those boxers who might be older than his 'official' age. A good amateur, he was beaten only twice and was Commonwealth Games gold medalist. He turned professional in December 1979 and soon won the African featherweight championship. In his tenth contest he knocked out the Australian Brian Roberts to become Commonwealth champion. In July 1982 he went to New York to challenge Salvador Sanchez for the WBC title, and gave Sanchez a good battle before being stopped in the last round. Sanchez was killed the following month, but Nelson had to wait nearly 2½ years to get another shot at the title. In San Juan in December 1984 he stopped the local idol Wilfredo Gomez in the 11th round to become champion.

Nelson proved to be one of the best champions, making six defences in two years, only regretting that he did not get an opportunity of a big-money match with Barry McGuigan. In February 1988 he moved up a division to super-featherweight by winning the vacant WBC title when he outpointed Mario Martinez in Los Angeles. In his third defence he stopped Jim McDonnell in London and in his fourth he outpointed Juan Laporte in Sydney. Between these bouts he tackled Pernell Whitaker for the undisputed lightweight title but, fighting soon after his wife died, he lacked fire and was outpointed.

In June 1991 Nelson defended his title against the tough Australian Jeff Fenech in Las Vegas. It was a terrific battle and ended a draw, with the Fenech supporters seeming the most aggrieved. A return was a natural and took place in the open air at Melbourne on 1 March 1992, before 38,000 spectators in the rain. The younger unbeaten Fenech was a big favourite but Nelson proved himself to be among the greats with a brilliant display which stopped Fenech in the eighth. It was Nelson's 17th world title fight.

Record: 38 contests; 35 wins; 1 draw; 2 defeats

RIGHT: Azumah Nelson.

BELOW: A spectacular knockout of Jim McDonnell in 1989.

ABOVE: Battling Nelson (right) before knocking out Eddie Hanlon in the 19th round, San Francisco, 1904.

LEFT: The 'Durable Dane'.

BATTLING NELSON

born: (Oscar Nielson) 5 June 1882, Copenhagen, Denmark
died: 7 February 1954, Chicago, Illinois, USA

Nelson was brought up in the United States and began boxing in booths when 14 years old. A crude boxer both in style and personal habits, his main asset was the ability to take punishment, a capacity which earned him the nickname the 'Durable Dane'. He had little regard for rules and won most of his contests by wearing down opponents with close-range blows to the body.

A knockout of Jimmy Britt in 1905 was advertised as for the 'white lightweight world title', Joe Gans then being supreme, but this enabled Tex Rickard to match Nelson with Gans in a very profitable encounter in 1906. Nelson lost on a 42nd round foul, but in the following year he beat the ageing Gans twice to become champion.

Nelson lost his title in 1910 to Ad Wolgast, who knocked him out in the 40th round. He continued boxing till 1917 before retiring.
Record: 132 contests; 59 wins; 19 draws; 19 defeats; 35 no-decision

See also: Gans v Nelson

NICKNAMES

Lots of boxers fight under assumed names. The real names of the famous boxers in this book are included in their entries. Many boxers also acquire nicknames – some have had more than one. The best are those which are given to boxers by the fans, and seem so apt that they immediately catch on. Sometimes the press invent a name which doesn't really stick. Sometimes boxers or their handlers try to obtain a nickname to improve their appeal on posters. Occasionally a boxer doesn't like his nickname and would like it changed. For example Nigel Benn disowned the 'Dark Destroyer' when he decided to adopt a more thoughtful, restrained style than that which earned the name.

Following is a list of some of the more established nicknames. Many are naturally preceded by 'the', but the definite article is omitted.

Nickname	Ring name	Nickname	Ring name
Ancient Archie	Archie Moore	Illinois	
Ambling Alp	Primo Carnera	Thunderbolt	Billy Papke
Astoria Assassin	Paul Berlenbach	Iron Mike	Mike Tyson
Baby Face	Jimmy McLarnin	Jack the Giant	
Barbados Demon	Joe Walcott	Killer	Jack Dillon
Basque		Jaws	Ossie Ocasio
Woodchopper	Paolino Uzcudun	Kansas Rube	Jim Ferns
Bazooka	Rafael Limon	Little Artha	Jack Johnson
Benicia Boy	John C. Heenan	Little Chocolate	George Dixon
Black Cloud	Larry Holmes	Little Hebrew	Abe Attell
Black Mamba	Roger	Livermore	
	Mayweather	Larruper	Max Baer
Black Panther	Harry Wills	Louisville Lip	Muhammad Ali
Black Uhlan	Max Schmeling	Macho Man	Hector Camacho
Body Snatcher	Mike McCallum	Mad Dog	Gene Hatcher
Boilermaker	Jim Jeffries	Madcap Maxie	Max Baer
Boom-Boom	Ray Mancini	Manassa Mauler	Jack Dempsey
Boston Gob	Jack Sharkey		(heavyweight)
Boston Strong		Man of Steel	Tony Zale
Boy	John L. Sullivan	Manos de Piedra	Roberto Duran
Boston Tar Baby	Sam Langford	Marvelous Marvin	Marvin Hagler
Boxing Marvel	Jack Britton	Michigan	
Box O' Tricks	Pedlar Palmer	Assassin	Stanley Ketchel
Brockton		Michigan Bearcat	Ad Wolgast
Blockbuster	Rocky Marciano	Mighty Atom	Jimmy Wilde
Bronx Bull	Jake LaMotta	Motor City Cobra	Thomas Hearns
Brown Bomber	Joe Louis	Nonpareil	Jack Dempsey
Cadillac Bearcat	Ad Wolgast		(middleweight)
California Grizzly		Old Bones	Joe Brown
Bear	Jim J. Jeffries	Old Master	Joe Gans
Camden Buzzsaw	Dwight	Old Mongoose	Archie Moore
	Muhammad	Old Smoke	John Morrissey
	Qawi	Orchid Man	Georges
Cincinnati Cobra	Ezzard Charles		Carpentier
Cincinatti Flash	Ezzard Charles	Peerless Jim	Jim Driscoll
Cinderella Man	James J.	Perpetual Motion	Henry Armstrong
	Braddock	Phainting Phil	Phil Scott
Cleveland Rubber		Pittsburgh Kid	Billy Conn
Man	Johnny Risko	Poison	David Kotey
Clones Cyclone	Barry McGuigan	Pottawatomie	
Clutch	Sammy Angott	Giant	Jess Willard
Corkscrew Kid	Charles 'Kid'	Pride of the	
	McCoy	Ghetto	Barney Ross
Cuban Bon Bon	Kid Chocolate	Real Deal	Evander
Cuban Hawk	Kid Gavilan		Holyfield
Durable Dane	Battling Nelson	Rochdale	
Fargo Express	Billy Petrolle	Thunderbolt	Jock McAvoy
Fighting		Ruby Robert	Bob Fitzsimmons
Blacksmith	Bob Fitzsimmons	Saginaw Kid	George 'Kid'
Fighting Marine	Gene Tunney		Lavigne
Galveston Giant	Jack Johnson	Scotch Wop	Johnny Dundee
Game Chicken	Hen Pearce	Slapsie Maxie	Maxie
Gentleman Jim	James J. Corbett		Rosenbloom
Georgia Deacon	Tiger Flowers	Smokin' Joe	Joe Frazier
Ghetto Wizard	Benny Leonard	Swaffham Gypsy	Jem Mace
Ghost with a		Sweet C	Colin McMillan
Hammer in His		Sweep Pea	Pernell Whitaker
Hand	Jimmy Wilde	Terrible Terry	Terry McGovern
Gunboat	Eddie Smith	Terrible Tim	Tim Witherspoon
Hands of Stone	Roberto Duran	Texas Cobra	Don Curry
Hard Rock from		Tipton Slasher	William Perry
Down Under	Tom Heeney	Toy Bulldog	Mickey Walker
Harlem Spider	Tommy Kelly	Two Ton	Tony Galento
Havana Bon Bon	Kid Chocolate	Tylerstown Terror	Jimmy Wilde
Hawk	Kid Gavilan	Welsh Wizard	Freddie Welsh
Herkimer		Whitechapel	
Hurricane	Lou Ambers	Whirlwind	Jack 'Kid' Berg
Hit Man	Thomas Hearns	Wild Bull of the	
Hoko	Paul Hodkinson	Pampas	Luis Firpo
Homicide Hank	Henry Armstrong	Will o' the Wisp	Willie Pep
Human Windmill	Harry Greb		

TERRY NORRIS

born: 17 June 1967, Lubbock, Texas, USA

Terry Norris started as a nine-year-old at 67lb, and had 295 amateur bouts, losing only four and winning a Texas Golden Gloves title at 139lb. His older brother Orlin Norris turned professional in June 1986. Terry had to choose between boxing and baseball, and turned professional two months after his brother. Two losses in 1987 did not stop Norris's progress to the North American light-middleweight championship in 1988. In 1989 he challenged for the WBA title but was knocked out in the second round by Julian Jackson.

Norris caused a big upset in March 1990 by knocking out John Mugabe in the first round in Tampa to win the WBC championship. In July he went to Annecy in France to outpoint Rene Jacquot in a defence and then, in February 1991, he really attracted world attention by comprehensively beating Sugar Ray Leonard in Madison Square Garden and ending Leonard's career.

Norris proved himself a good boxer and a hard puncher. Donald Curry was another ex-champion to fall under his fists in an eighth-round knockout in Palm Springs in June. Norris made two more defences in 1991 and one in February 1992 before he enhanced his status further by stopping the WBA welterweight champion Meldrick Taylor in the fourth round in Las Vegas in May.
Record: 35 contests; 32 wins; 3 defeats

TERRY NORRIS displays his WBC light-middleweight belt.

127

PHILADELPHIA JACK O'BRIEN

born: (Joseph Francis Hagen) **17 January 1878, Philadelphia, USA**
died: 12 November 1942, New York City

O'Brien could have made the middleweight limit for most of his career, but preferred to campaign as a light-heavyweight and heavyweight. He began boxing professionally in 1896 and became an excellent defensive boxer. With only one early loss on his record, he had 21 contests in Britain between 1901 and 1903 and won them all, including one against George Crisp, who was claiming the British heavyweight title. In 1905, in San Francisco, he won the world light-heavyweight championship when Bob Fitzsimmons was forced to retire in the 13th round. But O'Brien cared little for this title and relinquished it. The following year he challenged Tommy Burns for the world heavyweight title and was a little lucky to get a draw over 20 rounds. He was favourite in a return but was clearly outpointed.

In a contest with middleweight champion Stanley Ketchel in 1909 O'Brien was knocked out with his head lying in his resin tray, but was saved when the final bell rang when the round reached eight. It was a no-decision contest. However Ketchel and Sam Langford later knocked him out and he retired in 1912.
Record: 181 contests; 101 wins; 16 draws; 7 defeats; 57 no-decision

A CLEVER craftsman, Philadelphia Jack O'Brien won the light-heavyweight championship but was more interested in the heavyweight division, where he drew in a title challenge.

RUBEN OLIVARES

born: 14 January 1947, Mexico City

Olivares, the son of a well-off businessman, was an outstanding amateur who became a professional in 1964. A bantamweight, he did not look as if he had the power to be a destructive puncher, but he proved to be one of the hardest hitting ever seen in the division. Only two of his first 51 opponents lasted the distance, and in August 1969 he knocked out Lionel Rose in Los Angeles to become the undisputed world bantamweight champion. He suffered his first defeat in October 1970 when surprisingly stopped on a cut eye by Chucho Castillo in the 14th round. Olivares had defended successfully against him six months earlier, and within another six months 'Rockabye Ruben' had won the title back from him. Olivares lost the title for good in 1972 when, having difficulty making the weight, he was knocked out by a fellow Mexican Rafael Herrera.

Olivares moved up to featherweight and after winning the American title he won the vacant WBA crown when stopping Zensuke Utagawa in the seventh round in 1974. Later in the year he was knocked out by the great Alexis Arguello for this crown, but he soon took the WBC title with a quick stoppage of Bobby Chacon. However again his reign was short-lived, David Kotey outpointing him in Los Angeles. He had one more stab at the title in 1979 when Eusebio Pedroza stopped him. Two further losses forced him to retire in 1981, but in 1986 at 39 he made a one-match comeback, winning on points.

Record: 102 contests; 87 wins; 3 draws; 12 defeats

CARLOS ORTIZ was an outstanding lightweight who was at the top for six years before being knocked out by alcohol.

CARLOS ORTIZ

born: 9 September 1936, Ponce, Puerto Rico

Carlos Ortiz lived in New York from the age of nine and, after winning national amateur titles, turned professional there in 1959. He was unbeaten in his first 27 fights and made himself a contender for Joe Brown's lightweight title. While waiting for a shot at it, he took the vacant light-welterweight title with a second round knockout of Kenny Lane. He lost this title to Duilio Loi before outpointing Joe Brown in Las Vegas.

The hard-punching Ortiz held the lightweight title for three years before losing it on points to Ismael Laguna in Panama City. However the Puerto Rican won the title back in San Juan and held on for another 2½ years before being outpointed by Carlos Teo Cruz in June 1968. Despite his impressive record, Ortiz had been having a drinking problem for much of his later career. After losing his title he had only two fights in three years, but he began a serious comeback in December 1971. After nine wins, eight by the short route, he was stopped for the first time in his career by Ken Buchanan in 1972 and retired.

He entered politics, but then became a New York cab-driver saying: 'I'm not drinking when I'm driving, and when I'm not driving, I'm asleep.'

Record: 70 contests; 61 wins; 1 draw; 7 defeats; 1 no-contest

LASZLO PAPP

born: 25 March 1926, Hungary

Laszlo Papp was one of the greatest of the amateur boxers to come from behind the Iron Curtain in post-Second World War years. He first attracted world-wide attention when he won the Olympic middleweight title in London in 1948. He was really only a light-middleweight, but this class wasn't reintroduced into the Olympics until 1952, when Papp won it. In 1956 he retained the title, beating in the final Jose Torres, who was to become the world light-heavyweight champion as a professional. Papp was the first boxer to win three Olympic gold medals.

The following year when Papp was 31, the Hungarian government allowed him to become the country's first professional. Papp, a strong two-fisted southpaw with a particularly devastating left hook, earned a shot at the European middleweight title in 1962, when he stopped the Dane Chris Christensen in the seventh round in Vienna. Injuries to bones in his hands kept him inactive for spells but by 1965 he had beaten off six challengers and was scheduled to fight Joey Giardello for the world title. Unfortunately for Papp, the Hungarian government decided this was carrying capitalism too far and he was denied permission. Although unbeaten, he was by now 39, and decided to retire.
Record: 29 contests; 26 wins; 3 draws

JACKIE PATERSON

born: 5 September 1920, Springfield, Ayrshire, Scotland
died: 19 November 1966, South Africa

Paterson's family emigrated to the United States when he was eight but, five years later, Paterson returned to Glasgow where he joined the Anderton club. In 1938 he turned professional as a flyweight and quickly

became British and British Empire champion. In June 1943 he added the world flyweight title when he beat Peter Kane with a first-round knockout, maintaining Britain's long superiority in this division. He was the first southpaw to win the title.

Continuing a successful career, Paterson took the British Empire and then the European bantamweight titles. However in 1947 he failed to make the weight for a challenge by Dado Marino for his world flyweight title, and was stripped. He went to law against the BBBC and was 'reinstated' and matched with the new 'champion' Rinty Monaghan, but although he got down to eight stone he was knocked out in the seventh round in Belfast. Paterson then lost his European bantamweight title to Theo Medina, but collected the British title to add to the Empire one. These were taken from him eventually by Stan Rowan in 1949. He retired in 1951, having lost ten of his last 13 fights, including his world title. Paterson had lost much of his money gambling. He moved to South Africa where, in 1966, he was stabbed to death in a street fight.
Record: 91 contests; 63 wins; 3 draws; 25 defeats

FLOYD PATTERSON

born: 4 January 1935, Waco, North Carolina, USA

Patterson was the third son of a labourer who took his family to Brooklyn, where Floyd became a retarded pupil, in trouble with the law and sent to reform school. Here he learned to box, although when he joined his brothers' club he cried when hurt, one of those contradictions which make his career so fascinating.

Patterson proved more successful than his brothers, who also turned professional, winning a Golden Gloves and then, at 17, the 1952 Olympic middleweight gold medal, with a 74-second knockout of his opponent in the final. He turned professional and grew into the heavyweight class. When Marciano retired Patterson

had lost only once on his way up, to former light-heavyweight champion Joey Maxim. This was good enough to earn him a contest with Archie Moore for the vacant heavyweight crown, and he knocked out the older man in the fifth round. At 21 years, 10 months, 26 days, he was the youngest man (until Tyson) to win the title.

Patterson, at 6ft and less than 190lb, was not big as a heavyweight. His manager Cus d'Amato had given him a 'peek-a-boo' style which involved holding his gloves high and peering round his arms. He was very quick and put punches together very fast and, because his reach was relatively short, he often hurled himself into punches with his feet off the floor. D'Amato protected the champion and chose his opponents carefully, one being Pete Rademacher, making his professional debut. In 1959, however, Ingemar Johansson, a Swede, shook the Patterson camp by knocking him down seven times on the way to a third-round win.

Patterson hid for a year after this defeat and then showed his courage by bouncing back to regain the title a year later with a fourth-round knockout. Patterson thus created another record – he was the first heavyweight champion to regain the title. The rubber match, in March 1961, saw both men on the floor in turn,

but Patterson was the victor in the sixth, and resumed his safety-first ways.

Patterson showed both sides of his character in 1962 by over-ruling his manager and accepting a challenge from ex-jailbird Sonny Liston, who was regarded as

LEFT: Floyd Patterson, who was the youngest world heavyweight champion when he won in 1956.

BELOW: Patterson outpointing Oscar Bonavena in 1972.

being the best heavyweight around. But Patterson showed such apprehension that he was knocked out in 126 seconds. The humiliated ex-champion crept from the stadium in disguise and built up a stock of false beards and spectacles for future use when beaten. He badly needed them again in the return, when he lasted only four seconds longer.

Patterson rebuilt his career and challenged Muhammad Ali for the title in 1965 but although he showed bravery he was toyed with by Ali. He lost to Jerry Quarry in a WBA eliminating tournament for the title when Ali's Vietnam War stand lost him his licence, and was then outpointed by Jimmy Ellis, who won the WBA version

PATTERSON knocks out challenger Roy Harris in the 12th round in 1958.

of the title. He had only one fight between September 1968 and January 1971 but, in 1972, fought Ali again for the American heavyweight title. He was stopped in the seventh round and retired. He began to train boxers and when his adopted son Tracy Harris Patterson won the WBC light-featherweight title in 1992, pop Floyd said it was the proudest moment of his life.

Record: 64 contests; 55 wins; 1 draw; 8 defeats

See also: Patterson v Johansson

FLOYD PATTERSON V INGEMAR JOHANSSON

26 June 1959, New York
20 June 1960, New York
13 March 1961, Miami Beach

Floyd Patterson, at 13 stone, was not big enough to rank among the greatest heavyweights, but careful selection of opponents by his manager, Cus d'Amato, led to a lengthy reign as champion. When a top contender, Eddie Machen, was stopped in one round by a Swede, Ingemar Johansson, it seemed that Johansson would provide another authentic opponent without much chance of taking the title.

They first met at New York's Yankee Stadium, where only 18,215 attended but, for the first time, television receipts exceeded a million dollars. Patterson was a 4-1 favourite, as Johansson amazed the New York fight community by arriving with his father as his trainer, his mother as cook, brother as sparring partner, another brother and his sister as consultants, and his stunning fiancée as secretary. They all moved into a training camp together and training appeared to include plenty of lazes by the pool and evening meals with his secretary.

Johansson controlled the early exchanges with a long accurate jab and proved not to be the naive challenger Patterson's camp had expected. One typical leaping hook was the sum total of Patterson's success as the third round began. After about 30 seconds Johansson crossed his right for the first time. Down went Patterson, but instinct immediately got him up. Unfortunately, he was actually out on his feet, rubbing his nose like a little boy embarrassed in front of his friends. Later it was claimed he thought he had dropped the challenger and was searching for a neutral corner.

Johansson hit Patterson with a left and right while Patterson was looking the other way. Down he went again. Patterson had no idea what he was doing as seven times in all Johansson clubbed him to the floor. Patterson kept rising as if he were a mechanical toy until

132

finally referee Ruby Goldstein decided playtime couldn't last forever.

The media loved the new playboy champion and his right hand punch which allowed him to reign without, apparently, the necessity of the monk-like training ritual which other fighters needed. The right was called 'Ingo's Bingo', or the 'Hammer of Thor'.

The return, at the Polo Grounds, saw the new champion under-rate the old.

Nobody had reclaimed the heavyweight title before, and Johansson no doubt thought that a brush of his 'hammer' on Patterson's chin would be all that was necessary to keep that record intact. But Patterson went into seclusion and trained hard for a year, and was a different proposition. He had put on eight pounds.

This time the speedy and determined Patterson carried the fight to Johansson. The moment of truth came in the second round when Ingo's Bingo landed on his head. Patterson was shaken but backed away and survived the round. As the rounds passed and Johansson failed to get in a damaging right, Patterson's confidence visibly grew. In the fifth a right followed by a leaping left hook put Johansson down. This time it was Patterson who was the destroyer when Johansson rose at nine, cut over the eye and bleeding from the mouth. Several more left hooks found their target and sent Johansson crashing down again, his head thudding on the canvas. Referee Arthur Mercante counted him out.

Patterson was 4-1 favourite again in the third encounter at the Miami Beach Convention Hall. This was partly due to the folds of

LEFT: Ingemar Johansson knocks down Floyd Patterson to cause a big upset in 1959.

BELOW: Patterson wins the series in Miami Beach in 1961.

flesh around Johansson's waistline, which added nearly 12lb to the trimmer frame he had carried on the second encounter. Patterson, too, was slightly heavier.

Again the fight had an exciting start. Ingo's favourite right was crossed to Patterson's chin in the first round and dumped the champion on the canvas. Patterson rose quickly at 'three', but the new mandatory 'eight' count, in operation for the first time in a heavyweight title fight, helped him to clear the cobwebs away. But Johansson was on him, another right dropped him and Patterson's eyes were glazed. Perhaps the mandatory count kept him his title. As Johansson came in again to finish it, Patterson found a left and right which completely surprised Johansson, catching him in the face and knocking him down. Both men had been on the deck in the first round of a heavyweight title fight for the first time since Dempsey beat Firpo 38 years before.

In the second round both threw punches at each other as if they were old-time gladiators fighting with lethal weapons – the first to land

would annihilate the other. Both slipped to the floor but both survived. It was the same story in the next two rounds and, surprisingly, both boxers took savage blows which had befuddled them on earlier occasions. This time the effects were seen in cuts and puffiness around the eyes.

The fifth was quieter, mainly because Johansson was obviously tiring. In the sixth he launched a do-or-die assault, snapping Patterson's head back with a couple of hard rights and following strongly with other punches. But, although groggy, Patterson did not go down and suddenly Johansson appeared to have nothing left. One of Patterson's leaping hooks, followed by two rights, knocked him to the floor. Johansson was balanced on his knee when the referee reached 'nine' but, as he went to rise, he overbalanced and was counted out scrambling to get to his feet.

Patterson retained his title after the first three-match series in heavyweight boxing history. Charles and Walcott had met four times, but only two were consecutive.

WILLIE PEP

born: (Guglielmo Papaleo) 19 September 1922, Middletown, Connecticut, USA

Pep's father went to America from Sicily and Pep was brought up in a poor district where as a small boy he took up boxing as a protection against bullying. He won state titles as an amateur and turned professional in July 1940. Pep was a very fast featherweight, with dazzling skills, who frequently fought two or three times a month. In November 1942 he surprised everybody by outpointing Chalky Wright to win the New York version of the world featherweight title. Aged just over 20 he was the youngest world champion for over 40 years. Four months later he was outpointed by former lightweight champion Sammy Angott, who was beginning a comeback. This was to prove his only defeat in his first 137 contests.

In June 1943 Pep outpointed Sal Bartolo who

WILLIE PEP winning against Sandy Saddler, 1949.

later became the NBA world champion. In 1946 Pep knocked out Bartolo to become undisputed champion. Pep registered few knockouts, but he did occasionally stop opponents who became exhausted. He was nicknamed 'Will o' the Wisp' because he was so fast he seemed to appear and reappear in different places. He built up a tremendous following with discerning fans.

In January 1947 he was in a plane crash which claimed five lives, and he himself was told he would not box again after breaking two vertebrae in his back. However, less than six months later he was back, and continuing his winning ways.

Pep suffered his second defeat and lost his title in 1948 when he was knocked out by Sandy Saddler in the fourth round. Three months later he surprised the fans by winning it back in a tremendously skilful display, but he was stopped by Saddler in two subsequent title fights.

Naturally, Pep's talents waned as his career approached 200 contests and after a second successive defeat in January 1959 he

retired. He was persuaded to make a comeback in 1965, but retired again when, after nine wins, he lost his tenth contest. He became a referee.
Record: 242 contests; 230 wins; 1 draw; 11 defeats

See also: Saddler v Pep

PASCUAL PEREZ

**born: 4 March 1926, Tupungate, Mendoza, Argentina
died: 22 January 1977, Argentina**

Pascual Perez was a brilliant amateur who, in the London Olympics in 1948, was initially disqualified for being overweight. However this was an error – he had been confused with his bantamweight colleague Arnoldo Pares. This was amusing as Perez, at 4ft 10½ in and never more than 110lb was among the world's smallest flyweights. However, he was built like a miniature well-muscled heavyweight, and it had been his unusual strength that had first persuaded him to take up boxing. He came from a poor family of nine children and at the time of the Olympics was a clerk in the Chamber of

Deputies Office in Buenos Aires. He won the gold medal comfortably, but his family preferred him to keep his steady job rather than turn professional. It was only after his family discovered that he was continuing to box under an assumed name that he finally turned professional when nearer 27 than 26.

Only one man had gone the distance with the big-punching Perez when he fought the world champion Yoshio Shirai in a non-title fight in Buenos Aires in 1954. He drew, and was given a title shot in Tokyo four months later. Perez outpointed Shirai and won the championship. Perez made ten successful defences, six abroad, in the next five years before he surrendered his title to Pone Kingpetch, who outpointed him in Bangkok. There was a return in Los Angeles, but the younger Kingpetch this time stopped him in the eighth.

Perez, who loved the game, kept boxing for over three years more but after losing four of his last six contests he retired in 1964. Sadly he died when only 50.
Record: 91 contests; 83 wins; 1 draw; 7 defeats

PRIZE FIGHTING

Bare-knuckle fighting became popular in Britain in the 17th century. Travelling fairs helped spread the sport. The resident 'professionals' would put on exhibitions or issue challenges to the locals. Samuel Pepys described such an event in his diary for 1662. Gradually local champions emerged, and friends or sponsors would put up money to support challenges to other champions. As with cricketers, the aristocracy would take good fighters on the staff and bet on them in matches. The first report of a prize-fight, from the *Protestant Mercury* of January 1681, describes a match between the Duke of Albemarle's footman and a butcher.

Groups of boxers took to roaming the country and challenging locals on the village greens. The spectators would be asked to take a rope and form a circle with it. This was the 'ring'. A local would accept a challenge by 'throwing his hat into the ring'.

If there were no challengers the boxers would fight each other. Afterwards there would be a collection, where spectators would throw coins into the ring. This was the forerunner of the custom still just about alive of throwing 'nobbins' into the ring to show appreciation of the boxers. Gradually rules became necessary to govern these encounters (*see also* the section on Rules). Some rules grew out of custom. Boxers were stripped to the waist, and it became custom to ban lifting or grabbing below the waist. Biting and eye-gouging were never allowed, but otherwise hair-pulling, wrestling, throttling, practically anything was accepted in the earliest days. A popular throw was the cross-buttock, by which a boxer rammed his buttock into his opponent's crotch and grabbed his arm to toss him over his shoulder. After putting an opponent down, a boxer was allowed to fall on him as heavily as he could in an effort to knock the wind out of him.

As spectators holding

the rope became excitable and moved around, it became useful to drive stakes in the ground to take the ropes, so the 'ring' became square. The purses carrying the bets were often attached to these stakes, hence the use of the word 'stakes' to signify an amount bet or an amount won in a horserace, or in a sweepstake. Soon there were two rings – the centre one in which the boxers fought, and an outer one for the patrons, officials, timekeepers, boxers' seconds, umpires and 'whips'. The whips were men who were employed to keep order and prevent the spectators interfering. The small whips they carried were also used to persuade the public to contribute to collections, hence the 'whipround'. The seconds were also boxers who were prepared to put on a substitute or secondary bout if anything prevented the first. Hence their name – 'seconds'. One bent a knee for the boxer to sit on between rounds while the other was the 'bottle-man', who supplied mouthwash.

Fights were to a finish. Each round lasted until one or other man went to the floor, either from a punch or a throw. There was then a 30-second interval, at the end of which the timekeeper blew a whistle or struck a gong. The boxers had eight seconds from then to come up to a line scratched across the centre of the ring. If a boxer could not 'toe the line' in time, he was the loser. In other words, he 'failed to come up to scratch'. He was said to have been counted out of time. Boxing authorities still prefer the term 'count-out' to 'knockout'. 'Knockout' connotes being knocked out of one's senses, but the real meaning is knocked or counted out of time.

Boxing often went hand-in-hand with other forms of combat, such as the use of the backsword and quarterstaff. James Figg, or Fig, who opened an academy in Tottenham Court Road called 'Figg's Amphitheatre' to teach proficiency in all these things, was acknowledged as the first Champion of England, and it is possible to trace a line of champions from Figg down

to Mike Tyson and beyond. Figg challenged all-comers: 'For money, for love or a bellyful'. One of the first was Ned Sutton, the Gravesend pipe-maker, and they fought with bare fists and then cudgels.

After Figg, Jack Broughton was the next great champion, and he became so upset at the death of one challenger, George Stevenson the Coachman, that he invented a set of rules which took some of the savagery out of the sport. Broughton also had his academy attended by the nobility – even royalty took a keen interest in prize-fighting. In 1723 George I had a ring set up in Hyde Park for the benefit of the populace. This was finally demolished by the Bow Street police in 1820. During this time boxing was in the peculiar situation of being popular with all the influential people of the day, encouraged by royalty and yet illegal as a public spectacle. The authorities turned a blind eye except for the big fights which drew enormous crowds. The police and magistrates then moved to prevent disturbances of the peace. This led to matches being arranged near the borders of counties, so that everybody could nip over the border when the local police force arrived. The followers of the sport were known as 'The Fancy' and included many statesmen, politicians, writers and noblemen.

Tom Johnson, Ben Brain, Daniel Mendoza, 'The Star of the East', and Gentleman John Jackson were the most notable champions to follow Broughton. In 1814 Jackson formed the Pugilistic Club which brought more order to the sport, particularly by providing purses through its rich patrons and eliminating 'crossing' or fixing. The poet Byron and various princes were patrons of Jackson, and the Pugilistic Club provided a guard of 18 prizefighters at the coronation of George IV to prevent supporters of Queen Charlotte from entering the Abbey.

After Jackson, Jem Belcher, Hen Pearce, John Gully and Tom Cribb were great champions. Cribb saw

off the first challengers for the championship from America, beating Bill Richmond and Tom Molineaux in the early 19th century.

The greatest challenge from America came in 1860 when Tom Sayers kept the championship in England by getting a draw with John C. Heenan. Jem Mace was the last great British bare-knuckle champion, and he spread the popularity of boxing around the world. In fact with laws being enforced with more severity, Mace and many of the better boxers went to America in the second half of the 19th century, where two of them, Tom Allen and Joe Goss, became American champion.

The last big bare-knuckle fights both in American and Europe occurred in 1889. John L. Sullivan beat Jake Kilrain in Richburg, Mississippi, in July, and was in effect the champion of the world. In December Jem Smith, the British champion, drew with an Australian, Frank Slavin, in a fight arranged by the Pelican Club of London but which they were forced to stage overseas, in Bruges, Belgium. The worst aspects of the prize ring were shown by this encounter. Squire Abingdon Baird, a 'sportsman', wagered heavily on Smith and dispatched a gang of ruffians to Bruges to ensure he won. These men used sticks on Slavin whenever they could reach him during the fight

and when Slavin was, nevertheless, on the point of victory they invaded the ring and forced a timid referee to grant a draw. The Pelican Club insisted that Slavin have the £500-a-side stake money.

In America, Sullivan's next big bout was wearing gloves under Marquess of Queensberry rules, and the age of the prize-ring was over.

AARON PRYOR

born: 20 October 1955, Cincinnati, Ohio, USA

Aaron Pryor was a brilliant amateur lightweight who beat Thomas Hearns on his way to becoming American champion. He turned professional in November 1976 and, with his strength and skill and devastating punching, ran up a string of rapid wins, making him an obvious contender for world lightweight honours, especially when Elmer Kinty, whom he had beaten as an amateur, became WBA champion in March 1980. Tired of waiting for a chance, Pryor took the WBA light-welterweight title instead with a fourth-round knockout of Antonio Cervantes in his native Cincinnati.

Although still able to fight at lightweight, Pryor did not get a shot at this title, but defended the light-welter title eight times, winning all inside the distance including two against former lightweight great Alexis

Arguello. However Aaron Pryor became addicted to cocaine, and his title was taken away in 1983 when he retired. In 1984, however, he was given the opportunity to fight Nicky Furlano for the new IBF version of the title, and he won on points. He defended this title in 1985 and then was stripped through inactivity as his drugs problem worsened. He was shot in the left wrist in a drugs raid, getting a scar to match one on his right arm inflicted by his wife in a quarrel. He then underwent drug rehabilitation and in 1987 returned to the ring as a welterweight but was stopped by Bobby Joe Young. It was his first defeat. He began speaking to youth about drugs problems. In May 1990, after surgery for a detached retina and cataracts, he boxed in Wisconsin, which lacks a boxing commission, and scored a three-round stoppage.

Between 1978 and 1983 Pryor, called the 'Hawk', was virtually unbeatable, winning all his 25 contests, including nine world title fights by the short route.
Record: 38 contests; 37 wins; 1 defeat

AARON PRYOR celebrating possibly his greatest victory: a knockout of the great Alexis Arguello in 1983.

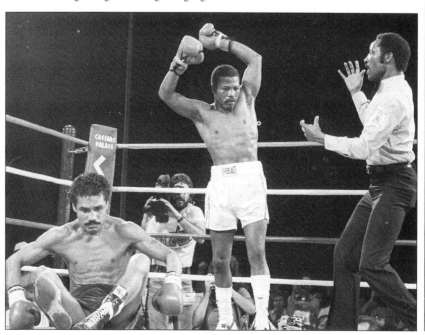

SUGAR RAY ROBINSON

born: (Walker Smith) 3 May 1921, Detroit, Michigan, USA
died: 12 April 1989, Los Angeles, California, USA

Young Walker Smith used to attend a gym in New York after his family moved there soon after he reached his teens, but his mother (his parents had separated) wouldn't allow him to box in tournaments. One day, however, he stood in for a boxer who failed his medical, helped by his friend and later trainer George Gainford who produced a licence – in the name of Ray Robinson. The boy kept going and was unbeaten as an amateur in 85 contests winning a Golden Gloves competition. He continued to use the name on his false licence, and when it was remarked that he was a sweet boxer, somebody replied: 'As sweet as sugar'. From then on he was always known as Sugar Ray Robinson.

Robinson turned professional in 1940 as a welterweight and won his first 40 contests. He was then outpointed by Jake LaMotta, but he was to avenge this defeat 21 days later and did not lose again for eight years and 91 fights. In December 1946 he won the vacant world welterweight title when outpointing Tommy Bell. In the next three years he proved himself unbeatable among the welters and increasing weight persuaded him to move up to middleweight. In June 1950 he beat Robert Villemain to be recognised in Pennsylvania as world middleweight champion, while two months later he retained his welterweight title in a defence against Charley Fusari. He defended both titles until in 1951 he stopped Jake LaMotta in the 13th round in Chicago to become undisputed world middleweight champion. He then relinquished the welter crown.

In 1951 Robinson toured Europe where, in July he surprisingly lost his title to Randolph Turpin, only his second defeat in 132 contests. In a return in New York two months later he won the title back in a desperate rally after his eye had been cut. After two successful defences in 1952 Robinson then challenged Joey Maxim for the world light-heavyweight title. Robinson was winning on an extraordinary night in the Yankee Stadium but, with the temperature at 104°F (40°C) first the referee, then Robinson, succumbed to heat exhaustion. Robinson could not come out for the 14th round, the greatest regret of his career. Six months later Robinson announced his retirement.

After trying a dancing career, Robinson returned to the ring in January 1955 after a gap of 2½ years. He lost his second fight, but by the end of the year had become middleweight champion for the third time with a second-round knockout of Carl (Bobo) Olson. He repeated this win in 1956 but in January 1957 was outpointed by Gene Fullmer. Four months later a knockout of Fullmer in the fifth round won him the title for a fourth time. Robinson then had two tremendous battles with Carmen Basilio, losing the first and winning the second. He thus had won the world middleweight title five times, easily a record.

In 1960 Robinson lost the title again when outpointed by Paul Pender, a result Pender repeated. But Robinson was still not finished in his attempts on the middleweight title. The title having now split he challenged Gene Fullmer, who held the NBA version, and got a draw. In 1961 his final attempt resulted in Fullmer outpointing him.

Robinson continued boxing for over four years more, spoiling his record a little with five defeats in his last 11 bouts before retiring in December 1965.

During his long career Robinson demonstrated a mastery of every facet of boxing. He was skilful, strong, had a basic instinct of tactics, and was always able to move up a gear when necessary. In 201 contests he was never knocked out, the retirement against Maxim being the only time he failed to make the final bell. Many critics rate him the best boxer, pound-for-pound, there has ever been.

Record: 201 contests; 174 wins; 6 draws; 19 defeats; 2 no-contest

See also: Turpin v Robinson

LEFT: The great Sugar Ray Robinson in training.

RIGHT: Robinson delivers a *coup de grace*.

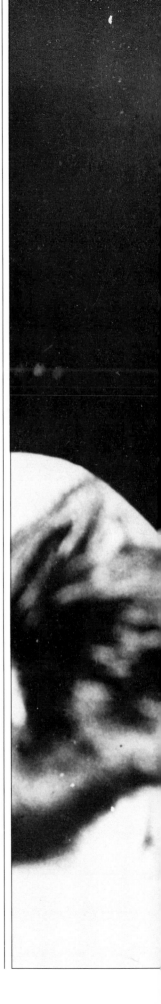

BARNEY ROSS

**born: (Beryl David Rosofsky) 23 December 1909, New York City, USA
died: 17 January 1967, Chicago, Illinois**

Ross's parents were Jews from Russia. Of their nine children, four died in infancy. The family moved to Chicago when Barney was two. Underweight, he was involved in street fights, being nearly blinded by a rock and suffering permanent injury to an arm through a blow with a crowbar. When he was 14 his father was shot and killed by two youths robbing his small grocery store. His mother suffered a miscarriage as a result. Barney became involved in dice games and ran errands for Al Capone. Eventually he got a proper job, joined a gym, became a fine amateur boxer and won a Golden Gloves tournament.

In September 1929, Ross turned professional and progressed into an outstanding lightweight. In 1932 he outpointed Battling Battalino and six months later Billy Petrolle. In June 1933 in Chicago he outpointed Tony Canzoneri to become undisputed world lightweight champion and NBA light-welterweight champion. Ross soon relinquished the lightweight title, but kept the other and in May 1934 he added the world welterweight title when he outpointed Jimmy McLarnin in New York.

Ross was a fast puncher rather than a destructive one. He kept up a constant attack on opponents, overwhelming them by the speed and number of punches which came from all angles, although there was nothing haphazard about them. Ross lost the welterweight title back to McLarnin in his first defence but, after successful defences of his light-welter title, he won the major title back in a third meeting with McLarnin. He defended against Ceferino Garcia, but lost his title to Henry Armstrong in 1938. He took tremendous punishment and retired. However Ross was on his feet at the end, and was never stopped during his 81-fight career.

Ross was decorated for bravery while serving in the Marines against Japan at Guadalcanal in the Second World War, but became addicted to the drugs given him to combat malaria. He was forced to go to hospital for a cure and spent much time later helping other addicts. He died from cancer after a long illness, aged 57.
Record: 81 contests; 73 wins; 3 draws; 4 defeats; 1 no-decision

RULES

The first rules of boxing were drawn up in 1743 by Jack Broughton in answer to demands to lessen the brutality of pugilism. Broughton needed no encouragement because he himself had been moved by the death of one of his opponents, George Stevenson. Stevenson was a young Yorkshire coachman having an affair with his mistress, whose husband sent him to London to challenge Broughton, the champion. Stevenson received the backing of the Prince of Wales, and the match took place in Figg's amphitheatre in 1741.

After both men had taken heavy blows, Broughton began the third round by crushing his opponent against the ring post while squeezing him in a mighty grip. Suddenly he let go and struck the coachman with a terrible blow under the heart. The gallant Yorkshireman fell and could not move. He was put to bed in the nearby Adam and Eve tavern, where a doctor diagnosed two broken ribs and an internal haemorrhage. Nothing could be done. He asked for Broughton to visit and Broughton continued to visit Stevenson each day, the two becoming great friends in the sad circumstances. Stevenson lived for nearly a month before he died, to Broughton's great distress. The Fancy sent the Coachman off with a magnificent funeral. Broughton had the tragedy in his mind when, two years later, he framed his rules.

Broughton's Rules were originally framed for one particular fight only, on 10 August 1743, at which he was to be the referee. They read:

Broughton's Rules

1. That a square of a yard be chalked in the middle of the stage; and every fresh set-to after a fall, or being parted from the rails, each second is to bring his man to the side of the square, and place him opposite to the other, and till they are fairly set to at the lines, it shall not be lawful for one to strike the other.
2. That, in order to prevent any disputes, the time a man lies after a fall, if the second does not bring his man to the side of the square within the space of half a minute, he shall be deemed a beaten man.
3. That in every main battle, no person whatever shall be upon the stage except the principals and their seconds; the same rule to be observed in by-battles, except that in the latter, Mr Broughton is allowed to be upon the stage to keep decorum, and to assist gentlemen in getting to their places, provided always he does not interfere in the battle; and whoever pretends to infringe these rules to be turned immediately out of the house. Everybody is to quit the stage as soon as the champions are stripped, before set-to.
4. That no champion be deemed beaten unless he fails coming up to the line in the limited time; or, that his own second declares him beaten. No second is to be allowed to ask his man's adversary any questions, or advise him to give out.
5. That in by-battles, the winning man to have two-thirds of the money given, which shall be publicly divided upon the stage notwithstanding any private agreements to the contrary.
6. That to prevent disputes in every main battle, the principals shall, on the coming on the stage, choose from among the gentleman present, two umpires, who shall absolutely decide all disputes that may arise about the battle; and if the two umpires cannot agree, the said umpires to choose a third, who is to determine it.
7. That no person is to hit his adversary when he is down, or seize him by the hair, the breeches, or any part below the waist; a man on his knees to be reckoned down.

Broughton's Rules received general acceptance and all the main contests were governed by them for nearly 100 years. Two deaths were the main reasons for their amendment. In 1833, after Jem Ward, the champion, retired, the title was claimed by James Burke, a River Thames waterman and a Londoner whose parents were Irish. He was very hard of hearing and was known as the 'Deaf 'Un'. On 30 May 1833 he fought a bitter battle with Simon Byrne, an Irishman. Burke was only 5ft 8½in and weighed about 12st 10lb. Byrne was a much bigger man, but Burke was a superior boxer. Byrne's strength kept him in the fight but he took a terrible beating over 99 rounds which lasted for three hours and 16 minutes. Byrne was in a coma at the end and did not recover, dying three days later. Byrne had already been acquitted of manslaughter himself after the death of an opponent three years before and now Burke was exonerated. However Burke decided to flee to America where, incidentally, he narrowly escaped death himself when he took on an old adversary, Sam O'Rourke, another Irishman and a gangster who planned to avenge Byrne's death by having his mob interrupt the fight and murder Burke. They rushed the ring in the third round, but Burke managed to get away.

In 1838 there was another high-profile death, when Bill Phelps, a lightweight boxer known as Brighton Bill, died after getting a beating from Owen Swift. It was decided that the rules needed to be examined to prevent such disasters.

In both fights in which a death occurred, and particularly in the Burke-Byrne contest, the boxers had at times been brought up to the mark by their seconds in a state of helplessness, whereupon they received another savage blow or throw to earn another 30 seconds recovery time. The main amendment to Broughton's Rules was that a boxer could not be carried by his seconds to the scratch at the beginning of a round. A man was considered beaten if he could not toe the line unaided.

The amended rules were known as the London Prize Ring Rules and they gained acceptance wherever prize-fighting was practised.

With prizefighting becoming more and more frowned upon as barbaric, and with the laws against it being enforced more and more under pressure from the church, something more drastic was required to humanise the sport.

To the rescue came John Sholto Douglas, the eighth Marquess of Queensberry. He gave his name to the new boxing rules which had largely been drawn up by a man who had been a student with him at Cambridge University, John Graham Chambers. Queensberry was an aggressive man who later played a major part in the downfall of Oscar Wilde, so he has two claims to notoriety.

The Queensberry Rules were published in 1867 and read as follows:
1. To be a fair stand-up boxing match in a twenty-four foot ring, or as near that size as practicable.
2. No wrestling or hugging allowed.
3. The rounds to be of three minutes' duration, and one minute's time between rounds.
4. If either man fall through weakness or otherwise, he must get up unassisted, ten seconds to be allowed him to do so; the other man meanwhile to return to his corner, and when the fallen man is on his legs the round is to be resumed, and continued till the three minutes have expired. If one man fails to come to the scratch in the ten seconds allowed, it shall be in the power of the referee to give his award in favour of the other man.
5. A man hanging on the ropes in a helpless state, with his toes off the ground, shall be considered down.
6. No seconds or any other person to be allowed in the ring during the rounds.
7. Should the contest be stopped by any unavoidable interference, the referee to name the time and place as soon as possible for finishing the contest; so that the match must be won and lost, unless the backers of both men agree to draw the stakes.

8. The gloves to be fair-sized boxing gloves of the best quality and new.

9. Should a glove burst, or come off, it must be replaced to the referee's satisfaction.

10. A man on one knee is considered down, and if struck is entitled to the stakes.

11. No shoes or boots with springs allowed.

12. The contest in all other respects to be governed by revised rules of the London Prize Ring.

These rules form the nucleus of those that govern all matches today. The three biggest differences from the Broughton/London Prize Ring rules concern (a) the use of gloves, (b) the rounds to last three minutes each instead of being variable and dependent upon knockdowns, and (c) the elimination of wrestling. No mention is made of the duration of a bout, and the idea was still that a contest should continue until one man gave best. When the idea of limiting the duration of a match was first implemented, the time limit was 45 rounds. With intervals, this meant a contest which went its full distance would last, with intervals, one minute short of three hours. No wonder few bouts went the whole way. Of course, putting a limit on a contest meant that the idea of a points win was born, and the need for somebody or some persons to render a decision. It tended at first to be the referee, and this is still the case in British rings, then two judges outside the ring were added, but in world title contests and in America now the convention is to use three judges outside the ring, with the referee's job solely to control the action, not to score.

The Queensberry Rules were updated by the National Sporting Club and further amended by various controlling bodies throughout the world to suit their own tastes and conditions. Variables are such things as the lengths of contests, and how the points are scored. The most common practice in points scoring is that the winner of each round, or both boxers if the round is drawn, is given

ten points, and his opponent usually nine. If a man is knocked down, however, or is completely beaten in the round, he might be given only eight points. In Britain in particular a five-point per round system was used with the loser scoring 4½ points. Scoring at boxing is primitive and it is no wonder there are controversies.

Other matters to be decided by the governing body with jurisdiction over the contest are such things as

whether a boxer suffering three knockdowns in one round is automatically adjudged a loser, and whether a boxer knocked down must accept a mandatory count of eight from the referee. Archie Moore claimed to have lost a heavyweight title fight when the referee gave Rocky Marciano a mandatory eight count which was not in the rules for that particular contest.

Procedures on fouls also

vary from one authority to another. In many cases it is impossible now to win a bout on a disqualification for a low blow. The development of protectors has rendered the low blow less dangerous, but a referee might give a recipient time to recover from one. An enforced retirement with a cut caused by a clash of heads does not now necessarily mean a defeat – under some authorities a decision might be rendered based on the

ROCKY MARCIANO defending against Archie Moore, when a referee's mistake over the rules helped him.

score cards up to the time of the cut.

The basic rules, however, are the same all over the world, allowing boxers to fight in foreign countries without handicap.

SANDY SADDLER

born: 23 June 1926,
Boston, Massachusetts,
USA

Saddler's father was a West Indian who moved to New York's Harlem when Saddler was a boy. Saddler took up boxing and, after a short amateur career, became a professional before his 18th birthday. He was knocked out in his second contest, but gradually built an impressive career as a featherweight.

Saddler was a freakish featherweight, standing 5ft 8½ in and having long skinny arms that gave him the reach of a much bigger man. Those thin arms packed a tremendous punch and, in his second year, he stopped 14 opponents in succession, mainly with body punches and uppercuts. His size made him look an awkward fighter and he was sometimes accused of being dirty and avoided by the top men, especially, he thought, by Willie Pep, the champion. However in October 1948 Saddler got his chance and knocked out Pep to take the title. Pep boxed brilliantly to reclaim it in a return but Saddler won two more bitter and dirty scraps to confirm himself as champion. He also won what Ohio regarded as the vacant world super-featherweight title with a win over Orlando Zulueta but, after he defended it twice, this division once again sank into disuse for a number of years.

Saddler was inducted into the army and was inactive for most of 1952 and 1953, during which time Teddy 'Red Top' Davis gained recognition in some quarters as an 'interim' featherweight champion, but Saddler outpointed him in 1955 to resume his reign. He stopped Flash Elorde in 1956 but soon afterwards suffered an eye injury when his taxi was involved in an accident, and was forced to retire.

Record: 162 contests; 144 wins; 2 draws; 16 defeats

See also: Saddler v Pep

SANDY SADDLER V WILLIE PEP

29 October 1948, New York
11 February 1949, New York
8 September 1950, New York
26 September 1951, New York

It seemed that Willie Pep owned the featherweight title in 1948. He had won a version of it back in 1942, and unified the division in 1946. He had lost only once in 137 fights. When he was challenged by Sandy Saddler, a man who had lost to Humberto Sierra, whom Willie had just knocked out in his previous defence, he was not worried. Pep thought Saddler was 'a thin, weak-looking guy'. Saddler, at 5ft 8½in, was three inches taller than Pep but slightly lighter when they met at Madison Square Garden.

Pep found that Saddler's thin arms were not weak at all, and in the fourth round Pep found the referee counting 'ten' over him for the first time in his career. So shocked were fight fans that some called it a fix, especially when it was known that Saddler had been heavily backed. Pep's story was that he had underestimated Saddler and then found himself thumbed, butted and grabbed. 'It will be different in the return', he said. Even so, before their second meeting at Madison Square Garden, New York's commissioner for boxing warned them that the good name of the sport was in their hands. The betting odds still favoured Willie, but very narrowly at 6-5. Only 19,000 could get into the Garden and thousands were turned away.

This was the classic puncher v boxer confrontation. Pep was such a clever boxer that he once claimed to have won a round after deliberately setting out not to throw a punch. Saddler, as Pep now knew, was a puncher. He was tall and awkward and his fights were consequently often untidy, but he could punch much harder than a featherweight should.

For three rounds the 'Will o' the Wisp' danced and prodded Saddler –

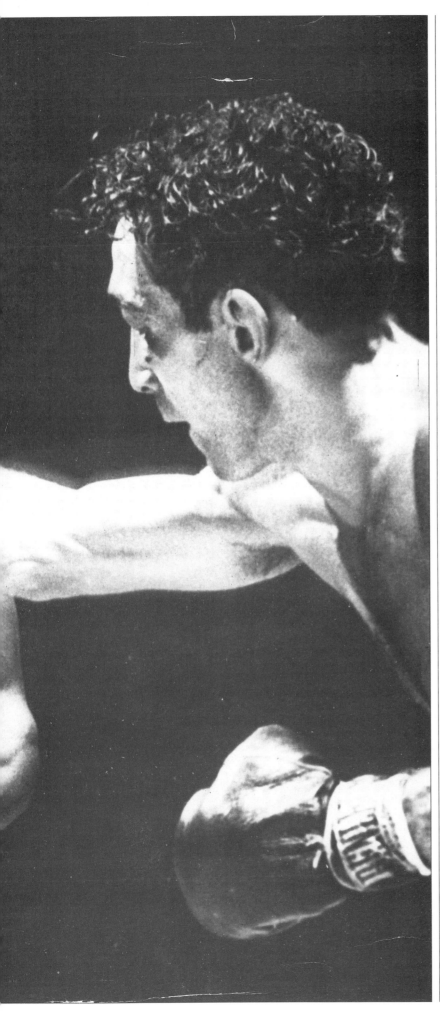

somebody counted 37 straight lefts in the first round alone found Saddler's face. In the fourth Saddler got home his first real blow, a jab to the body, and in the fifth he opened a cut under Pep's eye. From the sixth Saddler's hard punches seemed to be getting on top as Pep tired and his constant barrage eased up. Pep received a second cut in the eighth and, in both the ninth and tenth, was in trouble as rights were cracked to his jaw and combination punches ripped through his defences. But he refused to go down, and he kept his left peppering Saddler's face.

Suddenly Saddler became tired. The energy used trying to land a knockout blow and missing had left his thin arms without strength. From the 11th onwards Pep continued to dance and Saddler's assaults carried less and less conviction. By the 15th Saddler knew he needed a knockout to keep his crown and, digging into his reserves, he found a right which rocked Pep. But Pep boxed on auto-pilot to keep away from any more punches and at the end was peppering Saddler's face again. Pep took the decision although his face was a mess of bruises and cuts from Saddler's gloves. He had put up an exhibition of boxing *par excellence* and thoroughly answered the rumours about the first fight.

There had to be a third fight, and this time the Yankee Stadium was needed. Saddler had not been happy with the way the referee handled the close work in the second fight. In the third he kept on top of Pep. Pep would grab his arms and Saddler would try to pull them away, sometimes getting one free and punching while Pep held the other. Pep claimed all the dirty work started with Saddler holding him. Soon both boxers were using any

foul tactic they could, including tripping and wrestling. After seven rounds Pep claimed a dislocated shoulder, and retired.

They fought again a year later at the Polo Grounds. The fight began where the last had finished. Anything went. Eventually Pep had to retire again with a badly cut eye. Both men were banned by the commissioner from boxing in New York after this foul-ridden contest, Pep for ever, Saddler for 30 days. Pep's ban was lifted, but reimposed in 1954 following rumours after a loss to Lulu Perez.

On retirement, Pep and Saddler had proper respect for each other, but Saddler never came to terms with the way Pep is regarded as one of the greatest of all boxers while he himself, who beat him three times in four, is just another world champion.

VICENTE SALDIVAR

born: 3 May 1943, Mexico City
died: July 1985, Mexico

Saldivar was born into a big family in a tough area of Mexico City and developed from a street scrapper as a boy into a fine amateur boxer who was disappointed to be outpointed in an early round in the 1960 Olympics. He turned professional in 1961 and became a hard-hitting featherweight.

Saldivar, a southpaw, could punch equally hard with either fist and most of his opponents were beaten by the short route. In September 1964 the undisputed world champion, Sugar Ramos, was persuaded to accept a challenge from Saldivar in Mexico City. The local boy won when, after a tough battle, Ramos was unable to come out for the 12th round. Saldivar proved an excellent champion, putting his title at stake eight times in three years, including a series of three contests with the classy Welshman Howard Winstone. After winning the last of these the 24-year-old Saldivar surprisingly announced his retirement.

After 21 months Saldivar made a comeback, first beating Jose Legra who had held the WBC title in his

SANDY SADDLER (left) and Willie Pep in the second of their four bitter, dirty scraps.

absence then, in 1970, regaining this title by outpointing Johnny Famechon in Rome. Seven months later, however, he was stopped in the 12th round by Kuniaki Shibata of Japan. Except for a loss on a foul in his second year, it was his first defeat. He retired again but, in 1973, after over two years absence, he came back to try to regain the title from Eder Jofre in Brazil. He was knocked out in the fourth round and finally gave up for good.
Record: 40 contests; 37 wins; 3 defeats

SALVADOR SANCHEZ

born: 26 January 1959, Santiago Tianguistenco, Mexico
died: 12 August 1982, Queretaro, Mexico

Sanchez' brief professional career began in May 1975, and he quickly demonstrated that he was a strong bantamweight with 17 stoppages in his first 18 contests before being outpointed by Antonio Becerra for the Mexican title. It was to prove his only defeat.

Moving up to featherweight, Sanchez challenged Danny Lopez in Phoenix for the WBC title in February 1980 and stopped the brilliant champion in the 13th round. All but one of Sanchez' subsequent ten contests were successful defences. He was a brilliant boxer with a full repertoire of punches who possessed a knockout blow when the opportunity occurred.

Lopez, Juan LaPorte, Wilfredo Gomez and Azumah Nelson, four men whom he beat in title defences, were all world champions in their day. Tragically, Sanchez was killed in a car accident three weeks after stopping Azumah Nelson, an untimely death that cut short the career of one of the greatest of modern champions.
Record: 46 contests; 44 wins; 1 draw; 1 defeat

TOM SAYERS

born: 25 May 1826, Brighton, Sussex
died: 8 November 1865, Camden Town, London

Sayers was one of the greatest bare-knuckle prizefighters. He became a bricklayer who, after a successful scrap or two, was advised to go to London to seek his fortune. After some more 'unofficial' set-tos, he took part in his first fight in a ring on 19 March 1849, beating Abe Couch in 13 minutes, the fight having been stopped by the law at Edenbridge and Redhill before taking place at Greenhithe. Sayers began a succession of victories, his only setback coming when middleweight Nat Langham managed to close both his eyes and beat him over 61 rounds in a contest lasting just over two hours.

Sayers was only 5ft 8½in and weighed 152lb, so was usually giving weight away to his opponents. Soon he was forced to tackle the heavyweights to get fights, eventually challenging a claimant to the championship, William Perry, the 'Tipton Slasher', who was five inches taller and over two stone heavier. Sayers won in one hour, 42 minutes. He then beat the other claimant to the title, Tom Paddock, in an hour and 20 minutes.

Sayers' fame had reached the United States, where the champion was John C. Heenan, the 'Benicia Boy'. Backers sent Heenan to England in 1860 to challenge Sayers. Sayers again gave away 5½ inches and over three stone. The fight ended in confusion after two hours and 20 minutes when the ring was invaded, and a draw was announced. It was Sayers' last fight. He died five years later, and has a big memorial in Highgate cemetery.
See also: Sayers v Heenan

TOM SAYERS V JOHN C. HEENAN

17 April 1860, Farnborough Common

Tom Sayers was champion of England with 12 victories behind him. John Camel Heenan, known as the 'Benicia Boy', issued a challenge from America 'for £200 a side and the champion's belt'. Heenan and his entourage boarded the ss *Asia* on 4 January 1860 for Liverpool, backed by a newspaper, the *Spirit of the Times*. He was the third American to set sail for England in an attempt to win the championship.

Press interest in England, America and Europe was immense, yet prize-fighting was illegal. Special trains left London Bridge for the fight at 3.30 a.m., destination unknown by the fans who had bought tickets at £3 each. The Metropolitan Police boarded the trains but after 16 miles they were out of their jurisdiction. On board were statesmen, peers, judges, novelists, journalists, bookmakers, everybody who could afford the fare. The South Eastern Railroad and publicans who sold tickets made nearly £5000 for their night's work.

The destination of the train was Farnborough, Hampshire. At 7.30 a.m. the two principals threw their hats into the ring. Heenan had all the physical advantages. At 27 he was seven years younger, at 6ft 2in he was 5½ inches taller and at 14 stone he was three stone heavier. But Sayers had been used to fighting bigger men and was vastly the more experienced. Heenan had had only one formal ring battle and had lost it after breaking a hand, so his claim to be American champion was not to everybody's liking – in fact his conqueror, John Morrisey, helped Sayers, and backed him. It is estimated that £100,000 was bet on the outcome. Parliament debated its morality, but Queen Victoria insisted on being informed immediately of the result.

The men came up to the scratch line and the battle commenced. Sayers got in the first significant blow, a left which drew blood. But Heenan picked him up and threw him to the ground, falling heavily upon him. Round followed round with Heenan perhaps getting the best of it by using his strength to knock down or throw Sayers, but Sayers was the better hitter, and kept Heenan at bay with powerful punches to the body, neck and head.

In the sixth round Sayers deflected a blow with his right arm and broke a bone. He fought on, but the fracture grew worse and presented a big handicap. However Sayers was nothing if not brave and, with continued shots to Heenan's face, closed his right eye and made a bloody mess of his features. The advantage surged back and forth, and Heenan, in delivering a blow to Sayers' head, broke a bone in his own left hand. For about two hours the two fought for supremacy, Heenan trying to use his physical advantages to throw, maul and generally manhandle his opponent, while Sayers took it all and pumped blows to Heenan's face, attempting to shut his other eye and render him temporarily blind.

The 37th round proved a vital one. The Hampshire constabulary arrived and began to push through the crowd intending to stop the fight. Spectators were pushed forward into the ropes and a general melee ensued. What happened next is confused, but it appears that Heenan grabbed Sayers around the neck and forced his throat against a rope. It would have been legitimate for Sayers' seconds to lower the rope to prevent their man being strangled, but it seems more likely that the rope was cut, perhaps by Sayers' supporters seeing he was in difficulties. With the downing of the ropes and the pushing from the police spectators flooded into the ring and referee Francis Dowling announced a draw.

However, order was soon restored and the time-keeper called upon the men to continue. Five more rounds were fought but, with the constables persistently trying to intervene, the chaos could not be controlled and the fight ended. The crowd returned to London while the principals and their seconds beat a hasty retreat to avoid arrest. The world's greatest prize fight had lasted 2 hours and 20 minutes and covered 42 rounds.

Silversmiths made duplicate belts for the two men, presented at a grand ceremony. They became friends and toured England, giving exhibitions. Sayers became a national hero, with songs praising him sung all over the land. The Irish remarked Heenan's ancestry and praised him, while Heenan was met by 50,000 in a New York park when he finally returned home, and thousands feted him in other cities as he made a tour of honour. The American press, of course, claimed Heenan had been swindled on the point of victory.

It was Sayers' last fight, but Heenan returned to England in 1863 to challenge the new champion, Tom King. King won comparatively easily in 24 rounds lasting 35 minutes. This was Heenan's last battle. Sadly the two principals in the great Farnborough fight were both dead within 13 years, Sayers dying in 1865 and Heenan in 1873.

MAX SCHMELING

born: 28 September 1905, Klein Lukaw, Brandenburg, Germany

Schmeling was a good amateur boxer who turned professional in August 1924 just before his 19th birthday. He had a couple of defeats in his first two years, but in 1926 won the German light-heavyweight title, and the European title the following year. Schmeling won the German heavyweight title in 1928 and went to New York, where he had four impressive wins in 1929 and in June 1930 was matched with Jack Sharkey for the world title vacated by Gene Tunney. Schmeling won the title on a foul in the fourth round, becoming the only man to take the heavyweight championship of the world on a disqualification.

Schmeling was a dark beetle-browed boxer with some resemblance facially to Dempsey. He was a good tactician with a powerful right as his main weapon. This was too much for Young Stribling in his first defence, but in 1932 Sharkey took the title from him on a split decision – many thought the German the victim of a 'home-country' decision. In 1936 Schmeling was one of a succession of ex-champions matched with the new sensation Joe Louis, but Schmeling had worked out a weakness in Louis' technique, and he shocked the boxing world by knocking out Louis and inflicting on him his first defeat. Schmeling's reward should have been a match with James J. Braddock for the world title but, with war in the offing, he was side-stepped and Louis won the title instead.

Louis gave Schmeling an early shot at the title, but at 33 Schmeling could not contain the 24-year-old and was stopped in the first round. During the Second World War Schmeling joined the paratroops, was wounded and decorated for bravery. After an eight-year break, he had five post-war fights, losing two, and retired in 1948. He became a German executive of Coca-Cola. **Record: 70 contests; 56 wins; 4 draws; 10 defeats**

See also: Louis v Schmeling

THE veteran Max Schmeling (left) on his way to knocking out Wermer Vollmer in Frankfurt in 1947.

JACK SHARKEY

born: (Joseph Paul Zukauskas) 26 October 1902, Binghamton, New York, USA

Sharkey's parents were Lithuanian. He never boxed as an amateur and, flat broke, he enlisted for the US Navy in 1920. Punching a bag on board ship gave him the idea of becoming a boxer, and on shore leave in January 1924 he took his first fight, lying about his lack of previous experience, and won on a first-round knockout. In his sixth fight he beat Floyd Johnson, a heavyweight

contender, and began to get talked about. On being told to get a better name on his first engagement, he joined the names of Jack Dempsey, the champion and his idol, with Tom Sharkey, an earlier heavyweight from the navy, and came up with Jack Sharkey. Fans soon called him the 'Boston Gob', a gob being American slang for a sailor. He beat Harry Wills, whom Dempsey had avoided, and became a championship contender himself. He amused the fans with displays of temperament in the ring, even at times crying with

frustration, so that he picked up another nickname, the 'Sobbing Sailor'.

Sharkey was not a big puncher for a heavyweight but was a cagey boxer whose punishing body attacks were often on the borderline. The British heavyweight Phil Scott, known as 'Phainting' Phil, earned his nickname largely because of his inability to rise after Sharkey

JACK SHARKEY, the sailor who won the heavyweight championship.

had hit him low in a heavyweight eliminator in 1930. Controversy and Sharkey walked hand in hand, for in 1927 he had been knocked out by Dempsey, who thus earned a return title fight with Tunney, after Dempsey had punched him low. After winning the American title by beating Tommy Loughran and disposing of Scott, Sharkey was matched with Max Schmeling for the title vacated by Tunney. Sharkey fouled Schmeling in the fourth, and Schmeling's manager was so forcibly voluble that Sharkey was disqualified – surprisingly for the only time in his career. In 1931 he fought a draw with ex-middleweight Mickey Walker and outpointed Primo Carnera to get a return with Schmeling in 1932. He finally won the heavyweight championship, although even here there was a split decision and plenty to say he was lucky.

A year later Sharkey lost the title in his first defence – to Primo Carnera, whom he had previously easily beaten. Again there was a mystery. Sharkey claimed to have seen a vision of Eddie Schaaf, a companion who had died after fighting Carnera, and was knocked out while thus distracted. He subsided after this, losing four of his remaining seven bouts, the last a knockout by the up-and-coming Joe Louis in 1935.
Record: 55 contests; 38 wins; 3 draws; 13 defeats; 1 no-decision

BATTLING SIKI

**born: (Louis Phal) 16 September 1897, St Louis, Senegal
died: 15 December 1925, New York City**

Siki was brought to Paris from the French colony of Senegal as a boy by an actress who took pity on him. He was put to work doing chores like dishwashing in a restaurant, while he learned boxing in a club in Montmartre. At 16 he turned professional. From 1915 he served in the First World War and was decorated for bravery. He continued his boxing afterwards all over Europe and in September

1922 was given a title match with world light-heavyweight champion Georges Carpentier, his idol.

Siki was popular for his unorthodox, whirling style, but was not considered a serious match for Carpentier. A film was to be made of the fight, and it was planned that the fight would look good for six rounds or so whereupon Carpentier would knock out his man and everybody would be happy. It is in dispute, of course, as to who was party to the plan – Carpentier claimed he didn't train properly for this 'arranged' fixture. In the event, Carpentier obviously upset Siki somehow, the fight became real, and a wild Siki got in the deciding blow, knocking out Carpentier in the sixth. Even then the referee tried to right matters for the 'establishment' by considering disqualifying Siki, but was persuaded not to.

Success went to Siki's head. Walking round Paris with a lion cub was not too bad, but defending against Mike McTigue in Dublin during the 'troubles', with rifle-fire not too far away and on St Patrick's Day at that, was a severe error of judgement. McTigue won a 20-round points verdict.

In 1924 Siki transferred his career to the United States with mixed success. In 1925 he was in a street argument in New York, he was shot in the back and his body left in the gutter, just over three years after he won the title.
Record: 94 contests; 64 wins; 5 draws; 25 defeats

SIZE

Tallest

The tallest boxers are believed to be Gogea Mitu of Romania who fought in the 1930s, and Jim Culley, the Tipperary Giant, who fought a decade later. They were both 7ft 4in.

Henry Johnson, a Canadian, who fought in the 1890s, was 7ft 2in, and was called the 'Human Skyscraper'. Ewart Potgeiter, a South African who came to London in 1955, was also 7ft 2in.

All the above were heavyweights. The tallest

men to win the world heavyweight championship were:
6ft 6¼in Jess Willard
6ft 6in Ernie Terrell (WBA)
6ft 5¾in Primo Carnera
6ft 4in John Tate (WBA)
6ft 3½in Larry Holmes (WBC, IBF)
6ft 3in Muhammad Ali
6ft 3in Michael Dokes (WBA)
6ft 3in Tim Witherspoon (WBC, WBA)
6ft 3in Pinklon Thomas (WBC)
6ft 3in Greg Page (WBA)

Shortest

With weights getting lighter and lighter, and more fighters coming from the Far Eastern nations, it is hard to keep track of the shortest boxers. However, here are some world champions in the shake-up:
4ft 11in Netrnoi Vorasingh (WBC light-flyweight)
4ft 11½ Pascual Perez (flyweight)
4ft 11¾in Johnny Coulon (bantamweight)
The shortest world heavyweight champion was Tommy Burns at 5ft 7½ in. Two of the most destructive hitters in the division come next: Rocky Marciano at 5ft 10¼in and Mike Tyson at 5ft 11in. John L. Sullivan, the last bare-knuckle champion, was 5ft 10½ in.

Heaviest

The heaviest boxer is probably Ewart Potgeiter, the South African, who weighed 23st 13lb (335lb).

The heaviest boxers to win the world heavyweight championship are as follows (heaviest weights in a match won):
Primo Carnera, 19st 4lb (270lb)
John Tate (WBA), 17st 2lb (240lb)
Greg Page (WBA), 17st 1½lb (289½lb)
Mike Weaver (WBA) 16st 8lb (232lb)
Jess Willard, 16st 6lb (230lb)
Muhammad Ali, 16st 6lb (230lb)
The greatest combined weight in a heavyweight title bout was 488¾lb: Primo Carnera 259½lb) v Paulino Uzcudun (229¼lb), 22 October 1933, at Rome, Italy.

Next was 472¾lb: Max Baer (209½lb) v Primo Carnera (263¼lb), 14 June 1934, at Madison Square

Garden Bowl, New York.

The greatest weight difference in a world heavyweight title bout was 86lb: Primo Carnera (270lb) v Tommy Loughran (184lb), 1 March 1934, at Miami, Florida.

The greatest weight difference in which the lighter man was the winner in a championship bout was 58lb: Jack Dempsey (187lb) v Jess Willard (245lb), 4 July 1919, at Toledo. These official figures might be false and the true difference nearer 70lb.

The greatest weight difference in any contest was 140lb, when Bob Fitzsimmons (172lb) knocked out Ed Dunkhorst (312lb) in the second round at Brooklyn, New York, on 30 April 1900.

Lightest

There is now a proliferation of sub-flyweight classes. The lightest boxer to win the world flyweight championship was Jimmy Wilde, who weighed six stone 12lb (96lb) in one of his contests, which would make him eligible for the mini-flyweight class today.

The lightest man to win the world heavyweight championship was Bob Fitzsimmons, who weighed only 11st 13lb (167lb) when he beat James J. Corbett on 17 March 1897 at Carson City, Nevada.

Two lighter boxers than Fitzsimmons have challenged for the heavyweight title, the lighter being Charley Mitchell, who weighed only 11st 4lb (158lb) when he challenged James J. Corbett on 25 January 1894 at Jacksonville. The other was Philadelphia Jack O'Brien, who weighed 163½lb when challenging Tommy Burns on 28 November 1906 in Los Angeles. He was, in fact, given a rather lucky draw. Mitchell was below the middleweight limit, and indeed he, Fitzsimmons and O'Brien were all lighter than middleweight champion Stanley Ketchel when he challenged Jack Johnson in 1909.

MUHAMMAD ALI, a magnificent 6ft 3in and 230lb physique.

LEON SPINKS

born: 11 July 1953, St Louis, Missouri

Spinks was a good amateur who was a lance corporal in the US Marines when he completed an Olympic double in 1976 by adding the light-heavyweight gold medal to the middleweight medal won by his brother Michael in the previous contest. He turned professional in January 1977.

After six wins and a draw, Spinks found himself matched in February 1978 with Muhammad Ali for the world heavyweight title. Spinks, to whom nobody gave a chance, astonished fans by producing a frenetic non-stop display which seemed to rush the ageing Ali off his feet. Spinks got the verdict and was the new champion. There was a return clause in the contract which caused the WBC to strip Spinks for his failure to meet their challenger, Ken Norton. Instead Spinks faced Ali again in September 1978 and sanity returned as he was comfortably outpointed.

Spinks' career became somewhat erratic from then on. He was knocked out by Gerrie Coetzee in the first round of his next fight and when, in 1981, he challenged Larry Holmes for the WBC title he was stopped in the third. He retired in 1983 but resumed his career in 1985, without ever threatening to regain the heights of his first years.

Record: 38 contests; 23 wins; 3 draws; 12 defeats

MICHAEL SPINKS

born: 13 July 1956, St Louis, Missouri, USA

Three years younger than his brother Leon, Michael Spinks was taller (6ft 2½in) and lighter. He won the Olympic gold medal at middleweight in the 1976 Olympic Games and turned pro early in 1977. He proved to be a clever boxer who could also mix it and deliver a good punch, and he was immediately successful. In his 17th contest, in July 1981, he won the WBA light-heavyweight title with a

points win over Mustapha Muhammad at Las Vegas. He defended this title five times over the next 15 months and, in November 1982, he outpointed Dwight Muhammad Qawi (formerly Dwight Braxton) at Atlantic City to unify the division.

The busy Spinks defended his undisputed title five times, gaining IBF recognition on the way as their first champion and, having proved himself the best at his weight he relinquished his titles to tackle Larry Holmes for the IBF heavyweight title. Spinks proved too young and fast for Holmes and registered a first defeat for the champion. He also became the first light-heavyweight champion to take a version of the heavyweight crown. Spinks' points victory, and that in the return in April 1986,were both controversial.

Spinks agreed, with the other two heavyweight champions, to take part in the unification of the division, together with others like Mike Tyson, but Spinks decided to relinquish his claim to the title in favour of a big-money match with white hope Gerry Cooney. Spinks won with a fifth-round stoppage in 1987. A year later, still unbeaten, he challenged undisputed heavyweight champion Mike Tyson but fought apprehensively and was knocked out in 91 seconds. He retired. However with Tyson in prison and Foreman and Holmes, both much older than him, given lucrative title fights, he announced in 1992 his intention to make a comeback.
Record: 32 contests; 31 wins; 1 defeat

MICHAEL SPINKS (left) opted out of the heavyweight unification tournament by taking a lucrative contest with Gerry Cooney, whom he stopped early.

JOHN H. STRACEY (left), after losing the world title, was knocked out by Dave 'Boy' Green and had only one more contest.

JOHN H. STRACEY

born: 22 September 1950, Bethnal Green, London

Stracey represented Britain in the Olympics in 1968 when just 18, and was an ABA light-welterweight champion in 1969. He turned professional immediately, retaining an amateur style with his upright stance and straight left. But this and his young-looking face were misleading as he had a devastating punch and rarely let opponents recover when he had them beaten. In 1972 he fought Bobby Arthur for the vacant British welterweight title but suffered his second loss when he was disqualified. He won the title in a return eight months later with a fourth-round knockout.

Stracey took the European title in March 1974 when he stopped Roger Menetrey in Paris and, in December 1975, challenged the great Jose Napoles for the WBC title. The fight took place in Mexico City's 55,000 seat bull ring – the biggest in the world – and, although down in the first round, Stracey recovered to stop Napoles in the sixth. He made one successful defence of this title, against Hedgemon Lewis, before being surprisingly outpointed by Carlos Palomino at Wembley in 1976. Two years later he retired. Of his 45 wins, 37 were by the short route.

Record: 51 contests; 45 wins; 1 draw; 5 defeats

JOHN L. SULLIVAN

born: 15 October 1858, Roxbury, Massachusetts, USA

died: 2 February 1918, Abingdon, Massachusetts, USA

Sullivan's parents came from Ireland: Tralee and Athlone. Sullivan liked boxing from a youngster, for reportedly he played truant to watch the funeral of former champion John C. Heenan in 1873. He became a plumber's labourer and a tinsmith before beginning a fighting career.

Immensely strong he knocked out a local champion who challenged all-comers, and then began to challenge all-comers himself with the famous phrase he would issue in bars: 'I can lick any man in the house'. He was known as the 'Boston Strong Boy', and indeed used to perform strong-man acts like lifting street-cars.

In 1881 he had an important fight on a barge in New York, beating John Flood for a purse of 750 dollars and, in 1882, claimed the 'world championship' by stopping Paddy Ryan in Mississippi City. Ryan was a protégé of Richard K. Fox, the influential publisher of the *New York Police Gazette*, which shaped boxing opinion of the time, and Fox became a great enemy of Sullivan. Another enemy was the

Birmingham boxer Charlie Mitchell, not much more than a middleweight, who was the first man to put Sullivan on the floor. The two heartily disliked each other and, in 1888, fought for £500-a-side at Chantilly, France. After 39 rounds in three hours it was called a draw when the police arrived and arrested them both.

Meanwhile Fox proclaimed Jake Kilrain

world champion and presented him with a belt. Sullivan's Boston fans presented Sullivan with a much grander belt, with 397 diamonds spelling his name and carrying the legend 'Champion of Champions'.

Sullivan faced Kilrain in July 1889 at Richburg, Mississippi. Sullivan had been drinking seriously for years and it was a big effort to get the flabby body fit for this encounter. But it succeeded and, after 75 rounds and over two hours in scorching heat, Kilrain's corner retired him (to save him from being killed it was feared). It was the last great bare-knuckle fight, and Sullivan tossed Fox's Championship belt to a handler as a tip. Sullivan, now famous and immensely popular in areas far removed from Boston, toured the country in a melodrama, 'Honest Hearts and Willing Hands'. He was challenged for his title by James J. Corbett, eight years his junior, and once again had to shed his paunch and get in condition. This time it was once too many and, in 1892, the scientific Corbett outboxed John L. (for Lawrence) and inflicted his first defeat.

Sullivan made a generous speech and left weeping and the crowd booed Corbett. John L. was to fight twice more and in the meantime continued with his dramatic work and vaudeville acts. He had periods on and off the booze and in 1902 went bankrupt. His act enabled him to get out of debt, and one day he had a brainwave and gave up alcohol, becoming a fervent preacher against its evils. A Roman Catholic, he married his long-time companion in 1908, having finally got a divorce from the wife he had married 25 years earlier and had lived with for only a month or so. His second wife died in 1917 and a heartbroken John L. followed her the next year. He was America's first great sporting hero.

Record: 42 contests; 38 wins; 3 draws; 1 defeat

See also: Corbett v Sullivan

WILLIAM THOMPSON

born: 11 October 1811, Nottingham
died: 11 August 1880, Beeston, Notts

Thompson was one of triplets in a family of 21 children. Their mother, a coarse, violent pipe-smoking woman, nicknamed the three Meshack, Shadrack and Abednego. William was Abednego, and became known as Bendigo. When he began prizefighting he became famous all over the country as 'Bold Bendigo'. He was also a good cricketer, prize-winning fisherman and notable acrobat, this last proving useful in the ring at times.

By 1834 Bendigo had won over a dozen top battles and was followed by a bunch of supporters called the 'Nottingham Lambs', who were little more than ruffians. His greatest local rival was Ben Caunt, who was some 5½ inches taller and 45lb heavier than the 5ft 9¼in, 165lb Bendigo. The two met in 1835 when Bendigo, a master of psychological warfare, so taunted Caunt that after 22 rounds Caunt struck Bendigo in the interval, knocking him off his second's knee, and was disqualified. Bendigo continued his winning ways, temporarily blinding one opponent by lifting him up, after 99 rounds, and pile-driving his head into the ground. In 1838 Bendigo faced Caunt again and suffered his only defeat. He was disqualified in the 75th round for going down without being struck.

Bendigo won the Championship of England in 1839 when the holder Deaf Burke was disqualified for butting, an offence under the new London Prize Ring Rules. Bendigo then injured his knee when somersaulting to amuse children and retired, taking to whisky and running a pub. However Caunt won the vacant title, toured America, and came back to taunt and insult Bendigo. Bendigo's strong-willed mother insisted her son fight Caunt again. The fight inspired so much enthusiasm that the law took a close interest and the venue had to be changed three times. It was the dirtiest fight in history with Caunt banging Bendigo's head on the ring posts and throttling him while Bendigo used his acrobatics to get in flying kicks at sensitive parts of Caunt's body. After 93 rounds Caunt dropped without being hit, and Bendigo was declared the winner. However, it was said that Caunt was merely resting while Bendigo recovered and that the referee had been intimated by the 'Nottingham Lambs'. Riots ensued and Caunt was lucky to escape with his life, his carriage being overturned.

Five years later Tom Paddock challenged Bendigo, and Bendigo's mother insisted her son take up the cudgels again. Bendigo did, and beat his 15-years-younger challenger on a foul.

Bendigo's mother died aged 83, and Bendigo speeded up his life of assault and debauchery at the head of his Lambs, constantly in trouble with the law. During his 28th jail sentence he was impressed by the chaplain and afterwards was haunted by a preacher called 'Undaunted Dick', who peered at him through the window as he sat in pubs. One day Bendigo saved a woman from drowning and found Dick watching him like a ghostly conscience. He reformed and began to preach against drink in sermons which became so famous that he toured the whole country. These speeches he learned parrot fashion, as he was illiterate. He fell down his stairs in 1880, breaking three ribs, one of which punctured a lung, and he died, one of the the most colourful of boxing's champions.

DICK TIGER was an exciting fighter who won world titles at two weights but sadly died young.

DICK TIGER

born: (Richard Ihetu) 14 August 1929, Amaigbo, Orlu, Nigeria
died: 14 December 1971, Nigeria

After a short career as an amateur, Tiger turned professional in 1952 and fought for three years in Nigeria, winning the national middleweight title. In December 1955, at 26, he decided to try his luck in England, but lost his first four fights. The first indication that he might have something came when he stopped the promising Terry Downes in 1957. In 1958 he knocked out Pat McAteer to win the British Empire title.

Tiger went to America in 1959, again with mixed results at first, but in 1962 he outpointed Gene Fullmer in San Francisco for the NBA middleweight championship. After a draw in a Las Vegas return and a stoppage of Fullmer in Nigeria, Tiger was recognised by the other bodies as undisputed world champion. He lost the title to Joey Giardello in Atlantic City, but won it back in New York City. Tiger finally lost the middleweight title in 1966 when outpointed by Emile Griffith.

However, in his next contest, Tiger took the undisputed light-heavyweight title from Jose Torres, repeating his points win in the return. He was then 37 but made another successful defence against Roger Rouse, before he lost this title to Bob Foster, the only time in his career he was stopped. He had three more fights, including a win over Nino Benvenuti, a future middleweight champion, before retiring in 1971. The same year he died from cancer back home in Nigeria.

Record: 81 contests; 61 wins; 3 draws; 17 defeats

GENE TUNNEY

born: (James Joseph
Tunney) 25 May 1897, New
York City
died: 7 November 1978,
Greenwich, Connecticut

Gene Tunney was a self-
made, thinking champion.
From a well-off Greenwich
Village family he asked for
boxing gear when he was 11
years old. He studied the
game, boxed as an amateur,
and turned professional at
18. In 1918, after 11
unbeaten contests, he
enlisted in the US Marine
Corps, and won an Allied
Expeditionary Force light-
heavyweight championship
in France, beating 20
opponents in the various
rounds. Back in the States, he
won the American light-
heavyweight title by
outpointing Battling
Levinsky.

In May 1923 came one
of his most significant fights
when he lost his title on
points to Harry Greb, taking
such a bloody battering that
he was in bed for a week.
However, far from being
discouraged, the young
Tunney enlisted the help of
the great lightweight
champion Benny Leonard to
find a way to beat Greb, and
did so in a return in 1923. He
subsequently beat Greb
again, and had the newspaper
verdict over him in two more
no-decision bouts.

Tunney had a fixation on
heavyweight champion Jack
Dempsey, whom he was
convinced he could beat, and
in 1926 was given a chance
to prove it in a title fight in
Philadelphia. In a contest
mostly fought in pouring
rain, Tunney easily
outpointed the plodding
Dempsey over ten rounds to
take the title. There was
immense interest in the
return, the battle of the
famous 'long count', in
which Tunney was down for
14 seconds, but Tunney
clearly won again to end
Dempsey's career.

He fought once more, a
defence against Tom
Heeney, a New Zealander,
and then retired to become a
rich and successful
businessman. He refused all
offers to make a comeback,
the first heavyweight
champion to retire while still
a champion and stay retired.
His defeat against Greb was

his only one but sometimes
Tunney's 'no-decision'
contests are included in his
record of wins and losses,
according to the newspaper
verdict, although there is
great reluctance to make his
losses two despite Tommy
Loughran being said to have
had the best of a contest in
1922.

**Record: 77 contests; 58
wins; 1 draw; 1 defeat; 16
no-decision; 1 no-contest**

See also: Tunney v Dempsey

GENE TUNNEY V JACK DEMPSEY

**23 September 1926,
Philadelphia
22 September 1927,
Chicago**

Heavyweight champions
were not in the habit of
defending their titles twice a
year, or even once a year, in
the days before Joe Louis. In
fact after Jack Dempsey
disposed of Luis Firpo in
September 1923, he did not
defend again for three years
and nine days. In that time he
went to Hollywood, married
a film star and made films
himself. Dempsey had boxed
only exhibitions for over two
years before he next put his
title on the line against Gene
Tunney.

Dempsey was not a
popular champion in his
prime but he had built up
such an aura of toughness
and raw power that, even
after such a long lay-off, few
expected he could lose to
the ex-light-heavyweight Gene
Tunney, who had once been
badly beaten by Harry Greb.
Dempsey was barred from
boxing in New York because
he had pulled out of a contest
with the black challenger
Harry Wills, so the fight
went to the Sesquicentennial
Stadium at Philadelphia,
where the maximum distance
permitted for a bout was ten
rounds. Sadly for the
120,757 who comprised the
biggest paying attendance at
a boxing match, it poured
with rain throughout the
proceedings.

**GENE TUNNEY is
down for the famous
'long count' as
Dempsey stands
poised to attack.**

Tunney boxed better,
kept his feet better and
hardly allowed Dempsey an
opening, to win convincingly
on points. After Dempsey
had re-established himself
with a knockout of Jack
Sharkey, the return took
place a year later, again over
ten rounds at Soldiers Field,
Chicago. Such was the
reputation of Dempsey that
again he was expected to be
the winner. Interest was
enormous and the gate was
the first to exceed $2 million
– to be precise $2,658,660.
This was a record which
stood until inflation-assisted
1976.

The encounter had those
ingredients acknowledged to
make a classic: an out-and-
out unstoppable slugger
against a cool, calculating
boxer.

Tunney outboxed
Dempsey in the first, as the
challenger continually
circled the ring looking for
an opening, but not finding
one. In the second round,
however, Dempsey landed a
crunching left hook to
Tunney's head, followed by
a left to the body. But
Tunney was unhurt and
resumed his immaculate
boxing. In the fourth Tunney
landed a right to the eye
which drew blood and
followed up by battering
Dempsey round the ring.
Dempsey was dazed and
Tunney was ready to take
him in the fifth, but Dempsey
resumed as strong as ever.

After six rounds Tunney
was well ahead on points,
and Dempsey had been
warned as his punches got
more and more careless.

The seventh round is

possibly the most famous in
boxing, its incidents
examined and argued over
for years. The first minute
followed the pattern of
previous rounds, with
Tunney skilfully countering
Dempsey's rushes with
clinical hitting. Then
Dempsey caught Tunney
with a right counter and, as
the champion stepped
backwards towards the
ropes, Dempsey came
charging in like a bull, and
lashed a long left to
Tunney's jaw. This was
followed by a deadly right
and another left which sent
Tunney sliding down the
ropes. As he went, three
more lightning blows
crashed into Tunney, who
knew nothing of them. He
was out for a second or two.

Tunney quickly
recovered and grabbed the
middle rope with his left
hand. Dempsey then made
the mistake of standing over
Tunney in his usual manner
waiting for him to get up.
Referee Dave Barry moved
to take up the count, but first
motioned Dempsey to move
away from Tunney and go to
a neutral corner. Dempsey at
first ignored Barry and then
headed towards the wrong
corner. Barry only took up
the count when he was
satisfied that Dempsey was
properly positioned.

Meanwhile Tunney's
head cleared in time for him
to hear the count reach 'two'
and he rose when the referee
said 'nine'. Dempsey rushed
forward while Tunney
circled to his right. Tunney
dodged eight or nine wild
swings. Dempsey at last
stood in the centre of the ring

and beckoned Tunney in.
Tunney remained relaxed
and, as Dempsey missed
again, hit him with three
rights. Dempsey said later
that the first punch was the
hardest he received, and took
his breath away.

Tunney in the eighth
dropped a tired Dempsey
with a right to the chin and
harried him to the end of the
round. Tunney continued his
boxing through the last two
rounds and emerged an easy
winner.

There were violent
objections from Dempsey's
corner after the fight, which
became known as the 'Battle
of the Long Count'. There
was no doubt that all the
rules were obeyed correctly,
and indeed it was Dempsey's
behaviour in the Firpo fight
three years previously which
made boxing commissions
determined to enforce the
rule whereby a boxer must
retreat to a neutral corner
when his opponent is down.
Dempsey was reminded of
this rule in the pre-fight
instructions.

Tunney was estimated to
have been given at least a 14-
second rest. Many point to
his glassy eyes when he hit
the canvas and say that he
would never have beaten the
count and indeed Tunney has
said that he was unaware of
what was happening as he hit
the deck. But he has also said
that he could have risen
earlier, and pointed out that
he was entitled to stay on the
canvas as long as he was
allowed. And it was
Dempsey who declined a
third meeting between the
two.

RANDOLPH TURPIN

born: 7 June 1928, Leamington, Warwickshire
died: 17 May 1966, Leamington, Warwickshire

Turpin's black father died when Turpin was nine months old, and he and his two brothers and two sisters were brought up in hard times by their white mother.

Bronchitis as a child gave him the incentive to develop his body and he began boxing at 12. He became a bully and his first wife was to sue him for assault. He was by then a cook in the navy with ABA titles at both welter and middleweight. He turned professional in 1946 and outpointed Vince Hawkins, the British middleweight champion in 1948, when Randy was still not old enough to fight for a British title. But that year he was stopped by Jean Stock after claiming no interest in the fight on hearing that his wife had been given custody of his son. It was the first indication that Turpin's emotional frame of mind would have a big influence on the way he fought.

Turpin's brother Dick became the first black boxer to win a British title when the BBBC colour bar was broken, but Dick lost his middleweight title to Albert Finch in 1950. Six months later Randy won it back for the family and in 1951 added the European title with a 48-second knockout of Luc Van Dam.

In July 1971 came Turpin's biggest night, when he inflicted the first defeat in 91 contests on Sugar Ray Robinson to take the world middleweight title. Turpin was an unorthodox boxer, who planted his feet wide apart and often used a low stance. He had a long reach and could deliver knockout blows with a single punch of either hand. He held the title for only 64 days, losing it to Robinson in New York when the referee stopped the contest with Turpin helpless on the ropes with eight seconds of the tenth round remaining. Robinson, badly cut, had launched a do-or-die assault which succeeded.

Turpin was never so good again. An assault charge by an American showgirl arising out of this visit to New York, subsequent marriage problems and financial difficulties centred on tax demands undermined his desire. Turpin did, however, win six of eight further title fights. He won the British and Empire light-heavyweight title from Don Cockell, who later fought Rocky Marciano. He won the British Empire middleweight title from George Angelo. He was never to lose any of his British or Empire titles in the ring. But, in a very substandard display, he failed on points when tackling Carl Bobo Olson in New York for the vacant world middleweight title. He ran into his former American girlfriend on this trip and was arrested and charged with assault and rape, subsequently settled out of court. Later he was stopped in the first round when challenged by Tiberio Mitri for his European title in Rome. Neither Olson nor Mitri would have beaten him at his best.

A knockout by Yolande Pompey in 1958 convinced Turpin he should retire, but after nearly five years of inactivity he made a comeback with two wins before retiring again. He had been unlucky financially with the failure of a hotel and income tax demands were pressing again. He took up wrestling, worked in his manager's scrapyard and finally took a transport cafe to support his wife and four daughters. A compulsory purchase order was served on this, and in 1966 Turpin shot himself in the bedroom above the cafe.

Record: 75 contests; 67 wins; 8 defeats

See also: Turpin v Robinson

RANDOLPH TURPIN after exercising to make the weight for a contest with Charles Humez.

RANDOLPH TURPIN V SUGAR RAY ROBINSON

10 July 1951, London
12 September 1951, New York

Sugar Ray Robinson was not only the man many claim to be the best pound-for-pound fighter ever, he was also a flamboyant character. His trip to Europe after he won the middleweight title in 1951 took on the flavour of a royal tour. His entourage included sisters, manager, wife, trainers, secretary, court jester (a dwarf) and hairdresser. He drove round in an extended pink Cadillac and, with the top back, waved to the crowd and accepted their respects. Unlike royalty, though, Robinson did a little work on the way to pay the expenses, and took on opponents in Paris, Zurich, Antwerp, Liège, Berlin and Turin. When he got to London he took on Randolph Turpin, the young British champion, with his middleweight crown at stake.

Turpin was a much better boxer than Robinson expected. But the 18,000 British fans who packed the Exhibition Hall at Earls Court did not really expect him to beat the legend. Opinions began to change early on as Turpin's spearing straight left, launched from a low crouching stance, continually found Robinson's face. Robinson's flicks fell short and, when he did get in his famed uppercut, it had no effect on Turpin. Turpin manhandled Robinson in the clinches and was obviously the stronger man.

Halfway through the fight Robinson tired under the pressure. His left eye was split and he was reduced to desperate assaults in search of a lucky punch and a knockout. Turpin just continued to punish Robinson and, at the end of the 14th round the crowd cheered throughout the interval and sang 'for he's a jolly good fellow'.

This sounded strangely on the radio commentary which, famously, got the whole thing wrong as the two experienced commentators described what they had

expected to see rather than what was happening. It was a measure of the Robinson charisma and the unlikelihood of the beating which the 23-year-old Briton was giving him. The fans cheered throughout the final round and continued after the formality of the verdict. It was one of the most exciting nights in British boxing. Turpin received a civic reception back home, while Robinson's consolation was the return clause in the contract.

The two met again only 64 days later at the Polo Grounds, New York, where a record crowd for a non-heavyweight title fight of 61,437 turned out to see if the old master could regain his crown from the new young sensation.

After Robinson caught Turpin with a good right in the second round, Turpin went on the defensive and allowed Robinson to dictate the pace. It was a cagey decision because, after seven rounds, Robinson began to look tired as he had in the first contest. The stronger champion took over in the eighth and clearly won the round, as he did the ninth. He was fast catching up and was level on the referee's score-card, just behind on the two judges.

Early in the tenth Turpin landed a long right to Robinson's eye and the blood started to flow. It was probably his biggest mistake. Robinson felt the blood and knew his chances of regaining the title were rapidly going. He rushed in to Turpin and cracked home a right to the chin that forced the champion to hang on. Robinson got free and desperately launched a two-fisted attack. Finally a right got home and Turpin was spread-eagled on the canvas. However Turpin was up at 'nine' and retreated to the ropes as Robinson made his big effort to finish the fight before the end of the round. He might not be allowed another.

Robinson piled everything he could into Turpin, who rode much of it and then doubled up in a crouch. Robinson switched downstairs and tried to straighten Turpin up with vicious punches into the body. Turpin snapped himself upright and the assault continued to the head. Turpin took several other punches and then looked as if he would pitch to the floor. Referee Ruby Goldstein stepped in to shield him and waved the fight over.

But Turpin did not go down and was far from helpless or senseless as he weaved to avoid the blows. There were only eight seconds of the round left and, had he lasted it, he would still have had a chance to win, with Robinson injured the worst. He protested bitterly. Perhaps he should have gone down and taken the nine seconds rest.

Nothing could detract, though, from the performance of Robinson who, like a true champion, had snatched victory from the brink of defeat.

TURPIN gets home to Robinson's body on his way to the title in the most exciting night ever in Earl's Court.

MIKE TYSON

Born: 30 June 1966, Brooklyn, New York, USA

Mike Tyson was brought up in Brownsville, a tough area of New York. Immensely strong for his age, he first realised his power when he was ten years old, beating up an older boy who had killed one of his pigeons. He rapidly became a mugger and before he was 13 was living at the Tryon School, a reformatory for troubled juveniles. He was introduced to Cus d'Amato, trainer of world champions, and d'Amato, seeing the potential in the over-strength boy, developed a relationship with him that led to d'Amato becoming Tyson's legal guardian and mentor.

SWEAT drops off a happy-looking Mike Tyson.

Tyson became an amateur boxer but was disappointed at not making the 1984 Olympic team when outboxed twice by Henry Tillman. In March 1985 he turned professional, earning $500 for his first fight, a first-round knockout of Hector Mercedes. Tyson then proceeded to sweep through the heavyweight ranks so that in his first year he disposed of 18 opponents, all by knockout or stoppage. He had boxed only 34 rounds – less than two rounds per opponent.

Tyson, at only 5ft 11in and 218lb, was not tall for a heavyweight. His most obvious physical characteristic is a 19¾in neck, making his shoulders look as if they start to form just behind his ears. His main asset as a fighter, apart from his obviously devastating punching, was his hand speed. Tyson needed only half an opening and his fists were wreaking havoc.

By now d'Amato had died, but Tyson had two managers in Bill Cayton and Jim Jacobs who seemed well able to keep the young battler on the path to the heavyweight championship which d'Amato had confidently predicted for his protégé. The heavyweight division had become a joke, with three bodies proclaiming rapidly changing champions, and around 1985 a plan had been drawn up by promoter Don King, who controlled most of the top heavies, and HBO television, to rationalise the division and produce an undisputed champion by 1987. Tyson's instant success was such that he had to be incorporated into the shoot-out.

In November 1986 in Las Vegas, as part of this rationalisation programme, Tyson challenged Trevor Berbick, the WBC champion. Berbick, unwilling to go on the defensive against the young upstart, took the fight to Tyson, but was so staggered by a left hook in the first round that there was no going back. In the second a punch temporarily froze Berbick, who then reeled backwards, fell, groped his way up, reeled across the ring, fell, rose and reeled back again, like a child learning to walk in a playpen. He was incapable of carrying on. Tyson was 20 years, four months and 23 days old, the youngest-ever heavyweight champion.

Tyson disposed of the WBA champion James 'Bonecrusher' Smith, who became the third man to last the distance with him by going on the defensive until the last 30 seconds of the contest, and unified the title in August 1987 by outpointing Tony Tucker, who had won the vacant IBF title by stopping James 'Buster' Douglas. The previous champion, the unbeaten Michael Spinks, had wisely opted out of the unification tournament altogether. Tyson beat Tyrell Biggs and the comebacking Larry Holmes, but then his world began to fall apart.

Tyson's girlfriend, Robin Givens, allegedly pregnant, married him in February 1988, and immediately had a difference of opinion with Cayton over Tyson's contract. Jim Jacobs died of leukaemia days later. Don King attended the funeral and began to persuade Tyson to switch allegiance to him. Tyson and his wife, who was backed by her mother, began to row publicly. Soon Tyson dropped manager Cayton then, after a difference with Givens, crashed his Bentley, giving it to the investigating police officers (who were later disciplined). He seemed to suffer when his wife had a miscarriage.

In the ring Tyson at last caught up with Spinks and destroyed him in 91 seconds. Cayton won a compromise in court and remained his manager but Tyson's private life got worse. Tyson drove another car into a tree – there were suggestions of a suicide attempt which, true or not, at least demonstrated the turmoil of his life. His wife humiliated him by describing him as 'scary' on national television and then sued for divorce after a violent domestic incident.

At last it all showed professionally. Tyson sacked

his cornerman and mentor Kevin Rooney. He was less impressive than usual in allowing Frank Bruno to reach the fifth round, withdrew from a fight with Razor Ruddock and then went to Tokyo to meet Buster Douglas. Tyson was a shadow of his former self and was knocked out in the tenth. Although Tyson was knowledgable about boxing history and tradition, he then demeaned himself by appearing to support Don King in a disgusting attempt to get the verdict reversed or annulled on the grounds of an allegedly long count granted Douglas in the eighth round.

Tyson came back with wins over Henry Tillman, Alex Stewart and Razor Ruddock twice and a fight was fixed with champion Evander Holyfield. This fight was not to take place. Tyson's cavalier treatment of women had been the subject of talk before, and now two women brought cases against him, the more serious being for rape. In February 1992 Tyson was convicted and sent to prison. It seemed the career of one of the all-time great heavyweights might well have been self-destructed at 25.

Record: 42 contests; 41 wins; 1 defeat

See also: Douglas v Tyson

TYSON drops Razor Ruddock to the canvas. Tyson beat Ruddock twice between losing his title and losing his court case when charged with rape.

UPSETS

What constitutes an upset is, of course, largely a matter of opinion. And what is a great upset at the time can look to be fairly routine with the benefit of hindsight. Who could now be surprised that James J. Corbett beat John L. Sullivan in 1892 – one hundred years later he looks a good bet. But it came as a terrible shock to many at the time.

America's *Boxing Illustrated* listed the 15 greatest upsets in boxing history in their May 1990 issue. They were, in order of shock:

1. James Buster Douglas beating Mike Tyson on a tenth-round knockout for the world heavyweight championship in Tokyo, Japan, on 10 February 1990. Tyson was considered unbeatable at the time, already, at 23, an all-time great. Douglas was a journeyman. Who could tell that Tyson might have private emotions to get him in a turmoil?

2. Max Schmeling's 12th round knockout of Joe Louis on 19 June 1936 in New York. Schmeling was an ex-heavyweight champion, but Louis was the most complete fighting machine ever seen, marching unbeaten towards the title. This was a great performance by Schmeling on the day, which did not in fact interrupt Louis's march to his destiny.

3. James J. Braddock's points win over champion Max Baer to claim the heavyweight crown on 13 June 1935 at the Long Island Bowl, New York. Braddock was at the fag end of a disappointing career, not so much a has-been as a never-was, while super-confident Baer was reckoned to be the hardest puncher for years. Max took it too easy.

4. Cassius Clay's victory over Sonny Liston, who retired on his stool after seven rounds to give Clay the world heavyweight championship on 25 February 1964 at Miami Beach. Clay, who of course soon became Ali, a surprise winner? At the time Clay was thought to be a boy whistling in the dark, while Liston was regarded as the evil king at last risen to his throne to give his challengers and audience an appointment with fear. Clay brought the curtain down on this pantomime.

5. James J. Corbett's 21st round knockout of John L. Sullivan to become the first world heavyweight champion. Nobody could imagine the great John L. beaten, but Corbett ushered boxing into a new era where Sullivan's strength and bombast counted little against the new science.

6. Fritzie Zivic's points win over welterweight champion Henry Armstrong at New York on 4 October 1940. Armstrong was a recent world champion at three weights, but the clockwork that kept Mr Perpetual Motion going for 40 fights in the previous three years finally decided to run down a little and Fritzie bloodily took his chance.

7. Billy Papke's 12th round knockout of Stanley Ketchel to take his middleweight title on 7 September 1908 at Los Angeles. Ketchel was regarded as strong enough a year later to challenge the great heavyweight champion Jack Johnson. Some might say this fight doesn't count because Papke tricked Ketchel to get an unfair advantage, but it still shook the fans almost as much as Ketchel.

8. Randolph Turpin's points win over Sugar Ray Robinson to win the middleweight title on 10 July 1951 in London. Robinson was in his prime, unbeaten for years and regarded as the greatest all-round artist the ring had seen. Small wonder that the fans, many of whom had never heard of Randy Turpin before, were stunned when Robinson was trounced.

9. Jess Willard's 26th round knockout of Jack Johnson on 5 April 1915 at Havana, Cuba, to win the heavyweight title. Johnson was much bigger than just a boxer to white Americans, he was a threat to a whole way of life and seemed immovable. Had anybody beaten him it would have been a shock, but it was a mega-shock when the unco-ordinated cowboy did it. Johnson always claimed it was a fix to get him off the hook of prison, and many believed him as it provided an authentic explanation, but in truth he was a 37-year-old who'd been leading the easy life for five years, while Willard was as tough as rock. In the blazing heat, why shouldn't Johnson be glad of a lie down after 25 rounds?

10. Battling Siki's sixth round knockout of Georges Carpentier to win the world light-heavyweight title in Paris on 24 September 1922. One side or both believed this contest to be fixed for Carpentier to look good in a film being made of it. But somehow Carpentier upset Siki who wouldn't play any more and took matters into his own hands.

11. Leon Spinks' points win to take Muhammad Ali's world heavyweight title in Las Vegas on 18 February 1978. It was Spinks eighth fight only. The great Ali was already the 'greatest'. Did he lose it only in order to create a record by winning it back a third time? Was he lethargic and surprised by Spinks' frenetic pace? Or was Spinks at a peak that night while Ali's mind was temporarily elsewhere? This is one of the few shocks which is still fairly difficult to understand.

12. Eugene Criqui's sixth round knockout of Johnny Kilbane to win the featherweight title on 2 June 1923 in New York. Kilbane had had no difficulty holding the featherweight title for over 11 years, but Frenchman Criqui was no mug and was coming off a run of 21 knockouts in 22 straight wins. Kilbane was 34 and didn't fight again.

13. Muhammad Ali's eighth-round knockout of George Foreman on 30 October 1974, at Kinshasa, Zaire to regain the heavyweight title after seven years. That last phrase is the key to why the great Ali was a surprise winner. He was now 32 and in his absence from the big time the powerful George Foreman had knocked the world's heavyweights all over the place, including, in the case of former champion Joe Frazier, up in the air. Those who feared for Ali lived to wonder about his amazing Houdini powers.

14. Michael Spinks' points win over Larry Holmes to win the IBF heavyweight championship at Las Vegas on 20 September 1985. The surprise here was that never in boxing history had the light-heavyweight champion moved up to take the top crown, despite many tries. But Holmes *was* nearly 36, and might have retired happily unbeaten had he not had Rocky Marciano's 49 unbeaten contests dazzling his vision. This was to be the fight in which Holmes equalled it . . .

15. Ingemar Johansson's

MUHAMMAD ALI'S defeats of Liston and Foreman were both great upsets.

third round stoppage of Floyd Patterson on 26 June 1959 in New York to take his heavyweight title. Johansson was Swedish, he'd been thrown out of the Olympic Games final for not trying, forfeiting his silver medal, he trained with his girl friend. Enough said, but Ingo's Bingo had the last word.

VENUES

The most famous venue for world title fights is Madison Square Garden, New York. However, there have been four separate stadiums under the name.

The original Madison Square contained a railroad freight shed which, after serving its purpose, was leased by B.T. Barnum, the famous showman. Barnum built a wooden arena and opened his Hippodrome in 1874. In winter he put on boxing 'exhibitions'. When William Vanderbilt reclaimed the property in 1879 he found a new name for it, Madison Square Garden, and a star to pull in the crowds in John L.

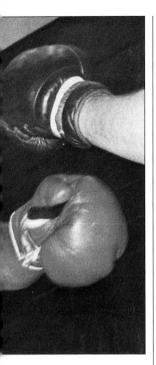

Sullivan. He packed the stadium when fighting the Britons Tug Wilson and Charley Mitchell. But genuine boxing was illegal and when police broke up a Sullivan-Paddy Ryan match in 1885 after one minute, before 11,000 customers, the place was doomed. It was demolished in 1889.

A magnificent new Madison Square Garden arose nearby on an old baseball field and covered a block bounded by Madison and Fourth Avenues. Amid its shows and other events it employed James J. Corbett to take on three opponents in one night in a boxing 'exhibition', but real prize-fighting was still forbidden in New York. Corbett won the world title – but in New Orleans. In 1908 the building passed into the hands of real estate and insurance companies, who kept proposing to turn it into offices, but bowed to public pressure not to.

Then along came Tex Rickard, successful boxing promoter. He leased the Garden and, in 1916, staged a contest between champion Jess Willard and Frank Moran. It was a 'no-decision' contest, but Moran could take the title with a knockout. It drew $152,000, the biggest gate in the Garden's history till then, and gave it a new lease of life. Jack Dempsey defended his title there. But, in 1924, the insurance company

decided to demolish the Garden and build an office block, so Tex Rickard raised capital to build a new arena, on the location of an old trolley barn on Eighth Avenue between 49th and 50th streets. Although it was many blocks away from Madison Square, Rickard kept the name of Madison Square Garden for his new showplace.

This was the most famous Madison Square Garden, where Joe Louis, Harry Greb, Sugar Ray Robinson, Henry Armstrong, Emile Griffith, Muhammad Ali and other great champions fought. Rickard died in 1929 but other promoters like James J. Johnston and Mike Jacobs carried on the work.

In 1960 the president of the Garden, Irving Mitchell Felt, announced the construction of a fourth Garden, above Penn Station, at 33rd Street between Seventh and Eighth Avenues. It would cost $120 million and embrace sports, offices, theatres, exhibitions etc. The new, fourth, Garden opened in 1968 and in 1971 staged the 'fight of the century' between unbeaten heavyweight champions Muhammad Ali and Joe Frazier.

But boxing diminished in the Garden, with the management concentrating on other entertainments in the face of competition from Las Vegas. The average attendance at its secondary Felt Forum arena dropped to below 750. But there has been a revival in the late 1980s, and Sugar Ray Leonard particularly wanted to fight there, such is the charisma of the name. In 1992 the new Paramount arena which replaced the Felt Forum began a schedule of regular fights again.

At the turn of the century San Francisco was a hub of boxing, and a large structure that looked like a barn but was called the Mechanics Pavilion was called the 'Madison Square Garden of the West'. James J. Jeffries made three of his heavyweight defences here. The earthquake and subsequent fire of 1906 destroyed the Mechanics Pavilion and Woodward's Pavilion, another boxing site.

That left the Mission Street Arena in nearby Colma, built by Jim Coffroth for the Battling Nelson – Jimmy Britt fight for the 'white lightweight title' in 1905. Colma became an important fight venue, the highlight of its era being the heavyweight title fight between Jack Johnson and middleweight champion Stanley Ketchel. It was also a good venue for Battling Nelson, who twice beat Joe Gans there to confirm himself as lightweight champion.

Big outdoor contests like heavyweight championship bouts were held from the 1930s in the Yankee Stadium in New York and from the 1940s also in the Polo Grounds, but from the mid-1970s Las Vegas took over as the main venue, with another gambling centre, Atlantic City, in competition.

Boxing matches are the best events to attract big spenders to the casinos. The casinos pay huge site fees for the big matches which they recoup because they keep anything up to 20 per cent of the money gambled by the fans who stay there. A big fight can increase their takings by over 50 per cent, or several million dollars over the week. Caesars Palace paid over $7 million for the privilege of staging the Hagler-Leonard middleweight fight, but the tourist turnover in Las Vegas for the week was estimated at $350 million.

Caesars Palace led the way in the boxing boom in Vegas, but the Hilton and Mirage are putting up competition.

In Britain, popular London centres in the early days of the century were Wonderland and The Ring. Wonderland was in Whitechapel Road in the East End and flourished under the control of matchmaker Harry Jacobs. Heavyweight champion of the world Tommy Burns defended his title there in 1908, but unfortunately the building was burned down in 1911. The Ring, an octagonal building in Blackfriars Road, promoted two or three boxing shows a week from 1910 and was a popular venue in the years around the First World War. It was staging a revival when the

Second World War arrived and it was destroyed by bombing.

The National Sporting Club was a powerful influence on boxing, and a great venue for British title fights, which the club controlled. It was founded in Covent Garden in 1891. There was a unique atmosphere as contests took place after dinner, with members and guests in dinner jackets. Talking and applause were forbidden during the rounds. At a benefit night for its co-founder A.F. 'Peggy' Bettinson in 1914 boxers on the bill included one-time world champions in Jim Driscoll, Jimmy Wilde, Ted 'Kid' Lewis, Georges Carpentier and Kid McCoy, as well as Digger Stanley and the great Sam Langford. The NSC was really the forerunner of the British Boxing Board of Control.

Wembley Arena, when known as the Empire Pool, staged the world title fight between Benny Lynch and Small Montana in 1937, and since the 1950s such champions as Terry Downes, John Conteh, Barry McGuigan and Emile Griffith have fought there, and Marvin Hagler beat Alan Minter for the world middleweight title there in 1980. Wembley Stadium drew 50,000 attendances for pre-war contests featuring such boxers as Len Harvey and Jack Petersen.

White City Stadium in West London staged some magnificent title fights in the 1930s and boasted the British record attendance in 1939 when Len Harvey and Jock McAvoy fought for the world light-heavyweight title before 82,000 spectators. After the war Freddie Mills regained the title for Britain at the White City when he beat Gus Lesnevich in 1948. The venue was later sold for development.

In the north of England, Liverpool Stadium staged fights from 1911 to 1985, although there were two buildings, the original one being forced to close in 1931. Favourite local fighters who packed them in were Nel Tarleton, Peter Kane and Ernie Roderick, but it had its share of shock results and was known as the 'graveyard

of champions'.

In Glasgow, the Kelvin Hall staged some great nights for Jim Watt's world title contests around 1980 and the King's Hall, Belfast performed the same function for the rising star Barry McGuigan.

PANCHO VILLA

born: (Francisco Guilledo) 1 August 1901, Iloilo, Philippines
died: 14 July 1925, San Francisco, California, USA

Villa took the name of the famous Mexican revolutionary as his ring name after picking up the taste for boxing at the US base in Manila. After turning professional in 1919 his first 54 bouts were in Manila, only two of which were losses, one on a foul. After winning the local flyweight and bantam titles he moved to New York in 1922.

Although only 5ft 1in, Villa was a tireless, all-action fighter who packed a knockout punch, and he soon became popular in the States for his exciting style. In only his eighth fight there he stopped Johnny Buff to become American champion, although Frankie Genaro took this title from him in 1923. In June of that year promoter Tex Rickard persuaded Jimmy Wilde to travel to New York to put the world title at stake against Villa, although Wilde had in fact retired two years earlier. Villa won with a seventh-round knockout. He then cashed in on the title, fighting 25 times in the next two years, including four successful defences of the world title, the last one back in Manila. His next fight was in Oakland in July 1925 against Jimmy McLarnin, an up-and-coming youngster who was to become world welterweight champion eight years later. Villa had a wisdom tooth removed the day before the bout and took considerable punishment to the jaw in a points defeat. More teeth were removed next day but Villa was forced to have a further operation and on 14 July died of blood poisoning from his ulcerated jaw.

Record: 105 contests; 88 wins; 5 draws; 9 loses; 3 no-decision

JERSEY JOE WALCOTT

born: (Arnold Raymond Cream) 31 January 1914, Merchantville, New Jersey, USA

Walcott's was one of those careers that began in such obscurity that its early days remain a mystery. Underprivileged but strong, he began boxing professionally at 16, his first recorded fight being in September 1930, although he claims there were earlier bouts. He did not think 'Cream' was a good name for a boxer so took the name of Joe Walcott, the 'Barbados Demon' and one time welterweight champion, to whom he bore a striking facial resemblance. He added 'Jersey', his state, to differentiate him from the old champ. Following his first bout there is a gap on his record till 1933 and another with no bouts traced for 1934. He was reasonably successful but, by 1941, he had lost eight contests in 34 and been knocked out by the two best known heavyweights he'd faced, Al Ettore and Abe Simon. He called it a day and took work in a soup factory as a steadier way to support his wife and six children.

However in 1945 a promoter in Camden persuaded him with $500 to top the bill for the opening of a new stadium. He was then 31, but he won and then took other fights. Throughout his career he had been box-office poison with his negative tactics aimed primarily at avoiding punishment. This proved an advantage when he was chosen as a safe opponent for Joe Louis to take on in New York in one of the exhibitions the long-reigning champion was giving at this time. Nobody wanted to see Walcott, so Louis decided to put his title on the line to provide some gate appeal. In December 1947 Walcott put up a great show against Louis, and it was only by courtesy of the two judges, who disagreed with the referee and just about everybody else in the stadium (including probably Louis), that Louis kept the title on a split decision.

Walcott had a good payday, and another the following year when Louis knocked him out in the return and, moreover, he was established as a contender. When Louis retired, he fought Ezzard Charles for the vacant title, but was outpointed. In 1951 he had another chance, and was outpointed again. But in July of that year he successfully took his fifth chance of the title by knocking out Charles in the seventh round. Walcott was 37½, the oldest man to become heavyweight champion.

Walcott was now coining the money, and he outpointed Charles again in a return a year later. In September 1952 he was beating the young Rocky Marciano until Marciano caught him in the 13th and knocked him out. Walcott had one more payday, a first-round knockout by Marciano in September 1953, when he was nearer 40 than 39. He retired but did not return to the soup factory. He was prosperous, became a referee, was mayor of Camden, and helped the New Jersey police fight juvenile delinquency.

Record: 69 contests; 50 wins; 1 draw; 18 defeats

See also: Marciano v Walcott

LEFT: Jersey Joe Walcott, 37-year-old champion

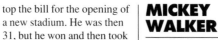

MICKEY WALKER

born: 13 July 1901, Elizabeth, New Jersey, USA
died: 28 April 1981, Freehold, New Jersey, USA

Walker's mother wanted a girl, and would arrange his hair in curls, so he became a scrapper at an early age. Sacked for fighting in an architect's office, he turned professional. His actual forenames were Edward Patrick and the 'Mickey' probably came because of his Irish ancestry. Because of a pug nose and his aggression and determination, he was called the 'Toy Bulldog'.

He began as a welter, most of his fights in his first two years being in his native Elizabeth. In 1921 he fought Jack Britton, the world champion, in Newark, but could not knock him out in a

MICKEY WALKER, the 'Toy Bulldog'.

'no-decision' match. In November 1922, however, he outpointed him in New York to become world champion. Strangely, he had lost four and won only two of his previous seven bouts. Walker held the title until May 1926, when he was outpointed by Pete Latzo. By then he was having weight trouble, and had already challenged Mike McTigue for the light-heavyweight crown (no-decision) and Harry Greb for the middleweight crown (lost on points). After the Greb bout, according to legend, the two briefly fought again outside a restaurant in the small hours. Although historians are sceptical, Walker was still able to describe this second encounter in an interview with Pete Heller 45 years later.

Walker won the world middleweight title from Tiger Flowers in December 1926. After two defences, including a knockout victory over British champion

Tommy Milligan in London, he challenged Tommy Loughran for the light-heavyweight title. He was outpointed.

Walker, who was only 5ft 7in, was among the hardest hitting of all middleweights. After another defence he relinquished his title in 1931 to tackle the heavyweights, seemingly a foolhardy decision. However he had already beaten Jimmy Risko twice, and Bearcat Wright, who weighed 20 stone. He drew with Jack Sharkey who was soon to win the world title, and beat King Levinsky and Paulino Uzcudun. He then had a terrific battle with ex-champion Max Schmeling, but was knocked out. He failed to outpoint Maxie Rosenbloom for the light-heavyweight title, although he beat him later. In retirement he earned some renown as a painter.
Record: 163 contests; 94 wins; 4 draws; 19 defeats; 45 no-decision; 1 no-contest

JIM WATT

born: 18 July 1948, Glasgow, Scotland

Jim Watt, a southpaw, began boxing professionally at 20, and apart from one cut-eye defeat, quickly avenged, he proceeded smoothly to contest the British lightweight title vacated by Ken Buchanan, but was stopped on another cut eye by Willie Reilly in Nottingham in 1972. Watt took the title soon afterwards by stopping Tony Riley, but, then fellow-Scot Buchanan took it back in Glasgow. Watt had to wait for Buchanan to relinquish the title again before he could claim it for a second time by stopping Johnny Cheshire in 1975. He failed to win the Commonwealth title in Lagos and in 1977 relinquished the British title, being unwilling to meet Charlie Nash in Northern Ireland. He soon won the vacant European title with a first-round cut-eye stoppage of Andre Holyk in Glasgow. He defended this three times before, in 1979, becoming WBC champion by stopping Alfredo Pitalua in Glasgow to take the title vacated by Roberto Duran.

Watt proved to be a brave, intelligent fighter with a good defence and a hard punch. His world title win began a series of great nights in Glasgow. He defended it successfully against Roberto Vasquez, Charlie Nash,

JIM WATT celebrates after a title defeat of Charlie Nash.

Howard Davis and Sean O'Grady. It is remarkable that of Watt's 16 title fights, 11 were stopped, usually because of cuts, and his defence against O'Grady was marred by the terrible cut O'Grady received to his head. Watt's last defence was in June 1981 when he fought at Wembley and was well outpointed by Alexis Arguello. He retired immediately but kept in the public eye as a television expert at the big fights.
Record: 46 contests; 38 wins; 8 defeats

WEIGHT DIVISIONS

In the earliest days of the prize ring there were not weight divisions – there was just the one champion. Around the 1850s the concept of a 'light' weight arose, and was quickly followed by 'middle' weight. These three divisions sufficed for a long time, although there was no formal recognition of them or agreement about the actual weights they embraced. Champions decided the weight at which they would accept challenges to suit themselves. Even when other

weights were invented, e.g. featherweight, and had acknowledged champions, there was still no agreement on the actual weights. For example, when Bob Fitzsimmons won the middleweight championship in 1891 he was quite happy to increase the limit to 158lb.

Standardisation came about in 1909 when the National Sporting Club decided on eight weight limits as follows:

Heavyweight above 12st 7lb (175lb)
Cruiserweight Not above 12st 7lb (175lb)
Middleweight Not above 11 stone (154lb)
Welterweight Not above 10st 2lb (142lb)
Lightweight Not above 9st 7lb (133lb)
Featherweight Not above 8st 10lb (122lb)
Bantamweight Not above 8st (112lb)
Flyweight Not above 7st 7lb (105lb)

There was soon agreement on the weights from America, except that they called the cruiserweight class 'light-heavy'. There had been such a category in America since 1903, and in fact British-born Bob Fitzsimmons (then weighing 168lb) had won it in its first year. Britain stuck to 'cruiserweight' until after the Second World War, when the BBBC agreed to adopt the American name. In 1979 a new cruiserweight division was introduced in America between heavyweight and light-heavyweight.

Gradually, other weights were added, although as late as 1968 there were still only the original eight divisions in British professional boxing. Also the weight limits increased. Nowadays there are 17 generally recognised weight divisions. With the proliferation of ruling bodies sanctioning world title fights, additional confusion arose in that sometimes they didn't agree on the weight limit (in particular the WBC raised the cruiserweight limit to 195lb in 1982). They also called the divisions by different names, for example the division between welterweight and middleweight is called either super-welterweight (the style of the WBC) or junior

middleweight (the style of the WBA and IBF). In this book we have called the division light-middleweight, following the system used in 1903 for light-heavyweights, the exceptions being the super-middleweight class (to avoid light-light-heavyweight) and the super-featherweight class (to avoid light-lightweight). This style is favoured by the British and Europeans.

The current 17 weight divisions and their limits, together with the year of the first world championship contest at the weight, are as follows:

Heavyweight Above 13st 8lb (190lb) : 1892
Cruiserweight Up to 13st 8lb (190lb) : 1979
Light-heavyweight Up to 12st 7lb (175lb) : 1903
Super-middleweight Up to 12st (168lb) : 1984
Middleweight Up to 11st 6lb (160lb) : 1891
Light-middleweight Up to 11st (154lb) : 1962
Welterweight Up to 10st 7lb (147lb) : 1892
Light-welterweight Up to 10st (140lb) : 1926
Lightweight Up to 9st 9lb (135lb) : 1896
Super-featherweight Up to 9st 4lb (130lb) : 1921
Featherweight Up to 9st (126lb) : 1890
Light featherweight Up to 8st 10lb (122lb) : 1922
Bantamweight Up to 8st 6lb (118lb) : 1892
Light bantamweight Up to 8st 3lb (115lb) : 1980
Flyweight Up to 8st (112lb) : 1913
Light-flyweight Up to 7st 10lb (108lb) : 1975
Mini-flyweight Up to 7st 7lb (105lb) : 1987

Some of these 'intermediate' weight divisions have not been in continuous use. In particular, the first light-featherweight champion in 1921, Jack Kid Wolfe, forfeited recognition through failure to make the weight without defending, and the division fell into disuse for over 50 years, being revived in 1976.

There were smaller gaps in the super-featherweight division between 1933 and 1949, and between 1951 and 1959; and in the light-welterweight division between 1935 and 1946, and between 1946 and 1959.

FREDDIE WELSH

born: (Frederick Hall Thomas) 5 March 1886, Pontypridd, Wales
died: 29 July 1927, New York, USA

Welsh went to America at 16 and worked in a sports shop, developing an interest in physical culture and then boxing. He was not robust, but cultivated an impregnable defence, and became a destructive in-fighter. In 1905, when he turned professional, he took the name Welsh to prevent his mother discovering what he was doing. In five years of boxing in the US, Wales and England he suffered only one defeat in 65 fights. He then took the British lightweight title from Johnny Summers in London. He beat Abe Attell, the world featherweight champion, but was carefully avoided by successive lightweight champions in Joe Gans, Battling Nelson and Ad Wolgast. In 1914, however, Willie Ritchie, whom Welsh had already beaten nearly three years earlier, was persuaded by a big fee that left hardly anything over for Welsh to put the title on the line in London. Welsh won a close decision. Many of Welsh's defences were of the 'no-decision' kind, including two against Benny Leonard. He did beat Ad Wolgast twice and Charley White, however.

When it seemed Welsh might go on forever he lost his title to Benny Leonard, who stopped him in the ninth round of a bout in New York to claim the crown. It was the only time Welsh was stopped in a career of 168 bouts. Welsh served as a captain in the US Army in the First World War, helping rehabilitate veterans at the Walter Reed Hospital. He resumed boxing in 1920, but a loss in 1922 persuaded him to give up. Continuing his interest in physical culture, he sank his money into a health farm which failed and he was penniless when he died five years later.

Record: 168 contests; 76 wins; 7 draws; 4 defeats; 81 no-decision

PERNELL WHITAKER

born: 2 January 1964, Norfolk, USA

Whitaker was an outstanding amateur who at the Los Angeles Olympics in 1984 won the lightweight gold medal with 5–0 margins in all his contests except the final, where his opponent retired. He turned professional in November and, in his 12th contest, won the vacant North American lightweight title with a points win over Roger Mayweather in his native Norfolk.

An outstanding boxer and a master of defensive ringcraft Whitaker is known as 'Sweet Pea' for his sweet moves. Sometimes he is outrageous and, in the win over Mayweather, was knocked down while playacting. In 1988 he challenged Jose Luis Ramirez for the WBC lightweight title and was outpointed in Paris in what was generally regarded as a perverse decision. A year later, in March 1989, Whitaker won the IBF version of the title with a points win at Hampton over Greg Haugen.

In August Whitaker gained revenge over Ramirez in Norfolk and became both IBF and WBC champion. In 1990 Whitaker continued to see off all-comers including the outstanding featherweight champion Azumah Nelson, who was unable to make any impression on the elusive Whitaker. In August, in Stateline, Whitaker knocked out in the first round the WBA champion Juan Nazario to unify the division. One of Whitaker's hardest contests in 1991 was with the European champion, Spain's Poli Diaz, but he was so superior to the world's lightweights that he again fought a featherweight, Jorge Paez, whom he outpointed in Reno.

Although still able to make the lightweight limit, Whitaker was forced to move up a division for competition. In his third contest at light-welter he outclassed Rafael Pineda in Barranquilla to take the IBF championship.

Record: 31 contests; 30 wins; 1 defeat

PERNELL WHITAKER stopping world title challenger Louis Lomeli in 1989.

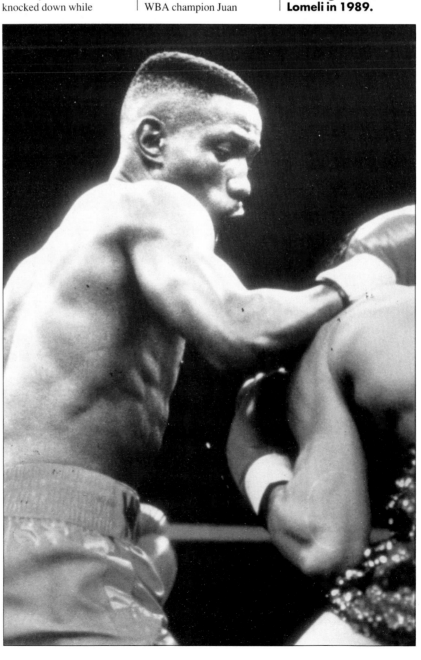

WHITE HOPE ERA

When John L. Sullivan challenged all-comers in 1892 for what became the heavyweight championship of the world, he made one exception. 'I will not fight a negro,' he said. The next four champions followed his lead and did not put their titles on the line against a black man.

Blacks were emerging from slavery but were far from free. They were kept very much in their place. They were tolerated as boxers but the heavyweight champion of the world was a man who transcended boxing. He was a symbol. He represented the physical peak of the world. To have a black man in that position was something that white society could not contemplate.

From the last days of the 19th century there were several outstanding black boxers who might have won the heavyweight championship but, by 1908, one man's chance was clear. He was Jack Johnson, a man who had been beaten five times in 77 contests, a man with the skill and power to succeed. The champion was Tommy Burns, a Canadian, who had gone on a tour of Europe and Australia to cash in on his title. Johnson followed him to Australia, and won the title.

From then on a search was made throughout America to find a 'White Hope' to beat Johnson. The middleweight champion Stanley Ketchel was given a try but stood no chance. The man in whom most hope was invested was James J. Jeffries, a former champion who had retired undefeated in 1904. Jack London, the famous writer, had written a report of the Burns-Johnson fight for the *New York Herald*, which finished with a plea to Jeffries. 'Jim Jeffries must emerge from his alfalfa farm and remove the golden smile from Jack Johnson's face. Jeff, it's up to you', wrote London.

Jeffries was reluctantly persuaded from his farm to fight Johnson in 1910. He was, very predictably, beaten – although the result was a tremendous shock to white America. There were savage riots for days and the search for a White Hope redoubled.

Among the men from whom it was hoped a challenger would emerge were Luther McCarty, a giant cowboy, Carl Morris, Tom Cowler, Fred Fulton, Arthur Pelkey, Gunboat Smith, Frank Morant, Al Palzer and Jess Willard, another huge cowboy.

Meanwhile Johnson infuriated the whites with his arrogance and his style of life, which included relationships with white women. His second wife Etta Duryea, who was white, committed suicide, and Johnson rapidly replaced her with a 19-year-old white mistress, Lucille Cameron. In 1912 Johnson accepted an offer from a Las Vegas syndicate to defend his title against 'Fireman' Jim Flynn, who had previously lost to Tommy Burns. Johnson easily disposed of Flynn.

Lucille Cameron's mother then charged Johnson with abducting her daughter across a state border for immoral purposes, an offence under the Mann Act. But Lucille, who later married Johnson, would not co-operate. Instead a white prostitute, Belle Schreiber, with whom Johnson had had a long-standing relationship, agreed to help the authorities convict him of the same offence regarding her. Johnson was sentenced to a year in prison, but fled the country while on bail.

Finally 21-year-old Luther McCarty emerged as the big hope to topple Johnson. He beat all the other contenders except Pelkey and called himself the white champion. Tommy Burns invited him to test this claim by meeting Pelkey in his new arena in Calgary, Alberta. They fought on 24 May 1913 for the 'white heavyweight championship'. Unfortunately McCarty collapsed after a light punch in the first round and never regained consciousness. The autopsy revealed that he had fought with a broken collarbone, and had neck injuries resulting from a recent fall from a stumbling horse, which he had not revealed before the match. A distressed Pelkey never won another match.

Gunboat Smith knocked out Pelkey on 1 June 1914 to become the White Hope heavyweight champion. In July Smith lost the white championship to Georges Carpentier in London. As Carpentier spent the next few years fighting the Germans in the First World War, the white heavyweight championship sank into oblivion.

At the outbreak of the war Johnson had fled from Paris, where he had twice defended his title and generally lived a full life, and gone to Buenos Aires. Promoter Jack Curley met him there and persuaded him to defend against Jess Willard. Johnson maintained that the most attractive part of the deal was Curley's promise that if he lost he would get a Federal pardon and be allowed back into the States.

Johnson was knocked out in the 26th round. There are still two views as to whether or not he lost deliberately, despite subsequent affidavits. Johnson did not get his pardon and served his sentence. The days of the White Hope were over.

It wasn't until 1936 that another black man got a chance to win the heavyweight title. Joe Louis was groomed not to show any delight in defeating white opponents, and took care that Johnson was not allowed into his training quarters. It was not until the Second World War that the white supremacists finally gave in.

JIMMY WILDE

born: 15 May 1892, Tylorstown, Glamorgan, Wales
died: 10 March 1969, Cardiff, Wales

Wilde began boxing in the booths around the mining area where he started work at 12. He nearly lost his right leg after a mining accident but, after getting married at 17, he returned to the booths to supplement his mining wages. Although in those days he scaled only 6 stone 6 pounds, his work in the narrow seams of the pit had developed great strength in his shoulders, and he packed a tremendous punch. He was called the 'Tylorstown Terror' and won a match in Glasgow styled as for the 'seven-stone championship of Britain'.

Wilde was only 5ft 2½in and looked boyish. His first recorded professional fight took place in February 1911. In 1913 Wilde left the mines. In March 1914 he fought Eugene Husson in London for the vacant European flyweight title and won on a sixth-round knockout. After two defences he lost the title in 1915 to the Scottish flyweight Tancy Lee, with the vacant British title also at stake. Percy Jones having forfeited recognition for the world title, being overweight for a match with Joe Symonds, some authorities claimed the fight was also for the world title. Wilde, who had been suffering from flu, was stopped in the 17th round.

In February 1916, Wilde challenged Joe Symonds, who had beaten Lee, for the British and world titles. The fight was stopped in Wilde's favour in the 12th. After three defences that same year, including a stoppage of Tancy Lee, from whom he won back the European title, Wilde was challenged by Young Zulu Kid, who was sent over from America. Wilde knocked out the Kid in the 11th round.

Wilde suffered his fourth defeat (he lost twice as a 19-year-old in 1911) against Memphis Pal Moore in 1918. At the time Wilde was a physical training instructor in the Army, and the contest was described as for the Inter-Allied Bantamweight title, over three rounds. The decision met with so much disapproval it nearly caused a riot. Seven months later Wilde outpointed Moore over 20 rounds. In 1919 Wilde went to America and had 11 contests, winning six with the others 'no-decision'.

The beginning of the end came for Wilde in 1921, when he agreed to meet Pete Herman for the American's world bantamweight championship. However, in the meantime, Herman lost his world title to Joe Lynch – a man Wilde had already beaten. Wilde claimed he had been tricked, especially when Herman weighed in early for the match and would not do so again just before the fight, a precaution

ABOVE: Jimmy Wilde.

Wilde had had put into the contract to prevent him giving away too much weight. It is estimated that, at the time of the fight, Herman was 8st 9lb, to Wilde's 7st 1lb. Wilde refused to fight, and was only persuaded to do so because the Prince of Wales was at the ringside. Even so Wilde was ahead at 15 rounds, but he was stopped in the 17th of a 20-rounder.

Wilde had a strange style of boxing with his hands low. He was adept at darting in and out quickly, punching with great power but not being there when the opponent tried to counter. The best of his many nicknames was the 'Ghost with a Hammer in his Hand'. After the beating by Herman, Wilde wanted to retire. However in 1923, when he had not fought for 2½ years, Wilde was persuaded by a huge purse offered by Tex Rickard to return to New York and defend his world title against Pancho Villa. Again he was unfortunate, this time with a vital refereeing decision. Having dropped his hands at the bell to end round 2, he was knocked out by a late blow from Villa. Wilde claimed not to remember the rest of the fight, but fought on to the seventh, when he was knocked out again, taking hours to come round and weeks to recover.

He retired, and became a manager, referee and promoter and wrote a newspaper column for many years.
Record: 153 contests; 132 wins; 2 draws; 6 defeats; 13 no-decision

JESS WILLARD

born: 29 December 1881, Pottawatomie County, Kansas, USA
died: 15 December 1965, Los Angeles, USA

Jess Willard, the 'Pottawatomie Giant' stood 6ft 6¼in and weighed for his contests anything from 16 stone up to 18 stone. He worked on a ranch before becoming a professional boxer and as he liked wearing the usual Western clothes he was also known as the 'Giant Cowboy'. He had his first professional fight in February 1911 when he was already in his 30th year. With an 83-inch reach he was hard to beat, and he had plenty of wins by stoppages, but was outpointed by Gunboat Smith in 1913.

When the search for a 'white hope' to beat the heavyweight champion Jack Johnson was proving fruitless, promoter Jack Curley thought Willard worth a try. In April 1915 Willard challenged Johnson in Havana over 45 rounds. There have been explanations for the surprising result of this fight. Johnson maintained later that he lost (a) for money and (b) because he had been promised he could re-enter the States as an ex-champion without having to serve a sentence given him years before for an offence against the Mann Act. It appeared that Willard survived the attacks of Johnson early on and that under the hot sun, the 37-year-old Johnson, probably out of condition, tired and was knocked out in the 26th round.

Willard became the white man's hero, but he was not a charismatic or even a natural fighter. He defended successfully once, but at 37 himself was mercilessly beaten by the young Jack Dempsey in July 1919. Down seven times in the first round, Willard showed tremendous bravery to last through the third round, but could not come out again. His purse was $100,000 and he could be heard muttering to himself: 'I have $100,000 and a farm' over and over again as consolation. A knockout by Luis Firpo in a 1923 comeback ended his career.
Record: 35 contests; 24 wins; 1 draw; 6 defeats; 4 no-contest

IKE WILLIAMS

born: 2 August 1923, Brunswick, Georgia, USA

Williams (first name Isiah) began boxing as an amateur when he was 15 and quickly won some inter-city titles. He turned professional in 1940 and with his defensive ringcraft and crisp punching he soon built up an impressive list of victories. There were many good lightweights around at the time, including Sammy Angott, who left the division in confusion when he retired as champion in 1942, but

then made a comeback.

Williams' chances of the title took a dive when he was hammered by Bob Montgomery and knocked out in the 12th round in 1944. However later that year Williams beat Angott, who had regained and since lost the NBA title, and in 1945 he knocked out Juan Zarita, who had succeeded Angott, to become NBA title-holder. Williams

defended the title in Cardiff against the British champion, Ronnie James, and then, in a grudge fight in 1946, he unified the world title by knocking out the New York title holder Bob Montgomery in the sixth round in Philadelphia.

Williams put the division back on an even keel by successfully defending five times. He was twice outpointed by Kid Gavilan,

the welterweight champion, in 1949 and was experiencing difficulty with the lightweight limit when he lost his title to Jimmy Carter on a 14th round stoppage in 1951. He retired in 1955.
Record: 153 contests; 124 wins; 5 draws; 24 defeats

IKE WILLIAMS came back from a beating to become champion.

WINS AND DEFEATS

The question of how many wins a boxer has recorded is complicated by the 'no-decision' matches fought in the USA around the First World War, when boxing was legal in some states only if verdicts were not rendered. In such matches a knockout would go into each boxer's record as a win or defeat accordingly, and other matches as 'no-decision'. However, the press would give their decisions on a match and these press decisions carried enough weight for bets to be decided upon them. In some cases *The Ring Record Book*, the authority on results of the day, registered the newspaper verdict, thus causing confusion. Further confusion is added by researchers converting 'no-decisions' into results and finding records of more bouts than previously recorded for a fighter, so records tend to be amended as time goes on.

The boxer credited with most wins in a career is Young Stribling. Stribling, born in Bainbridge, Georgia, USA, on 26 December 1904, fought from 1921 to 1933, when he was killed in a motor cycle accident. His first names were William Lawrence. The high spot of his career was when he challenged Max Schmeling for the world heavyweight title in July 1931. Stribling had 286 contests, taking part at times in over 30 a year. He registered 222 wins, a record.

Maxie Rosenbloom (born 6 September 1904, New York) was world light-heavyweight champion from 1930 to 1934, and from 1923 to 1939 he recorded 210 wins. Without 'no-decision' bouts his total would have been higher. Remarkably only 18 of these opponents were stopped. Five were won on fouls and 187 on points, which must be a record in itself.

Archie Moore had 199 wins between 1936 and 1963, and Sugar Ray Robinson 174 between 1940 and 1965.

The most consecutive wins is credited to a Spanish boxer, Pedro Carrasco (born 11 July 1943, Huelva) who was WBC lightweight champion for three months in 1971–72. He won 83 consecutive contests between April 1964 and September 1970, losing his record when boxing a draw.

Whereas 'no-decision' bouts hamper runs of consecutive wins they help unbeaten runs.

The longest unbeaten run is recognised as 97, recorded by the Irish American lightweight Packey McFarland, who remained unbeaten from a defeat in 1904 aged 16 to his retirement in 1915. In fact McFarland lost only once in his career of 104 bouts, of which he won 64 and drew five. The other 34 were 'no-decision' contests.

The longest unbeaten run without the aid of 'no-decision' contests is 93 by Pedro Carrasco (see above). He was unbeaten from March 1964 until he won the WBC lightweight championship in November 1971. His run ended on his first defence in February 1972, when he was outpointed by Mando Ramos.

Sugar Ray Robinson was unbeaten in 90 contests between February 1943 and July 1951, when he lost his world middleweight title to Randolph Turpin. This included two draws. The figure is often given as 91 but a match in Berlin was declared 'no-contest' and should not count.

When Nino Benvenuti lost to Ki-Soo Kim on 25 June 1966 it ended a run of 185 contests without defeat by the 1960 Olympic Games welterweight gold medalist: his last 120 as an amateur and his first 65 as a professional.

Hal Bagwell, a lightweight from Gloucester, was undefeated in 183 matches between 15 August 1938 and 29 November 1948, but as most of these contests were wartime ones their status is questionable.

Among amateur boxers, the Englishman Harold Mallin, who won the Olympic Games gold medal at middleweight in both 1920 and 1924, was unbeaten in over 300 contests.

Defeats

Four world champions are credited with having completed their careers without a single defeat in their record.

Rocky Marciano, world heavyweight champion from September 1952 to September 1955, retired with the perfect record of 49 contests, 49 wins.

Terry Marsh, IBF light-welterweight champion from 4 March 1987 to 2 February 1988, retired with a record of 27 contests, 26 wins, 1 draw.

Jimmy Barry (born 7 March 1870, Chicago), who was an American claimant to the bantamweight championship in the 1890s, retired in 1899 with a record of 70 bouts, 59 wins, 9 draws, 2 no-decision.

Jack McAuliffe (born 24 March 1866, Cork, Ireland) who fought in New York and was a claimant for the world lightweight championship in the 1880s and 1890s, retired in 1897 with a record of 36 bouts, 31 wins and 5 draws. However, this record was preserved only by his supporters breaking up a fight with the English champion Jem Carney, who had the fight won in the 74th round when the ring was invaded and the referee awarded McAuliffe a draw.

The most defeats in a career are the 146 believed to have been suffered by Arnold Sheppard of the USA between 1926 and 1939, although boxers defeated this often do not keep records like winners, and confirmed 'opponents' have been known to travel around America boxing under a variety of names and usually losing.

Of world champions, the most defeats were suffered by Fritzie Zivic, the world welterweight champion in 1940–41. He lost 65 contests out of 230 between 1931 and 1949.

Other world champions to lose over 50 contests are Johnny Dundee (feather and super featherweight) 56 out of 330 bouts (and he would have had more defeats but for 32 'no-decision' bouts), Lauro Salas (lightweight) 52 out of 148, and Johnny Jadick (light-welterweight) 51 out of 140.

The boxer with the worst percentage of defeats to bouts among world champions is Joey Archibald (featherweight), 44 out of 106 (39 per cent).

The most defeats suffered by a world heavyweight champion is the 25 out of 122 of Ezzard Charles.

The worst percentage of defeats to bouts among the heavyweight champions is the 23 defeats in 86 contests suffered by James J. Braddock (27 per cent). However, 11 of Braddock's bouts were no-decision and two no-contest, so the percentage of his defeats to bouts decided is 32 per cent.

HOWARD WINSTONE

born: 15 April 1939, Merthyr Tydfil, Wales

Howard Winstone lost the tops of three fingers of his right hand in an accident with a machine when he was a youngster. He was determined to be a great boxer, so he developed one of the best lefts in the history of the game. A brilliant amateur, he had a great year in 1958 when he won the ABA and Commonwealth Games bantamweight titles. He turned pro as a featherweight in February 1959 and, after 24 straight wins, took the British title from Terry Spinks, who retired in the tenth. In 1963, after three defences, Winstone added the European title by stopping Alberto Serti in the 14th in Porthcawl.

Although Winstone had no trouble with British and European opponents, it was a different story when he challenged Vicente Saldivar for the undisputed world title in London in 1965. He tried to outpunch the strong Saldivar and lost on points after Saldivar got right on top in the closing rounds. At Cardiff two years later Winstone used all his boxing skill against Saldivar but again lost the narrowest of decisions. Four months later Winstone went to Mexico City to try again, but this time was forced to retire at the end of the 12th with a badly cut eye. Saldivar had his measure, but the two men remained firm friends. Saldivar surprisingly retired and in January 1968 Winstone was able to realise his dream and become world champion when he stopped Mitsunori Seki in the ninth round in London. This was the WBC title, but he lost it six months later when stopped by Jose Legra in Porthcawl, and retired, relinquishing the British title he had held for nearly eight years.

Record: 67 contests; 61 wins; 6 defeats

HOWARD WINSTONE (right) and Vicente Saldivar at Earl's Court, 1965. Half of Winstone's six defeats were at the hands of the great Saldivar in world title fights.

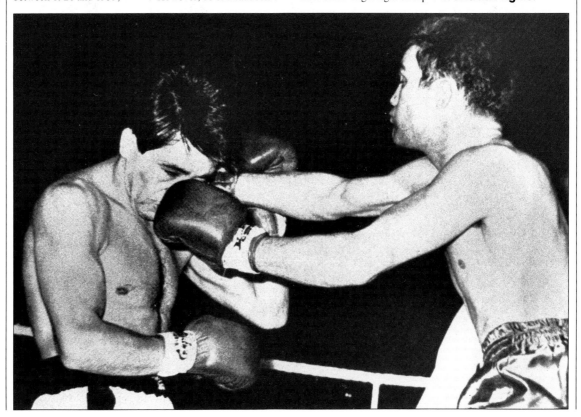

AD WOLGAST V JOE RIVERS

4 July 1912, Vernon, California
28 January 1914, Milwaukee

Ad Wolgast was one of the toughest lightweights of his era. Born in Cadillac, Michigan, in 1888, he fought with such ferocity that he was called the 'Cadillac Bearcat'. His only equal in ferocity was Battling Nelson from whom Wolgast won the world title in 1910. It was scheduled as a fight to a finish, and Wolgast was declared winner when the referee decided in the 40th round that a snarling but blood-masked Nelson should not take any further battering.

In 1912 Wolgast faced a challenge from 19-year-old Mexican Joe Rivers (real name Joe Ybarra), a former featherweight moving up a division. In the light of what followed, it was as well that the contest was refereed by his own favourite official, Jack Welch. Welch refereed many famous fights of the time and was known to tolerate a certain amount of roughness. Champions often had their own pet ref.

Rivers was a good, fast puncher who cut Wolgast on his ear and near his eye and, although Wolgast fought back in his own rough style, Rivers edged ahead. As the bout developed, a rough and tumble took shape and, in the 11th round they managed almost to wrestle each other out of the ring.

The event which singles this fight out occurred in the 13th round. By then Wolgast had taken the more punishment and indeed looked as if he might not come out for the round. As the two mauled in the centre of the ring, Rivers delivered a perfect right to Wolgast's chin. At the same time Wolgast fired a powerful left to Rivers' groin, a not unusual shot in his locker. The blows landed more or less together and both men crumpled to the floor. Wolgast landed on top of Rivers, with both looking as if they might not get up.

At this point, referee Welch began to count, but as he did so he helped Wolgast to his feet and stood holding him up with one arm while beating the count over Rivers with the other. Rivers scrambled to his haunches and knelt on one knee while he clutched his groin and protested he'd been fouled. Welch reached 'ten', raised the groggy Wolgast's arm, and got away from the vicinity as quickly as he could.

A twist to the tale is that the time-keeper, and several witnesses confirmed it, asserted afterwards that the bell had rung before the count-out, so it is possible to look at the outcome in three ways: Rivers was knocked out, which is what the record books say; both men were knocked out; or neither man was knocked out, as both were saved by the bell.

Welch's explanation of his actions, given much later, was that Rivers was down first, so he counted over him, and there was no reason why he should not remove Wolgast from the scene and prop him up.

Strangely Wolgast lost his title in similar circumstances on his next defence. Wolgast was winning in the 16th round against Willie Ritchie when a wild swing caught him flush on the jaw. Wolgast dropped to his knees but, before subsiding onto the canvas completely, he drove two blows at Ritchie's groin. Wolgast was disqualified. The following year Rivers and Wolgast met again over ten rounds in a no-decision contest.

Sadly Wolgast, who had 138 mostly tough contests between 1906 and 1920, lost his memory soon afterwards and in 1927 was committed to an asylum for the insane. He suffered from the hallucination that he was to meet Joe Gans, the legendary champion of 1902 to 1908, for the lightweight title, and he spent his time training and preparing accordingly. Gans had actually died in 1910. Wolgast lived to 1935 and his most regular visitor in the asylum was Mexican Joe Rivers.

WORLD CHAMPIONSHIP FACTS

The boxers who have taken part in the most world title fights are:

27 Joe Louis (heavyweight)
25 Henry Armstrong (featherweight, lightweight, welterweight, middleweight)
25 Muhammad Ali (heavyweight)
24 Larry Holmes (heavyweight)
23 Manuel Ortiz (bantamweight)
22 Emile Griffith (welterweight, light-middleweight, middleweight)

The boxers who have made the most successful defences in one division are:

25 Joe Louis (heavyweight)
20 Larry Holmes (heavyweight)
19 Henry Armstrong (welterweight)
19 Muhammad Ali (heavyweight)
19 Eusebio Pedroza (featherweight)
19 Kaosai Galaxy (light-bantamweight)
19 Manuel Ortiz (bantamweight, in two spells)

The boxers with the longest reign as world champions are:

Heavyweight Joe Louis, 11 years 252 days (22 June 1937 to 1 March 1949) : 25 successful defences
Light-heavyweight Archie Moore, 9 years 55 days (17 December 1952 to 10 February 1962) : 9 successful defences
Middleweight Tommy Ryan, 9 years 285 days (24 October 1898 to 5 August 1907) : 4 successful defences
Welterweight Red Cochrane, 4 years 187 days (29 July 1941 to 1 February 1946). Because of the Second World War Cochrane did not defend until he lost the title on the first defence. After him is Jose Napoles, 4 years 185 days (4 June 1971 to 6 December 1975) : 10 successful defences
Lightweight Benny Leonard, 7 years 260 days (28 May 1917 to 15 January 1925) : 7 successful defences
Featherweight Johnny Kilbane, 11 years 103 days (22 February 1912 to 2 June 1923): 10 successful defences
Bantamweight Panama Al Brown, 5 years 348 days (18 June 1929 to 1 June 1935) : 9 successful defences
Flyweight Jimmy Wilde, 7 years 125 days (14 February 1916 to 18 June 1923) : 4

successful defences

The boxers with the shortest reign as world champions are:

Heavyweight Greg Page, 150 days (1 December 1984 to 29 April 1985). Ken Norton was proclaimed champion by the WBC on 29 March 1978, but lost the title on his first defence 72 days later on 9 June 1978. He is not usually recognised as a champion, never having won the title in the ring.
Light-heavyweight Bob Goodwin, 23 days (1 March 1933 to 24 March 1933)
Middleweight Randolph Turpin, 64 days (10 July 1951 to 12 September 1951)
Welterweight Johnny Bratton, 65 days (14 March 1951 to 18 May 1951)
Lightweight Erubey Carmona, 56 days (15 September 1972 to 10 November 1972)
Featherweight Dave Sullivan, 46 days (26 September 1898 to 11 November 1972)
Bantamweight Takuya Muguruma, 56 days (29 March 1987 to 24 May 1987)
Flyweight Emile Pladner, 47 days (2 March 1929 to 18 April 1929)

The world champions who had the most contests during their career were:
Heavyweight Ezzard Charles, 122
Light-heavyweight Maxie Rosenbloom, 289
Middleweight Harry Greb, 294
Welterweight Jack Britton, 327
Lightweight Benny Leonard, 210
Featherweight Johnny Dundee, 330
Bantamweight Kid Williams, 204
Flyweight Valentin Angelmann, 176

TONY ZALE

born: (Anthony Florian Zaleski) 29 May 1913, Gary, Indiana, USA

Zale joined an amateur club as a youth and had 95 amateur bouts (won 50) while he built up his muscles in the steel mills. He turned professional at 21 in June 1934 and by the end of the year had had 21 contests, the last three of which he lost. He lost interest and had only six fights in the next 2½ years. He was now a middleweight, as hard as the steel he helped manufacture, and he began putting together some wins including, in January 1940, a defeat of Al Hostak, the NBA middleweight champion. It earned him a title shot and in July Zale won a hard-hitting fight when Hostak retired in the 13th round. After two defences, Zale unified the division when he outpointed the New York champion Georgie Abrams in November 1941. In Zale's only contest in 1942 he failed to give the weight to heavyweight contender Billy Conn and lost the decision. Zale then served in the US Navy and his title was frozen until 1946, when he found the nine-years-younger Rocky Graziano was a challenger. After half-a-dozen warm-up fights Zale beat Graziano in September 1946 with a sixth-round knockout. This was an outstanding contest which forced a rematch in July 1947, the result being an equally exciting sixth-round stoppage win for Graziano. Zale won the rubber match a year later, but the two men's names will be forever linked by these fights. Zale fought only once more, losing his title three months later to Marcel Cerdan on a 12th round stoppage in Jersey City in 1948.
Record: 87 contests; 67 wins; 2 draws; 18 defeats

See also: Zale v Graziano

TONY ZALE V ROCKY GRAZIANO

27 September 1946, New York
16 July 1947, Chicago
10 June 1948, Newark

After the Second World War many of boxing's world titles had been held for a few years. The middleweight title was one. Tony Zale the 'Man of Steel' had won the title in 1941 and had fought only once again before 1946. After six warm-up bouts in 1946 the 33-year-old Zale was ready to face Rocky Graziano, a charismatic 24-year-old challenger whose career hadn't even begun when Zale won the championship. The two were to have three fierce battles which linked their names forever in boxing history.

The two men were equally tough but in opposite ways. Zale was clean-living, durable, stolid, unflappable, whereas Graziano was an ex-delinquent, excitable and reckless with never a thought of giving best to anybody, and never happier than when swapping punches. Zale, a counter-puncher, loved boxers who came at him and Graziano knew nothing else. It promised to be a bloody encounter and 30,000 poured through the gates of the Yankee Stadium to see the mutual slaughter.

They were not disappointed. Graziano poured himself at Zale from the bell but Zale speared fierce counters to the ribs and halfway through he decked the challenger for a count of four. But Graziano rose and by the end of the round was bombarding Zale who staggered under the attack. The pattern was set.

In the second round Graziano continued his non-stop assault and punched Zale all round the ring, splitting his lip before dropping him with a succession of rights to the head. The bell came to Zale's rescue as the count reached 'three', and Zale's handlers had to help him back to his corner. The surprise of the third round was that Zale survived the constant battering Graziano gave him. The surprise of the fourth round was that Zale began to fight back. Body punches at last forced the challenger backwards. It was becoming a great fight.

In the fifth round Zale continued to press with savage body punches, but halfway through the round Graziano leaped in and drove Zale back with lefts and rights to the head, and the round ended with Zale groggily hanging on. Both men had taken plenty of punishment but Graziano hurled himself into the attack again at the start of the sixth and Zale was groggy again. But Zale crashed over a right

which sank into Graziano's body under his heart and a following left hook put him down on his haunches, where he couldn't get his breath to rise. Graziano was knocked out for the first time in his career, with the title in his grasp. He was furious. After such a see-saw battle there had to be a return.

Ten months later, at the Chicago Stadium, the slugfest was resumed before a record indoor attendance of 18,457. Zale had fought five times in the interim. Graziano in the meantime had been in trouble with the New York authorities for not reporting an attempted bribe, and another defeat could have seen his chances of a title disappear for good. Zale this time took the fight to Graziano, whose fate looked ominous when Zale's attacks had closed his left eye by the end of the round. Zale concentrated on the eye in the second round, but Graziano retaliated with a long swipe to the jaw that so shook Zale that he went to

the wrong corner at the end.

In the third round Zale appeared to have the battle won. He worsened Graziano's left eye, dropped him with a right to the head, and punched him around the ring. It was the same treatment in the fourth which ended with Graziano halfblinded in both eyes and with the referee asking him if he wanted to continue. He did, and his corner somehow restored vision to his left eye by breaking the skin and reducing the swelling.

Graziano now banked on a final desperate assault, swinging at random. A bewildered Zale was caught by a long right. Graziano piled in more and more rights and, at the bell, Zale was probably even rockier than Rocky, and this extraordinary series was taking another twist. Zale fought back in the sixth until another right found his jaw. He wavered, and a succession of blows put him down. When he rose Graziano went berserk and

fought as if through a red mist. Screaming to himself 'I'll kill the sonofabitch' he tore into Zale as if mad. Suddenly Zale was draped helpless over the middle rope with Graziano pouring in blows and referee Johnny Behr trying to pull him off. Graziano was in a trance and his seconds had to slap his face to bring him round.

The battered Graziano was champion, and taking the microphone he screamed: 'Hey, ma, your bad boy done it. Somebody up there likes me.' The last sentence became the title of his autobiography, and of the film based on it.

There was, of course, a rubber match, 11 months later at Newark, New Jersey. Graziano this time was a 12–5 favourite. But Zale came out attacking and had Graziano down within a minute. Zale kept up the attack and, apart from a flurry in the second, Graziano could not recapture his old zest. In the third a left hook floored Graziano and,

as Rocky rose and leaned on the ropes, Zale knocked him out with another left.

The great war between Zale and Graziano took a lot out of both men. The 35-year-old Zale fought only once more, losing his title to Marcel Cerdan. Graziano got one more chance of the crown four years later, but was no match for Sugar Ray Robinson.

TONY ZALE stands over the fallen Rocky Graziano in their third fight at Newark, where Zale regained his title and ended the most famous series of matches in boxing history.

World Title Bouts, 1890–1992

The following records attempt to set out by weight division every champion and championship bout contested under Queensberry Rules since the beginning of gloves (2 oz minimum)

Boxing grew up in Great Britain, and quickly spread to the USA, but it was not until the champions of these two countries came together in the latter part of the last century that it developed on an international scale. Organisations then came into existence solely for the purpose of controlling professional boxing. The National Sporting Club of Britain was formed in 1891, later to be amalgamated into the British Boxing Board of Control during 1929. By the early part of the century the sport had also begun to boom among the French, who in 1911 were instrumental in setting up the International Boxing Union to look after the interests of boxing in Europe. Following the Second World War the body became known as the European Boxing Union. In America many states had allowed boxing to take place, but in 1920 the New York State Athletic Commission was legally constituted under the Walker Law to govern the sport. Also at the same time several of the independent states of America became affiliated to form the National Boxing Association, which by 1962 was re-named the World Boxing Association. In an effort to create a balance of power, Britain supported the setting up of the World Boxing Council, formed in 1963, which brought together New York and its satellite states, with the BBBC, the Commonwealth and the EBU. Recently the International Boxing Federation, an offshoot of the WBA, and the World Boxing Organisation have sprung into prominence on the world boxing stage.

Over the years many new weight divisions have been formed and original classes have been restructured. For example the bantamweight division limit, which in 1890 stood at 112 lb, was gradually increased until it reached an internationally accepted 118 lb in 1909. Similarly other weight limits rose, e.g. featherweight: 1890 (118 lb) – 1909 (126 lb); welterweight: 1892 (142 lb) – 1909 (147 lb); middleweight; 1891 (154 lb) – 1909 (160 lb).

The following data does not include 'No Decision' bouts, champions awarded titles without a contest, or claimants with no realistic backing. Note that the champions in **bold** are accorded universal recognition.

Also, country codes relate to place of domicile, not necessarily the birthplace.

Championship status code

AUSTR = Australia; CALIF = California; EBU = European Boxing Union; FR = France; GB = Great Britain; IBF = International Boxing Federation; IBU = International Boxing Union; LOUIS = Louisiana; MARY = Maryland; MASS = Massachusetts; NBA = National Boxing Association; NY = New York; PEN = Pennsylvania; USA = United States; WBA = World Boxing Association; WBC = World Boxing Council; WBD = World Boxing Organisation.

Country Code

A = Australia; ARG = Argentine; Au = Austria; BAH = Bahamas; BAR =Barbados; BEL = Belgium; BR = Brazil; C = Canada; CH = Chile; CIS; COL = Colombia; CR = Costa Rica; CUB = Cuba; CZ = Czechoslovakia; DEN = Denmark; DOM = Dominican Republic; EC = Ecuador; FIN = Finland; FR = France; GB = Great Britain; GER = Germany; GH = Ghana; GRE = Greece; GU = Guyana; HOL = Holland; I = Ireland; IC = Ivory Coast; INDON = Indonesia; ITA = Italy; J = Jamaica; JAP = Japan; K = Kenya; MEX = Mexico; MOR = Morocco; N = Nigeria; NIC = Nicaragua; NOR = Norway; NZ = New Zealand; PAN = Panama; PAR = Paraguay; PERU; PH = Philippines; PNG = Papua New Guinea; PR = Puerto Rico; SA = South Africa; SK = South Korea; SP = Spain; SWE = Sweden; SWI = Switzerland; TH = Thailand; TOGO; TR = Trinidad; TUN = Tunisia; U = Uganda; UR = Uruguay; USA; VEN = Venezuela; YUG = Yugoslavia; ZA = Zambia.

Heavyweight

07.09.92	**James J. Corbett** (USA) W CO 21 John L. Sullivan (USA), New Orleans
25.01.94	**James J. Corbett** (USA) W CO 3 Charlie Mitchell (GB), Jacksonville
17.03.97	**Bob Fitzsimmons** (A) W CO 14 James J. Corbett (USA), Carson City
09.06.99	**James J. Jeffries** (USA) W CO 11 Bob Fitzsimmons (A), New York City
03.11.99	**James J. Jeffries** (USA) W PTS 25 Tom Sharkey (USA), New York City
06.04.00	**James J. Jeffries** (USA) W CO 1 Jack Finnegan (USA), Detroit
11.05.00	**James J. Jeffries** (USA) W CO 23 James J. Corbett (USA), New York City
15.11.01	**James J. Jeffries** (USA) W RTD 5 Gus Ruhlin (USA), San Francisco
25.07.02	**James J. Jeffries** (USA) W CO 8 Bob Fitzsimmons (A), San Francisco
14.08.03	**James J. Jeffries** (USA) W CO 10 James J. Corbett (USA), San Francisco
26.08.04	**James J. Jeffries** (USA) W CO 2 Jack Munroe (USA), San Francisco. *James J. Jeffries relinquished title*
03.07.05	**Marvin Hart** (USA) W RSC 12 Jack Root (USA), Reno
23.02.06	**Tommy Burns** (C) W PTS 20 Marvin Hart (USA), Los Angeles
02.10.06	**Tommy Burns** (C) W CO 15 Jim Flynn (USA), Los Angeles
28.11.06	**Tommy Burns** (C) DREW 20 Jack O'Brien (USA), Los Angeles
08.05.07	**Tommy Burns** (C) W PTS 20 Jack O'Brien (USA), Los Angeles
04.07.07	**Tommy Burns** (C) W CO 1 Bill Squires (A), Los Angeles
02.12.07	**Tommy Burns** (C) W CO 10 Gunner Moir (GB), NSC, London
10.02.08	**Tommy Burns** (C) W CO 4 Jack Palmer (GB), Wonderland, London
17.03.08	**Tommy Burns** (C) W CO 1 Jem Roche (GB), Dublin
18.04.08	**Tommy Burns** (C) W CO 5 Jewey Smith (GB), Paris
13.06.08	**Tommy Burns** (C) W CO 8 Bill Squires (A), Paris
24.08.08	**Tommy Burns** (C) W CO 13 Bill Squires (A), Sydney
02.09.08	**Tommy Burns** (C) W CO 6 Bill Lang (A), Melbourne
26.12.08	**Jack Johnson** (USA) W RSC 14 Tommy Burns (C), Sydney
16.10.09	**Jack Johnson** (USA) W CO 12 Stanley Ketchel (USA), Los Angeles
04.07.10	**Jack Johnson** (USA) W RSC 15 James J. Jeffries (USA), Reno
04.07.12	**Jack Johnson** (USA) W RSC 9 Jim Flynn (USA), Las Vegas
19.12.13	**Jack Johnson** (USA) DREW 10 Jim Johnson (USA), Paris
27.06.14	**Jack Johnson** (USA) W PTS 20 Frank Moran (USA), Paris
05.04.15	**Jess Willard** (USA) W CO 26 Jack Johnson (USA), Havana
04.07.19	**Jack Dempsey** (USA) W RTD 3 Jess Willard (USA), Toledo
06.09.20	**Jack Dempsey** (USA) W CO 3 Billy Miske (USA), Benton Harbor
14.12.20	**Jack Dempsey** (USA) W CO 12 Bill Brennan (USA), New York City
02.07.21	**Jack Dempsey** (USA) W CO 4 Georges Carpentier (FR), Jersey City
04.07.23	**Jack Dempsey** (USA) W PTS 15 Tommy Gibbons (USA), Shelby
14.09.23	**Jack Dempsey** (USA) W CO 2 Angel Firpo (ARG), New York City
23.09.26	**Gene Tunney** (USA) W PTS 10 Jack Dempsey (USA), Philadelphia
22.09.27	**Gene Tunney** (USA) W PTS 10 Jack Dempsey (USA), Chicago
26.07.28	**Gene Tunney** (USA) W RSC 11 Tom Heeney (NZ), New York City. *Gene Tunney relinquished title*
12.06.30	**Max Schmeling** (GER) W DIS 4 Jack Sharkey (USA), New York City
03.07.31	**Max Schmeling** (GER) W RSC 15 Young Stribling (USA), Cleveland
21.06.32	**Jack Sharkey** (USA) W PTS 15 Max Schmeling (GER), New York City
29.06.33	**Primo Carnera** (ITA) W CO 6 Jack Sharkey (USA), New York City
22.10.33	**Primo Carnera** (ITA) W PTS 15 Paolino Uzcudun (SP), Rome
01.03.34	**Primo Carnera** (ITA) W PTS 15 Tommy Loughran (USA), Miami
14.06.34	**Max Baer** (USA) W RSC 11 Primo Carnera (ITA), New York City
13.06.35	**James J. Braddock** (USA) W PTS 15 Max Baer (USA), New York City
22.06.37	**Joe Louis** (USA) W CO 8 James J. Braddock (USA), Chicago
30.08.37	**Joe Louis** (USA) W PTS 15 Tommy Farr (GB), New York City
23.02.38	**Joe Louis** (USA) W CO 3 Nathan Mann (USA), New York City
01.04.38	**Joe Louis** (USA) W CO 5 Harry Thomas (USA), Chicago
22.06.38	**Joe Louis** (USA) W CO 1 Max Schmeling (GER), New York City
25.01.39	**Joe Louis** (USA) W RSC 1 John Henry Lewis (USA), New York City
17.04.39	**Joe Louis** (USA) W CO 1 Jack Roper (USA), Los Angeles
28.06.39	**Joe Louis** (USA) W RSC 4 Tony Galento (USA), New York City
20.09.39	**Joe Louis** (USA) W CO 11 Bob Pastor (USA), Detroit
09.02.40	**Joe Louis** (USA) W PTS 15 Arturo Godoy (CH), New York City
29.03.40	**Joe Louis** (USA) W CO 2 Johnny Paychek (USA), New York City
20.06.40	**Joe Louis** (USA) W RSC 8 Arturo Godoy (CH), New York City
16.12.40	**Joe Louis** (USA) W RTD 6 Al McCoy (USA), Boston
31.01.41	**Joe Louis** (USA) W CO 5 Red Burman (USA), New York City
17.02.41	**Joe Louis** (USA) W CO 2 Gus Dorazio (USA), Philadelphia
21.03.41	**Joe Louis** (USA) W RSC 13 Abe Simon (USA), Detroit
08.04.41	**Joe Louis** (USA) W RSC 9 Tony Musto (USA), St Louis
23.05.41	**Joe Louis** (USA) W DIS 7 Buddy Baer (USA), Washington
18.06.41	**Joe Louis** (USA) W CO 13 Billy Conn (USA), New York City
29.09.41	**Joe Louis** (USA) W RSC 6 Lou Nova (USA), New York City
09.01.42	**Joe Louis** (USA) W CO 1 Buddy Baer (USA), New York City
27.03.42	**Joe Louis** (USA) W CO 6 Abe Simon (USA), New York City
19.06.46	**Joe Louis** (USA) W CO 8 Billy Conn (USA), New York City
18.09.46	**Joe Louis** (USA) W CO 1 Tami Mauriello (USA), New York City
05.12.47	**Joe Louis** (USA) W PTS 15 Jersey Joe Walcott (USA), New York City
25.06.48	**Joe Louis** (USA) W CO 11 Jersey Joe Walcott (USA), New York City. *Joe Louis relinquished title*
22.06.49	**Ezzard Charles** (USA) W PTS 15 Jersey Joe Walcott (USA), Chicago – NBA
10.08.49	**Ezzard Charles** (USA) W RSC 7 Gus Lesnevich (USA), New York City – NBA
14.10.49	**Ezzard Charles** (USA) W CO 8 Pat Valentino (USA), San Francisco – NBA
06.06.50	Lee Savold (USA) W RTD 4 Bruce Woodcock (GB), White City, London – GB/EBU. *Lee Savold forfeited GB/EBU recognition following an announcement that Joe Louis was making a comeback*
15.08.50	**Ezzard Charles** (USA) W RSC 14 Freddie Beshore (USA), Buffalo – NBA
27.09.50	**Ezzard Charles** (USA) W PTS 15 Joe Louis (USA), New York City
05.12.50	**Ezzard Charles** (USA) W CO 11 Nick Barone (USA), Cincinnati
12.01.51	**Ezzard Charles** (USA) W RSC 10 Lee Oma (USA), New York City

07.03.51 Ezzard Charles (USA) W PTS 15 Jersey Joe Walcott (USA), Detroit

30.05.51 Ezzard Charles (USA) W PTS 15 Joey Maxim (USA), Chicago

18.07.51 Jersey Joe Walcott (USA) W CO 7 Ezzard Charles (USA), Pittsburgh

05.06.52 Jersey Joe Walcott (USA) W PTS 15 Ezzard Charles (USA), Philadelphia

23.09.52 Rocky Marciano (USA) W CO 13 Jersey Joe Walcott (USA), Philadelphia

15.05.53 Rocky Marciano (USA) W CO 1 Jersey Joe Walcott (USA), Chicago

24.09.53 Rocky Marciano (USA) W RSC 11 Roland la Starza (USA), New York City

17.06.54 Rocky Marciano (USA) W PTS 15 Ezzard Charles (USA), New York City

17.09.54 Rocky Marciano (USA) W CO 8 Ezzard Charles (USA), New York City

16.05.55 Rocky Marciano (USA) W RSC 9 Don Cockell (GB), San Francisco

21.09.55 Rocky Marciano (USA) W CO 9 Archie Moore (USA), New York City. *Rocky Marciano relinquished title*

30.11.56 Floyd Patterson (USA) W CO 5 Archie Moore (USA), Chicago

29.07.57 Floyd Patterson (USA) W RSC 10 Tommy Jackson (USA), New York City

22.08.57 Floyd Patterson (USA) W CO 6 Pete Rademacher (USA), Seattle

18.08.58 Floyd Patterson (USA) W RTD 12 Roy Harris (USA), Los Angeles

01.05.59 Floyd Patterson (USA) W CO 11 Brian London (GB), Indianapolis

26.06.59 Ingemar Johansson (SWE) W RSC 3 Floyd Patterson (USA), New York City

20.06.60 Floyd Patterson (USA) W CO 5 Ingemar Johansson (SWE), New York City

13.03.61 Floyd Patterson (USA) W CO 6 Ingemar Johansson (SWE), Miami

04.12.61 Floyd Patterson (USA) W CO 4 Tom McNeeley (USA), Toronto

25.09.62 Sonny Liston (USA) W CO 1 Floyd Patterson (USA), Chicago

22.07.63 Sonny Liston (USA) W CO 1 Floyd Patterson (USA), Las Vegas

25.02.64 Muhammad Ali (USA) W RTD 6 Sonny Liston (USA), Miami. *Muhammad Ali forfeited WBA recognition due to a contractual dispute*

05.03.65 Ernie Terrell (USA) W PTS 15 Eddie Machen (USA), Chicago – WBA

25.05.65 Muhammad Ali (USA) W CO 1 Sonny Liston (USA), Lewiston – WBC

01.11.65 Ernie Terrell (USA) W PTS 15 George Chuvalo (C), Toronto – WBA

22.11.65 Muhammad Ali (USA) W RSC 12 Floyd Patterson (USA), Las Vegas – WBC

29.03.66 Muhammad Ali (USA) W PTS 15 George Chuvalo (C), Toronto – WBC

21.05.66 Muhammad Ali (USA) W RSC 6 Henry Cooper (GB), Highbury Stadium, London – WBC

28.06.66 Ernie Terrell (USA) W PTS 15 Doug Jones (USA), Houston – WBA

06.08.66 Muhammad Ali (USA) W CO 3 Brian London (GB), Earls Court, London – WBC

10.09.66 Muhammad Ali (USA) W RSC 12 Karl Mildenberger (GER), Frankfurt – WBC

14.11.66 Muhammad Ali (USA) W RSC 3 Cleveland Williams (USA), Houston – WBC

06.02.67 Muhammad Ali (USA) W PTS 15 Ernie Terrell (USA), Houston

22.03.67 Muhammad Ali (USA) W CO 7 Zora Folley (USA), New York City. *Muhammad Ali forfeited title due to inactivity*

04.03.68 Joe Frazier (USA) W RSC 11 Buster Mathis (USA), New York City – WBC

27.04.68 Jimmy Ellis (USA) W PTS 15 Jerry Quarry (USA), Oakland – WBA

24.06.68 Joe Frazier (USA) W RTD 2 Manuel Ramos (MEX), New York City – WBC

14.09.68 Jimmy Ellis (USA) W PTS 15 Floyd Patterson (USA), Stockholm – WBA

10.12.68 Joe Frazier (USA) W PTS 15 Oscar Bonavena (ARG), Philadelphia – WBC

22.04.69 Joe Frazier (USA) W CO 1 Dave Zyglewicz (USA), Houston – WBC

23.06.69 Joe Frazier (USA) W RSC 7 Jerry Quarry (USA), New York City – WBC

16.02.70 Joe Frazier (USA) W RTD 4 Jimmy Ellis (USA), New York City

18.11.70 Joe Frazier (USA) W CO 2 Bob Foster (USA), Detroit

08.03.71 Joe Frazier (USA) W PTS 15 Muhammad Ali (USA), New York City

15.01.72 Joe Frazier (USA) W RSC 4 Terry Daniels (USA), New Orleans

26.05.72 Joe Frazier (USA) W RSC 4 Ron Stander (USA), Omaha

22.01.73 George Foreman (USA) W RSC 2 Joe Frazier (USA), Kingston

01.09.73 George Foreman (USA) W CO 1 Jose Roman (PR), Tokyo

26.03.74 George Foreman (USA) W RSC 2 Ken Norton (USA), Caracas

30.10.74 Muhammad Ali (USA) W CO 8 George Foreman (USA), Kinshasha

24.03.75 Muhammad Ali (USA) W RSC 15 Chuck Wepner (USA), Cleveland

16.05.75 Muhammad Ali (USA) W RSC 11 Ron Lyle (USA), Las Vegas

01.07.75 Muhammad Ali (USA) W PTS 15 Joe Bugner (GB), Kuala Lumpur

01.10.75 Muhammad Ali (USA) W RTD 14 Joe Frazier (USA), Manila

20.02.76 Muhammad Ali (USA) W CO 5 Jean-Pierre Coopman (BEL), San Juan

30.04.76 Muhammad Ali (USA) W PTS 15 Jimmy Young (USA), Landover

25.05.76 Muhammad Ali (USA) W RSC 5 Richard Dunn (GB), Munich

28.09.76 Muhammad Ali (USA) W PTS 15 Ken Norton (USA), New York City

16.05.77 Muhammad Ali (USA) W PTS 15 Alfredo Evangelista (SP), Landover

29.09.77 Muhammad Ali (USA) W PTS 15 Earnie Shavers (USA), New York City

15.02.78 Leon Spinks (USA) W PTS 15 Muhammad Ali (USA), Las Vegas. *Leon Spinks forfeited WBC recognition for failing to defend against Ken Norton*

09.06.78 Larry Holmes (USA) W PTS 15 Ken Norton (USA), Las Vegas – WBC

15.09.78 Muhammad Ali (USA) W PTS 15 Leon Spinks (USA), New Orleans – WBA. *Muhammad Ali relinquished WBA version of title*

10.11.78 Larry Holmes (USA) W CO 7 Alfredo Evangelista (SP), Las Vegas – WBC

23.03.79 Larry Holmes (USA) W RSC 7 Ossie Ocasio (PR), Las Vegas – WBC

22.06.79 Larry Holmes (USA) W RSC 12 Mike Weaver (USA), New York City – WBC

28.09.79 Larry Holmes (USA) W RSC 11 Earnie Shavers (USA), Las Vegas – WBC

20.10.79 John Tate (USA) W PTS 15 Gerrie Coetzee (SA), Pretoria – WBA

03.02.80 Larry Holmes (USA) W CO 6 Lorenzo Zanon (ITA), Las Vegas – WBC

31.03.80 Mike Weaver (USA) W CO 15 John Tate (USA), Knoxville – WBA

31.03.80 Larry Holmes (USA) W RSC 8 Leroy Jones (USA), Las Vegas – WBC

07.07.80 Larry Holmes (USA) W RSC 7 Scott Ledoux (USA), Minneapolis – WBC

02.10.80 Larry Holmes (USA) W RTD 10 Muhammad Ali (USA), Las Vegas – WBC

25.10.80 Mike Weaver (USA) W CO 13 Gerrie Coetzee (SA), Sun City – WBA

11.04.81 Larry Holmes (USA) W PTS 15 Trevor Berbick (C), Las Vegas – WBC

12.06.81 Larry Holmes (USA) W RSC 3 Leon Spinks (USA), Detroit – WBC

03.10.81 Mike Weaver (USA) W PTS 15 James Tillis (USA), Rosemont – WBA

06.11.81 Larry Holmes (USA) W RSC 11 Renaldo Snipes (USA), Pittsburgh – WBC

11.06.82 Larry Holmes (USA) W RSC 13 Gerry Cooney (USA), Las Vegas – WBC

26.11.82 Larry Holmes (USA) W PTS 15 Tex Cobb (USA), Houston – WBC

10.12.82 Michael Dokes (USA) W RSC 1 Mike Weaver (USA), Las Vegas – WBA

27.03.83 Larry Holmes (USA) W PTS 12 Lucien Rodriguez (FR), Scranton – WBC

20.05.83 Michael Dokes (USA) DREW 15 Mike Weaver (USA), Las Vegas – WBA

20.05.83 Larry Holmes (USA) W PTS 12 Tim Witherspoon (USA), Las Vegas – WBC

10.09.83 Larry Holmes (USA) W RSC 5 Scott Frank (USA), Atlantic City – WBC

23.09.83 Gerrie Coetzee (SA) W CO 10 Michael Dokes (USA), Richfield – WBA

25.11.83 Larry Holmes (USA) W RSC 1 Marvis Frazier (USA), Las Vegas – WBC. *Larry Holmes relinquished WBC version of title*

09.03.84 Tim Witherspoon (USA) W PTS 12 Greg Page (USA), Las Vegas – WBC

31.08.84 Pinklon Thomas (USA) W PTS 12 Tim Witherspoon (USA), Las Vegas – WBC

09.11.84 Larry Holmes (USA) W RSC 12 James Smith (USA), Las Vegas – IBF

01.12.84 Greg Page (USA) W CO 8 Gerrie Coetzee (SA), Sun City – WBA

15.03.85 Larry Holmes (USA) W RSC 10 David Bey (USA), Las Vegas – IBF

29.04.85 Tony Tubbs (USA) W PTS 15 Greg Page (USA), Buffalo – WBA

20.05.85 Larry Holmes (USA) W PTS 15 Carl Williams (USA), Reno – IBF

15.06.85 Pinklon Thomas (USA) W CO 8 Mike Weaver (USA), Las Vegas – WBC

21.09.85 Michael Spinks (USA) W PTS 15 Larry Holmes (USA), Las Vegas – IBF

17.01.86 Tim Witherspoon (USA) W PTS 15 Tony Tubbs (USA), Atlanta – WBA

22.03.86 Trevor Berbick (C) W PTS 12 Pinklon Thomas (USA), Las Vegas – WBC

19.04.86 Michael Spinks (USA) W PTS 15 Larry Holmes (USA), Las Vegas – IBF

19.07.86 Tim Witherspoon (USA) W RSC 11 Frank Bruno (GB), The Stadium, Wembley – WBA

06.09.86 Michael Spinks (USA) W RSC 4 Steffen Tangstad (NOR), Las Vegas – IBF. *Michael Spinks forfeited IBF version of title when refusing to defend against Tony Tucker*

22.11.86 Mike Tyson (USA) W RSC 2 Trevor Berbick (C), Las Vegas – WBC

12.12.86 James Smith (USA) W RSC 1 Tim Witherspoon (USA), New York City – WBA

07.03.87 Mike Tyson (USA) W PTS 12 James Smith (USA), Las Vegas – WBA/WBC

30.05.87 Mike Tyson (USA) W RSC 6 Pinklon Thomas (USA), Las Vegas – WBA/WBC

30.05.87 Tony Tucker (USA) W RSC 10 James Douglas (USA), Las Vegas – IBF

01.08.87 Mike Tyson (USA) W PTS 12 Tony Tucker (USA), Las Vegas

16.10.87 Mike Tyson (USA) W RSC 7 Tyrell Biggs (USA), Atlantic City

22.01.88 Mike Tyson (USA) W RSC 4 Larry Holmes (USA), Atlantic City

21.03.88 Mike Tyson (USA) W RSC 2 Tony Tubbs (USA), Tokyo

27.06.88 Mike Tyson (USA) W CO 1 Michael Spinks (USA), Atlantic City

25.02.89 Mike Tyson (USA) W RSC 5 Frank Bruno (GB), Las Vegas. *Mike Tyson forfeited WBO recognition when they decided to support the winner of a Damiani v du Plooy bout as their champion.*

06.05.89 Francesco Damiani (ITA) W CO 3 Johnny du Plooy (SA), Syracuse – WBO

21.07.89 Mike Tyson (USA) W RSC 1 Carl Williams (USA), Atlantic City – IBF/WBA/WBC

16.12.89 Francesco Damiani (ITA) W RTD 2 Daniel Netto (ARG), Cesena – WBO

11.02.90 James Douglas (USA) W CO 10 Mike Tyson (USA), Tokyo – IBF/WBA/WBC

25.10.90 Evander Holyfield (USA) W CO 3 James Douglas (USA), Las Vegas – IBF/WBA/WBC

11.01.91 Ray Mercer (USA) W CO 9 Francesco Damiani (ITA), Atlantic City – WBO

19.04.91 Evander Holyfield (USA) W PTS 12 George Foreman (USA), Atlantic City – IBF/WBA/WBC

18.10.91 Ray Mercer (USA) W RSC 5 Tommy Morrison (USA), Atlantic City – WBO. *Ray Mercer forfeited title when refusing to defend against Michael Moorer*

23.11.91 Evander Holyfield (USA) W RSC 7 Bert Cooper (USA), Atlanta – IBF/WBA/WBA

15.05.92 Michael Moorer (USA) W RSC 5 Bert Cooper (USA), Atlantic City – WBO

19.06.92 Evander Holyfield (USA) W PTS 12 Larry Holmes (USA), Las Vegas – IBF/WBA/WBC

Cruiserweight

08.12.79 Marvin Camel (USA) DREW 15 Mate Parlov (YUG), Split – WBC

31.03.80 Marvin Camel (USA) W PTS 15 Mate Parlov (YUG), Las Vegas – WBC

25.11.80 Carlos de Leon (PR) W PTS 15 Marvin Camel (USA), New Orleans – WBC

13.02.82 Ossie Ocasio (PR) W PTS 15 Robbie Williams (SA), Johannesburg – WBA

24.02.82 Carlos de Leon (PR) W RSC 8 Marvin Camel (USA), Atlantic City – WBC

27.06.82 S. T. Gordon (USA) W RSC 2 Carlos de Leon (PR), Cleveland – WBC

15.12.82 Ossie Ocasio (PR) W PTS 15 Young Joe Louis (USA), Chicago – WBA

16.02.83 S. T. Gordon (USA) W RSC 8 Jesse Burnett (USA), East Rutherford – WBC

20.05.83 Ossie Ocasio (PR) W PTS 15 Randy Stephens (USA), Las Vegas – WBA

21.05.83 Marvin Camel (USA) W RSC 9 Rick Sekorski (USA), Billings – IBF

17.07.83 Carlos de Leon (PR) W PTS 12 S. T. Gordon (USA), Las Vegas – WBC

21.09.83 Carlos de Leon (PR) W RSC 4 Yaqui Lopez (USA), San Jose – WBC

13.12.83 Marvin Camel (USA) W RSC 5 Rod MacDonald (C), Halifax – IBF

09.03.84 Carlos de Leon (PR) W PTS 12 Anthony Davis (USA), Las Vegas – WBC

05.05.84 Ossie Ocasio (PR) W RSC 15 John Odhiambo (U), San Juan – WBA

02.06.84 Carlos de Leon (PR) W PTS 12 Bash Ali (N), Oakland – WBC

06.10.84 Lee Roy Murphy (USA) W RSC 14 Marvin Camel (USA), Billings – IBF

01.12.84 Piet Crous (SA) W PTS 15 Ossie Ocasio (PR), Sun City – WBA

20.12.84 Lee Roy Murphy (USA) W RSC 12 Young Joe Louis (USA), Chicago – IBF

30.03.85 Piet Crous (SA) W RSC 3 Randy Stephens (USA), Sun City – WBA

06.06.85 Alfonso Ratliff (USA) W PTS 12 Carlos de Leon (PR), Las Vegas – WBC

27.07.85 Dwight Muhammad Qawi (USA) W CO 11 Piet Crous (SA), Sun City – WBA

21.09.85 Bernard Benton (USA) W PTS 12 Alfonso Ratliff (USA), Las Vegas – WBC

19.10.85 Lee Roy Murphy (USA) W CO 12 Chisanda Mutti (ZA), Monaco – IBF

22.03.86 Carlos de Leon (PR) W PTS 12 Bernard Benton (USA), Las Vegas – WBC

23.03.86 Dwight Muhammad Qawi (USA) W RSC 6 Leon Spinks (USA), Reno – WBA

19.04.86 Lee Roy Murphy (USA) W CO 9 Dorcey Gaymon (USA), San Remo – IBF

12.07.86 Evander Holyfield (USA) W PTS 15 Dwight Muhammad Qawi (USA), Atlanta – WBA

10.08.86 Carlos de Leon (PR) W RSC 8 Michael Greer (USA), Giardini Naxos – WBC

25.10.86 Rickey Parkey (USA) W RSC 10 Lee Roy Murphy (USA), Marsala – IBF

14.02.87 Evander Holyfield (USA) W RSC 7 Henry Tillman (USA), Reno – WBA

21.02.87 Carlos de Leon (PR) W RTD 4 Angelo Rottoli (ITA), Bergamo – WBC

28.03.87 Rickey Parkey (USA) W RSC 12 Chisanda Mutti (ZA), Camaiore – IBF

15.05.87 Evander Holyfield (USA) W RSC 3 Rickey Parkey (USA), Las Vegas – IBF/WBA

15.08.87 Evander Holyfield (USA) W RSC 11 Ossie Ocasio (PR), St Tropez – IBF/WBA

05.12.87 Evander Holyfield (USA) W CO 4 Dwight Muhammad Qawi (USA), Atlantic City – IBF/WBA

22.01.88 Carlos de Leon (PR) W PTS 12 Jose Mario Flores (UR), Atlantic City – WBC

09.04.88 **Evander Holyfield** (USA) W RSC 8 Carlos de Leon (PR), Las Vegas. *Evander Holyfield relinquished title*

25.03.89 Taoufik Belbouli (FR) W RSC 8 Michael Greer (USA), Casablanca – WBA. *Taoufik Belbouli relinquished WBA version of title*

17.05.89 Carlos de Leon (PR) W RSC 9 Sam Reeson (GB), London Arena, London – WBC

03.06.89 Glenn McCrory (GB) W PTS 12 Patrick Lumumba (K), Louisa Centre, Stanley – IBF

21.10.89 Glenn McCrory (GB) W CO 11 Siza Makhatini (SA), Eston Leisure Centre, Middlesbrough – IBF

28.11.89 Robert Daniels (USA) W PTS 12 Dwight Muhammad Qawi (USA), Noget Sur Marne – WBA

03.12.89 Boone Pultz (USA) W PTS 12 Magne Havnaa (NOR), Copenhagen – WBO

27.01.90 Carlos de Leon (PR) DREW 12 Johnny Nelson (GB), City Hall, Sheffield – WBC

22.03.90 Jeff Lampkin (USA) W CO 3 Glenn McCrory (GB), Leisure Centre, Gateshead – IBF

17.05.90 Magne Havnaa (NOR) W RSC 5 Boone Pultz (USA), Aars – WBO

19.07.90 Robert Daniels (USA) W PTS 12 Craig Bodzianowski (USA), Seattle – WBA

27.07.90 Masimilliano Duran (ITA) W DIS 11 Carlos de Leon (PR), Capo d'Orlando – WBC

29.07.90 Jeff Lampkin (USA) W CO 8 Siza Makhatini (SA), St Petersburg – IBF. *Jeff Lampkin relinquished title*

22.11.90 Robert Daniels (USA) DREW 12 Taoufik Belbouli (FR), Madrid – WBA

08.12.90 Masimilliano Duran (ITA) W DIS 12 Anaclet Wamba (FR), Ferrara – WBC

08.12.90 Magne Havnaa (NOR) W PTS 12 Daniel Netto (ARG), Aalborg – WBO

15.02.91 Magne Havnaa (NOR) W PTS 12 Tyrone Booze (USA), Randers – WBO. *Magne Havnaa relinquished WBO version of title*

09.03.91 Bobby Czyz (USA) W PTS 12 Robert Daniels (USA), Atlantic City – WBA

20.07.91 Anaclet Wamba (FR) W RSC 11 Masimilliano Duran (ITA), Palermo – WBC

09.08.91 Bobby Czyz (USA) W PTS 12 Bash Ali (N), Atlantic City – WBA

06.09.91 James Warring (USA) W CO 1 James Pritchard (USA), Salemi – IBF

15.11.91 James Warring (USA) W CO 5 Donnell Wingfield (USA), Roanoke – IBF

13.12.91 Anaclet Wamba (FR) W RSC 11 Masimilliano Duran (ITA), Paris – WBC

08.05.92 Bobby Czyz (USA) W PTS 12 Don Lalonde (C), Las Vegas – WBA

16.05.92 James Warring (USA) W PTS 12 Johnny Nelson (GB), Fredricksburg – IBF

13.06.92 Anaclet Wamba (FR) W RSC 5 Andrei Rudenko (CIS), Levallois – WBC

Light-Heavyweight

22.04.03 Jack Root (USA) W PTS 10 Kid McCoy (USA), Detroit – USA

04.07.03 George Gardner (USA) W CO 12 Jack Root (USA), Fort Erie – USA

25.11.03 Bob Fitzsimmons (A) W PTS 20 George Gardner (USA), San Francisco

20.12.05 Jack O'Brien (USA) W RTD 13 Bob Fitzsimmons (A), San Francisco

28.11.06 Jack O'Brien (USA) DREW 20 Tommy Burns (C), Los Angeles. *Jack O'Brien relinquished title*

28.05.12 Jack Dillon (USA) W CO 3 Hugo Kelly (USA), Indianapolis

14.04.14 Jack Dillon (USA) W PTS 12 Battling Levinsky (USA), Butte

28.04.14 Jack Dillon (USA) W PTS 10 Al Norton (USA), Kansas City

15.06.14 Jack Dillon (USA) W PTS 12 Bob Moha (USA), Butte

25.04.16 Jack Dillon (USA) W PTS 15 Battling Levinsky (USA), Kansas City

24.10.16 Battling Levinsky (USA) W PTS 12 Jack Dillon (USA), Boston

03.05.20 Battling Levinsky (USA) W PTS 12 Clay Turner (USA), Portland

12.10.20 Georges Carpentier (FR) W CO 4 Battling Levinsky (USA), Jersey City

11.05.22 Georges Carpentier (FR) W CO 1 Ted Kid Lewis (GB), Olympia, London

24.09.22 Battling Siki (FR) W CO 6 Georges Carpentier (FR), Paris

17.03.23 Mike McTigue (USA) W PTS 20 Battling Siki (FR), Dublin

04.10.23 Mike McTigue (USA) DREW 10 Young Stribling (USA), Columbus

30.05.25 Paul Berlenbach (USA) W PTS 15 Mike McTigue (USA), New York City

11.09.25 Paul Berlenbach (USA) W RSC 11 Jimmy Slattery (USA), New York City

11.12.25 Paul Berlenbach (USA) W PTS 15 Jack Delaney (C), New York City

10.06.26 Paul Berlenbach (USA) W PTS 15 Young Stribling (USA), New York City

16.07.26 Jack Delaney (C) W PTS 15 Paul Berlenbach (USA), New York City. *Jack Delaney relinquished title*

30.08.27 Jimmy Slattery (USA) W PTS 10 Maxie Rosenbloom (USA), Hartford – NBA

07.10.27 Tommy Loughran (USA) W PTS 15 Mike McTigue (USA), New York City – NY

12.12.27 Tommy Loughran (USA) W PTS 15 Jimmy Slattery (USA), New York City

06.01.28 Tommy Loughran (USA) W PTS 15 Leo Lomski (USA), New York City

01.06.28 Tommy Loughran (USA) W PTS 15 Pete Latzo (USA), New York City

16.07.28 Tommy Loughran (USA) W PTS 10 Pete Latzo (USA), Wilkes Barre

08.03.29 **Tommy Loughran** (USA) W PTS 10 Mickey Walker (USA), Chicago

18.07.29 **Tommy Loughran** (USA) W PTS 15 James J. Braddock (USA), New York City. *Tommy Loughran relinquished title*

10.02.30 Jimmy Slattery (USA) W PTS 15 Lou Scozza (USA), Buffalo – NY

25.06.30 Maxie Rosenbloom (USA) W PTS 15 Jimmy Slattery (USA), Buffalo – NY

22.10.30 Maxie Rosenbloom (USA) W RSC 11 Abe Bain (USA), New York City – NY

05.08.31 Maxie Rosenbloom (USA) W PTS 15 Jimmy Slattery (USA), New York City – NY

18.03.32 George Nichols (USA) W PTS 10 Dave Maier (USA), Chicago – NBA. *George Nichols forfeited NBA recognition following a defeat by Lou Scozza in May, 1932*

14.07.32 Maxie Rosenbloom (USA) W PTS 15 Lou Scozza (USA), Buffalo – NY

22.02.33 Maxie Rosenbloom (USA) W PTS 10 Al Stillman (USA), St Louis – NY

01.03.33 Bob Godwin (USA) W PTS 10 Joe Knight (USA), Palm Beach – NBA

10.03.33 Maxie Rosenbloom (USA) W PTS 15 Adolf Heuser (GER), New York City – NY

24.03.33 **Maxie Rosenbloom** (USA) W RSC 4 Bob Godwin (USA), New York City

03.11.33 **Maxie Rosenbloom** (USA) W PTS 15 Mickey Walker (USA), New York City

05.02.34 **Maxie Rosenbloom** (USA) DREW 15 Joe Knight (USA), Miami

16.11.34 **Bob Olin** (USA) W PTS 15 Maxie Rosenbloom (USA), New York City

31.10.35 **John Henry Lewis** (USA) W PTS 15 Bob Olin (USA), St Louis

13.03.36 **John Henry Lewis** (USA) W PTS 15 Jock McAvoy (GB), New York City

09.11.36 **John Henry Lewis** (USA) W PTS 15 Len Harvey (GB), The Arena, Wembley

03.06.37 **John Henry Lewis** (USA) W RSC 8 Bob Olin (USA), St Louis

25.04.38 **John Henry Lewis** (USA) W CO 4 Emilio Martinez (USA), Minneapolis

28.10.38 **John Henry Lewis** (USA) W PTS 15 Al Gainer (USA), New Haven. *John Henry Lewis relinquished title*

29.11.38 Tiger Jack Fox (USA) W PTS 15 Al Gainer (USA), New York City – NY

03.02.39 Melio Bettina (USA) W RSC 9 Tiger Jack Fox (USA), New York City – NY

10.07.39 Len Harvey (GB) W PTS 15 Jock McAvoy (GB), White City, London – GB

13.07.39 Billy Conn (USA) W PTS 15 Melio Bettina (USA), New York City – NY/ NBA

25.09.39 Billy Conn (USA) W PTS 15 Melio Bettina (USA), Pittsburgh – NY/NBA

17.11.39 Billy Conn (USA) W PTS 15 Gus Lesnevich (USA), New York City – NY/NBA

05.06.40 Billy Conn (USA) W PTS 15 Gus Lesnevich (USA), Detroit – NY/NBA. *Billy Conn relinquished NY/NBA version of title*

13.01.41 Anton Christoforidis (GRE) W PTS 15 Melio Bettina (USA), Cleveland – NBA

22.05.41 Gus Lesnevich (USA) W PTS 15 Anton Christoforidis (GRE), New York City – NY/NBA

26.08.41 Gus Lesnevich (USA) W PTS 15 Tami Mauriello (USA), New York City – NY/NBA

14.11.41 Gus Lesnevich (USA) W PTS 15 Tami Mauriello (USA), New York City – NY/NBA

20.06.42 Freddie Mills (GB) W CO 2 Len Harvey (GB), White Hart Lane, London – GB

14.05.46 Gus Lesnevich (USA) W RSC 10 Freddie Mills (GB), Harringay Arena, London

28.02.47 Gus Lesnevich (USA) W RSC 10 Billy Fox (USA), New York City

05.03.48 Gus Lesnevich (USA) W CO 1 Billy Fox (USA), New York City

26.07.48 Freddie Mills (GB) W PTS 15 Gus Lesnevich (USA), White City, London

24.01.50 Joey Maxim (USA) W CO 10 Freddie Mills (GB), Earls Court, London

22.08.51 Joey Maxim (USA) W PTS 15 Bob Murphy (USA), New York City

25.06.52 Joey Maxim (USA) W RTD 13 Sugar Ray Robinson (USA), New York City

17.12.52 Archie Moore (USA) W PTS 15 Joey Maxim (USA), St Louis

24.06.53 **Archie Moore** (USA) W PTS 15 Joey Maxim (USA), Ogden

27.01.54 **Archie Moore** (USA) W PTS 15 Joey Maxim (USA), Miami

11.08.54 **Archie Moore** (USA) W RSC 14 Harold Johnson (USA), New York City

22.06.55 **Archie Moore** (USA) W CO 3 Carl Bobo Olson (USA), New York City

05.06.56 **Archie Moore** (USA) W RSC 10 Yolande Pompey (TR), Harringay Arena, London

20.09.57 **Archie Moore** (USA) W RSC 7 Tony Anthony (USA), Los Angeles

10.12.58 **Archie Moore** (USA) W CO 11 Yvon Durelle (C), Montreal

12.08.59 **Archie Moore** (USA) W CO 3 Yvon Durelle (C), Montreal. *Archie Moore forfeited NBA recognition due to inactivity*

07.02.61 Harold Johnson (USA) W RSC 9 Jesse Bowdry (USA), Miami – NBA

24.04.61 Harold Johnson (USA) W RSC 2 Von Clay (USA), Philadelphia – NBA

10.06.61 Archie Moore (USA) W PTS 15 Giulio Rinaldi (ITA), New York City – NY/ EBU. *Archie Moore forfeited NY/EBU recognition for failing to defend against either Harold Johnson or Doug Jones*

29.08.61 Harold Johnson (USA) W PTS 15 Eddie Cotton (USA), Seattle – NBA

12.05.62 **Harold Johnson** (USA) W PTS 15 Doug Jones (USA), Philadelphia

23.06.62 **Harold Johnson** (USA) W PTS 15 Gustav Scholz (GER), Berlin

01.06.63 **Willie Pastrano** (USA) W PTS 15 Harold Johnson (USA), Las Vegas

10.04.64 **Willie Pastrano** (USA) W RSC 5 Greg Peralta (ARG), New Orleans

30.11.64 **Willie Pastrano** (USA) W RSC 11 Terry Downes (GB), Belle Vue, Manchester

30.03.65 **Jose Torres** (PR) W RSC 9 Willie Pastrano (USA), New York City

21.05.66 **Jose Torres** (PR) W PTS 15 Wayne Thornton (USA), New York City

15.08.66 **Jose Torres** (PR) W PTS 15 Eddie Cotton (USA), Las Vegas

15.10.66 **Jose Torres** (PR) W CO 2 Chic Calderwood (GB), San Juan

16.12.66 **Dick Tiger** (N) W PTS 15 Jose Torres (PR), New York City

16.05.67 **Dick Tiger** (N) W PTS 15 Jose Torres (PR), New York City

17.11.67 **Dick Tiger** (N) W RSC 12 Roger Rouse (USA), Las Vegas

24.05.68 **Bob Foster** (USA) W CO 4 Dick Tiger (N), New York City

23.01.69 **Bob Foster** (USA) W RSC 1 Frankie de Paula (USA), New York City

24.05.69 **Bob Foster** (USA) W RSC 4 Andy Kendall (USA), Springfield

04.04.70 **Bob Foster** (USA) W RSC 3 Roger Rouse (USA), Missoula

27.06.70 **Bob Foster** (USA) W CO 10 Mark Tessman (USA), Baltimore. *Bob Foster forfeited WBA recognition for failing to defend against Jimmy Dupree*

27.02.71 Vicente Rondon (VEN) W RSC 6 Jimmy Dupree (USA), Caracas – WBA

02.03.71 Bob Foster (USA) W CO 4 Hal Carroll (USA), Scranton – WBC

24.04.71 Bob Foster (USA) W PTS 15 Ray Anderson (USA), Tampa – WBC

05.06.71 Vicente Rondon (VEN) W CO 1 Piero del Papa (ITA), Caracas – WBA

21.08.71 Vicente Rondon (VEN) W PTS 15 Eddie Jones (USA), Caracas – WBA

26.10.71 Vicente Rondon (VEN) W RSC 12 Gomeo Brennan (BAH), Miami – WBA

29.10.71 Bob Foster (USA) W RSC 8 Tommy Hicks (USA), Scranton – WBC

15.12.71 Vicente Rondon (VEN) W CO 8 Doyle Baird (USA), Cleveland – WBA

16.12.71 Bob Foster (USA) W RSC 3 Brian Kelly (USA), Oklahoma City – WBC

07.04.72 **Bob Foster** (USA) W CO 2 Vicente Rondon (VEN), Miami

27.06.72 **Bob Foster** (USA) W CO 4 Mike Quarry (USA), Las Vegas

26.09.72 **Bob Foster** (USA) W CO 14 Chris Finnegan (GB), The Arena, Wembley

21.08.73 **Bob Foster** (USA) W PTS 15 Pierre Fourie (SA), Alburquerque

01.12.73 **Bob Foster** (USA) W PTS 15 Pierre Fourie (SA), Johannesburg

17.06.74 **Bob Foster** (USA) DREW 15 Jorge Ahumada (ARG), Alburquerque. *Bob Foster relinquished title*

01.10.74 John Conteh (GB) W PTS 15 Jorge Ahumada (ARG), The Arena, Wembley – WBC

07.12.74 Victor Galindez (ARG) W RTD 12 Len Hutchins (USA), Buenos Aires – WBA

11.03.75 John Conteh (GB) W RSC 5 Lonnie Bennett (USA), The Arena, Wembley – WBC

07.04.75 Victor Galindez (ARG) W PTS 15 Pierre Fourie (SA), Johannesburg – WBA

30.06.75 Victor Galindez (ARG) W PTS 15 Jorge Ahumada (ARG), New York City – WBA

13.09.75 Victor Galindez (ARG) W PTS 15 Pierre Fourie (SA) Johannesburg – WBA

28.03.76 Victor Galindez (ARG) W RTD 3 Harald Skog (NOR), Oslo – WBA

22.05.76 Victor Galindez (ARG) W CO 15 Richie Kates (USA), Johannesburg – WBA

05.10.76 Victor Galindez (ARG) W PTS 15 Kosie Smith (SA), Johannesburg – WBA

09.10.76 John Conteh (GB) W PTS 15 Yaqui Lopez (USA), Copenhagen – WBC

05.03.77 John Conteh (GB) W RSC 3 Len Hutchins (USA), The Stadium, Liverpool – WBC. *John Conteh forfeited WBC version of title when he withdrew from a scheduled defence against Miguel Cuello*

21.05.77 Miguel Cuello (ARG) W CO 9 Jesse Burnett (USA), Monaco – WBC

18.06.77 Victor Galindez (ARG) W PTS 15 Richie Kates (USA), Rome – WBA

17.09.77 Victor Galindez (ARG) W PTS 15 Yaqui Lopez (USA), Rome – WBA

20.11.77 Victor Galindez (ARG) W PTS 15 Mustapha Muhammad (USA), Turin – WBA

07.01.78 Mate Parlov (YUG) W CO 9 Miguel Cuello (ARG), Milan – WBC

06.05.78 Victor Galindez (ARG) W PTS 15 Yaqui Lopez (USA), Reggio – WBA

17.06.78 Mate Parlov (YUG) W PTS 15 John Conteh (GB), Belgrade – WBC

15.09.78 Mike Rossman (USA) W RSC 13 Victor Galindez (ARG), New Orleans – WBA

02.12.78 Marvin Johnson (USA) W RSC 10 Mate Parlov (YUG), Marsala – WBC

05.12.78 Mike Rossman (USA) W RSC 6 Aldo Traversaro (ITA), Philadelphia – WBA

14.04.79 Victor Galindez (ARG) W RTD 9 Mike Rossman (USA), New Orleans – WBA

22.04.79 Matt Saad Muhammad (USA) W RSC 8 Marvin Johnson (USA), Indianapolis – WBC

18.08.79 Matt Saad Muhammad (USA) W PTS 15 John Conteh (GB), Atlantic City – WBC

30.11.79 Marvin Johnson (USA) W RSC 11 Victor Galindez (ARG), New Orleans – WBA

29.03.80 Matt Saad Muhammad (USA) W RSC 4 John Conteh (GB), Atlantic City – WBC

31.03.80 Mustapha Muhammad (USA) W RSC 11 Marvin Johnson (USA), Knoxville – WBA

11.05.80 Matt Saad Muhammad (USA) W RSC 5 Louis Pergaud (FR), Halifax – WBC

13.07.80 Matt Saad Muhammad (USA) W RSC 14 Yaqui Lopez (USA), McAfee – WBC

20.07.80 Mustapha Muhammad (USA) W RSC 10 Jerry Martin (USA), McAfee – WBA

28.11.80 Matt Saad Muhammad (USA) W CO 4 Lotte Mwale (U), San Diego – WBC

29.11.80 Mustapha Muhammad (USA) W RSC 3 Rudi Koopmans (HOL), Los Angeles – WBA

28.02.81 Matt Saad Muhammad (USA) W RSC 11 Vonzell Johnson (USA), Atlantic City – WBC

25.04.81 Matt Saad Muhammad (USA) W CO 9 Murray Sutherland (C), Atlantic City – WBC

18.07.81 Michael Spinks (USA) W PTS 15 Mustapha Muhammad (USA), Las Vegas – WBA

26.09.81 Matt Saad Muhammad (USA) W RSC 11 Jerry Martin (USA), Atlantic City – WBC

07.11.81 Michael Spinks (USA) W RSC 7 Vonzell Johnson (USA), Atlantic City – WBA

19.12.81 Dwight Muhammad Qawi (USA) W RSC 10 Matt Saad Muhammad (USA), Atlantic City – WBC

13.02.82 Michael Spinks (USA) W RSC 6 Mustapha Wasajja (U). Atlantic City – WBA

21.03.82 Dwight Muhammad Qawi (USA) W RSC 6 Jerry Martin (USA), Las Vegas – WBC

11.04.82 Michael Spinks (USA) W RSC 8 Murray Sutherland (C), Atlantic City – WBA

12.06.82 Michael Spinks (USA) W RSC 8 Jerry Celestine (USA), Atlantic City – WBA

07.08.82 Dwight Muhammad Qawi (USA) W RSC 6 Matt Saad Muhammad (USA), Philadelphia – WBC

18.09.82 Michael Spinks (USA) W RSC 9 Johnny Davis (USA), Atlantic City – WBA

20.11.82 Dwight Muhammad Qawi (USA) W RSC 11 Eddie Davis (USA), Atlantic City – WBC

18.03.83 **Michael Spinks** (USA) W PTS 15 Dwight Muhammad Qawi (USA), Atlantic City

25.11.83 **Michael Spinks** (USA) W RSC 10 Oscar Rivadeneyra (PERU), Vancouver

25.02.84 **Michael Spinks** (USA) W PTS 12 Eddie Davis (USA), Atlantic City

23.02.85 **Michael Spinks** (USA) W RSC 3 David Sears (USA), Atlantic City

06.06.85 **Michael Spinks** (USA) W RSC 8 Jim MacDonald (USA), Las Vegas. *Michael Spinks relinquished title*

10.12.85 J. B. Williamson (USA) W PTS 12 Prince Muhammed (GH), Los Angeles – WBC

21.12.85 Slobodan Kacar (YUG) W PTS 15 Mustafa Muhammad (USA), Pesaro – IBF

09.02.86 Marvin Johnson (USA) W RSC 7 Leslie Stewart (TR), Indianapolis – WBA

30.04.86 Dennis Andries (GB) W PTS 12 J. B. Williamson (USA), Picketts Lock Leisure Centre, London – WBC

06.09.86 Bobby Czyz (USA) W RSC 5 Slobodan Kacar (YUG), Las Vegas – IBF

10.09.86 Dennis Andries (GB) W RSC 9 Tony Sibson (GB), Alexandra Pavilion, London – WBC

20.09.86 Marvin Johnson (USA) W RSC 13 Jean-Marie Emebe (FR), Indianapolis – WBA

26.12.86 Bobby Czyz (USA) W RSC 1 David Sears (USA), West Orange – IBF

21.02.87 Bobby Czyz (USA) W CO 2 Willie Edwards (USA), Atlantic City – IBF

07.03.87 Thomas Hearns (USA) W RSC 10 Dennis Andries (GB), Detroit – WBC. *Thomas Hearns relinquished WBC version of title*

03.05.87 Bobby Czyz (USA) W RSC 6 Jim MacDonald (USA), Atlantic City – IBF

23.05.87 Leslie Stewart (TR) W RTD 8 Marvin Johnson (USA), Port of Spain – WBA

05.09.87 Virgil Hill (USA) W RSC 4 Leslie Stewart (TR), Atlantic City – WBA

29.10.87 Charles Williams (USA) W RTD 9 Bobby Czyz (USA), Las Vegas – IBF

21.11.87 Virgil Hill (USA) W PTS 12 Rufino Angulo (FR), Paris – WBA

27.11.87 Don Lalonde (C) W RSC 2 Eddie Davis (USA), Port of Spain – WBC

03.04.88 Virgil Hill (USA) W RSC 11 Jean-Marie Emebe (FR), Bismark – WBA

29.05.88 Don Lalonde (C) W RSC 5 Leslie Stewart (TR), Port of Spain – WBC

06.06.88 Virgil Hill (USA) W PTS 12 Ramzi Hassan (USA), Las Vegas – WBA

10.06.88 Charles Williams (USA) W RTD 11 Richard Caramanolis (FR), Annecy – IBF

21.10.88 Charles Williams (USA) W RSC 3 Rufino Angulo (FR), Villeneuve d'Ornon – IBF

07.11.88 Sugar Ray Leonard (USA) W RSC 9 Don Lalonde (C), Las Vegas – WBC. *Sugar Ray Leonard relinquished WBC version of title*

11.11.88 Virgil Hill (USA) W RSC 10 Willie Featherstone (C), Bismark – WBA

03.12.88 Michael Moorer (USA) W RSC 5 Ramzi Hassan (USA), Cleveland – WBO

14.01.89 Michael Moorer (USA) W RSC 2 Victor Claudio (PR), Detroit – WBO

19.02.89 Michael Moorer (USA) W RSC 6 Frankie Swindell (USA), Monessen – WBO

21.02.89 Dennis Andries (GB) W RSC 5 Tony Willis (USA), Tucson – WBC

04.03.89 Virgil Hill (USA) W PTS 12 Bobby Czyz (USA), Bismark – WBA

169

22.04.89 Michael Moorer (USA) W RSC 1 Freddie Delgado (PR), Detroit – WBO
27.05.89 Virgil Hill (USA) W RSC 7 Joe Lasisi (N), Bismark – WBA
24.06.89 Jeff Harding (A) W RSC 12 Dennis Andries (GB), Atlantic City – WBC
25.06.89 Charles Williams (USA) W RSC 10 Bobby Czyz (USA), Atlantic City – IBF
25.06.89 Michael Moorer (USA) W RSC 8 Leslie Stewart (TR), Atlantic City – WBO
24.10.89 Jeff Harding (A) W RTD 2 Tom Collins (GB), Brisbane – WBC
24.10.89 Virgil Hill (USA) W RSC 1 James Kinchen (USA), Bismark – WBA
16.11.89 Michael Moorer (USA) W RSC 1 Jeff Thompson (USA), Atlantic City – WBO
22.12.89 Michael Moorer (USA) W RSC 6 Mike Sedillo (USA), Detroit – WBO
07.01.90 Charles Williams (USA) W RSC 8 Frankie Swindell (USA), Atlantic City – IBF
03.02.90 Michael Moorer (USA) W RSC 9 Marcellus Allen (USA), Atlantic City – WBO
25.02.90 Virgil Hill (USA) W PTS 12 David Vedder (USA), Bismark – WBA
18.03.90 Jeff Harding (A) W RSC 11 Nestor Giovannini (ARG), Atlantic City – WBC
28.04.90 Michael Moorer (USA) W CO 1 Mario Melo (ARG), Atlantic City – WBO
07.07.90 Virgil Hill (USA) W PTS 12 Tyrone Frazier (USA), Bismark – WBA
28.07.90 Dennis Andries (GB) W CO 7 Jeff Harding (A), Melbourne – WBC
10.10.90 Dennis Andries (GB) W RTD 4 Sergio Merani (ARG), Albert Hall, London – WBC
15.12.90 Michael Moorer (USA) W CO 8 Danny Lindstrom (C), Pittsburgh – WBO. *Michael Moorer relinquished WBO version of title*
06.01.91 Virgil Hill (USA) W PTS 12 Mike Peak (USA), Bismark – WBA
12.01.91 Charles Williams (USA) W PTS 12 Mwehu Beya (ITA), St Vincent – IBF
19.01.91 Dennis Andries (GB) W PTS 12 Guy Waters (A), Adelaide – WBC
20.04.91 Charles Williams (USA) W RSC 2 James Kinchen (USA), Atlantic City – IBF
09.05.91 Leonzer Barber (USA) W RTD 5 Tom Collins (GB), Town Hall, Leeds – WBO
03.06.91 Thomas Hearns (USA) W PTS 12 Virgil Hill (USA), Las Vegas – WBA
20.07.91 Charles Williams (USA) W CO 3 Vince Boulware (USA), San Remo – IBF
11.09.91 Jeff Harding (A) W PTS 12 Dennis Andries (GB), Hammersmith Odeon, London – WBC
19.10.91 Charles Williams (USA) W RSC 2 Freddie Delgado (PR), Williamsburg – IBF
07.01.92 Leonzer Barber (USA) W PTS 12 Anthony Hembrick (USA), Detroit – WBO
20.03.92 Iran Barkley (USA) W PTS 12 Thomas Hearns (USA), Las Vegas – WBA
05.06.92 Jeff Harding (A) W RSC 8 Christophe Tiozzo (FR), Marseille – WBC

Super-Middleweight
28.03.84 Murray Sutherland (C) W PTS 15 Ernie Singletary (USA), Atlantic City – IBF
22.07.84 Chong-Pal Park (SK) W CO 11 Murray Sutherland (C), Seoul – IBF
02.01.85 Chong-Pal Park (SK) W CO 2 Roy Gumbs (GB), Seoul – IBF
30.06.85 Chong-Pal Park (SK) W PTS 15 Vinnie Curto (USA), Seoul – IBF
11.04.86 Chong-Pal Park (SK) W CO 15 Vinnie Curto (USA), Los Angeles – IBF
06.07.86 Chong-Pal Park (SK) TD 2 Lindell Holmes (USA), Chungju – IBF
14.09.86 Chong-Pal Park (SK) W PTS 15 Marvin Mack (USA), Pusan – IBF
25.01.87 Chong-Pal Park (SK) W RSC 15 Doug Sam (A), Seoul – IBF
03.05.87 Chong-Pal Park (SK) W PTS 15 Lindell Holmes (USA), Inchon – IBF
26.07.87 Chong-Pal Park (SK) W RSC 4 Emmanuel Otti (U), Kwangju – IBF. *Chong-Pal Park relinquished IBF version of title*
06.12.87 Chong-Pal Park (SK) W RSC 2 Jesus Gallardo (MEX), Seoul – WBA
01.03.88 Chong-Pal Park (SK) W CO 5 Polly Pasieron (INDON), Chungju – WBA

12.03.88 Graciano Rocchigiani (GER) W RSC 8 Vince Boulware (USA) Dusseldorf – IBF
23.05.88 Fully Obelmejias (VEN) W PTS 12 Chong-Pal Park (SK), Suanbao – WBA
03.06.88 Graciano Rocchigiani (GER) W PTS 15 Nicky Walker (USA), Berlin – IBF
07.10.88 Graciano Rocchigiani (GER) W RTD 11 Chris Reid (USA), Berlin – IBF
07.11.88 Sugar Ray Leonard (USA) W RSC 9 Don Lalonde (C), Las Vegas – WBC
14.11.88 Thomas Hearns (USA) W PTS 12 James Kinchen (USA), Las Vegas – WBO
27.01.89 Graciano Rocchigiani (GER) W PTS 12 Thulani Malinga (SA), Berlin – IBF. *Graciano Rocchigiani relinquished IBF version of title*
27.05.89 In-Chul Baek (SK) W RSC 11 Fully Obelmejias (VEN), Seoul – WBA
12.06.89 Sugar Ray Leonard (USA) DREW 12 Thomas Hearns (USA), Las Vegas – WBC
08.10.89 In-Chul Baek (SK) W RSC 11 Ronnie Essett (USA), Seoul – WBA
07.12.89 Sugar Ray Leonard (USA) W PTS 12 Roberto Duran (PAN), Las Vegas – WBC. *Sugar Ray Leonard relinquished WBC version of title*
13.01.90 In-Chul Baek (SK) W RSC 7 Yoshiaki Tajima (JAP), Seoul – WBA
27.01.90 Lindell Holmes (USA) W PTS 12 Frank Tate (USA), New Orleans – IBF
30.03.90 Christophe Tiozzo (FR) W RSC 6 In-Chul Baek (SK), Lyon – WBA
28.04.90 Thomas Hearns (USA) W PTS 12 Michael Olajide (C), Atlantic City – WBO. *Thomas Hearns relinquished WBO version of title*
19.07.90 Lindell Holmes (USA) W RSC 9 Carl Sullivan (USA), Seattle – IBF
20.07.90 Christophe Tiozzo (FR) W RSC 8 Paul Whittaker (USA), Arles – WBA
23.11.90 Christophe Tiozzo (FR) W RSC 2 Danny Morgan (USA), Cergy Pontoise – WBA
15.12.90 Mauro Galvano (ITA) W PTS 12 Dario Matteoni (ARG), Monaco – WBC
16.12.90 Lindell Holmes (USA) W PTS 12 Thulani Malinga (SA), Marino – IBF
07.03.91 Lindell Holmes (USA) W PTS 12 Antoine Byrd (USA), Madrid – IBF
05.04.91 Victor Cordoba (PAN) W RSC 9 Christophe Tiozzo (FR), Marseille – WBA
18.05.91 Darrin van Horn (USA) W CO 11 Lindell Holmes (USA), Verbania – IBF
27.07.91 Mauro Galvano (ITA) W PTS 12 Ronnie Essett (USA), Capo d'Orlando – WBC
17.08.91 Darrin van Horn (USA) W RSC 3 John Jarvis (USA), Irvine – IBF
21.09.91 Chris Eubank (GB) W RSC 12 Michael Watson (GB), White Hart Lane, London – WBO
13.12.91 Victor Cordoba (PAN) W RSC 11 Vincenzo Nardiello (ITA), Paris – WBA
10.01.92 Iran Barkley (USA) W RSC 2 Darrin van Horn (USA), New York – IBF
06.02.92 Mauro Galvano (ITA) W PTS 12 Juan Carlos Gimenez (PAR), Marino – WBC
07.02.92 Chris Eubank (GB) W PTS 12 Thulani Malinga (SA), National Indoor Centre, Birmingham – WBO
25.04.92 Chris Eubank (GB) W CO 3 John Jarvis (USA), G-Mex Leisure Centre, Manchester – WBO
27.06.92 Chris Eubank (GB) W PTS 12 Ronnie Essett (USA), Quinta do Lago – WBO.

Middleweight
18.02.90 **Nonpareil Jack Dempsey** (USA) W RSC 28 Billy McCarthy (A), San Francisco
14.01.91 **Bob Fitzsimmons** (A) W CO 13 Nonpareil Jack Dempsey (USA), New Orleans
26.09.94 **Bob Fitzsimmons** (A) W CO 2 Dan Creedon (NZ), New Orleans. *Bob Fitzsimmons relinquished title*
17.12.97 **Kid McCoy** (USA) W PTS 15 Dan Creedon (NZ), New York City. *Kid McCoy forfeited title when electing to campaign in the heavyweight division*
25.02.98 **Tommy Ryan** (USA) W CO 18 George Green (USA), San Francisco
13.06.98 **Tommy Ryan** (USA) W RSC 14 Tommy West (GB), New York City

24.10.98 **Tommy Ryan** (USA) W PTS 20 Jack Bonner (USA), New York City
18.09.99 **Tommy Ryan** (USA) W 10 Frank Craig (USA), New York City
04.03.01 **Tommy Ryan** (USA) W RTD 17 Tommy West (GB), Louisville
24.06.02 **Tommy Ryan** (USA) W CO 3 Johnny Gorman (GB), NSC, London
15.09.02 **Tommy Ryan** (USA) W CO 6 Kid Carter (USA), Fort Erie. *Tommy Ryan relinquished title*
04.07.07 **Stanley Ketchel** (USA) DREW 20 Joe Thomas (USA), Marysville
02.09.07 **Stanley Ketchel** (USA) W CO 32 Joe Thomas (USA), San Francisco
12.12.07 **Stanley Ketchel** (USA) W PTS 20 Joe Thomas (USA), San Francisco
22.02.08 **Stanley Ketchel** (USA) W CO 1 Mike Twin Sullivan (USA), San Francisco
09.05.08 **Stanley Ketchel** (USA) W CO 20 Jack Twin Sullivan (USA), San Francisco
04.06.08 **Stanley Ketchel** (USA) W PTS 10 Billy Papke (USA), Milwaukee
31.07.08 **Stanley Ketchel** (USA) W CO 3 Hugo Kelly (USA), San Francisco
18.08.08 **Stanley Ketchel** (USA) W CO 2 Joe Thomas (USA), San Francisco
07.09.08 **Billy Papke** (USA) W RSC 12 Stanley Ketchel (USA), Los Angeles
26.11.08 **Stanley Ketchel** (USA) W CO 11 Billy Papke (USA), San Francisco
02.06.09 **Stanley Ketchel** (USA) W CO 4 Tony Caponi (USA), Schnectady
09.06.09 **Stanley Ketchel** (USA) W RSC 3 Jack O'Brien (USA), Philadelphia
05.07.09 **Stanley Ketchel** (USA) W PTS 20 Billy Papke (USA), San Francisco
27.05.10 **Stanley Ketchel** (USA) W CO 2 Willie Lewis (USA), New York City
10.06.10 **Stanley Ketchel** (USA) W CO 5 Jim Smith (USA), New York City. *Stanley Ketchel left title vacant after being murdered in shooting incident*
08.06.11 Billy Papke (USA) W RTD 9 Jim Sullivan (GB), The Paladium, London – GB
22.02.12 Frank Mantell (USA) W PTS 20 Billy Papke (USA), Sacramento – USA
30.03.12 Frank Mantell (USA) W PTS 20 Jack Henrick (USA), Los Angeles – USA. *Frank Mantell forfeited USA recognition following several bad defeats*
29.06.12 Billy Papke (USA) W RSC 16 Marcel Moreau (FR), Paris – IBU
23.10.12 Billy Papke (USA) W DIS 17 Georges Carpentier (FR), Paris – IBU
04.12.12 Billy Papke (USA) W CO 7 George Bernard (FR), Paris – IBU
05.03.13 Frank Klaus (USA) W DIS 15 Billy Papke (USA), Paris – IBU
11.10.13 George Chip (USA) W CO 6 Frank Klaus (USA), Pittsburgh – USA
23.12.13 George Chip (USA) W CO 5 Frank Klaus (USA), Pittsburgh – USA
01.01.14 Eddie McGoorty (USA) W CO 1 Dave Smith (A), Sydney – AUSTR
07.02.14 Eddie McGoorty (USA) W PTS 20 Pat Bradley (A), Sydney – AUSTR
14.03.14 Jeff Smith (USA) W PTS 20 Eddie McGoorty (USA), Sydney – AUSTR
06.04.14 Al McCoy (USA) W CO 1 George Chip (USA), New York City – USA
13.04.14 Jeff Smith (USA) W CO 16 Pat Bradley (A), Sydney – AUSTR
06.06.14 Jeff Smith (USA) W PTS 20 Jimmy Clabby (USA), Sydney – AUSTR
28.11.14 Mick King (A) W PTS 20 Jeff Smith (USA), Sydney – AUSTR
26.12.14 Jeff Smith (USA) W PTS 20 Mick King (A), Sydney – AUSTR
23.01.15 Jeff Smith (USA) W DIS 5 Les Darcy (A), Sydney – AUSTR
20.02.15 Jeff Smith (USA) W PTS 20 Mick King (A), Melbourne – AUSTR
23.05.15 Les Darcy (A) W DIS 2 Jeff Smith (USA), Sydney – AUSTR
12.06.15 Les Darcy (A) W RTD 10 Mick King (A), Sydney – AUSTR
31.07.15 Les Darcy (A) W RSC 15 Eddie McGoorty (USA), Sydney – AUSTR
04.09.15 Les Darcy (A) W PTS 20 Billy Murray (USA), Sydney – AUSTR
09.10.15 Les Darcy (A) W RTD 6 Fred Dyer (GB), Sydney – AUSTR
23.10.15 Les Darcy (A) W PTS 20 Jimmy Clabby (USA), Sydney – AUSTR
27.12.15 Les Darcy (A) W RTD 8 Eddie McGoorty (USA), Sydney – AUSTR
15.01.16 Les Darcy (A) W PTS 20 George Brown (USA), Sydney – AUSTR

25.03.16 Les Darcy (A) W CO 7 Les O'Donnell (A), Sydney – AUSTR

08.04.16 Les Darcy (A) W PTS 20 George Brown (USA), Sydney – AUSTR

13.05.16 Les Darcy (A) W RTD 4 Alex Costica (ROM), Sydney – AUSTR

03.06.16 Les Darcy (A) W CO 2 Buck Crouse (USA) Sydney – AUSTR

24.06.16 Les Darcy (A) W CO 12 Dave Smith (A), Sydney – AUSTR

26.06.16 Al McCoy (USA) W PTS 15 Hugh Ross (USA), Bridgeport – USA

09.09.16 Les Darcy (A) W PTS 20 Jimmy Clabby (USA), Sydney – AUSTR

30.09.16 Les Darcy (A) W CO 9 George Chip (USA), Sydney – AUSTR. *Les Darcy left Australian version of the title vacant when he died of pneumonia*

14.11.17 Mike O'Dowd (USA) W CO 6 Al McCoy (USA), New York City

17.07.19 Mike O'Dowd (USA) W CO 3 Al McCoy (USA), St Paul

06.11.19 Mike O'Dowd (USA) W CO 2 Billy Kramer (USA), Paterson

01.03.20 Mike O'Dowd (USA) W CO 2 Jack McCarron (USA), Philadelphia

30.03.20 Mike O'Dowd (USA) W CO 5 Joe Eagan (USA), Boston

06.05.20 Johnny Wilson (USA) W PTS 12 Mike O'Dowd (USA), Boston

17.03.21 Johnny Wilson (USA) W PTS 15 Mike O'Dowd (USA), New York City

27.07.21 Johnny Wilson (USA) W DIS 7 Bryan Downey (USA), Cleveland. *Johnny Wilson forfeited NY/OHIO recognition following the disputed win over Bryan Downey*

22.02.22 Bryan Downey (USA) W PTS 12 Frank Carbone (USA), Canton – OHIO

15.05.22 Bryan Downey (USA) W PTS 12 Mike O'Dowd (USA), Columbus – OHIO

14.08.22 Dave Rosenberg (USA) W PTS 15 Phil Krug (USA), New York City – NY

18.09.22 Jock Malone (USA) W PTS 12 Bryan Downey (USA), Columbus – OHIO

30.11.22 Mike O'Dowd (USA) W DIS 8 Dave Rosenberg (USA), New York City – NY. *Mike O'Dowd relinquished NY version of title*

09.01.23 Lou Bogash (USA) W RSC 11 Charley Nashert (USA), New York City – NY. *Lou Bogash relinquished NY version of title*

24.07.23 Jock Malone (USA) W PTS 12 Bryan Downey (USA), Columbus – OHIO. *Jock Malone relinquished Ohio version of title*

31.08.23 Harry Greb (USA) W PTS 15 Johnny Wilson (USA), New York City

03.12.23 Harry Greb (USA W PTS 10 Bryan Downey (USA), Pittsburgh

18.01.24 Harry Greb (USA) W PTS 15 Johnny Wilson (USA), New York City

24.03.24 Harry Greb (USA) W RSC 12 Fay Keiser (USA), Baltimore

26.06.24 Harry Greb (USA) W PTS 15 Ted Moore (GB), New York City

02.07.25 Harry Greb (USA) W PTS 15 Mickey Walker (USA), New York City

13.11.25 Harry Greb (USA) W PTS 15 Tony Marullo (USA), New Orleans

26.02.26 Tiger Flowers (USA) W PTS 15 Harry Greb (USA), New York City

19.08.26 Tiger Flowers (USA) W PTS 15 Harry Greb (USA), New York City

03.12.26 Mickey Walker (USA) W PTS 10 Tiger Flowers (USA), Chicago

30.06.27 Mickey Walker (USA) W CO 10 Tommy Milligan (GB), Olympia, London

21.06.28 Mickey Walker (USA) W PTS 10 Ace Hudkins (USA), Chicago

29.10.29 Mickey Walker (USA) W PTS 10 Ace Hudkins (USA), Los Angeles

30.07.30 Mickey Walker (USA) W CO 3 Willie Oster (USA), Newark. *Mickey Walker relinquished title*

25.08.31 Gorilla Jones (USA) W PTS 10 Tiger Thomas (USA), Milwaukee – NBA

25.01.32 Gorilla Jones (USA) W RSC 6 Oddone Piazza (ITA), Milwaukee – NBA

26.04.32 Gorilla Jones (USA) W PTS 12 Young Terry (USA), Trenton – NBA

11.06.32 Marcel Thil (FR) W DIS 11 Gorilla Jones (USA), Paris – NBA/IBU

04.07.32 Marcel Thil (FR) W PTS 15 Len Harvey (GB), White City, London – NBA/IBU. *Marcel Thil forfeited NBA recognition when the authority once again supported the claims of Gorilla Jones*

11.11.32 Ben Jeby (USA) W PTS 15 Chuck Devlin (USA), New York City – NY

13.01.33 Ben Jeby (USA) W RSC 12 Frank Battaglia (C), New York City – NY

30.01.33 Gorilla Jones (USA) W CO 7 Sammy Slaughter (USA), Cleveland – NBA. *Gorilla Jones forfeited NBA recognition for failing to defend*

17.03.33 Ben Jeby (USA) DREW 15 Vince Dundee (USA), New York City – NY

10.07.33 Ben Jeby (USA) W PTS 15 Young Terry (USA), Newark – NY

09.08.33 Lou Brouillard (C) W CO 7 Ben Jeby (USA), New York City – NY/NBA

02.10.33 Marcel Thil (FR) W PTS 15 Kid Tunero (CUB), Paris – IBU

30.10.33 Vince Dundee (USA) W PTS 15 Lou Brouillard (C), Boston – NY/NBA

08.12.33 Vince Dundee (USA) W PTS 15 Andy Callahan (USA), Boston – NY/NBA

26.02.34 Marcel Thil (FR) W PTS 15 Ignacio Ara (SP), Paris – IBU

01.05.34 Vince Dundee (USA) W PTS 15 Al Diamond (USA), Paterson – NY/NBA

03.05.34 Marcel Thil (FR) W PTS 15 Gustav Roth (BEL), Paris – IBU

11.09.34 Teddy Yarosz (USA) W PTS 15 Vince Dundee (USA), Pittsburgh – NY/NBA

15.10.34 Marcel Thil (FR) DREW 15 Carmelo Candel (FR), Paris – IBU

04.05.35 Marcel Thil (FR) W RTD 14 Kid Jaks (CZ), Paris – IBU

03.06.35 Marcel Thil (FR) W PTS 15 Ignacio Ara (SP), Madrid – IBU

28.06.35 Marcel Thil (FR) W PTS 10 Carmelo Candel (FR), Paris – IBU

19.09.35 Babe Risko (USA) W PTS 15 Teddy Yarosz (USA), Pittsburgh – NY/NBA

20.01.36 Marcel Thil (FR) W DIS 4 Lou Brouillard (C), Paris – IBU

10.02.36 Babe Risko (USA) W PTS 15 Tony Fisher (USA), Newark – NY/NBA

11.07.36 Freddie Steele (USA) W PTS 15 Babe Risko (USA), Seattle – NY/NBA

01.01.37 Freddie Steele (USA) W PTS 10 Gorilla Jones (USA), Milwaukee – NY/NBA

15.02.37 Marcel Thil (FR) W DIS 6 Lou Brouillard (C), Paris – IBU

19.02.37 Freddie Steele (USA) W PTS 15 Babe Risko (USA), New York City – NY/NBA

11.05.37 Freddie Steele (USA) W CO 3 Frank Battaglia (C), Seattle – NY/NBA

11.09.37 Freddie Steele (USA) W CO 4 Ken Overlin (USA), Seattle – NY/NBA. *Freddie Steele forfeited NY recognition for failing to defend against Fred Apostoli*

23.09.37 Fred Apostoli (USA) W RSC 10 Marcel Thil (FR), New York City – IBU. *Fred Apostoli forfeited IBU recognition when the authority decided to recognise the winner of the Tenet v Besselmann contest*

19.02.38 Freddie Steele (USA) W RTD 7 Carmen Barth (USA) Cleveland – NBA

01.04.38 Fred Apostoli (FR) W PTS 15 Glen Lee (USA) New York City – NY

07.04.38 Edouard Tenet (FR) W RTD 12 Josef Besselmann (GER), Berlin – IBU. *Edouard Tenet forfeited IBU recognition following a defeat by Bep van Klaveren in July 1938*

26.07.38 Al Hostak (USA) W CO 1 Freddie Steele (USA), Seattle – NBA

01.11.38 Solly Krieger (USA) W PTS 15 Al Hostak (USA) Seattle – NBA

18.11.38 Fred Apostoli (USA) W RSC 8 Young Corbett III (USA), New York City – NY

27.06.39 Al Hostak (USA) W RSC 4 Solly Krieger (USA) Seattle – NBA

02.10.39 Ceferino Garcia (PH) W RSC 7 Fred Apostoli (USA), New York City – NY

11.12.39 Al Hostak (USA) W CO 1 Eric Seelig (GER), Cleveland – NBA

23.12.39 Ceferino Garcia (PH) W CO 13 Glen Lee (USA) Manila – NY

01.03.40 Ceferino Garcia (PH) DREW 10 Henry Armstrong (USA), Los Angeles – NY

23.05.40 Ken Overlin (USA) W PTS 15 Ceferino Garcia (PH) New York City – NY

19.07.40 Tony Zale (USA) W RTD 13 Al Hostak (USA), Seattle – NBA

01.11.40 Ken Overlin (USA) W PTS 15 Steve Belloise (USA) New York City – NY

13.12.40 Ken Overlin (USA) W PTS 15 Steve Belloise (USA) New York City – NY

21.02.41 Tony Zale (USA) W CO 14 Steve Mamakos (USA) Chicago – NBA

09.05.41 Billy Soose (USA) W PTS 15 Ken Overlin (USA) New York City – NY. *Billy Soose forfeited NY recognition following a defeat by George Abrams in July, 1941 and increasing weight problems*

28.05.41 Tony Zale (USA) W CO 2 Al Hostak (USA), Chicago – NBA

28.11.41 Tony Zale (USA) W PTS 15 Georgie Abrams (USA), New York City

27.09.46 Tony Zale (USA) W CO 6 Rocky Graziano (USA), New York City

16.07.47 Rocky Graziano (USA) W RSC 6 Tony Zale (USA), Chicago

10.06.48 Tony Zale (USA) W CO 3 Rocky Graziano (USA), Newark

21.09.48 Marcel Cerdan (FR) W RSC 12 Tony Zale (USA), Jersey City

16.06.49 Jake la Motta (USA) W RTD 10 Marcel Cerdan (FR), Detroit. *Jake la Motta forfeited Pennsylvanian recognition when ignoring the outstanding claim of Sugar Ray Robinson*

05.06.50 Sugar Ray Robinson (USA) W PTS 15 Robert Villemain (FR), Philadelphia – PEN

12.07.50 Jake la Motta (USA) W PTS 15 Tiberio Mitri (ITA), New York City – NY/NBA

25.08.50 Sugar Ray Robinson (USA) W CO 1 Jose Basora (PR), Scranton – PEN

13.09.50 Jake la Motta (USA) W CO 15 Laurent Dauthuille (FR), Detroit – NY/NBA

26.10.50 Sugar Ray Robinson (USA) W CO 12 Carl Bobo Olson (USA), Philadelphia – PEN

14.02.51 Sugar Ray Robinson (USA) W RSC 13 Jake la Motta (USA), Chicago

10.07.51 Randy Turpin (GB) W PTS 15 Sugar Ray Robinson (USA), Earls Court London

12.09.51 Sugar Ray Robinson (USA) W RSC 10 Randy Turpin (GB), New York City

13.03.52 Sugar Ray Robinson (USA) W PTS 15 Carl Bobo Olson (USA), San Francisco

16.04.52 Sugar Ray Robinson (USA) W CO 3 Rocky Graziano (USA), Chicago. *Sugar Ray Robinson relinquished title*

09.06.53 Randy Turpin (GB) W PTS 15 Charles Humez (FR), White City London – EBU

21.10.53 Carl Bobo Olson (USA) W PTS 15 Randy Turpin (GB), New York City

02.04.54 Carl Bobo Olson (USA) W PTS 15 Kid Gavilan (CUB), Chicago

20.08.54 Carl Bobo Olson (USA) W PTS 15 Rocky Castellani (USA), San Francisco

15.12.54 Carl Bobo Olson (USA) W RSC 11 Pierre Langlois (FR), San Francisco

09.12.55 Sugar Ray Robinson (USA) W CO 2 Carl Bobo Olson (USA), Chicago

18.05.56 Sugar Ray Robinson (USA) W CO 4 Carl Bobo Olson (USA), Los Angeles

02.01.57 Gene Fullmer (USA) W PTS 15 Sugar Ray Robinson (USA), New York City

01.05.57 Sugar Ray Robinson (USA) W CO 5 Gene Fullmer (USA), Chicago

23.09.57 Carmen Basilio (USA) W PTS 15 Sugar Ray Robinson (USA), New York City

25.03.58 Sugar Ray Robinson (USA) W PTS 15 Carmen Basilio (USA), Chicago. *Sugar Ray Robinson forfeited NBA recognition due to inactivity*

28.08.59 Gene Fullmer (USA) W RSC 14 Carmen Basilio (USA), San Francisco – NBA

04.12.59 Gene Fullmer (USA) W PTS 15 Spider Webb (USA), Logan – NBA

22.01.60 Paul Pender (USA) W PTS 15 Sugar Ray Robinson (USA), Boston – NY/EBU

20.04.60 Gene Fullmer (USA) DREW 15 Joey Giardello (USA), Bozeman – NBA

10.06.60 Paul Pender (USA) W PTS 15 Sugar Ray Robinson (USA), Boston – NY/EBU

29.06.60 Gene Fullmer (USA) W RSC 12 Carmen Basilio (USA), Salt Lake City – NBA

03.12.60 Gene Fullmer (USA) DREW 15 Sugar Ray Robinson (USA), Los Angeles – NBA

14.01.61 Paul Pender (USA) W RSC 7 Terry Downes (GB), Boston – NY/EBU

04.03.61 Gene Fullmer (USA) W PTS 15 Sugar Ray Robinson (USA), Las Vegas – NBA

22.04.61 Paul Pender (USA) W PTS 15 Carmen Basilio (USA), Boston – NY/EBU

11.07.61 Terry Downes (GB) W RTD 9 Paul Pender (USA), The Arena, Wembley – NY/EBU

05.08.61 Gene Fullmer (USA) W PTS 15 Florentino Fernandez (CUB), Ogden – NBA

09.12.61 Gene Fullmer (USA) W CO 10 Benny Kid Paret (CUB), Las Vegas – NBA

07.04.62 Paul Pender (USA) W PTS 15 Terry Downes (GB), Boston – NY/EBU. *Paul Pender forfeited NY/EBU recognition for failing to defend within stipulated period*

23.10.62 Dick Tiger (N) W PTS 15 Gene Fullmer (USA), San Francisco – NBA

23.02.63 Dick Tiger (N) DREW 15 Gene Fullmer (USA), Las Vegas – NBA

10.08.63 Dick Tiger (N) W RTD 7 Gene Fullmer (USA), Ibadan, Nigeria

07.12.63 Joey Giardello (USA) W PTS 15 Dick Tiger (N), Atlantic City

14.12.64 Joey Giardello (USA) W PTS 15 Ruben Carter (USA), Philadelphia

21.10.65 Dick Tiger (N) W PTS 15 Joey Giardello (USA), New York City

25.04.66 Emile Griffith (USA) W PTS 15 Dick Tiger (N), New York City

13.07.66 Emile Griffith (USA) W PTS 15 Joey Archer (USA), New York City

23.01.67 Emile Griffith (USA) W PTS 15 Joey Archer (USA), New York City

17.04.67 Nino Benvenuti (ITA) W PTS 15 Emile Griffith (USA), New York City

29.09.67 Emile Griffith (USA) W PTS 15 Nino Benvenuti (ITA), New York City

04.03.68 Nino Benvenuti (ITA) W PTS 15 Emile Griffith (USA), New York City

14.12.68 Nino Benvenuti (ITA) W PTS 15 Don Fullmer (USA), San Remo

04.10.69 Nino Benvenuti (ITA) W DIS 7 Fraser Scott (USA), Naples

22.11.69 Nino Benvenuti (ITA) W CO 1 Luis Rodriguez (CUB), Rome

23.05.70 Nino Benvenuti (ITA) W CO 8 Tom Bethea (USA), Umag

07.11.70 Carlos Monzon (ARG) W CO 12 Nino Benvenuti (ITA), Rome

08.05.71 Carlos Monzon (ARG) W RSC 3 Nino Benvenuti (ITA), Monaco

25.09.71 Carlos Monzon (ARG) W RSC 14 Emile Griffith (USA), Buenos Aires

04.03.72 Carlos Monzon (ARG) W RSC 5 Denny Moyer (USA), Rome

17.06.72 Carlos Monzon (ARG) W RTD 12 Jean-Claude Bouttier (FR), Colombes

19.08.72 Carlos Monzon (ARG) W RSC 5 Tom Bogs (DEN), Copenhagen

11.11.72 Carlos Monzon (ARG) W PTS 15 Bennie Briscoe (USA), Buenos Aires

02.06.73 Carlos Monzon (ARG) W PTS 15 Emile Griffith (USA), Monaco

29.09.73 Carlos Monzon (ARG) W PTS 15 Jean-Claude Bouttier (FR), Paris

09.02.74 Carlos Monzon (ARG) W RTD 6 Jose Napoles (CUB), Paris. *Carlos Monzon forfeited WBC recognition for failing to defend against Rodrigo Valdez*

25.05.74 Rodrigo Valdez (COL) W CO 7 Bennie Briscoe (USA), Monaco – WBC

05.10.74 Carlos Monzon (ARG) W CO 7 Tony Mundine (A), Buenos Aires – WBA

30.11.74 Rodrigo Valdez (COL) W CO 11 Gratien Tonna (FR), Paris – WBC

31.05.75 Rodrigo Valdez (COL) W RSC 8 Ramon Mendez (ARG), Cali – WBC

30.06.75 Carlos Monzon (ARG) W RSC 10 Tony Licata (USA), New York City – WBA

16.08.75 Rodrigo Valdez (COL) W PTS 15 Rudy Robles (MEX), Cartagena – WBC

13.12.75 Carlos Monzon (ARG) W CO 5 Gratien Tonna (FR), Paris – WBA

28.03.75 Rodrigo Valdez (COL) W RTD 4 Nessim Cohen (FR), Paris – WBC

26.06.76 Carlos Monzon (ARG) W PTS 15 Rodrigo Valdez (COL), Monaco

30.07.77 Carlos Monzon (ARG) W PTS 15 Rodrigo Valdez (COL), Monaco. *Carlos Monzon relinquished title*

05.11.77 Rodrigo Valdez (COL) W PTS 15 Bennie Briscoe (USA), Campione

22.04.78 Hugo Corro (ARG) W PTS 15 Rodrigo Valdez (COL), San Remo

05.08.78 Hugo Corro (ARG) W PTS 15 Ronnie Harris (USA), Buenos Aires

11.11.78 Hugo Corro (ARG) W PTS 15 Rodrigo Valdez (COL), Buenos Aires

30.06.79 Vito Antuofermo (ITA) W PTS 15 Hugo Corro (ARG), Monaco

30.11.79 Vito Antuofermo (ITA) DREW 15 Marvin Hagler (USA), Las Vegas

16.03.80 Alan Minter (GB) W PTS 15 Vito Antuofermo (ITA), Las Vegas

28.06.80 Alan Minter (GB) W RTD 8 Vito Antuofermo (ITA), The Arena, Wembley

27.09.80 Marvin Hagler (USA) W RSC 3 Alan Minter (GB), The Arena, Wembley

17.01.81 Marvin Hagler (USA) W RSC 8 Fully Obelmejias (VEN), Boston

13.06.81 Marvin Hagler (USA) W RTD 4 Vito Antuofermo (ITA), Boston

03.10.81 Marvin Hagler (USA) W RSC 11 Mustafa Hamsho (USA), Rosemont

07.03.82 Marvin Hagler (USA) W RSC 1 Caveman Lee (USA), Atlantic City

30.10.82 Marvin Hagler (USA) W RSC 5 Fully Obelmejias (VEN), San Remo

11.02.83 Marvin Hagler (USA) W RSC 6 Tony Sibson (GB), Worcester

27.05.83 Marvin Hagler (USA) W CO 4 Wilford Scypion (USA), Providence

10.11.83 Marvin Hagler (USA) W PTS 15 Roberto Duran (PAN), Las Vegas

30.03.84 Marvin Hagler (USA) W RSC 10 Juan Domingo Roldan (ARG), Las Vegas

19.10.84 Marvin Hagler (USA) W RSC 3 Mustafa Hamsho (USA), New York City

16.04.85 Marvin Hagler (USA) W RSC 3 Thomas Hearns (USA), Las Vegas

10.03.86 Marvin Hagler (USA) W CO 11 John Mugabi (U), Las Vegas. *Margin Hagler forfeited WBA/IBF recognition for failing to meet Herol Graham inside the stipulated period and subsequently boxing Sugar Ray Leonard*

06.04.87 Sugar Ray Leonard (USA) W PTS 12 Marvin Hagler (USA), Las Vegas – WBC. *Sugar Ray Leonard relinquished WBC version of title*

10.10.87 Frank Tate (USA) W PTS 15 Michael Olajide (C), Las Vegas – IBF

23.10.87 Sumbu Kalambay (ITA) W PTS 15 Iran Barkley (USA), Livorno – WBA

29.10.87 Thomas Hearns (USA) W CO 4 Juan Domingo Roldan (ARG), Las Vegas – WBC

07.02.88 Frank Tate (USA) W CO 10 Tony Sibson (GB), Stafford – IBF

01.03.88 Sumbu Kalambay (ITA) W PTS 12 Mike McCallum (J), Pesaro – WBA

06.06.88 Iran Barkley (USA) W RSC 3 Thomas Hearns (USA), Las Vegas – WBC

12.06.88 Sumbu Kalambay (ITA) W PTS 12 Robbie Sims (USA), Ravenna – WBA

28.07.88 Michael Nunn (USA) W RSC 9 Frank Tate (USA), Las Vegas – IBF

04.11.88 Michael Nunn (USA) W CO 8 Juan Domingo Roldan (ARG), Las Vegas – IBF

08.11.88 Sumbu Kalambay (ITA) W RSC 7 Doug de Witt (USA), Monaco – WBA. *Sumbu Kalambay forfeited WBA recognition when failing to sign for defence against Herol Graham*

24.02.89 Roberto Duran (PAN) W PTS 12 Iran Barkley (USA), Atlantic City – WBC. *Roberto Duran forfeited WBC recognition for failing to give a written undertaking to defend his title*

25.03.89 Michael Nunn (USA) W CO 1 Sumbu Kalambay (ITA), Las Vegas – IBF

18.04.89 Doug de Witt (USA) W PTS 12 Robbie Sims (USA), Atlantic City – WBO

10.05.89 Mike McCallum (J) W PTS 12 Herol Graham (GB), Albert Hall, London – WBA

14.08.89 Michael Nunn (USA) W PTS 12 Iran Barkley (USA), Reno – IBF

15.01.90 Doug de Witt (USA) W RTD 11 Matthew Hilton (C), Atlantic City – WBO

03.02.90 Mike McCallum (J) W PTS 12 Steve Collins (I), Boston – WBA

14.04.90 Michael Nunn (USA) W PTS 12 Marlon Starling (USA), Las Vegas – IBF

14.04.90 Mike McCallum (J) W CO 11 Michael Watson (GB), Albert Hall, London – WBA

29.04.90 Nigel Benn (GB) W RSC 8 Doug de Witt (USA), Atlantic City – WBO

18.08.90 Nigel Benn (GB) W RSC 1 Iran Barkley (USA), Las Vegas – WBO

18.10.90 Michael Nunn (USA) W RSC 10 Don Curry (USA), Paris – IBF

18.11.90 Chris Eubank (GB) W RSC 9 Nigel Benn (GB), Exhibition Centre, Birmingham – WBO

24.11.90 Julian Jackson (USA) W CO 4 Herol Graham (GB), Benalmadena – WBC

23.02.91 Chris Eubank (GB) W TD 10 Dan Sherry (C), Conference Centre, Brighton – WBO

01.04.91 Mike McCallum (J) W PTS 12 Sumbu Kalambay (ITA), Monaco – WBA. *Mike McCallum forfeited WBA recognition when challenging James Toney for IBF version of title*

18.04.91 Chris Eubank (GB) W RSC 6 Gary Stretch (GB), Olympia, London – WBO

10.05.91 James Toney (USA) W RSC 11 Michael Nunn (USA), Davenport – IBF

22.06.91 Chris Eubank (GB) W PTS 12 Michael Watson (GB), Earls Court Exhibition Centre, London – WBO. *Chris Eubank relinquished WBO version of title*

29.06.91 James Toney (USA) W PTS 12 Reggie Johnson (USA), Las Vegas – IBF

14.09.91 Julian Jackson (USA) W CO 1 Dennis Milton (USA), Las Vegas – WBC

12.10.91 James Toney (USA) W RSC 4 Francisco Dell' Aquila (ITA), Monaco – IBF

20.11.91 Gerald McClellan (USA) W RSC 1 John Mugabi (U), Albert Hall, London – WBO

13.12.91 James Toney (USA) DREW 12 Mike McCallum (J), Atlantic City – IBF

08.02.92 James Toney (USA) W PTS 12 Dave Tiberi (USA), Atlantic City – IBF

15.02.92 Julian Jackson (USA) W CO 1 Ismael Negron (USA), Las Vegas – WBC

10.04.92 Julian Jackson (USA) W RSC 5 Ron Collins (USA), Mexico City – WBC

11.04.92 James Toney (USA) W PTS 12 Glenn Wolfe (USA), Las Vegas – IBF

22.04.92 Reggie Johnson (USA) W PTS 12 Steve Collins (I), East Rutherford – WBA

Light-Middleweight

20.10.62 Denny Moyer (USA) W PTS 15 Joey Giambra (USA), Portland – WBA

19.02.63 Denny Moyer (USA) W PTS 15 Stan Harrington (USA), Honolulu – WBA

29.04.63 Ralph Dupas (USA) W PTS 15 Denny Moyer (USA), New Orleans – WBA

17.06.63 Ralph Dupas (USA) W PTS 15 Denny Moyer (USA), Baltimore – WBA

07.09.63 Sandro Mazzinghi (ITA) W CO 9 Ralph Dupas (USA), Milan – WBA

02.12.63 Sandro Mazzinghi (ITA) W RSC 13 Ralph Dupas (USA), Sydney – WBA

11.12.64 Sandro Mazzinghi (ITA) W PTS 15 Fortunato Manca (ITA), Rome – WBA

18.06.65 Nino Benvenuti (ITA) W CO 6 Sandro Mazzinghi (ITA), Milan – WBA

17.12.65 Nino Benvenuti (ITA) W PTS 15 Sandro Mazzinghi (ITA), Rome – WBA

25.06.66 Ki-Soo Kim (SK) W PTS 15 Nino Benvenuti (ITA), Seoul – WBA

17.12.66 Ki-Soo Kim (SK) W PTS 15 Stan Harrington (USA), Seoul – WBA

03.10.67 Ki-Soo Kim (SK) W PTS 15 Freddie Little (USA), Seoul – WBA

25.05.68 Sandro Mazzinghi (ITA) W PTS 15 Ki-Soo Kim (SK), Milan – WBA

25.10.68 Sandro Mazzinghi (ITA) NC 9 Freddie Little (USA), Rome – WBA. *Sandro Mazzinghi forfeited WBA recognition for failing to defend against Freddie Little*

17.03.69 Freddie Little (USA) W PTS 15 Stan Hayward (USA), Las Vegas – WBA

09.09.69 Freddie Little (USA) W CO 2 Hisao Minami (JAP), Osaka – WBA

20.03.70 Freddie Little (USA) W PTS 15 Gerhard Piaskowy (GER), Berlin – WBA

09.07.70 Carmelo Bossi (ITA) W PTS 15 Freddie Little (USA), Monza – WBA

29.04.71 Carmelo Bossi (ITA) DREW 15 Jose Hernandez (SP), Madrid – WBA

31.10.71 Koichi Wajima (JAP) W PTS 15 Carmelo Bossi (ITA), Tokyo – WBA

07.05.72 Koichi Wajima (JAP) W CO 1 Domenico Tiberia (ITA), Tokyo – WBA

03.10.72 Koichi Wajima (JAP) W CO 3 Matt Donovan (TR), Tokyo – WBA

09.01.73 Koichi Wajima (JAP) DREW 15 Miguel de Oliviera (BR), Tokyo – WBA

19.04.73 Koichi Wajima (JAP) W PTS 15 Ryu Sorimachi (JAP), Osaka – WBA

14.08.73 Koichi Wajima (JAP) W RTD 12 Silvani Bertini (ITA), Sapporo – WBA

05.02.74 Koichi Wajima (JAP) W PTS 15 Miguel de Oliviera (BR), Tokyo – WBA

03.06.74 Oscar Albarado (USA) W CO 15 Koichi Wajima (JAP), Tokyo – WBA

08.10.74 Oscar Albarado (USA) W RSC 7 Ryu Sorimachi (JAP), Tokyo – WBA

21.01.75 Koichi Wajima (JAP) W PTS 15 Oscar Albarado (USA), Tokyo – WBA

07.05.75 Miguel de Oliviera (BR) W PTS 15 Jose Duran (SP), Monaco – WBC

07.06.75 Jae-Do Yuh (SK) W RSC 7 Koichi Wajima (JAP), Kitakyushi – WBA

11.11.75 Jae-Do Yuh (SK) W RSC 6 Masahiro Misako (JAP), Shizuoka – WBA

13.11.75 Elisha Obed (BAH) W RTD 10 Miguel de Oliviera (BR), Paris – WBC

17.02.76 Koichi Wajima (JAP) W CO 15 Jae-Do Yuh (SK), Tokyo – WBA

28.02.76 Elisha Obed (BAH) W CO 2 Tony Gardner (USA), Nassau – WBC

25.04.76 Elisha Obed (BAH) W PTS 15 Sea Robinson (IC), Abidjan – WBC

18.05.76 Jose Duran (SP) W CO 14 Koichi Wajima (JAP), Tokyo – WBA

18.06.76 Eckhard Dagge (GER) W RTD 10 Elisha Obed (BAH), Berlin – WBC

18.09.76 Eckhard Dagge (GER) W PTS 15 Emile Griffith (USA), Berlin – WBC

08.10.76 Miguel Castellini (ARG) W PTS 15 Jose Duran (SP), Madrid – WBA

05.03.77 Eddie Gazo (NIC) W PTS 15 Miguel Castellini (ARG), Managua – WBA

15.03.77 Eckhard Dagge (GER) DREW 15 Maurice Hope (GB), Berlin – WBC

07.06.77 Eddie Gazo (NIC) W RSC 11 Koichi Wajima (JAP), Tokyo – WBA

06.08.77 Rocky Mattioli (ITA) W CO 5 Eckhard Dagge (GER), Berlin – WBC

13.09.77 Eddie Gazo (NIC) W PTS 15 Kenji Shibata (JAP), Tokyo – WBA

18.12.77 Eddie Gazo (NIC) W PTS 15 Chae-Keun Lim (SK), Inchon – WBA

11.03.78 Rocky Mattioli (ITA) W CO 7 Elisha Obed (BAH), Melbourne – WBC

14.05.78 Rocky Mattioli (ITA) W RSC 5 Jose Duran (SP), Pescara – WBC

09.08.78 Masashi Kudo (JAP) W PTS 15 Eddie Gazo (NIC), Akita – WBA

13.12.78 Masashi Kudo (JAP) W PTS 15 Ho-In Joo (SK), Osaka – WBA

04.03.79 Maurice Hope (GB) W RTD 8 Rocky Mattioli (ITA), San Remo – WBC

13.03.79 Masashi Kudo (JAP) W PTS 15 Manuel Gonzalez (USA), Tokyo – WBA

20.06.79 Masashi Kudo (JAP) W RSC 12 Manuel Gonzalez (USA), Yokkaichi – WBA

25.09.79 Maurice Hope (GB) W RSC 7 Mike Baker (USA), The Arena, Wembley – WBC

24.10.79 Ayub Kalule (U) W PTS 15 Masashi Kudo (JAP), Akita – WBA

06.12.79 Ayub Kalule (U) W PTS 15 Steve Gregory (USA), Copenhagen – WBA

17.04.80 Ayub Kalule (U) W RTD 11 Emiliano Villa (COL), Copenhagen – WBA

12.06.80 Ayub Kalule (U) W PTS 15 Marijan Benes (YUG), Randers – WBA

12.07.80 Maurice Hope (GB) W RSC 11 Rocky Mattioli (ITA), Grand Hall, Wembley – WBC

06.09.80 Ayub Kalule (U) W PTS 15 Bushy Bester (SA), Aarhus – WBA

26.11.80 Maurice Hope (GB) W PTS 15 Carlos Herrera (ARG), Grand Hall Wembley – WBC

24.05.81 Wilfred Benitez (PR) W CO 12 Maurice Hope (GB), Las Vegas – WBC

25.06.81 Sugar Ray Leonard (USA) W RSC 9 Ayub Kalule (U), Houston – WBA. Sugar Ray Leonard relinquished WBA version of title

07.11.81 Tadashi Mihara (JAP) W PTS 15 Rocky Fratto (USA), Rochester – WBA

14.11.81 Wilfred Benitez (PR) W PTS 15 Carlos Santos (PR), Las Vegas – WBC

30.01.82 Wilfred Benitez (PR) W PTS 15 Roberto Duran (PAN), Las Vegas – WBC

02.02.82 Davey Moore (USA) W RSC 6 Tadashi Mihara (JAP), Tokyo – WBA

26.04.82 Davey Moore (USA) W CO 5 Charlie Weir (SA), Johannesburg – WBA

17.07.82 Davey Moore (USA) W RSC 10 Ayub Kalule (U), Atlantic City – WBA

03.12.82 Thomas Hearns (USA) W PTS 15 Wilfred Benitez (PR), New Orleans – WBC

29.01.83 Davey Moore (USA) W CO 4 Gary Guiden (USA), Atlantic City – WBA

16.06.83 Roberto Duran (PAN) W RSC 8 Davey Moore (USA), New York City – WBA.

Roberto Duran relinquished WBA version of title

11.02.84 Thomas Hearns (USA) W PTS 12 Luigi Minchillo (ITA), Detroit – WBC

11.03.84 Mark Medal (USA) W RSC 5 Earl Hargrove (USA), Atlantic City – IBF

15.06.84 Thomas Hearns (USA) W CO 2 Roberto Duran (PAN), Las Vegas – WBC

15.09.84 Thomas Hearns (USA) W RSC 3 Fred Hutchings (USA), Saginaw – WBC

19.10.84 Mike McCallum (J) W PTS 15 Sean Mannion (USA), New York City – WBA

02.11.84 Carlos Santos (PR) W PTS 15 Mark Medal (USA), New York City – IBF

01.12.84 Mike McCallum (J) W RSC 14 Luigi Minchillo (ITA), Milan – WBA

01.06.85 Carlos Santos (PR) W PTS 15 Louis Acaries (FR), Paris – IBF. *Carlos Santos forfeited IBF recognition for failing to defend against Davey Moore*

28.07.85 Mike McCallum (J) W RSC 8 David Braxton (USA), Miami – WBA

04.06.86 Buster Drayton (USA) W PTS 15 Carlos Santos (PR), East Rutherford – IBF

23.06.86 Thomas Hearns (USA) W RSC 8 Mark Medal (USA), Las Vegas – WBC. *Thomas Hearns relinquished WBC version of title*

23.08.86 Mike McCallum (J) W RSC 2 Julian Jackson (USA), Miami – WBA

24.08.86 Buster Drayton (USA) W RSC 10 Davey Moore (USA), Juan les Pins – IBF

25.10.86 Mike McCallum (J) W CO 9 Said Skouma (FR), Paris – WBA

05.12.86 Duane Thomas (USA) W RSC 3 John Mugabi (U), Las Vegas – WBC

27.03.87 Buster Drayton (USA) W RTD 10 Said Skouma (FR), Cannes – IBF

19.04.87 Mike McCallum (J) W RSC 10 Milton McCrory (USA), Phoenix – WBA

27.06.87 Matthew Hilton (C) W PTS 15 Buster Drayton (USA), Montreal – IBF

12.07.87 Lupe Aquino (MEX) W PTS 12 Duane Thomas (USA), Bordeaux – WBC

18.07.87 Mike McCallum (J) W CO 5 Don Curry (USA), Las Vegas – WBA. *Mike McCallum relinquished WBA version of title*

02.10.87 Gianfranco Rosi (ITA) W PTS 12 Lupe Aquino (MEX), Perugia – WBC

16.10.87 Matthew Hilton (C) W RTD 2 Jack Callahan (USA), Atlantic City – IBF

21.11.87 Julian Jackson (USA) W RSC 3 In-Chul Baek (SK), Las Vegas – WBA

03.01.88 Gianfranco Rosi (ITA) W RSC 7 Duane Thomas (USA), Genoa – WBC

08.07.88 Don Curry (USA) W RTD 9 Gianfranco Rosi (ITA), San Remo – WBC

30.07.88 Julian Jackson (USA) W RSC 3 Buster Drayton (USA), Atlantic City – WBA

04.11.88 Robert Hines (USA) W PTS 12 Matthew Hilton (C), Las Vegas – IBF

08.12.88 John David Jackson (USA) W RTD 7 Lupe Aquino (MEX), Detroit – WBO

05.02.89 Darrin van Horn (USA) W PTS 12 Robert Hines (USA), Atlantic City – IBF

11.02.89 Rene Jacquot (FR) W PTS 12 Don Curry (USA), Grenoble – WBC

25.02.89 Julian Jackson (USA) W CO 8 Francisco de Jesus (BR), Las Vegas – WBA

22.04.89 John David Jackson (USA) W RSC 8 Steve Little (USA), Detroit – WBO

08.07.89 John Mugabi (U) W RSC 1 Rene Jacquot (FR), Paris – WBC

15.07.89 Gianfranco Rosi (ITA) W PTS 12 Darrin van Horn (USA), Atlantic City – IBF

30.07.89 Julian Jackson (USA) W RSC 2 Terry Norris (USA), Atlantic City – WBA. *Julian Jackson forfeited WBA recognition when challenging Herol Graham for the WBC middleweight title*

27.10.89 Gianfranco Rosi (ITA) W PTS 12 Troy Waters (A), St Vincent – IBF

17.02.90 John David Jackson (USA) NC 11 Martin Camara (FR), Deauville – WBO

31.03.90 Terry Norris (USA) W CO 1 John Mugabi (U), Tampa – WBC

14.04.90 Gianfranco Rosi (ITA) W RSC 7 Kevin Daigle (USA), Monaco – IBF

13.07.90 Terry Norris (USA) W PTS 12 Rene Jacquot (FR), Annecy – WBC

21.07.90 Gianfranco Rosi (ITA) W PTS 12 Darrin van Horn (USA), Marino – IBF

23.11.90 John David Jackson (USA) W PTS 12 Chris Pyatt (GB), Granby Halls, Leicester – WBO

30.11.90 Gianfranco Rosi (ITA) W PTS 12 Rene Jacquot (FR), Marsala – IBF

09.02.91 Terry Norris (USA) W PTS 12 Sugar Ray Leonard (USA), New York City – WBC

23.02.91 Gilbert Dele (FR) W RSC 7 Carlos Elliott (USA), Point a Pitre – WBA

16.03.91 Gianfranco Rosi (ITA) W PTS 12 Ron Amundsen (USA), St Vincent – IBF

05.05.91 Gilbert Dele (FR) W PTS 12 Jun-Suk Hwang (SK), Paris – WBA

01.06.91 Terry Norris (USA) W CO 8 Don Curry USA, Palm Springs – WBC

13.07.91 Gianfranco Rosi (ITA) W PTS 12 Glenn Wolfe (USA), Avezzano – IBF

20.07.91 John David Jackson (USA) W PTS 12 Tyrone Trice (USA), McKee City – WBO

16.08.91 Terry Norris (USA) W RSC 1 Brett Lally (USA), San Diego – WBC

03.10.91 Vinnie Pazienza (USA) W RSC 12 Gilbert Dele (FR), Providence – WBA

21.11.91 Gianfranco Rosi (ITA) W PTS 12 Gilbert Baptist (USA), Perugia – IBF

13.12.92 Terry Norris (USA) W PTS 12 Jorge Castro (ARG), Paris – WBC

22.02.92 Terry Norris (USA) W RSC 9 Carl Daniels (USA), San Diego – WBC

09.04.92 Gianfranco Rosi (ITA) W RSC 6 Angel Hernandez (SP), Celano – IBF

09.05.92 Terry Norris (USA) W RSC 4 Meldrick Taylor (USA), Las Vegas – WBC

09.06.92 John David Jackson (USA) W RTD 9 Pat Lawlor (USA), San Francisco – WBO

Welterweight

14.12.92 **Mysterious Billy Smith** (USA) W CO 14 Danny Needham (USA), San Francisco

17.04.93 **Mysterious Billy Smith** (USA) W CO 2 Tom Williams (A), New York City

26.07.94 **Tommy Ryan** (USA) W PTS 20 Mysterious Billy Smith (USA), Minneapolis

18.01.95 **Tommy Ryan** (USA) W 3 Nonpareil Jack Dempsey (USA), New York City

27.05.95 **Tommy Ryan** (USA) NC 18 Mysterious Billy Smith (USA), New York City

25.11.96 **Tommy Ryan** (USA) W DIS 9 Mysterious Billy Smith (USA), New York City

23.12.96 **Tommy Ryan** (USA) W CO 4 Bill Payne (USA), Syracuse

24.02.97 **Tommy Ryan** (USA) W CO 9 Tom Tracey (A), Syracuse. *Tommy Ryan relinquished title*

04.04.98 Mysterious Billy Smith (USA) DREW 25 Joe Walcott (USA), Bridgeport

29.07.98 **Mysterious Billy Smith** (USA) W PTS 25 George Green (USA), New York City

25.08.98 **Mysterious Billy Smith** (USA) W PTS 25 Matty Matthews (USA), New York City

05.09.98 **Mysterious Billy Smith** (USA) DREW 25 Andy Walsh (USA), New York City

03.10.98 **Mysterious Billy Smith** (USA) W CO 20 Jim Judge (USA), Scranton

07.10.98 **Mysterious Billy Smith** (USA) W PTS 25 Charley McKeever (USA), New York City

06.12.98 **Mysterious Billy Smith** (USA) W PTS 20 Joe Walcott (USA), New York City

24.01.99 **Mysterious Billy Smith** (USA) W CO 14 Billy Edwards (A), New York City

10.03.99 **Mysterious Billy Smith** (USA) W RSC 14 George Lavigne (USA), San Francisco

29.06.99 **Mysterious Billy Smith** (USA) DREW 20 Charley McKeever (USA), New York City

04.08.99 **Mysterious Billy Smith** (USA) DREW 25 Andy Walsh (USA), New York City

08.11.99 **Mysterious Billy Smith** (USA) W PTS 20 Charley McKeever (USA), New York City

17.04.00 **Matty Matthews** (USA) W CO 19 Mysterious Billy Smith (USA), New York City

05.06.00 **Eddie Connolly** (C) W PTS 25 Matty Matthews (USA), Coney Island

13.08.00 **Rube Ferns** (USA) W RTD 15 Eddie Connolly (C), Buffalo

01.09.00 **Rube Ferns** (USA) W PTS 15 Matty Matthews (USA), Detroit

16.10.00	**Matty Matthews** (USA) W PTS 15 Rube Ferns (USA), Detroit
29.04.01	**Matty Matthews** (USA) W PTS 20 Tom Couhig (USA), Louisville
24.05.01	**Rube Ferns** (USA) W CO 10 Matty Matthews (USA), Toronto
23.09.01	**Rube Ferns** (USA) W CO 9 Frank Erne (USA), Fort Erie
18.12.01	**Joe Walcott** (USA) W RSC 5 Rube Ferns (USA), Fort Erie
23.06.02	**Joe Walcott** (USA) W PTS 15 Tommy West (GB), NSC, London
02.04.03	**Joe Walcott** (USA) DREW 20 Billy Woods (USA), Los Angeles
29.04.04	**Dixie Kid** (USA) W DIS 20 Joe Walcott (USA), San Francisco
12.05.04	**Dixie Kid** (USA) DREW 20 Joe Walcott (USA), San Francisco. *Dixie Kid forfeited title for failing to defend within a reasonable period*
30.09.04	Joe Walcott (USA) DREW 20 Joe Gans (USA), San Francisco
16.10.06	**Honey Mellody** (USA) W PTS 15 Joe Walcott (USA), Chelsea, Mass
29.11.06	**Honey Mellody** (USA) W RSC 12 Joe Walcott (USA), Chelsea, Mass
23.04.07	**Mike Twin Sullivan** (USA) W PTS 20 Honey Mellody (USA), Los Angeles. *Mike Twin Sullivan forfeited national recognition when Frank Mantell also defeated Honey Mellody*
01.11.07	**Frank Mantell** (USA) W CO 15 Honey Mellody (USA), Dayton – OHIO
01.11.07	**Mike Twin Sullivan** (USA) W PTS 20 Frank Field (USA), Goldfield – CALIF
27.11.07	**Mike Twin Sullivan** (USA) W CO 13 Kid Farmer (USA), Los Angeles – CALIF
23.01.08	**Harry Lewis** (USA) W CO 3 Frank Mantell (USA), New Haven – OHIO
23.04.08	**Mike Twin Sullivan** (USA) W PTS 25 Jimmy Gardner (USA), Los Angeles – CALIF. *Mike Twin Sullivan relinquished Californian version of title*
07.11.08	**Jimmy Gardner** (USA) W PTS 15 Jimmy Clabby (USA), New Orleans – LOUIS
26.11.08	**Jimmy Gardner** (USA) DREW 20 Jimmy Clabby (USA), New Orleans – LOUIS. *Jimmy Gardner forfeited Louisianan recognition when unable to make the weight*
19.02.10	**Harry Lewis** (USA) DREW 25 Willie Lewis (USA), Paris – FR
23.04.10	**Harry Lewis** (USA) DREW 25 Willie Lewis (USA), Paris – FR
04.05.10	**Harry Lewis** (USA) W CO 3 Peter Brown (GB), Paris – FR
27.06.10	**Harry Lewis** (USA) W RTD 7 Young Joseph (GB), Wonderland, London – GB/FR
05.09.10	**Jimmy Clabby** (USA) W CO 13 Guy Buckles (USA), Sheridan – USA
02.11.10	**Jimmy Clabby** (USA) W RSC 7 Bob Bryant (A), Sydney – USA/AUSTR
26.12.10	**Jimmy Clabby** (USA) W CO 1 Gus Devitt (A), Brisbane – USA/AUSTR. *Jimmy Clabby forfeited USA/Australian recognition when unable to make the weight*
25.01.11	**Harry Lewis** (USA) W CO 4 Johnny Summers (GB), Olympia, London – GB/FR. *Harry Lewis forfeited GB/French recognition following losing contests against Johnny Mathieson in 1912*
01.01.14	**Waldemar Holberg** (DEN) W PTS 20 Ray Bronson (USA), Melbourne – AUSTR
24.01.14	**Tom McCormick** (GB) W DIS 6 Waldemar Holberg (DEN), Melbourne – AUSTR
14.02.14	**Tom McCormick** (GB) W CO 1 Johnny Summers (GB), Sydney – AUSTR
21.03.14	**Matt Wells** (GB) W PTS 20 Tom McCormick (GB), Sydney – AUSTR
01.06.15	**Mike Glover** (USA) W PTS 12 Matt Wells (GB), Boston – USA
22.06.15	**Jack Britton** (USA) W PTS 12 Mike Glover (USA), Boston – USA
31.08.15	**Ted Kid Lewis** (GB) W PTS 12 Jack Britton (USA), Boston
27.09.15	**Ted Kid Lewis** (GB) W PTS 12 Jack Britton (USA), Boston
26.10.15	**Ted Kid Lewis** (GB) W PTS 12 Joe Mandot (USA), Boston
02.11.15	**Ted Kid Lewis** (GB) W PTS 12 Milburn Saylor (USA), Boston
23.11.15	**Ted Kid Lewis** (GB) W CO 1 Jimmy Duffy (USA), Boston
01.03.16	**Ted Kid Lewis** (GB) W PTS 20 Harry Stone (USA), New Orleans
24.04.16	**Jack Britton** (USA) W PTS 20 Ted Kid Lewis (GB), New Orleans
06.06.16	**Jack Britton** (USA) W PTS 12 Mike O'Dowd (USA), Boston
17.10.16	**Jack Britton** (USA) W PTS 12 Ted Kid Lewis (GB), Boston
14.11.16	**Jack Britton** (USA) DREW 12 Ted Kid Lewis (GB), Boston
21.11.16	**Jack Britton** (USA) W PTS 12 Charley White (USA), Boston
25.06.17	**Ted Kid Lewis** (GB) W PTS 20 Jack Britton (USA), Dayton
13.11.17	**Ted Kid Lewis** (GB) W RSC 4 Johnny McCarthy (USA), San Francisco
17.05.18	**Ted Kid Lewis** (GB) W PTS 20 Johnny Tillman (USA), Denver
17.03.19	**Jack Britton** (USA) W CO 9 Ted Kid Lewis (GB), Canton
01.12.19	**Jack Britton** (USA) W CO 11 Billy Ryan (USA), Canton
31.05.20	**Jack Britton** (USA) W PTS 15 Johnny Griffiths (USA), Akron
23.08.20	**Jack Britton** (USA) DREW 12 Lou Bogash (USA), Bridgeport
06.09.20	**Jack Britton** (USA) W PTS 10 Ray Bronson (USA), Cedar Point
07.02.21	**Jack Britton** (USA) W PTS 15 Ted Kid Lewis (GB), New York City
03.06.21	**Jack Britton** (USA) DREW 10 Dave Shade (USA), Portland
10.06.21	**Jack Britton** (USA) DREW 10 Frank Barrieau (USA), Portland
17.02.22	**Jack Britton** (USA) DREW 15 Dave Shade (USA), New York City
26.06.22	**Jack Britton** (USA) W DIS 13 Benny Leonard (USA), New York City
01.11.22	**Mickey Walker** (USA) W PTS 15 Jack Britton (USA), New York City
08.10.23	**Mickey Walker** (USA) NC 9 Jimmy Jones (USA), Newark
02.06.24	**Mickey Walker** (USA) W PTS 10 Lew Tendler (USA), Philadelphia
01.10.24	**Mickey Walker** (USA) W CO 6 Bobby Barrett (USA), Philadelphia
21.09.25	**Mickey Walker** (USA) W PTS 15 Dave Shade (USA), New York City
20.05.26	**Pete Latzo** (USA) W PTS 10 Mickey Walker (USA), Scranton
29.06.26	**Pete Latzo** (USA) W CO 5 Willie Harmon (USA), Newark
09.07.26	**Pete Latzo** (USA) W DIS 4 George Levine (USA), New York City
03.06.27	**Joe Dundee** (USA) W PTS 15 Pete Latzo (USA), New York City
07.07.28	**Joe Dundee** (USA) W CO 8 Hilario Martinez (SP), Philadelphia. *Joe Dundee forfeited NBA recognition when not defending against Jackie Fields*
25.03.29	Jackie Fields (USA) W PTS 10 Young Jack Thompson (USA), Chicago – NBA
25.07.29	**Jackie Fields** (USA) W DIS 2 Joe Dundee (USA), Detroit
09.05.30	**Young Jack Thompson** (USA) W PTS 15 Jackie Fields (USA), Detroit
05.09.30	**Tommy Freeman** (USA) W PTS 15 Young Jack Thompson (USA), Cleveland
09.01.31	**Tommy Freeman** (USA) W PTS 10 Pete August (USA), Hot Springs
26.01.31	**Tommy Freeman** (USA) W PTS 10 Eddie Murdock (USA), Oklahoma City
05.02.31	**Tommy Freeman** (USA) W CO 5 Duke Tramel (USA), Memphis
09.02.31	**Tommy Freeman** (USA) W CO 5 Al Kid Kober (USA), New Orleans
01.03.31	**Tommy Freeman** (USA) W PTS 10 Alfredo Gaona (MEX), Mexico City
14.04.31	**Young Jack Thompson** (USA) W RTD 12 Tommy Freeman (USA), Cleveland
23.10.31	**Lou Brouillard** (C) W PTS 15 Young Jack Thompson (USA), Boston
28.01.32	**Jackie Fields** (USA) W PTS 10 Lou Brouillard (C), Chicago
22.02.33	**Young Corbett III** (USA) W PTS 10 Jackie Fields (USA), San Francisco
29.05.33	**Jimmy McLarnin** (USA) W CO 1 Young Corbett III (USA), Los Angeles
28.05.34	**Barney Ross** (USA) W PTS 15 Jimmy McLarnin (USA), New York City
17.09.34	**Jimmy McLarnin** (USA) W PTS 15 Barney Ross (USA), New York City
28.05.35	**Barney Ross** (USA) W PTS 15 Jimmy McLarnin (USA), New York City
27.11.36	**Barney Ross** (USA) W PTS 15 Izzy Jannazzo (USA), New York City
23.09.37	**Barney Ross** (USA) W PTS 15 Ceferino Garcia (PH), New York City
31.05.38	**Henry Armstrong** (USA) W PTS 15 Barney Ross (USA), New York City
25.11.38	**Henry Armstrong** (USA) W PTS 15 Ceferino Garcia (PH), New York City
05.12.38	**Henry Armstrong** (USA) W RSC 3 Al Manfredo (USA), Cleveland
10.01.39	**Henry Armstrong** (USA) W PTS 10 Baby Arizmendi (MEX), Los Angeles
04.03.39	**Henry Armstrong** (USA) W RSC 4 Bobby Pacho (USA), Havana
16.03.39	**Henry Armstrong** (USA) W CO 1 Lew Feldman (USA), St Louis
31.03.39	**Henry Armstrong** (USA) W CO 12 Davey Day (USA), New York City
25.05.39	**Henry Armstrong** (USA) W PTS 15 Ernie Roderick (GB), Harringay Arena, London
09.10.39	**Henry Armstrong** (USA) W RSC 4 Al Manfredo (USA), Des Moines
13.10.39	**Henry Armstrong** (USA) W CO 2 Howard Scott (USA), Minneapolis
20.10.39	**Henry Armstrong** (USA) W CO 3 Richie Fontaine (USA), Seattle
24.10.39	**Henry Armstrong** (USA) W PTS 10 Jimmy Garrison (USA), Los Angeles
30.10.39	**Henry Armstrong** (USA) W RSC 4 Bobby Pacho (USA), Denver
11.12.39	**Henry Armstrong** (USA) W CO 7 Jimmy Garrison (USA), Cleveland
04.01.40	**Henry Armstrong** (USA) W CO 5 Joe Ghnouly (USA), St Louis
24.01.40	**Henry Armstrong** (USA) W RSC 9 Pedro Montanez (PR), New York City
26.04.40	**Henry Armstrong** (USA) W RSC 7 Paul Junior (C), Boston
24.05.40	**Henry Armstrong** (USA) W RSC 5 Ralph Zanelli (USA), Boston
21.06.40	**Henry Armstrong** (USA) W RSC 3 Paul Junior (C), Portland
23.09.40	**Henry Armstrong** (USA) W CO 4 Phil Furr (USA), Washington
04.10.40	**Fritzie Zivic** (USA) W PTS 15 Henry Armstrong (USA), New York City
17.01.41	**Fritzie Zivic** (USA) W RSC 12 Henry Armstrong (USA), New York City
29.07.41	**Red Cochrane** (USA) W PTS 15 Fritzie Zivic (USA), Newark
01.02.46	**Marty Servo** (USA) W CO 4 Red Cochrane (USA), New York City. *Marty Servo relinquished title*
20.12.46	**Sugar Ray Robinson** (USA) W PTS 15 Tommy Bell (USA), New York City
24.06.47	**Sugar Ray Robinson** (USA) W RSC 8 Jimmy Doyle (USA), Cleveland
19.12.47	**Sugar Ray Robinson** (USA) W RSC 6 Chuck Taylor (USA), Detroit
28.06.48	**Sugar Ray Robinson** (USA) W PTS 15 Bernard Docusen (USA), Chicago
11.07.49	**Sugar Ray Robinson** (USA) W PTS 15 Kid Gavilan (CUB), Philadelphia
09.08.50	**Sugar Ray Robinson** (USA) W PTS 15 Charlie Fusari (USA), Jersey City. *Sugar Ray Robinson relinquished title*
14.03.51	Johnny Bratton (USA) W PTS 15 Charlie Fusari (USA), Chicago – NBA
18.05.51	**Kid Gavilan** (CUB) W PTS 15 Johnny Bratton (USA), New York City – NBA/NY
29.08.51	**Kid Gavilan** (CUB) W PTS 15 Billy Graham (USA), New York City – NBA/NY
04.02.52	Kid Gavilan (CUB) W PTS 15 Bobby Dykes (USA), Miami – NBA/NY
07.07.52	**Kid Gavilan** (CUB) W RSC 11 Gil Turner (USA), Philadelphia
05.10.52	**Kid Gavilan** (CUB) W PTS 15 Billy Graham (USA), Havana
11.02.53	**Kid Gavilan** (CUB) W RTD 9 Chuck Davey (USA), Chicago
18.09.53	**Kid Gavilan** (CUB) W PTS 15 Carmen Basilio (USA), Syracuse
13.11.53	**Kid Gavilan** (CUB) W PTS 15 Johnny Bratton (USA), Chicago
20.10.54	**Johnny Saxton** (USA) W PTS 15 Kid Gavilan (CUB), Philadelphia
01.04.55	**Tony de Marco** (USA) W RSC 14 Johnny Saxton (USA), Boston
10.06.55	**Carmen Basilio** (USA) W RSC 12 Tony de Marco (USA), Syracuse
30.11.55	**Carmen Basilio** (USA) W RSC 12 Tony de Marco (USA), Boston
14.03.56	**Johnny Saxton** (USA) W PTS 15 Carmen Basilio (USA), Chicago
12.09.56	**Carmen Basilio** (USA) W RSC 9 Johnny Saxton (USA), Syracuse
22.02.57	**Carmen Basilio** (USA) W CO 2 Johnny Saxton (USA), Cleveland. *Carmen Basilio relinquished title*

05.06.58 **Virgil Akins** (USA) W RSC 4 Vince Martinez (USA), St Louis

05.12.58 **Don Jordan** (USA) W PTS 15 Virgil Akins (USA), Los Angeles

24.04.59 **Don Jordan** (USA) W PTS 15 Virgil Akins (USA), St Louis

10.07.59 **Don Jordan** (USA) W PTS 15 Denny Moyer (USA), Portland

27.05.60 **Benny Kid Paret** (CUB) W PTS 15 Don Jordan (USA), Las Vegas

10.12.60 **Benny Kid Paret** (CUB) W PTS 15 Federico Thompson (PAN), New York City

01.04.61 **Emile Griffith** (USA) W CO 13 Benny Kid Paret (CUB), Miami

03.06.61 **Emile Griffith** (USA) W RSC 12 Gaspar Ortega (MEX), Los Angeles

30.09.61 **Benny Kid Paret** (CUB) W PTS 15 Emile Griffith (USA), New York City

24.03.62 **Emile Griffith** (USA) W RSC 12 Benny Kid Paret (CUB), New York City

13.07.62 **Emile Griffith** (USA) W PTS 15 Ralph Dupas (USA), Las Vegas

08.12.62 **Emile Griffith** (USA) W RTD 9 Jorge Fernandez (ARG), Las Vegas

21.03.63 **Luis Rodriguez** (CUB) W PTS 15 Emile Griffith (USA), Los Angeles

08.06.63 **Emile Griffith** (USA) W PTS 15 Luis Rodriguez (CUB), New York City

12.06.64 **Emile Griffith** (USA) W PTS 15 Luis Rodriguez (CUB), Las Vegas

22.09.64 **Emile Griffith** (USA) W PTS 15 Brian Curvis (GB), The Arena, Wembley

30.03.65 **Emile Griffith** (USA) W PTS 15 Jose Stable (CUB), New York City

10.12.65 **Emile Griffith** (USA) W PTS 15 Manuel Gonzalez (USA), New York City. *Emile Griffith relinquished title*

24.08.66 Curtis Cokes (USA) W PTS 15 Manuel Gonzalez (USA), New Orleans – WBA

28.11.66 Curtis Cokes (USA) W PTS 15 Jean Josselin (FR), Dallas – WBA

07.12.66 Charlie Shipes (USA) W RSC 10 Percy Manning (USA), Hayward – CALIF

19.05.67 Curtis Cokes (USA) W RSC 10 Francois Pavilla (FR), Dallas – WBA

02.10.67 **Curtis Cokes** (USA) W RSC 8 Charlie Shipes (USA), Oakland

16.04.68 **Curtis Cokes** (USA) W RSC 5 Willie Ludick (SA), Dallas

21.10.68 **Curtis Cokes** (USA) W PTS 15 Ramon la Cruz (ARG), New Orleans

18.04.69 **Jose Napoles** (CUB) W RSC 13 Curtis Cokes (USA), Los Angeles

29.06.69 **Jose Napoles** (CUB) W RTD 10 Curtis Cokes (USA) Mexico City

17.10.69 **Jose Napoles** (CUB) W PTS 15 Emile Griffith (USA), Los Angeles

15.02.70 **Jose Napoles** (CUB) W RSC 15 Ernie Lopez (USA), Los Angeles

03.12.70 **Billy Backus** (USA) W RSC 4 Jose Napoles (CUB), Syracuse

04.06.71 **Jose Napoles** (CUB) W RSC 8 Billy Backus (USA), Los Angeles

14.12.71 **Jose Napoles** (CUB) W PTS 15 Hedgemon Lewis (USA), Los Angeles

28.03.72 **Jose Napoles** (CUB) W CO 7 Ralph Charles (GB), The Arena, Wembley

10.06.72 **Jose Napoles** (CUB) W RSC 2 Adolph Pruitt (USA), Monterrey. *Jose Napoles forfeited NY recognition when failing to defend title against Hedgemon Lewis in a return match*

16.06.72 Hedgemon Lewis (USA) W PTS 15 Billy Backus (USA), Syracuse – NY

08.12.72 Hedgemon Lewis (USA) W PTS 15 Billy Backus (USA), Syracuse – NY

28.02.73 Jose Napoles (CUB) W CO 7 Ernie Lopez (USA), Los Angeles – WBA/WBC

23.06.73 Jose Napoles (CUB) W PTS 15 Roger Menetrey (FR), Grenoble – WBA/WBC

22.09.73 Jose Napoles (CUB) W PTS 15 Clyde Gray (C), Toronto – WBA/WBC

03.08.74 **Jose Napoles** (CUB) W RSC 9 Hedgemon Lewis (USA), Mexico City

14.12.74 **Jose Napoles** (CUB) W CO 3 Horacio Saldano (ARG), Mexico City

30.03.75 **Jose Napoles** (CUB) W TD 12 Armando Muniz (MEX), Acapulco. *Jose Napoles relinquished WBA version of title*

28.06.75 Angel Espada (PR) W PTS 15 Clyde Gray (C), San Juan – WBA

12.07.75 Jose Napoles (CUB) W PTS 15 Armando Muniz (MEX), Mexico City – WBC

11.10.75 Angel Espada (PR) W PTS 15 Johnny Gant (USA), San Juan – WBA

06.12.75 John H. Stracey (GB) W RSC 6 Jose Napoles (CUB), Mexico City – WBC

20.03.76 John H. Stracey (GB) W RSC 10 Hedgemon Lewis (USA), The Arena, Wembley – WBC

27.04.76 Angel Espada (PR) W RSC 8 Alfonso Hayman (USA), San Juan – WBA

22.06.76 Carlos Palomino (MEX) W RSC 12 John H. Stracey (GB), The Arena Wembley – WBC

17.07.76 Pipino Cuevas (MEX) W RSC 2 Angel Espada (PR), Mexicali – WBA

27.10.76 Pipino Cuevas (MEX) W CO 2 Shoji Tsujimoto (JAP), Kanazawa – WBA

22.01.77 Carlos Palomino (MEX) W RSC 15 Armando Muniz (MEX), Los Angeles – WBC

12.03.77 Pipino Cuevas (MEX) W CO 2 Miguel Campanino (ARG), Mexico City – WBA

14.06.77 Carlos Palomino (MEX) W CO 11 Dave Boy Green (GB), The Arena, Wembley – WBC

06.08.77 Pipino Cuevas (MEX) W CO 2 Clyde Gray (C), Los Angeles – WBA

13.09.77 Carlos Palomino (MEX) W PTS 15 Everaldo Azevedo (BR), Los Angeles – WBC

19.11.77 Pipino Cuevas (MEX) W RSC 11 Angel Espada (PR), San Juan – WBA

10.12.77 Carlos Palomino (MEX) W CO 13 Jose Palacios (MEX), Los Angeles – WBC

11.02.78 Carlos Palomino (MEX) W CO 7 Ryu Sorimachi (JAP), Las Vegas – WBC

04.03.78 Pipino Cuevas (MEX) W RSC 9 Harold Weston (USA), Los Angeles – WBA

18.03.78 Carlos Palomino (MEX) W RSC 9 Mimoun Mohatar (MOR), Las Vegas – WBC

20.05.78 Pipino Cuevas (MEX) W RSC 1 Billy Backus (USA), Los Angeles – WBA

27.05.78 Carlos Palomino (MEX) W PTS 15 Armando Muniz (MEX), Los Angeles – WBC

09.09.78 Pipino Cuevas (MEX) W RSC 2 Pete Ranzany (USA), Sacramento – WBA

14.01.79 Wilfred Benitez (PR) W PTS 15 Carlos Palomino (MEX), San Juan – WBC

29.01.79 Pipino Cuevas (MEX) W RSC 2 Scott Clark (USA), Los Angeles – WBA

25.03.79 Wilfred Benitez (PR) W PTS 15 Harold Weston (USA), San Juan – WBC

30.07.79 Pipino Cuevas (MEX) W PTS 15 Randy Shields (USA), Chicago – WBA

30.11.79 Sugar Ray Leonard (USA) W RSC 15 Wilfred Benitez (PR), Las Vegas – WBC

08.12.79 Pipino Cuevas (MEX) W RSC 10 Angel Espada (PR), Los Angeles – WBA

31.03.80 Sugar Ray Leonard (USA) W CO 4 Dave Boy Green (GB), Landover – WBC

06.04.80 Pipino Cuevas (MEX) W CO 5 Harold Volbrecht (SA), Houston – WBA

20.06.80 Roberto Duran (PAN) W PTS 15 Sugar Ray Leonard (USA), Montreal – WBC

02.08.80 Thomas Hearns (USA) W RSC 2 Pipino Cuevas (MEX), Detroit – WBA

25.11.80 Sugar Ray Leonard (USA) W RTD 8 Roberto Duran (PAN), New Orleans – WBC

06.12.80 Thomas Hearns (USA) W CO 6 Luis Primera (VEN), Detroit – WBA

28.03.81 Sugar Ray Leonard (USA) W RSC 10 Larry Bonds (USA), Syracuse – WBC

25.04.81 Thomas Hearns (USA) W RSC 12 Randy Shields (USA), Phoenix – WBA

25.06.81 Thomas Hearns (USA) W RSC 4 Pablo Baez (USA), Houston – WBA

16.09.81 **Sugar Ray Leonard** (USA) W RSC 14 Thomas Hearns (USA), Las Vegas

15.02.82 **Sugar Ray Leonard** (USA) W RSC 3 Bruce Finch (USA), Reno. *Sugar Ray Leonard relinquished title*

13.02.83 Don Curry (USA) W PTS 15 Jun-Sok Hwang (SK), Fort Worth – WBA

19.03.83 Milton McCrory (USA) DREW 12 Colin Jones (GB), Reno – WBC

13.08.83 Milton McCrory (USA) W PTS 12 Colin Jones (GB), Las Vegas – WBC

03.09.83 Don Curry (USA) W RSC 1 Roger Stafford (USA), Marsala – WBA

14.01.84 Milton McCrory (USA) W RSC 6 Milton Guest (USA), Detroit – WBC

04.02.84 Don Curry (USA) W PTS 15 Marlon Starling (USA), Atlantic City – WBA/IBF

15.04.84 Milton McCrory (USA) W RSC 6 Gilles Ebilia (FR), Detroit – WBC

21.04.84 Don Curry (USA) W RTD 7 Elio Diaz (VEN), Fort Worth – WBA/IBF

22.09.84 Don Curry (USA) W RSC 6 Nino la Rocca (ITA), Monaco – WBA/IBF

19.01.85 Don Curry (USA) W RSC 4 Colin Jones (GB), National Exhibition Centre, Birmingham – WBA/IBF

09.03.85 Milton McCrory (USA) W PTS 12 Pedro Vilella (PR), Paris – WBC

14.07.85 Milton McCrory (USA) W RSC 3 Carlos Trujillo (PAN), Monaco – WBC

06.12.85 **Don Curry** (USA) W CO 2 Milton McCrory (USA), Las Vegas

09.03.86 **Don Curry** (USA) W CO 2 Eduardo Rodriguez (PAN), Forth Worth

27.09.86 **Lloyd Honeyghan** (GB) W RTD 6 Don Curry (USA), Atlantic City. *Lloyd Honeyghan relinquished WBA version of title*

06.02.87 Mark Breland (USA) W CO 7 Harold Volbrecht (SA), Atlantic City – WBA

22.02.87 Lloyd Honeyghan (GB) W RSC 2 Johnny Bumphus (USA), Grand Hall, Wembley – IBF/WBC

18.04.87 Lloyd Honeyghan (GB) W PTS 12 Maurice Blocker (USA), Albert Hall, London – IBF/WBC

22.08.87 Marlon Starling (USA) W CO 11 Mark Breland (USA), Columbia – WBA

30.08.87 Lloyd Honeyghan (GB) W RSC 1 Gene Hatcher (USA), Marbella – IBF/WBC

28.10.87 Jorge Vaca (MEX) W TD 8 Lloyd Honeyghan (GB), Grand Hall, Wembley – IBF/WBC. *Jorge Vaca forfeited IBF recognition due to the duration of the bout being over twelve rounds and not fifteen as required by that body*

05.02.88 Marlon Starling (USA) W PTS 12 Fujio Ozaki (JAP), Atlantic City – WBA

29.03.88 Lloyd Honeyghan (GB) W CO 3 Jorge Vaca (MEX), The Arena, Wembley – WBC

16.04.88 Marlon Starling (USA) DREW 12 Mark Breland (USA), Las Vegas – WBA

23.04.88 Simon Brown (USA) W RSC 14 Tyrone Trice (USA), Berck sur Mer – IBF

16.07.88 Simon Brown (USA) W RSC 3 Jorge Vaca (MEX), Kingston – IBF

29.07.88 Tomas Molinares (COL) W CO 6 Marlon Starling (USA), Atlantic City – WBA. *Tomas Molinares forfeited WBA recognition when unable to make the weight*

29.07.88 Lloyd Honeyghan (GB) W RSC 5 Yung-Kil Chung (SK), Atlantic City – WBC

14.10.88 Simon Brown (USA) W PTS 12 Mauro Martelli (SWI), Lausanne – IBF

05.02.89 Mark Breland (USA) W RSC 1 Seung-Soon Lee (SK), Las Vegas – WBA

05.02.89 Marlon Starling (USA) W RSC 9 Lloyd Honeyghan (GB), Las Vegas – WBC

18.02.89 Simon Brown (USA) W RSC 3 Jorge Maysonet (PR), Budapest – IBF

22.04.89 Mark Breland (USA) W RSC 5 Rafael Pineda (COL), Atlantic City – WBA

27.04.89 Simon Brown (USA) W CO 7 Al Long (USA), Washington – IBF

08.05.89 Genaro Leon (MEX) W CO 1 Danny Garcia (PR), Santa Ana – WBO. *Genaro Leon relinquished WBO version of title*

15.09.89 Marlon Starling (USA) W PTS 12 Yung-Kil Chung (SK), Hartford – WBC

20.09.89 Simon Brown (USA) W RSC 2 Bobby Jo Brown (USA), Rochester – IBF

13.10.89 Mark Breland (USA) W RSC 2 Mauro Martelli (SWI), Geneva – WBA

09.11.89 Simon Brown (USA) W PTS 12 Luis Santana (DOM), Springfield – IBF

10.12.89 Mark Breland (USA) W RSC 4 Fujio Ozaki (JAP), Tokyo – WBA

15.12.89 Manning Galloway (USA) W PTS 12 Al Hamza (USA), Yabucoa – WBO

03.03.90 Mark Breland (USA) W RSC 3 Lloyd Honeyghan (GB), The Arena, Wembley – WBA

01.04.90 Simon Brown (USA) W RSC 10 Tyrone Trice (USA), Washington – IBF

08.07.90 Aaron Davis (USA) W CO 9 Mark Breland (USA), Reno – WBA

19.08.90 Maurice Blocker (USA) W PTS 12 Marlon Starling (USA), Reno – WBC

25.08.90 Manning Galloway (USA) W PTS 12 Nika Khumalo (SA), Lewiston – WBO

19.01.91 Meldrick Taylor (USA) W PTS 12 Aaron Davis (USA), Atlantic City – WBA

15.02.91 Manning Galloway (USA) W RTD 8 Gert Bo Jacobsen (DEN), Randers – WBO

18.03.91 Simon Brown (USA) W RSC 10 Maurice Blocker (USA), Las Vegas – IBF/WBC. *Simon Brown relinquished IBF version of title*

17.05.91 Manning Galloway (USA) W RTD 7 Racheed Lawal (DEN), Copenhagen – WBO

01.06.91 Meldrick Taylor (USA) W PTS 12 Luis Garcia (VEN), Palm Springs – WBA

15.09.91 Manning Galloway (USA) W PTS 12 Jeff Malcolm (A), Broadbeach – WBO

04.10.91 Maurice Blocker (USA) W PTS 12 Glenwood Brown (USA), Atlantic City – IBF

29.11.91 James McGirt (USA) W PTS 12 Simon Brown (USA), Las Vegas – WBC

14.12.91 Manning Galloway (USA) W PTS 12 Nika Khumalo (SA), Cape Town – WBO

18.01.92 Meldrick Taylor (USA) W PTS 12 Glenwood Brown (USA), Philadelphia – WBA

25.06.92 James McGirt (USA) W PTS 12 Patrizio Oliva (ITA), Naples – WBC

Light-Welterweight

21.09.26 Mushy Callahan (USA) W PTS 10 Pinkey Mitchell (USA), Los Angeles – NY/NBA

14.03.27 Mushy Callahan (USA) W CO 2 Andy Divodi (USA), New York City – NY/NBA

31.05.27 Mushy Callahan (USA) W PTS 10 Spug Myers (USA), Chicago – NY/NBA

28.05.29 Mushy Callahan (USA) W CO 3 Fred Mahan (USA), Los Angeles NY/NBA. *Mushy Callahan ceased to be recognised by NY*

18.02.30 Jackie Kid Berg (GB) W RTD 10 Mushy Callahan (USA), Albert Hall, London – NBA

29.05.30 Jackie Kid Berg (GB) W RSC 4 Al Delmont (USA), Newark – NBA

03.09.30 Jackie Kid Berg (GB) W PTS 10 Buster Brown (USA), Newark – NBA

23.01.31 Jackie Kid Berg (GB) W PTS 10 Goldie Hess (USA), Chicago – NBA

10.04.31 Jackie Kid Berg (GB) W PTS 10 Billy Wallace (USA), Detroit – NBA

24.04.31 Tony Canzoneri (USA) W CO 3 Jackie Kid Berg (GB), Chicago – NBA

13.07.31 Tony Canzoneri (USA) W PTS 10 Cecil Payne (USA), Los Angeles – NBA

29.10.31 Tony Canzoneri (USA) W PTS 10 Phillie Griffin (USA), Newark – NBA

18.01.32 Johnny Jadick (USA) W PTS 10 Tony Canzoneri (USA), Philadelphia – NBA

18.07.32 Johnny Jadick (USA) W PTS 10 Tony Canzoneri (USA), Philadelphia – NBA

20.02.33 Battling Shaw (MEX) W PTS 10 Johnny Jadick (USA), New Orleans – NBA

21.05.33 Tony Canzoneri (USA) W PTS 10 Battling Shaw (MEX), New Orleans – NBA

23.06.33 Barney Ross (USA) W PTS 10 Tony Canzoneri (USA), Chicago – NBA

26.07.33 Barney Ross (USA) W RSC 6 Johnny Farr (USA), Kansas City – NBA

17.11.33 Barney Ross (USA) W PTS 10 Sammy Fuller (USA), Chicago – NBA

07.02.34 Barney Ross (USA) W PTS 12 Pete Nebo (USA), New Orleans – NBA

05.03.34 Barney Ross (USA) DREW 10 Frankie Klick (USA), San Francisco – NBA

27.03.34 Barney Ross (USA) W PTS 10 Bobby Pacho (USA), Los Angeles – NBA

10.12.34 Barney Ross (USA) W PTS 12 Bobby Pacho (USA), Cleveland – NBA

28.01.35 Barney Ross (USA) W PTS 10 Frankie Klick (USA), Miami – NBA

09.04.35 Barney Ross (USA) W PTS 12 Harry Woods (USA), Seattle – NBA. *Barney Ross relinquished NBA version of title*

29.04.46 Tippy Larkin (USA) W PTS 12 Willie Joyce (USA), Boston – MASS

13.09.46 Tippy Larkin (USA) W PTS 12 Willie Joyce (USA), New York City – MASS/NY. *Tippy Larkin forfeited NY/Massachusetts recognition following a defeat by Ike Williams in a non-title bout June 1947*

12.06.59 Carlos Ortiz (PR) W RTD 2 Kenny Lane (USA), New York City – NBA

04.02.60 Carlos Ortiz (PR) W CO 10 Battling Torres (MEX), Los Angeles – NBA

15.06.60 Carlos Ortiz (PR) W PTS 15 Duillio Loi (ITA), San Francisco – NBA

01.09.60 Duillio Loi (ITA) W PTS 15 Carlos Ortiz (PR), Milan – NBA

10.05.61 Duillio Loi (ITA) W PTS 15 Carlos Ortiz (PR), Milan – NBA

21.10.61 Duillio Loi (ITA) DREW 15 Eddie Perkins (USA), Milan – NBA

14.09.62 Eddie Perkins (USA) W PTS 15 Duillio Loi (ITA), Milan – NBA

15.12.62 Duillio Loi (ITA) W PTS 15 Eddie Perkins (USA), Milan – NBA. *Duillio Loi relinquished NBA version of title*

21.03.63 Roberto Cruz (PH) W CO 1 Battling Torres (MEX), Los Angeles – WBA

15.06.63 Eddie Perkins (USA) W PTS 15 Roberto Cruz (PH), Manila – WBA

04.01.64 Eddie Perkins (USA) W RSC 13 Yoshinori Takahashi (JAP), Tokyo – WBA

18.04.64 Eddie Perkins (USA) W PTS 15 Bunny Grant (J), Kingston – WBA

18.01.65 Carlos Hernandez (VEN) W PTS 15 Eddie Perkins (USA), Caracas – WBA

15.05.65 Carlos Hernandez (VEN) W RSC 4 Mario Rossito (COL), Maracaibo – WBA

10.07.65 Carlos Hernandez (VEN) W CO 3 Percy Hayles (J), Kingston – WBA

30.04.66 Sandro Lopopolo (ITA) W PTS 15 Carlos Hernandez (VEN), Rome – WBA

21.10.66 Sandro Lopopolo (ITA) W RSC 7 Vicente Rivas (VEN), Rome – WBA

30.04.67 Paul Fujii (USA) W RTD 2 Sandro Lopopolo (ITA), Tokyo – WBA

16.11.67 Paul Fujii (USA) W CO 4 Willi Quatuor (GER), Tokyo – WBA

12.12.68 Nicolino Loche (ARG) W RTD 9 Paul Fujii (USA), Tokyo – WBA

14.12.68 Pedro Adigue (PH) W PTS 15 Adolph Pruitt (USA), Quezon City – WBC

03.05.69 Nicolino Loche (ARG) W PTS 15 Carlos Hernandez (VEN), Buenos Aires – WBA

11.10.69 Nicolino Loche (ARG) W PTS 15 Joao Henrique (BR), Buenos Aires – WBA

01.02.70 Bruno Arcari (ITA) W PTS 15 Pedro Adigue (PH), Rome – WBC

16.05.70 Nicolino Loche (ARG) W PTS 15 Adolph Pruitt (USA), Buenos Aires – WBA

10.07.70 Bruno Arcari (ITA) W DIS 6 Rene Roque (FR), Lignano – WBC

30.10.70 Bruno Arcari (ITA) W CO 3 Raymundo Dias (BR), Genoa – WBC

06.03.71 Bruno Arcari (ITA) W PTS 15 Joao Henrique (BR), Rome – WBC

03.04.71 Nicolino Loche (ARG) W PTS 15 Domingo Barrera (SP), Buenos Aires – WBA

26.06.71 Bruno Arcari (ITA) W RSC 9 Enrique Jana (ARG), Palermo – WBC

10.10.71 Bruno Arcari (ITA) W CO 10 Domingo Barrera (SP), Genoa – WBC

11.12.71 Nicolino Loche (ARG) W PTS 15 Antonio Cervantes (COL), Buenos Aires – WBA

10.03.72 Alfonso Frazer (PAN) W PTS 15 Nicolino Loche (ARG), Panama City – WBA

10.06.72 Bruno Arcari (ITA) W CO 12 Joao Henrique (BR), Genoa – WBC

17.06.72 Alfonso Frazer (PAN) W RTD 4 Al Ford (C), Panama City – WBA

28.10.72 Antonio Cervantes (COL) W CO 10 Alfonso Frazer (PAN), Panama City – WBA

02.12.72 Bruno Arcari (ITA) W PTS 15 Costa Azevedo (BR), Turin – WBC

16.02.73 Antonio Cervantes (COL) W PTS 15 Josua Marquez (PR), San Juan – WBA

17.03.73 Antonio Cervantes (COL) W RTD 9 Nicolino Loche (ARG), Maracay – WBA

19.05.73 Antonio Cervantes (COL) W RSC 5 Alfonso Frazer (PAN), Panama City – WBA

08.09.73 Antonio Cervantes (COL) W RSC 5 Carlos Giminez (ARG), Bogota – WBA

04.12.73 Antonio Cervantes (COL) W PTS 15 Lion Furuyama (JAP), Panama City – WBA

16.02.74 Bruno Arcari (ITA) W DIS 8 Tony Ortiz (SP), Turin – WBC. *Bruno Arcari relinquished WBC version of title*

02.03.74 Antonio Cervantes (COL) W CO 6 Chang-Kil Lee (SK), Cartagena – WBA

27.07.74 Antonio Cervantes (COL) W CO 2 Victor Ortiz (PR), Cartagena – WBA

21.09.74 Perico Fernandez (SP) W PTS 15 Lion Furuyama (JAP), Rome – WBC

26.10.74 Antonio Cervantes (COL) W CO 8 Shinchi Kadoto (JAP), Tokyo – WBA

19.04.75 Perico Fernandez (SP) W CO 9 Joao Henrique (BR), Barcelona – WBC

17.05.75 Antonio Cervantes (COL) W PTS 15 Esteban de Jesus (PR), Panama City – WBA

15.07.75 Saensak Muangsurin (TH) W RTD 8 Perico Fernandez (SP), Bangkok – WBC

15.11.75 Antonio Cervantes (COL) W RTD 7 Hector Thompson (A), Panama City – WBA

25.01.76 Saensak Muangsurin (TH) W PTS 15 Lion Furuyama (JAP), Tokyo – WBC

06.03.76 Wilfred Benitez (PR) W PTS 15 Antonio Cervantes (COL), San Juan – WBA

31.05.76 Wilfred Benitez (PR) W PTS 15 Emiliano Villa (COL), San Juan – WBA

30.06.76 Miguel Velasquez (SP) W DIS 4 Saensak Muangsurin (TH), Madrid – WBC

16.10.76 Wilfred Benitez (PR) W RSC 3 Tony Petronelli (USA), San Juan – WBA. *Wilfred Benitez forfeited WBA recognition for failing to defend against Antonio Cervantes*

29.10.76 Saensak Muangsurin (TH) W RSC 2 Miguel Velasquez (SP), Segovia – WBC

05.01.77 Saensak Muangsurin (TH) W RSC 15 Monroe Brooks (USA), Chiang – WBC

02.04.77 Saensak Muangsurin (TH) W CO 6 Guts Ishimatsu (JAP), Tokyo – WBC

17.06.77 Saensak Muangsurin (TH) W PTS 15 Perico Fernandez (SP), Madrid – WBC

25.06.77 Antonio Cervantes (COL) W RSC 5 Carlos Giminez (ARG), Maracaibo – WBA

03.08.77 Wilfred Benitez (PR) W RSC 15 Guerrero Chavez (C), New York City – NY. *Wilfred Benitez forfeited NY recognition when boxing regularly in the welterweight division*

20.08.77 Saensak Muangsurin (TH) W RSC 6 Mike Everett (USA), Roi-Et – WBC

22.10.77 Saensak Muangsurin (TH) W PTS 15 Saoul Mamby (USA), Korat – WBC

05.11.77 Antonio Cervantes (COL) W PTS 15 Adriano Marrero (DOM), Maracay – WBA

29.12.77 Saensak Muangsurin (TH) W RTD 13 Jo Kimpuani (FR), Chanthabun – WBC

08.04.78 Saensak Muangsurin (TH) W CO 13 Francisco Moreno (VEN), Hat Yai – WBC

28.04.78 Antonio Cervantes (COL) W CO 6 Tonga Kiatvayupakdi (TH), Udon – WBA

26.08.78 Antonio Cervantes (COL) W RSC 9 Norman Sekgapane (SA), Botswana – WBA

30.12.78 Sang-Hyun Kim (SK) W CO 13 Saensak Muangsurin (TH), Seoul – WBC

18.01.79 Antonio Cervantes (COL) W PTS 15 Miguel Montilla (DOM), New York City – WBA

03.06.79 Sang-Hyun Kim (SK) W PTS 15 Fitzroy Guisseppi (TR), Seoul – WBC

25.08.79 Antonio Cervantes (COL) W PTS 15 Kwang-Min Kim (SK), Seoul – WBA

04.10.79 Sang-Hyun Kim (SK) W CO 11 Masahiro Yokai (JAP), Tokyo – WBC

23.02.80 Saoul Mamby (USA) W CO 14 Sang-Hyun Kim (SK), Seoul – WBC

29.03.80 Antonio Cervantes (COL) W RSC 7 Miguel Montilla (DOM), Cartagena – WBA

07.07.80 Saoul Mamby (USA) W RSC 13 Esteban de Jesus (PR), Bloomington – WBC

02.08.80 Aaron Pryor (USA) W CO 4 Antonio Cervantes (COL), Cincinnati – WBA

02.10.80 Saoul Mamby (USA) W PTS 15 Maurice Watkins (USA), Las Vegas – WBC

22.11.80 Aaron Pryor (USA) W RSC 6 Gaetan Hart (USA), Cincinnati – WBA

12.06.81 Saoul Mamby (USA) W PTS 15 Jo Kimpuani (FR), Detroit – WBC

27.06.81 Aaron Pryor (USA) W RSC 2 Lennox Blackmore (GU), Las Vegas – WBA

29.08.81 Saoul Mamby (USA) W PTS 15 Thomas Americo (INDON), Jakarta – WBC

14.11.81 Aaron Pryor (USA) W RSC 7 Dujuan Johnson (USA), Cleveland – WBA

20.12.81 Saoul Mamby (USA) W PTS 15 Obisia Nwankpa (N), Lagos – WBC

21.03.82 Aaron Pryor (USA) W RSC 12 Miguel Montilla (DOM), Atlantic City – WBA

26.06.82 Leroy Haley (USA) W PTS 15 Saoul Mamby (USA), Cleveland – WBC

04.07.82 Aaron Pryor (USA) W RSC 6 Akio Kameda (JAP), Cincinnati – WBA

20.10.82 Leroy Haley (USA) W PTS 15 Juan Giminez (ARG), Cleveland – WBC

12.11.82 Aaron Pryor (USA) W RSC 14 Alexis Arguello (NIC), Miami – WBA

13.02.83 Leroy Haley (USA) W PTS 12 Saoul Mamby (USA), Cleveland – WBC

02.04.83 Aaron Pryor (USA) W RSC 3 Sang-Hyun Kim (SK), Atlantic City – WBA

18.05.83 Bruce Curry (USA) W PTS 12 Leroy Haley (USA), Las Vegas – WBC

07.07.83 Bruce Curry (USA) W RSC 7 Hidekazu Akai (JAP), Osaka – WBC

09.09.83 Aaron Pryor (USA) W CO 10 Alexis Arguello (NIC), Las Vegas – WBA. *Aaron Pryor relinquished WBA version of title*

19.10.83 Bruce Curry (USA) W PTS 12 Leroy Haley (USA), Las Vegas – WBC

22.01.84 Johnny Bumphus (USA) W PTS 15 Lorenzo Garcia (ARG), Atlantic City – WBA

29.01.84 Bill Costello (USA) W RSC 10 Bruce Curry (USA), Beaumont – WBC

01.06.84 Gene Hatcher (USA) W RSC 11 Johnny Bumphus (USA), Buffalo – WBA

22.06.84 Aaron Pryor (USA) W PTS 15 Nicky Furlano (C), Toronto – IBF

15.07.84 Bill Costello (USA) W PTS 12 Ronnie Shields (USA), Kingston, NY – WBC

03.11.84 Bill Costello (USA) W PTS 12 Saoul Mamby (USA), Kingston, NY – WBC

15.12.84 Gene Hatcher (USA) W PTS 15 Ubaldo Sacco (ARG), Fort Worth – WBA

16.02.85 Bill Costello (USA) W PTS 12 Leroy Haley (USA), Kingston, NY – WBC

02.03.85 Aaron Pryor (USA) W PTS 15 Gary Hinton (USA), Atlantic City – IBF. *Aaron Pryor forfeited IBF recognition due to inactivity*

21.07.85 Ubaldo Sacco (ARG) W RSC 9 Gene Hatcher (USA), Campione – WBA

21.08.85 Lonnie Smith (USA) W RSC 8 Bill Costello (USA), New York City – WBC

15.03.86 Patrizio Oliva (ITA) W PTS 15 Ubaldo Sacco (ARG), Monaco – WBA

26.04.86 Gary Hinton (USA) W PTS 15 Antonio Reyes Cruz (DOM), Lucca – IBF

05.05.86 Rene Arredondo (MEX) W RSC 5 Lonnie Smith (USA), Los Angeles – WBC

24.07.86 Tsuyoshi Hamada (JAP) W CO 1 Rene Arredondo (MEX), Tokyo – WBC

06.09.86 Patrizio Oliva (ITA) W RSC 3 Brian Brunette (USA), Naples – WBA

30.10.86 Joe Manley (USA) W CO 10 Gary Hinton (USA), Hartford – IBF

02.12.86 Tsuyoshi Hamada (JAP) W PTS 12 Ronnie Shields (USA), Tokyo – WBC

10.01.87 Patrizio Oliva (ITA) W PTS 15 Rodolfo Gonzalez (MEX), Agrigento – WBA

04.03.87 Terry Marsh (GB) W RSC 10 Joe Manley (USA), Festival Hall Super Tent, Basildon – IBF

01.07.87 Terry Marsh (GB) W RTD 6 Akio Kameda (JAP), Albert Hall, London – IBF. *Terry Marsh relinquished IBF version of title*

04.07.87 Juan M. Coggi (ARG) W CO 3 Patrizio Oliva (ITA), Ribera – WBA

22.07.87 Rene Arredondo (MEX) W RSC 6 Tsuyoshi Hamada (JAP), Tokyo – WBC

12.11.87 Roger Mayweather (USA) W RSC 6 Rene Arredondo (MEX), Los Angeles – WBC

14.02.88 James McGirt (USA) W RSC 12 Frankie Warren (USA), Corpus Christi – IBF

24.03.88 Roger Mayweather (USA) W CO 3 Mauricio Aceves (MEX), Los Angeles – WBC

07.05.88 Juan M. Coggi (ARG) W CO 2 Sang-Ho Lee (SK), Roseto – WBA

06.06.88 Roger Mayweather (USA) W PTS 12 Harold Brazier (USA), Las Vegas – WBC

31.07.88 James McGirt (USA) W CO 1 Howard Davis (USA), New York City – IBF

03.09.88 Meldrick Taylor (USA) W RSC 12 James McGirt (USA), Atlantic City – IBF

22.09.88 Roger Mayweather (USA) W RSC 12 Rodolfo Gonzalez (MEX), Los Angeles – WBC

07.11.88 Roger Mayweather (USA) W PTS 12 Vinny Pazienza (USA), Las Vegas – WBC

21.01.89 Juan M. Coggi (ARG) W PTS 12 Harold Brazier (USA), Vasto – WBA

21.01.89 Meldrick Taylor (USA) W RSC 7 John Meekins (USA), Atlantic City – IBF

06.03.89 Hector Camacho (PR) W PTS 12 Ray Mancini (USA), Reno – WBO

29.04.89 Juan M. Coggi (ARG) W PTS 12 Akinobu Hiranaka (JAP), Vasto – WBA

13.05.89 Julio Cesar Chavez (MEX) W RTD 10 Roger Mayweather (USA), Los Angeles – WBC

11.09.89 Meldrick Taylor (USA) W PTS 12 Courtney Hooper (USA), Atlantic City – IBF

18.11.89 Julio Cesar Chavez (MEX) W RSC 10 Sammy Fuentes (USA), Las Vegas – WBC

16.12.89 Julio Cesar Chavez (MEX) W CO 3 Alberto Cortes (ARG), Mexico City – WBC

03.02.90 Hector Camacho (PR) W PTS 12 Vinny Pazienza (USA), Atlantic City – WBO

17.03.90 Julio Cesar Chavez (MEX) W RSC 12 Meldrick Taylor (USA), Las Vegas – IBF/WBC

24.03.90 Juan M. Coggi (ARG) W PTS 12 Jose Luis Ramirez (MEX), Arjaccio – WBA

11.08.90 Hector Camacho (PR) W PTS 12 Tony Baltazar (USA), Stateline – WBO

17.08.90 Loreta Garza (USA) W PTS 12 Juan M. Coggi (ARG), Nice – WBA

01.12.90 Loreta Garza (USA) W DIS 11 Vinny Pazienza (USA), Sacramento – WBA

08.12.90 Julio Cesar Chavez (MEX) W RSC 3 Kyung-Duk Ahn (SK), Atlantic City – IBF/WBC

23.02.91 Greg Haugen (USA), W PTS 12 Hector Camacho (PR), Las Vegas – WBO. *Greg Haugen forfeited title when failing post-fight drug test*

18.03.91 Julio Cesar Chavez (MEX) W RSC 4 John Duplessis (USA), Las Vegas – IBF/WBC. *Julio Cesar Chavez relinquished IBF version of title*

18.05.91 Hector Camacho (PR) W PTS 12 Greg Haugen (USA), Reno – WBO. *Hector Camacho relinquished WBO version of title*

14.06.91 Edwin Rosario (PR) W RSC 3 Loreta Garza (USA), Sacramento – WBA

14.09.91 Julio Cesar Chavez (MEX) W PTS 12 Lonny Smith (USA), Las Vegas – WBC

07.12.91 Rafael Pineda (COL) W RSC 9 Roger Mayweather (USA), Reno – IBF

10.04.92 Julio Cesar Chavez (MEX) W CO 5 Angel Hernandez (PR), Mexico City – WBC

10.04.92 Akinobu Hiranaka (JAP) W RSC 1 Edwin Rosario (PR), Mexico City – WBA

22.05.92 Rafael Pineda (COL) W RSC 7 Clarence Coleman (USA), Mexico City – IBF

30.06.92 Carlos Gonzalez (MEX) W RSC 2 Jimmy Paul (USA), Los Angeles – WBO

Lightweight

31.03.90 Jack McAuliffe (USA) W CO 47 Jimmy Carroll (GB) San Francisco – USA

05.09.92 Jack McAuliffe (USA) W CO 15 Billy Myer (USA), New Orleans – USA. *Jack McAuliffe retired*

01.06.96 George Lavigne (USA) W CO 17 Dick Burge (GB), NSC, London

27.10.96 George Lavigne (USA) W CO 24 Jack Everhardt (USA), New York City

08.02.97 George Lavigne (USA) W PTS 25 Kid McPartland (USA), New York City

28.04.97 George Lavigne (USA) W CO 11 Eddie Connolly (C), New York City

29.10.97 George Lavigne (USA) W RTD 12 Joe Walcott (USA), San Francisco

17.03.98 George Lavigne (USA) DREW 20 Jack Daly (USA), Cleveland

28.09.98 George Lavigne (USA) DREW 20 Frank Erne (USA) New York City

25.11.98 George Lavigne (USA) W PTS 20 Tom Tracey (A), San Francisco

03.07.99 Frank Erne (USA) W PTS 20 George Lavigne (USA), Buffalo

04.12.99 Frank Erne (USA) DREW 25 Jack O'Brien (USA), New York City

23.03.00 Frank Erne (USA) W RTD 12 Joe Gans (USA), New York City

12.05.02 Joe Gans (USA) W CO 1 Frank Erne (USA), Fort Erie

27.06.02 Joe Gans (USA) W CO 3 George McFadden (USA), San Francisco

24.07.02 Joe Gans (USA) W CO 15 Rufe Turner (USA), Oakland

17.09.02 Joe Gans (USA) W CO 5 Gus Gardner (USA), Baltimore

13.10.02 Joe Gans (USA) W CO 5 Kid McPartland (USA), Fort Erie

01.01.03 Joe Gans (USA) W DIS 11 Gus Gardner (USA), New Britain

11.03.03 Joe Gans (USA) W RTD 11 Steve Crosby (USA) Hot Springs

29.05.03 Joe Gans (USA) W CO 10 Willie Fitzgerald (USA), San Francisco

04.07.03 Joe Gans (USA) W CO 5 Buddy King (USA), Butte

12.01.04 Joe Gans (USA) W PTS 10 Willie Fitzgerald (USA), Detroit

31.10.04 Joe Gans (USA) W DIS 5 Jimmy Britt (USA), San Francisco. *Joe Gans forfeited title when refusing to make the weight*

20.12.04 Jimmy Britt (USA) W PTS 20 Battling Nelson (USA) San Francisco

05.05.05 Jimmy Britt (USA) W PTS 20 Jabez White (GB) San Francisco

21.07.05 Jimmy Britt (USA) W PTS 20 Kid Sullivan (USA), San Francisco

09.09.05 Battling Nelson (USA) W CO 18 Jimmy Britt (USA), San Francisco

03.09.06 Joe Gans (USA) W DIS 42 Battling Nelson (USA) Goldfield

01.01.07 Joe Gans (USA) W CO 8 Kid Herman (USA), Tonopah

09.09.07 Joe Gans (USA) W RTD 6 Jimmy Britt (USA), San Francisco

27.09.07 Joe Gans (USA) W PTS 20 George Memsic (USA), Los Angeles

01.04.08 Joe Gans (USA) W CO 3 Spike Robson (GB), Philadelphia

14.05.08 Joe Gans (USA) W RSC 11 Rudy Unholz (GER), San Francisco

04.07.08 Battling Nelson (USA) W CO 17 Joe Gans (USA), San Francisco

09.09.08 Battling Nelson (USA) W CO 21 Joe Gans (USA), San Francisco

29.05.09 Battling Nelson (USA) W CO 23 Dick Hyland (USA), San Francisco

22.06.09 Battling Nelson (USA) W CO 5 Jack Clifford (USA), Oklahoma City

22.02.10 Ad Wolgast (USA) W RSC 40 Battling Nelson (USA), Richmond

17.03.11 Ad Wolgast (USA) W RSC 9 George Memsic (USA), Los Angeles

31.03.11 Ad Wolgast (USA) W RTD 5 Antonio Ia Grave (USA), San Francisco

26.04.11 Ad Wolgast (USA) W RSC 2 One-Round Hogan (USA), New York City

27.05.11 Ad Wolgast (USA) W RTD 17 Frankie Burns (USA), San Francisco

04.07.11 Ad Wolgast (USA) W CO 13 Owen Moran (GB), San Francisco

04.07.12 Ad Wolgast (USA) W CO 13 Joe Rivers (USA), Los Angeles

28.11.12 Willie Ritchie (USA) W DIS 16 Ad Wolgast (USA), San Francisco

04.07.13 Willie Ritchie (USA) W CO 11 Joe Rivers (USA), San Francisco

17.04.14 Willie Ritchie (USA) W PTS 20 Tommy Murphy (USA), San Francisco

07.07.14 Freddie Welsh (GB) W PTS 20 Willie Ritchie (USA), Olympia, London

04.07.16 Freddie Welsh (GB) W DIS 11 Ad Wolgast (USA), Denver

04.09.16 Freddie Welsh (GB) W PTS 20 Charley White (USA), Colorado Springs

28.05.17 Benny Leonard (USA) W RSC 9 Freddie Welsh (GB), New York City

25.07.17 Benny Leonard (USA) W CO 3 Johnny Kilbane (USA), Philadelphia

05.07.20 Benny Leonard (USA) W CO 9 Charley White (USA), Benton Harbor

26.11.20 Benny Leonard (USA) W RSC 14 Joe Welling (USA), New York City

14.01.21 Benny Leonard (USA) W RSC 6 Richie Mitchell (USA), New York City

10.02.22 Benny Leonard (USA) W PTS 15 Rocky Kansas (USA), New York City

04.07.22 Benny Leonard (USA) W RSC 8 Rocky Kansas (USA), Michigan City

23.07.23 Benny Leonard (USA) W PTS 15 Lew Tendler (USA), New York City. *Benny Leonard relinquished title*

13.07.25 Jimmy Goodrich (USA) W RSC 2 Stanislaus Loayza (CH), New York City – NY

07.12.25 **Rocky Kansas** (USA) W PTS 15 Jimmy Goodrich (USA), Buffalo

03.07.26 **Sammy Mandell** (USA) W PTS 10 Rocky Kansas (USA), Chicago

21.05.28 **Sammy Mandell** (USA) W PTS 15 Jimmy McLarnin (USA), New York City

02.08.29 **Sammy Mandell** (USA) W PTS 10 Tony Canzoneri (USA), Chicago

17.07.30 **Al Singer** (USA) W CO 1 Sammy Mandell (USA), New York City

14.11.30 **Tony Canzoneri** (USA) W CO 1 Al Singer (USA), New York City

24.04.31 **Tony Canzoneri** (USA) W CO 3 Jackie Kid Berg (GB), Chicago

10.09.31 **Tony Canzoneri** (USA) W PTS 15 Jackie Kid Berg (GB), New York City

20.11.31 **Tony Canzoneri** (USA) W PTS 15 Kid Chocolate (CUB), New York City

04.11.32 **Tony Canzoneri** (USA) W PTS 15 Billy Petrolle (USA), New York City

23.06.33 **Barney Ross** (USA) W PTS 10 Tony Canzoneri (USA), Chicago

12.09.33 **Barney Ross** (USA) W PTS 15 Tony Canzoneri (USA), New York City. *Barney Ross relinquished title*

10.05.35 **Tony Canzoneri** (USA) W PTS 15 Lou Ambers (USA), New York City

04.10.35 **Tony Canzoneri** (USA) W PTS 15 Al Roth (USA), New York City

03.09.36 **Lew Ambers** (USA) W PTS 15 Tony Canzoneri (USA), New York City

07.05.37 **Lou Ambers** (USA) W PTS 15 Tony Canzoneri (USA), New York City

23.09.37 **Lou Ambers** (USA) W PTS 15 Pedro Montanez (PR), New York City

17.08.38 **Henry Armstrong** (USA) W PTS 15 Lou Ambers (USA), New York City

22.08.39 **Lou Ambers** (USA) W PTS 15 Henry Armstrong (USA), New York City. *Lou Ambers forfeited NBA recognition for failing to defend against Davey Day*

03.05.40 Sammy Angott (USA) W PTS 15 Davey Day (USA), Louisville – NBA

10.05.40 Lew Jenkins (USA) W RSC 3 Lou Ambers (USA), New York City – NY

22.11.40 Lew Jenkins (USA) W RSC 2 Pete Lello (USA), New York City – NY

02.05.41 Sammy Angott (USA) W PTS 12 Dave Castilloux (C), Louisville – NBA

19.12.41 **Sammy Angott** (USA) W PTS 15 Lew Jenkins (USA), New York City

15.05.42 **Sammy Angott** (USA) W PTS 15 Allie Stolz (USA), New York City. *Sammy Angott relinquished title*

18.12.42 Beau Jack (USA) W CO 3 Tippy Larkin (USA), New York City – NY

04.01.43 Slugger White (USA) W PTS 15 Willie Joyce (USA), Baltimore – MARY

21.05.43 Bob Montgomery (USA) W PTS 15 Beau Jack (USA), New York City – NY

27.10.43 Sammy Angott (USA) W PTS 15 Slugger White (USA), Los Angeles – NBA

19.11.43 Beau Jack (USA) W PTS 15 Bob Montgomery (USA), New York City – NY

03.03.44 Bob Montgomery (USA) W PTS 15 Beau Jack (USA), New York City – NY

08.03.44 Juan Zurita (MEX) W PTS 15 Sammy Angott (USA), Los Angeles – NBA

18.04.45 Ike Williams (USA) W CO 2 Juan Zurita (MEX), Mexico – NBA

30.04.46 Ike Williams (USA) W RSC 8 Enrique Bolanos (USA), Los Angeles – NBA

28.06.46 Bob Montgomery (USA) W CO 13 Allie Stolz (USA), New York City – NY

04.09.46 Ike Williams (USA) W CO 9 Ronnie James (GB), Ninian Park, Cardiff – NBA

26.11.46 Bob Montgomery (USA) W CO 8 Wesley Mouzon (USA), Philadelphia – NY

04.08.47 **Ike Williams** (USA) W CO 6 Bob Montgomery (USA), Philadelphia

25.05.48 **Ike Williams** (USA) W PTS 15 Enrique Bolanos (USA), Los Angeles

12.07.48 **Ike Williams** (USA) W RSC 6 Beau Jack (USA), Philadelphia

23.09.48 **Ike Williams** (USA) W CO 10 Jesse Flores (USA), New York City

21.07.49 **Ike Williams** (USA) W RSC 4 Enrique Bolanos (USA), Los Angeles

05.12.49 **Ike Williams** (USA) W PTS 15 Freddie Dawson (USA), Philadelphia

25.05.51 **Jimmy Carter** (USA) W RSC 14 Ike Williams (USA), New York City

14.11.51 **Jimmy Carter** (USA) W PTS 15 Art Aragon (USA), Los Angeles

01.04.52 **Jimmy Carter** (USA) W PTS 15 Lauro Salas (MEX), Los Angeles

14.05.52 **Lauro Salas** (MEX) W PTS 15 Jimmy Carter (USA), Los Angeles

15.10.52 **Jimmy Carter** (USA) W PTS 15 Lauro Salas (MEX), Chicago

24.04.53 **Jimmy Carter** (USA) W RSC 4 Tommy Collins (USA), Boston

12.06.53 **Jimmy Carter** (USA) W RSC 13 George Araujo (USA), New York City

11.11.53 **Jimmy Carter** (USA) W CO 5 Armand Savoie (C), Montreal

05.03.54 **Paddy de Marco** (USA) W PTS 15 Jimmy Carter (USA), New York City

17.11.54 **Jimmy Carter** (USA) W RSC 15 Paddy de Marco (USA), San Francisco

29.06.55 **Wallace Bud Smith** (USA) W PTS 15 Jimmy Carter (USA), Boston

19.10.55 **Wallace Bud Smith** (USA) W PTS 15 Jimmy Carter (USA), Cincinnati

24.08.56 **Joe Brown** (USA) W PTS 15 Wallace Bud Smith (USA), New Orleans

13.02.57 **Joe Brown** (USA) W RSC 10 Wallace Bud Smith (USA), Miami

19.06.57 **Joe Brown** (USA) W RSC 15 Orlando Zulueta (CUB), Denver

04.12.57 **Joe Brown** (USA) W RSC 11 Joey Lopes (USA), Chicago

07.05.58 **Joe Brown** (USA) W RSC 8 Ralph Dupas (USA), Houston

23.07.58 **Joe Brown** (USA) W PTS 15 Kenny Lane (USA), Houston

11.02.59 **Joe Brown** (USA) W PTS 15 Johnny Busso (USA), Houston

03.06.59 **Joe Brown** (USA) W RTD 8 Paolo Rossi (ITA), Washington

02.12.59 **Joe Brown** (USA) W RTD 5 Dave Charnley (GB), Houston

28.10.60 **Joe Brown** (USA) W PTS 15 Cisco Andrade (USA), Los Angeles

18.04.61 **Joe Brown** (USA) W PTS 15 Dave Charnley (GB), Earls Court, London

28.10.61 **Joe Brown** (USA) W PTS 15 Bert Somodio (PH), Quezon City

21.04.62 **Carlos Ortiz** (PR) W PTS 15 Joe Brown (USA), Las Vegas

03.12.62 **Carlos Ortiz** (PR) W CO 5 Teruo Kosaka (JAP), Tokyo

07.04.63 **Carlos Ortiz** (PR) W RSC 13 Doug Vaillant (CUB), San Juan

15.02.64 **Carlos Ortiz** (PR) W RSC 14 Flash Elorde (PH), Manila

11.04.64 **Carlos Ortiz** (PR) W PTS 15 Kenny Lane (USA), San Juan

10.04.65 **Ismael Laguna** (PAN) W PTS 15 Carlos Ortiz (PR), Panama City

13.11.65 **Carlos Ortiz** (PR) W PTS 15 Ismael Laguna (PAN), San Juan

20.06.66 **Carlos Ortiz** (PR) W RSC 12 Johnny Bizzaro (USA), Pittsburgh

22.10.66 **Carlos Ortiz** (PR) W RSC 5 Sugar Ramos (CUB), Mexico City

28.11.66 **Carlos Ortiz** (PR) W CO 14 Flash Elorde (PH), New York City

01.07.67 **Carlos Ortiz** (PR) W RSC 4 Sugar Ramos (CUB), San Juan

16.08.67 **Carlos Ortiz** (PR) W PTS 15 Ismael Laguna (PAN), New York City

29.06.68 **Carlos Teo Cruz** (DOM) W PTS 15 Carlos Ortiz (PR), St Domingo

28.09.68 **Carlos Teo Cruz** (DOM) W PTS 15 Mando Ramos (USA), Los Angeles

18.02.69 **Mando Ramos** (USA) W RSC 11 Carlos Teo Cruz (DOM), Los Angeles

04.10.69 **Mando Ramos** (USA) W RSC 6 Yoshiaki Numata (JAP), Los Angeles

03.03.70 **Ismael Laguna** (PAN) W RTD 9 Mando Ramos (USA), Los Angeles

07.06.70 **Ismael Laguna** (PAN) W RSC 13 Guts Ishimatsu (JAP), Panama City

26.09.70 **Ken Buchanan** (GB) W PTS 15 Ismael Laguna (PAN), San Juan

12.02.71 **Ken Buchanan** (GB) W PTS 15 Ruben Navarro (USA), Los Angeles. *Ken Buchanan forfeited WBC recognition for failing to defend against Pedro Carrasco*

13.09.71 Ken Buchanan (GB) W PTS 15 Ismael Laguna (PAN), New York City – WBA

05.11.71 Pedro Carrasco (SP) W DIS 11 Mando Ramos (USA), Madrid – WBC

18.02.72 Mando Ramos (USA) W PTS 15 Pedro Carrasco (SP), Los Angeles – WBC

26.06.72 Roberto Duran (PAN) W RSC 13 Ken Buchanan (GB), New York City – WBA

28.06.72 Mando Ramos (USA) W PTS 15 Pedro Carrasco (SP), Madrid – WBC

15.09.72 Chango Carmona (MEX) W RSC 8 Mando Ramos (USA), Los Angeles – WBC

10.11.72 Rodolfo Gonzalez (MEX) W RTD 12 Chango Carmona (MEX), Los Angeles – WBC

20.01.73 Roberto Duran (PAN) W CO 5 Jimmy Robertson (USA), Panama City – WBA

17.03.73 Rodolfo Gonzalez (MEX) W RSC 9 Ruben Navarro (USA), Los Angeles – WBC

02.06.73 Roberto Duran (PAN) W RSC 8 Hector Thompson (A), Panama City – WBA

08.09.73 Roberto Duran (PAN) W RSC 10 Guts Ishimatsu (JAP), Panama City – WBA

27.10.73 Rodolfo Gonzalez (MEX) W RTD 10 Antonio Puddu (ITA), Los Angeles – WBC

16.03.74 Roberto Duran (PAN) W RSC 11 Esteban de Jesus (PR), Panama City – WBA

11.04.74 Guts Ishimatsu (JAP) W CO 8 Rodolfo Gonzalez (MEX), Tokyo – WBC

13.09.74 Guts Ishimatsu (JAP) DREW 15 Tury Pineda (MEX), Nagoya – WBC

28.11.74 Guts Ishimatsu (JAP) W CO 12 Rodolfo Gonzalez (MEX), Osaka – WBC

21.12.74 Roberto Duran (PAN) W RSC 1 Masataka Takayama (JAP), San Jose – WBA

27.02.75 Guts Ishimatsu (JAP) W PTS 15 Ken Buchanan (GB), Tokyo – WBC

02.03.75 Roberto Duran (PAN) W CO 14 Ray Lampkin (USA), Panama City – WBA

05.06.75 Guts Ishimatsu (JAP) W PTS 15 Tury Pineda (MEX), Osaka – WBC

04.12.75 Guts Ishimatsu (JAP) W CO 14 Alvaro Rojas (CR), Tokyo – WBC

14.12.75 Roberto Duran (PAN) W CO 15 Leoncio Ortiz (MEX), San Juan – WBA

08.05.76 Esteban de Jesus (PR) W PTS 15 Guts Ishimatsu (JAP), Bayamon – WBC

22.05.76 Roberto Duran (PAN) W CO 14 Lou Bizzarro (USA), Fort Erie – WBA

10.09.76 Esteban de Jesus (PR) W CO 7 Hector Medina (DOM), Bayamon – WBC

15.10.76 Roberto Duran (PAN) W CO 1 Alvaro Rojas (CR), Los Angeles – WBA

29.01.77 Roberto Duran (PAN) W CO 13 Vilomar Fernandez (DOM), Miami – WBA

12.02.77 Esteban de Jesus (PR) W RSC 6 Buzzsaw Yamabe (JAP), Bayamon – WBC

25.06.77 Esteban de Jesus (PR) W CO 11 Vicente Mijares (MEX), Bayamon – WBC

17.09.77 Roberto Duran (PAN) W PTS 15 Edwin Viruet (PR), Philadelphia – WBA

21.01.78 **Roberto Duran** (PAN) W CO 12 Esteban de Jesus (PR), Las Vegas. *Roberto Duran relinquished title*

17.04.79 Jim Watt (GB) W RSC 12 Alfredo Pitalua (COL), Kelvin Hall, Glasgow – WBC

16.06.79 Ernesto Espana (VEN) W CO 13 Claude Noel (TR), San Juan – WBA

04.08.79 Ernesto Espana (VEN) W RSC 9 Johnny Lira (USA), Chicago – WBA

03.11.79 Jim Watt (GB) W RSC 9 Roberto Vasquez (USA), Kelvin Hall, Glasgow – WBC

02.03.80 Hilmer Kenty (USA) W RSC 9 Ernesto Espana (VEN), Detroit – WBA

14.03.80 Jim Watt (GB) W RSC 4 Charlie Nash (GB), Kelvin Hall, Glasgow – WBC

07.06.80 Jim Watt (GB) W PTS 15 Howard Davis (USA), Ibrox Park, Glasgow – WBC

02.08.80 Hilmer Kenty (USA) W RSC 9 Yong-Ho Oh (SK), Detroit – WBA

20.09.80 Hilmer Kenty (USA) W RSC 4 Ernesto Espana (VEN), San Juan – WBA

01.11.80 Jim Watt (GB) W RSC 12 Sean O'Grady (USA), Kelvin Hall, Glasgow – WBC

08.11.80 Hilmer Kenty (USA) W PTS 15 Vilomar Fernandez (DOM), Detroit – WBA

12.04.81 Sean O'Grady (USA) W PTS 15 Hilmer Kenty (USA), Atlantic City – WBA. *Sean O'Grady forfeited WBA recognition following a contractual dispute*

20.06.81 Alexis Arguello (NIC) W PTS 15 Jim Watt (GB) The Arena, Wembley – WBC

12.09.81 Claude Noel (TR) W PTS 15 Gato Gonzalez (MEX), Atlantic City – WBA

03.10.81 Alexis Arguello (NIC) W RSC 14 Ray Mancini (USA), Atlantic City – WBC

21.11.81	Alexis Arguello (NIC) W CO 7 Robert Elizondo (USA), Las Vegas – WBC
05.12.81	Arturo Frias (USA) W CO 8 Claude Noel (TR), Las Vegas – WBA
30.01.82	Arturo Frias (USA) W TD 9 Ernesto Espana (VEN), Atlantic City – WBA
13.02.82	Alexis Arguello (NIC) W RSC 6 Bubba Busceme (USA), Beaumont – WBC
08.05.82	Ray Mancini (USA) W RSC 1 Arturo Frias (USA), Las Vegas – WBA
22.05.82	Alexis Arguello (NIC) W CO 5 Andy Ganigan (USA), Las Vegas – WBC. *Alexis Arguello relinquished WBC version of title*
24.07.82	Ray Mancini (USA) W RSC 6 Ernesto Espana (VEN), Warren – WBA
13.11.82	Ray Mancini (USA) W RSC 14 Deuk-Koo Kim (SK), Las Vegas – WBA
01.05.83	Edwin Rosario (PR) W PTS 12 Jose Luis Ramirez (MEX), San Juan – WBC
15.09.83	Ray Mancini (USA) W CO 9 Orlando Romero (PERU), New York City – WBA
14.01.84	Ray Mancini (USA) W RSC 3 Bobby Chacon (USA), Reno – WBA
30.01.84	Charlie Choo Choo Brown (USA) W PTS 15 Melvin Paul (USA), Atlantic City – IBF
17.03.84	Edwin Rosario (PR) W RSC 1 Robert Elizondo (USA), San Juan – WBC
15.04.84	Harry Arroyo (USA) W RSC 14 Charlie Choo Choo Brown (USA), Atlantic City – IBF
01.06.84	Livingstone Bramble (USA) W RSC 14 Ray Mancini (USA), Buffalo – WBA
23.06.84	Edwin Rosario (PR) W PTS 12 Howard Davis (USA), San Juan – WBC
01.09.84	Harry Arroyo (USA) W RSC 8 Charlie White Lightning Brown (USA), Youngstown – IBF
03.11.84	Jose Luis Ramirez (MEX) W RSC 4 Edwin Rosario (PR), San Juan – WBC
12.01.85	Harry Arroyo (USA) W RSC 11 Terrence Alli (GU), Atlantic City – IBF
16.02.85	Livingstone Bramble (USA) W PTS 15 Ray Mancini (USA), Reno – WBA
06.04.85	Jimmy Paul (USA) W PTS 15 Harry Arroyo (USA), Atlantic City – IBF
30.06.85	Jimmy Paul (USA) W RSC 14 Robin Blake (USA), Las Vegas – IBF
10.08.85	Hector Camacho (PR) W PTS 12 Jose Luis Ramirez (MEX), Las Vegas – WBC
16.02.86	Livingstone Bramble (USA) W RSC 13 Tyrone Crawley (USA), Reno – WBA
04.06.86	Jimmy Paul (USA) W PTS 15 Irleis Perez (CUB), East Rutherford – IBF
13.06.86	Hector Camacho (PR) W PTS 12 Edwin Rosario (PR), New York City – WBC
15.08.86	Jimmy Paul (USA) W PTS 15 Darryl Tyson (USA), Detroit – IBF
26.09.86	Hector Camacho (PR) W PTS 12 Cornelius Boza-Edwards (GB), Miami – WBC. *Hector Camacho relinquished WBC version of title*
26.09.86	Edwin Rosario (PR) W CO 2 Livingstone Bramble (USA), Miami – WBA
05.12.86	Greg Haugen (USA) W PTS 15 Jimmy Paul (USA), Las Vegas – IBF
07.06.87	Vinny Pazienza (USA) W PTS 15 Greg Haugen (USA), Providence – IBF
19.07.87	Jose Luis Ramirez (MEX) W PTS 12 Terrence Alli (GU), St Tropez – WBC
11.08.87	Edwin Rosario (PR) W CO 8 Juan Nazario (PR), Chicago – WBA
10.10.87	Jose Luis Ramirez (MEX) W CO 5 Cornelius Boza-Edwards (GB), Paris – WBC
21.11.87	Julio Cesar Chavez (MEX) W RSC 11 Edwin Rosario (PR), Las Vegas – WBA
06.02.88	Greg Haugen (USA) W PTS 15 Vinny Pazienza (USA), Atlantic City – IBF
12.03.88	Jose Luis Ramirez (MEX) W PTS 12 Pernell Whitaker (USA), Paris – WBC
11.04.88	Greg Haugen (USA) W TD 11 Miguel Santana (PR), Tacoma – IBF
16.04.88	Julio Cesar Chavez (MEX) W RSC 6 Rodolfo Aguilar (PAN), Las Vegas – WBA
28.10.88	Greg Haugen (USA) W RTD 10 Gert Bo Jacobsen (DEN), Copenhagen – IBF
29.10.88	Julio Cesar Chavez (MEX) W TD 11 Jose Luis Ramirez (MEX), Las Vegas – WBA/WBC. *Julio Cesar Chavez relinquished WBA/WBC versions of title*
21.01.89	Mauricio Aceves (MEX) DREW 12 Amancio Castro (COL), Monteria – WBO
18.02.89	Pernell Whitaker (USA) W PTS 12 Greg Haugen (USA), Hampton – IBF
30.04.89	Pernell Whitaker (USA) W RSC 3 Louie Lomeli (USA), Norfolk – IBF
08.05.89	Mauricio Aceves (MEX) W PTS 12 Amancio Castro (COL), Santa Ana – WBO
09.07.89	Edwin Rosario (PR) W RSC 6 Anthony Jones (USA), Atlantic City – WBA
20.08.89	Pernell Whitaker (USA) W PTS 12 Jose Luis Ramirez (MEX), Norfolk – IBF/WBC
30.08.89	Mauricio Aceves (MEX) W RSC 10 Oscar Bejines (MEX), Los Angeles – WBO
03.02.90	Pernell Whitaker (USA) W PTS 12 Freddie Pendleton (USA), Atlantic City – IBF/WBC
04.04.90	Juan Nazario (PR), W RSC 8 Edwin Rosario (PR), New York City – WBA
19.05.90	Pernell Whitaker (USA) W PTS 12 Azumah Nelson (GH), Las Vegas – IBF/WBC
11.08.90	Pernell Whitaker (USA) W CO 1 Juan Nazario (PR), Stateline – IBF/WBA/WBC
22.09.90	Dingaan Thobela (SA) W PTS 12 Mauricio Aceves (MEX), Brownsville – WBO
02.02.91	Dingaan Thobela (SA) W PTS 12 Mario Martinez (MEX), San Jose – WBO
23.02.91	Pernell Whitaker (USA) W PTS 12 Anthony Jones (USA), Las Vegas – IBF/WBA/WBC
27.07.91	Pernell Whitaker (USA) W PTS 12 Policarpo Diaz (SP), Norfolk – IBF/WBA/WBC
14.09.91	Dingaan Thobela (SA) W PTS 12 Antonio Rivera (PR), Johannesburg – WBO
05.10.91	Pernell Whitaker (USA) W PTS 12 Jorge Paez (MEX), Reno – IBF/WBA/WBC. *Pernell Whitaker relinquished IBF/WBA/WBC versions of title*
12.06.92	Joey Gamache (USA) W RTD 8 Chil-Sung Chun (SK), Portland – WBA

Super-Featherweight

18.11.21	Johnny Dundee (USA) W DIS 5 K. O. Chaney (USA), New York – NY
06.07.22	Johnny Dundee (USA) W PTS 15 Jackie Sharkey (USA), New York City – NY
28.08.22	Johnny Dundee (USA) W PTS 15 Pepper Martin (USA), New York City – NY
02.02.23	Johnny Dundee (USA) W PTS 15 Elino Flores (PH), New York City – NY
30.05.23	Jack Bernstein (USA) W PTS 15 Johnny Dundee (USA), New York City NY/NBA
25.06.23	Jack Bernstein (USA) W CO 5 Freddie Jacks (GB), Philadelphia – NY/NBA
17.12.23	Johnny Dundee (USA) W PTS 15 Jack Bernstein (USA), New York City – NY/NBA
20.06.24	Kid Sullivan (USA) W PTS 10 Johnny Dundee (USA), New York City – NY/NBA
18.08.24	Kid Sullivan (USA) W PTS 15 Pepper Martin (USA), New York City – NY/NBA
15.10.24	Kid Sullivan (USA) W CO 5 Mike Ballerino (USA), New York City – NY/NBA
01.04.25	Mike Ballerino (USA) W PTS 10 Kid Sullivan (USA), Philadelphia – NY/NBA
06.07.25	Mike Ballerino (USA) W PTS 15 Pepper Martin (USA), New York City – NY/NBA
02.12.25	Tod Morgan (USA) W RTD 10 Mike Ballerino (USA), Los Angeles – NY/NBA
03.06.26	Tod Morgan (USA) W RTD 6 Kid Sullivan (USA), New York City – NY/NBA
30.09.26	Tod Morgan (USA) W PTS 15 Joe Glick (USA), New York City – NY/NBA
19.10.26	Tod Morgan (USA) W PTS 10 Johnny Dundee (USA), San Francisco – NY/NBA
19.11.26	Tod Morgan (USA) W PTS 15 Carl Duane (USA), New York City – NY/NBA
28.05.27	Tod Morgan (USA) W PTS 12 Vic Foley (C), Vancouver – NY/NBA
16.12.27	Tod Morgan (USA) W DIS 14 Joe Glick (USA), New York City – NY/NBA
24.05.28	Tod Morgan (USA) W PTS 15 Eddie Martin (USA), New York City – NY/NBA
18.07.28	Tod Morgan (USA) W PTS 15 Eddie Martin (USA), New York City – NY/NBA
03.12.28	Tod Morgan (USA) DREW 10 Santiago Zorilla (PAN), San Francisco – NY/NBA
05.04.29	Tod Morgan (USA) W PTS 10 Santiago Zorilla (PAN), Los Angeles – NY/NBA
20.05.29	Tod Morgan (USA) W PTS 10 Baby Sal Sorio (USA), Los Angeles – NY/NBA
20.12.29	Benny Bass (USA) W CO 2 Tod Morgan (USA), New York City NY/NBA. *Benny Bass forfeited NY recognition when the State abolished weight division*
03.02.30	Benny Bass (USA) W RSC 4 Davey Abad (PAN), St Louis – NBA
05.01.31	Benny Bass (USA) W PTS 10 Lew Massey (USA), Philadelphia – NBA
15.07.31	Kid Chocolate (CUB) W RSC 7 Benny Bass (USA), Philadelphia – NBA
10.04.32	Kid Chocolate (CUB) W PTS 15 Davey Abad (PAN), Havana – NBA
04.08.32	Kid Chocolate (CUB) W PTS 10 Eddie Shea (USA), Chicago – NBA
01.05.33	Kid Chocolate (CUB) W PTS 10 Johnny Farr (USA), Philadelphia – NBA
04.12.33	Kid Chocolate (CUB) W PTS 10 Frankie Wallace (USA), Cleveland – NBA
25.12.33	Frankie Klick (USA) W RSC 7 Kid Chocolate (CUB), Philadelphia – NBA. *Frankie Klick relinquished NBA version of title*
06.12.49	Sandy Saddler (USA) W PTS 10 Orlando Zulueta (CUB), Cleveland – OHIO
18.04.50	Sandy Saddler (USA) W RSC 9 Lauro Salas (MEX), Cleveland – OHIO
28.02.51	Sandy Saddler (USA) W CO 2 Diego Sosa (CUB), Havana – OHIO. *Sandy Saddler forfeited Ohio recognition for failing to defend after regaining the featherweight title*
20.07.59	Harold Gomes (USA) W PTS 15 Paul Jorgensen (USA), Providence – NBA
16.03.60	Flash Elorde (PH) W CO 7 Harold Gomes (USA), Quezon City – NBA
17.08.60	Flash Elorde (PH) W CO 1 Harold Gomes (USA), San Francisco – NBA
19.03.61	Flash Elorde (PH) W PTS 15 Joey Lopes (USA), Manila – NBA
16.12.61	Flash Elorde (PH) W RSC 1 Sergio Caprari (ITA), Manila – NBA
23.06.62	Flash Elorde (PH) W PTS 15 Auburn Copeland (USA), Manila – NBA
16.02.63	Flash Elorde (PH) W PTS 15 Johnny Bizzarro (USA), Manila – WBA
16.11.63	Flash Elorde (PH) W DIS 11 Love Allotey (GH), Quezon City – WBA
27.07.64	Flash Elorde (PH) W RSC 12 Teruo Kosaka (JAP), Tokyo – WBA
05.06.65	Flash Elorde (PH) W CO 15 Teruo Kosaka (JAP), Quezon City – WBA
04.12.65	Flash Elorde (PH) W PTS 15 Kang-Il Suh (SK), Quezon City – WBA
22.10.66	Flash Elorde (PH) W PTS 15 Vincente Derado (ARG), Quezon City – WBA
15.06.67	Flash Elorde (PH), Tokyo – WBA
14.12.67	Hiroshi Kobayashi (JAP) W CO 12 Yoshiaki Numata (JAP), Tokyo – WBA
30.03.68	Hiroshi Kobayashi (JAP) DREW 15 Rene Barrientos (PH), Tokyo – WBA
06.10.68	Hiroshi Kobayashi (JAP) W PTS 15 Jaime Valladeres (EC), Tokyo – WBA
15.02.69	Rene Barrientos (PH) W PTS 15 Ruben Navarro (USA), Quezon City – WBC
06.04.69	Hiroshi Kobayashi (JAP) W PTS 15 Antonio Amaya (PAN), Tokyo – WBA
09.11.69	Hiroshi Kobayashi (JAP) W PTS 15 Carlos Canete (ARG), Tokyo – WBA
05.04.70	Yoshiaki Numata (JAP) W PTS 15 Rene Barrientos (PH), Tokyo – WBC
23.08.70	Hiroshi Kobayashi (JAP) W PTS 15 Antonio Amaya (PAN), Tokyo – WBA
27.09.70	Yoshiaki Numata (JAP) W CO 5 Raul Rojas (USA), Tokyo – WBC
03.01.71	Yoshiaki Numata (JAP) W PTS 15 Rene Barrientos (PH), Shizuaka – WBC
03.03.71	Hiroshi Kobayashi (JAP) W PTS 15 Ricardo Arredondo (MEX), Tokyo – WBA
30.05.71	Yoshiaki Numata (JAP) W PTS 15 Lionel Rose (A), Hiroshima – WBC

29.07.71 Alfredo Marcano (VEN) W RTD 10 Hiroshi Kobayashi (JAP), Aomori – WBA

10.10.71 Ricardo Arredondo (MEX) W CO 10 Yoshiaki Numata (JAP), Sendai – WBC

07.11.71 Alfredo Marcano (VEN) W RSC 4 Kenji Iwata (JAP), Caracas – WBA

29.01.72 Ricardo Arredondo (MEX) W PTS 15 Jose Marin (CR), San Jose – WBC

22.04.72 Ricardo Arredondo (MEX) W CO 5 William Martinez (NIC), Mexico City – WBC

25.04.72 Ben Villaflor (PH) W PTS 15 Alfredo Marcano (VEN), Honolulu – WBA

05.09.72 Ben Villaflor (PH) DREW 15 Victor Echegaray (ARG), Honolulu – WBA

15.09.72 Ricardo Arredondo (MEX) W CO 12 Susumu Okabe (JAP), Tokyo – WBC

06.03.73 Ricardo Arredondo (MEX) W PTS 15 Apollo Yoshio (JAP), Fukuoka City – WBC

12.03.73 Kuniaki Shibata (JAP) W PTS 15 Ben Villaflor (PH), Honolulu – WBA

19.06.73 Kuniaki Shibata (JAP) W PTS 15 Victor Echegaray (ARG), Tokyo – WBA

01.09.73 Ricardo Arredondo (MEX) W RSC 6 Morito Kashiwaba (JAP), Tokyo – WBC

18.10.73 Ben Villaflor (PH) W CO 1 Kuniaki Shibata (JAP), Honolulu – WBA

28.02.74 Kuniaki Shibata (JAP) W PTS 15 Ricardo Arredondo (MEX), Tokyo – WBC

14.03.74 Ben Villaflor (PH) DREW 15 Apollo Yoshio (JAP), Toyama – WBA

27.06.74 Kuniaki Shibata (JAP) W PTS 15 Antonio Amaya (PAN), Tokyo – WBC

03.08.74 Kuniaki Shibata (JAP) W RSC 15 Ramiro Bolanos (EC), Tokyo – WBC

24.08.74 Ben Villaflor (PH) W RSC 2 Yasutsune Uehara (JAP), Honolulu – WBA

13.03.75 Ben Villaflor (PH) W PTS 15 Hyun-Chi Kim (SK), Quezon City – WBA

27.03.75 Kuniaki Shibata (JAP) W PTS 15 Ould Makloufi (FR), Fukuoka City – WBC

05.07.75 Alfredo Escalera (PR) W CO 2 Kuniaki Shibata (JAP), Kasamatsu – WBC

20.09.75 Alfredo Escalera (PR) DREW 15 Leonel Hernandez (VEN), Caracas – WBC

12.12.75 Alfredo Escalera (PR) W RSC 9 Sven-Erik Paulsen (NOR), Oslo – WBC

12.01.76 Ben Villaflor (PH) W RSC 13 Morito Kashiwaba (JAP), Tokyo – WBA

20.02.76 Alfredo Escalera (PR) W RSC 13 Jose Fernandez (DOM), San Juan – WBC

01.04.76 Alfredo Escalera (PR) W RSC 6 Buzzsaw Yamabe (JAP), Nara – WBC

13.04.76 Ben Villaflor (PH) DREW 15 Sam Serrano (PR), Honolulu – WBA

01.07.76 Alfredo Escalera (PR) W PTS 15 Buzzsaw Yamabe (JAP), Nara – WBC

18.09.76 Alfredo Escalera (PR) W RTD 12 Ray Lunny (USA), San Juan – WBC

16.10.76 Sam Serrano (PR) W PTS 15 Ben Villaflor (PH), San Juan – WBA

30.11.76 Alfredo Escalera (PR) W PTS 15 Tyrone Everett (USA), Philadelphia – WBC

15.01.77 Sam Serrano (PR) W RSC 11 Alberto Herrera (EC), Guayaquil – WBA

17.03.77 Alfredo Escalera (PR) W RSC 6 Ronnie McGarvey (USA), San Juan – WBC

16.05.77 Alfredo Escalera (PR) W CO 8 Carlos Becerril (MEX), Landover – WBC

26.06.77 Sam Serrano (PR) W PTS 15 Leonel Hernandez (VEN), Cruz – WBA

27.08.77 Sam Serrano (PR) W PTS 15 Apollo Yoshio (JAP), San Juan – WBA

10.09.77 Alfredo Escalera (PR) W PTS 15 Sigfredo Rodriguez (MEX), San Juan – WBC

19.11.77 Sam Serrano (PR) W RSC 10 Tae-Ho Kim (SK), San Juan – WBA

28.01.78 Alexis Arguello (NIC) W RSC 13 Alfredo Escalera (PR), Bayamon – WBC

18.02.78 Sam Serrano (PR) W PTS 15 Mario Martinez (NIC), San Juan – WBA

29.04.78 Alexis Arguello (NIC) W RSC 5 Rey Tam (PH), Los Angeles – WBC

03.06.78 Alexis Arguello (NIC) W CO 1 Diego Alcala (PAN), San Juan – WBC

08.07.78 Sam Serrano (PR) W RSC 9 Yong-Ho Oh (SK), San Juan – WBA

10.11.78 Alexis Arguello (NIC) W PTS 15 Arturo Leon (MEX), Las Vegas – WBC

29.11.78 Sam Serrano (PR) W PTS 15 Takas Maruki (JAP), Nagoya – WBA

04.02.79 Alexis Arguello (NIC) W CO 13 Alfredo Escalera (PR), Rimini – WBC

18.02.79 Sam Serrano (PR) W PTS 15 Julio Valdez (DOM), San Juan – WBA

14.04.79 Sam Serrano (PR) W RSC 8 Nkosana Mgxaji (SA), Capetown – WBA

08.07.79 Alexis Arguello (NIC) W RSC 11 Rafael Limon (MEX), New York City – WBC

16.11.79 Alexis Arguello (NIC) W RTD 7 Bobby Chacon (USA), Los Angeles – WBC

20.01.80 Alexis Arguello (NIC) W RSC 11 Ruben Castillo (USA), Tucson – WBC

03.04.80 Sam Serrano (PR) W RSC 13 Battle Hawk Kazama (JAP), Nara – WBA

27.04.80 Alexis Arguello (NIC) W RSC 4 Rolando Navarrete (PH), San Juan – WBC. *Alexis Arguello relinquished WBC version of title*

02.08.80 Yasutsune Uehara (JAP) W CO 6 Sam Serrano (PR), Detroit – WBA

20.11.80 Yasutsune Uehara (JAP) W PTS 15 Leonel Hernandez (VEN), Tokyo – WBA

11.12.80 Rafael Limon (MEX) W RSC 15 Ildefonso Bethelmy (VEN), Los Angeles – WBC

08.03.81 Cornelius Boza-Edwards (GB) W PTS 15 Rafael Limon (MEX), Stockton – WBC

09.04.81 Sam Serrano (PR) W PTS 15 Yasutsune Uehara (JAP), Wakayama – WBA

30.05.81 Cornelius Boza-Edwards (GB) W RTD 13 Bobby Chacon (USA), Las Vegas – WBC

29.06.81 Sam Serrano (PR) W PTS 15 Leonel Hernandez (VEN), Caracas – WBA

29.08.81 Rolando Navarrete (PH) W CO 5 Cornelius Boza-Edwards (GB), Reggio – WBC

10.12.81 Sam Serrano (PR) W RSC 12 Hikaru Tomonari (JAP), San Juan – WBA

16.01.82 Rolando Navarrete (PH) W CO 11 Chung-Il Choi (SK), Manila – WBC

29.05.82 Rafael Limon (MEX) W CO 12 Rolando Navarrete (PH), Las Vegas – WBC

05.06.82 Sam Serrano (PR) NC 11 Benedicto Villablanca (CH), Santiago – WBA

18.09.82 Rafael Limon (MEX) W RSC 7 Chung-Il Choi (SK), Los Angeles – WBC

11.12.82 Bobby Chacon (USA) W PTS 15 Rafael Limon (MEX), Sacramento – WBC

19.01.83 Roger Mayweather (USA) W CO 8 Sam Serrano (PR), San Juan – WBA

20.04.83 Roger Mayweather (USA) W RSC 8 Jorge Alvarado (PAN), San Jose – WBA

15.05.83 Bobby Chacon (USA) W PTS 12 Cornelius Boza-Edwards (GB), Las Vegas – WBC. *Bobby Chacon forfeited WBC recognition following a contractual dispute*

07.08.83 Hector Camacho (PR) W RSC 5 Rafael Limon (MEX), San Juan – WBC

17.08.83 Roger Mayweather (USA) W CO 1 Benedicto Villablanca (CH), Las Vegas – WBA

18.11.83 Hector Camacho (PR) W CO 5 Rafael Solis (PR), San Juan – WBC. *Hector Camacho relinquished WBC version of title*

26.02.84 Rocky Lockridge (USA) W CO 1 Roger Mayweather (USA), Beaumont – WBA

22.04.84 Hwan-Kil Yuh (SK) W PTS 15 Rod Sequenan (PH), Seoul – IBF

12.06.84 Rocky Lockridge (USA) W RSC 11 Taej-ln Moon (SK), Anchorage – WBA

13.09.84 Julio Cesar Chavez (MEX) W RSC 8 Mario Martinez (MEX), Los Angeles – WBC

16.09.84 Hwan-Kil Yuh (SK) W CO 6 Sak Galexi (TH), Pohang – IBF

27.01.85 Rocky Lockridge (USA) W RSC 6 Kamel Bou Ali (TUN), Riva del Garda – WBA

15.02.85 Lester Ellis (A) W PTS 15 Hwan-Kil Yuh (SK), Melbourne – IBF

19.04.85 Julio Cesar Chavez (MEX) W RSC 6 Ruben Castillo (USA), Los Angeles – WBC

26.04.85 Lester Ellis (A) W CO 13 Rod Sequenan (PH), Melbourne – IBF

19.05.85 Wilfredo Gomez (PR) W PTS 15 Rocky Lockridge (USA), San Juan – WBA

07.07.85 Julio Cesar Chavez (MEX) W RSC 2 Roger Mayweather (USA), Las Vegas – WBC

12.07.85 Barry Michael (A) W PTS 15 Lester Ellis (A), Melbourne – IBF

22.09.85 Julio Cesar Chavez (MEX) W PTS 12 Dwight Pratchett (USA), Las Vegas – WBC

18.10.85 Barry Michael (A) W RSC 4 Jin-Shik Choi (SK), Darwin – IBF

15.05.86 Julio Cesar Chavez (MEX) W RSC 5 Faustino Barrios (ARG), Paris – WBC

23.05.86 Barry Michael (A) W RSC 4 Mark Fernandez (USA), Melbourne – IBF

24.05.86 Alfredo Layne (PAN) W RSC 9 Wilfredo Gomez (PR), San Juan – WBA

13.06.86 Julio Cesar Chavez (MEX) W RSC 7 Refugio Rojas (USA), New York City – WBC

03.08.86 Julio Cesar Chavez (MEX) W PTS 12 Rocky Lockridge (USA), Monaco – WBC

23.08.86 Barry Michael (A) W PTS 12 Najib Daho (GB), Granada Studio, Manchester – IBF

27.09.86 Brian Mitchell (SA) W RSC 10 Alfredo Layne (PAN), Sun City – WBA

12.12.86 Julio Cesar Chavez (MEX) W PTS 12 Juan Laporte (PR), New York City – WBC

27.03.87 Brian Mitchell (SA) DREW 15 Jose Rivera (PR), San Juan – WBA

18.04.87 Julio Cesar Chavez (MEX) W RSC 3 Francisco Tomas Cruz (BR), Nimes – WBC

31.07.87 Brian Mitchell (SA) W RSC 14 Francisco Fernandez (PAN), Panama City – WBA

09.08.87 Rocky Lockridge (USA) W RTD 8 Barry Michael (A), Blazer's Night Club, Windsor – IBF

21.08.87 Julio Cesar Chavez (MEX) W PTS 12 Danilo Cabrera (DOM), Tijuana – WBC. *Julio Cesar Chavez relinquished WBC version of title*

03.10.87 Brian Mitchell (SA) W PTS 15 Daniel Londas (FR), Gravelines – WBA

25.10.87 Rocky Lockridge (USA) W RSC 10 Johnny de la Rosa (DOM), Tucson – IBF

19.12.87 Brian Mitchell (SA) W RTD 8 Salvatore Curcetti (ITA), Capo d'Orlando – WBA

29.02.88 Azumah Nelson (GH) W PTS 12 Mario Martinez (MEX), Los Angeles – WBC

02.04.88 Rocky Lockridge (USA) W PTS 15 Harold Knight (USA), Atlantic City – IBF

26.04.88 Brian Mitchell (SA) W PTS 12 Jose Rivera (PR), Madrid – WBA

25.06.88 Azumah Nelson (GH) W RSC 9 Lupe Suarez (USA), Atlantic City – WBC

27.07.88 Tony Lopez (USA) W PTS 12 Rocky Lockridge (USA), Sacramento – IBF

27.10.88 Tony Lopez (USA) W PTS 12 Juan Molina (PR), Sacramento – IBF

02.11.88 Brian Mitchell (SA) W PTS 12 Jim McDonnell (GB), Elephant & Castle Recreation Centre, London – WBA

10.12.88 Azumah Nelson (GH) W CO 3 Sydnei dal Rovere (BR), Accra – WBC

10.02.89 Brian Mitchell (SA) W RSC 8 Salvatore Bottiglieri (ITA), Capo d'Orlando – WBA

25.02.89 Azumah Nelson (GH) W RSC 12 Mario Martinez (MEX), Las Vegas – WBC

05.03.89 Tony Lopez (USA) W PTS 12 Rocky Lockridge (USA), Sacramento – IBF

29.04.89 Juan Molina (PR) W PTS 12 Juan Laporte (PR), San Juan – WBO. *Juan Molina relinquished WBO version of title*

18.06.89 Tony Lopez (USA) W CO 8 Tyrone Jackson (USA), Stateline – IBF

01.07.89 Brian Mitchell (SA) W TD 9 Jackie Beard (USA), Crotone – WBA

28.09.89 Brian Mitchell (SA) W RSC 7 Irving Mitchell (USA), Lewiston – WBA

07.10.89 Juan Molina (PR) W RSC 10 Tony Lopez (USA), Sacramento – IBF

05.11.89 Azumah Nelson (GH) W CO 12 Jim McDonnell (GB), Albert Hall, London – WBC

09.12.89 Kamel Bou Ali (TUN) W CO 8 Antonio Rivera (PR), Terano – WBO

28.01.90 Juan Molina (PR) W RSC 6 Lupe Suarez (USA), Atlantic City – IBF

14.03.90 Brian Mitchell (SA) W PTS 12 Jackie Beard (USA), Grossetto – WBA

20.05.90 Tony Lopez (USA) W PTS 12 Juan Molina (PR), Reno – IBF

22.09.90 Tony Lopez (USA) W PTS 12 Jorge Paez (MEX), Sacramento – IBF

29.09.90 Brian Mitchell (SA) W PTS 12 Frankie Mitchell (USA), Aosta – WBA

13.10.90 Azumah Nelson (GH) W PTS 12 Juan Laporte (PR), Sydney – WBC

20.10.90 Kamel Bou Ali (TUN) NC 2 Pedro Villegas (ARG), Cesena – WBO

15.03.91 Brian Mitchell (SA) DREW 12 Tony Lopez (USA), Sacramento – WBA/IBF. *Brian Mitchell relinquished WBA version of title*

01.06.91 Kamel Bou Ali (TUN) W CO 3 Joey Jacobs (GB), Ragusa – WBO

28.06.91 Azumah Nelson (GH) DREW 12 Jeff Fenech (A), Las Vegas – WBC

28.06.91 Joey Gamache (USA) W RSC 10 Jerry N'Gobeni (SA), Lewiston – WBA. *Joey Gamache relinquished title*

12.07.91 Tony Lopez (USA) W RSC 6 Lupe Guttierez (USA), Lake Tahoe – IBF

13.09.91 Brian Mitchell (SA) W PTS 12 Tony Lopez (USA), Sacramento – IBF. *Brian Mitchell relinquished IBF version of title*

22.11.91 Genaro Hernandez (USA) W RTD 9 Daniel Londas (FR), Epernay – WBA

22.02.92 Juan Molina (PR) W RSC 4 Jackie Gunguluza (SA), Sun City – IBF

24.02.92 Genaro Hernandez (USA) W PTS 12 Omar Catari (VEN) Los Angeles – WBA

01.03.92 Azumah Nelson (GH) W RSC 8 Jeff Fenech (A), Melbourne – WBC

21.03.92 Daniel Londas (FR) W PTS 12 Kamel Bou Ali (TUN), San Rufo – WBO

Featherweight

13.01.90 Billy Murphy (NZ) W CO 14 Ike Weir (GB), San Francisco – AUST

02.02.90 Young Griffo (A) W RSC 15 Billy Murphy (NZ), Sydney – AUST

12.03.91 Young Griffo (A) W DIS 20 George Powell (A), Sydney – AUST. *Young Griffo forfeited Australian version of title due to increasing weight problems*

31.03.91 George Dixon (C) W RSC 22 Cal McCarthy (USA), Troy – USA

28.07.91 George Dixon (C) W CO 5 Abe Willis (A), San Francisco – USA

27.06.92 **George Dixon** (C) W CO 14 Fred Johnson (GB), New York City

06.09.92 **George Dixon** (C) W CO 8 Jack Skelly (USA), New Orleans

07.08.93 **George Dixon** (C) W CO 3 Eddie Pierce (USA), New York City

25.09.93 **George Dixon** (C) W CO 7 Solly Smith (USA), New York City

27.08.95 **George Dixon** (C) W PTS 25 Johnny Griffin (USA), Boston

05.12.95 **George Dixon** (C) DREW 10 Frank Erne (USA), New York City

17.03.96 **George Dixon** (C) W 8 Jerry Marshall (USA), Boston

16.06.96 **George Dixon** (C) DREW 20 Martin Flaherty (USA), Boston

25.09.96 **George Dixon** (C) DREW 20 Tommy White (USA), New York City

22.01.97 **George Dixon** (C) W CO 6 Billy Murphy (NZ), New York City

15.02.97 **George Dixon** (C) DREW 20 Jack Downey (USA), New York City

26.04.97 **George Dixon** (C) W PTS 20 Johnny Griffin (USA), New York City

23.07.97 **George Dixon** (C) DREW 20 Dal Hawkins (USA), San Francisco

04.10.97 **Solly Smith** (USA) W PTS 20 George Dixon (C), San Francisco – USA. *Solly Smith forfeited GB recognition following Ben Jordan's victory over George Dixon in July, 1898*

01.07.98 Ben Jordan (GB) W PTS 25 George Dixon (C), New York City – GB

07.07.98 Solly Smith (USA) W DIS 7 Billy O'Donnell (USA), Buffalo – USA

01.08.98 Solly Smith (USA) DREW 25 Tommy White (USA), New York City – USA

26.09.98 Dave Sullivan (USA) W RTD 5 Solly Smith (USA), New York City – USA

11.11.98 George Dixon (C) W DIS 10 Dave Sullivan (USA), New York City – USA

29.11.98 George Dixon (C) W PTS 25 Oscar Gardner (USA), New York City – USA

17.01.99 George Dixon (C) W CO 10 Young Pluto (A), New York City – USA

15.05.99 George Dixon (C) W PTS 20 Kid Broad (USA), Buffalo – USA

29.05.99 Ben Jordan (GB) W CO 9 Harry Greenfield (GB), NSC, London – GB. *Ben Jordan forfeited GB recognition following a defeat by Eddie Santry in October, 1899*

02.06.99 George Dixon (C) W PTS 25 Joe Bernstein (USA), New York City – USA

11.07.99 George Dixon (C) W PTS 20 Tommy White (USA), Denver – USA

11.08.99 George Dixon (C) DREW 20 Eddie Santry (USA), New York City – USA

02.11.99 **George Dixon** (C) W PTS 25 Will Curley (GB), New York City

21.11.99 **George Dixon** (C) W PTS 25 Eddie Lenny (USA), New York City

09.01.00 **Terry McGovern** (USA) W RSC 9 George Dixon (C), New York City

01.02.00 **Terry McGovern** (USA) W CO 5 Eddie Santry (USA), Chicago

09.03.00 **Terry McGovern** (USA) W CO 3 Oscar Gardner (USA), New York City

12.06.00 **Terry McGovern** (USA) W CO 3 Tommy White (USA), New York City

02.11.00 **Terry McGovern** (USA) W CO 7 Joe Bernstein (USA), Louisville

30.04.01 **Terry McGovern** (USA) W CO 4 Oscar Gardner (USA), San Francisco

29.05.01 **Terry McGovern** (USA) W CO 5 Aurelio Herrera (USA), San Francisco

28.11.01 **Young Corbett II** (USA) W CO 2 Terry McGovern (USA), Hartford

16.10.02 **Young Corbett II** (USA) W RTD 8 Joe Bernstein (USA), Baltimore

14.01.03 **Young Corbett II** (USA) W 18 Austin Rice (USA), Hot Springs

26.02.03 **Young Corbett II** (USA) DREW 20 Eddie Hanlon (USA), San Francisco

31.03.03 **Young Corbett II** (USA) W CO 11 Terry McGovern (USA), San Francisco. *Young Corbett II relinquished title*

03.09.03 **Abe Attell** (USA) W PTS 20 Johnny Reagan (USA), St Louis

01.02.04 **Abe Attell** (USA) W RSC 5 Harry Forbes (USA), St Louis

23.06.04 **Abe Attell** (USA) W PTS 20 Johnny Reagan (USA), St Louis

13.10.04 **Tommy Sullivan** (USA) W CO 5 Abe Attell (USA), St Louis. *Tommy Sullivan forfeited title due to inactivity*

22.02.06 **Abe Attell** (USA) W PTS 15 Jimmy Walsh (USA), Chelsea, Mass

15.03.06 **Abe Attell** (USA) W DIS 3 Tony Moran (USA), Baltimore

11.05.06 **Abe Attell** (USA) DREW 20 Kid Herman (USA), Los Angeles

04.07.06 **Abe Attell** (USA) W PTS 20 Frankie Neil (USA), Los Angeles

30.10.06 **Abe Attell** (USA) W PTS 20 Harry Baker (USA), Los Angeles

16.11.06 **Abe Attell** (USA) W PTS 15 Billy de Coursey (USA), San Diego

07.12.06 **Abe Attell** (USA) W CO 8 Jimmy Walsh (USA), Los Angeles

18.01.07 **Abe Attell** (USA) W CO 8 Harry Baker (USA), Los Angeles

24.05.07 **Abe Attell** (USA) W PTS 20 Kid Solomon (USA), Los Angeles

29.10.07 **Abe Attell** (USA) W CO 4 Freddie Weeks (USA), Los Angeles

01.01.08 **Abe Attell** (USA) DREW 25 Owen Moran (GB), San Francisco

31.01.88 **Abe Attell** (USA) W RTD 13 Frankie Neil (USA), San Francisco

28.02.08 **Abe Attell** (USA) W CO 7 Eddie Kelly (USA), San Francisco

30.04.08 **Abe Attell** (USA) W CO 4 Tommy Sullivan (USA), San Francisco

07.09.08 **Abe Attell** (USA) DREW 23 Owen Moran (GB), San Francisco

14.01.09 **Abe Attell** (USA) W CO 10 Freddie Weeks (USA), Goldfield

04.02.09 **Abe Attell** (USA) W CO 7 Eddie Kelly (USA), New Orleans

26.03.09 **Abe Attell** (USA) W CO 8 Frankie White (USA), Dayton

28.02.10 **Abe Attell** (USA) W CO 6 Harry Forbes (USA), New York City

22.08.10 **Abe Attell** (USA) W CO 3 Eddie Merino (C), Calgary

05.09.10 **Abe Attell** (USA) W CO 17 Billy Lauder (C), Winnipeg

24.10.10 **Abe Attell** (USA) W PTS 10 Johnny Kilbane (USA), Kansas City

13.11.10 **Abe Attell** (USA) DREW 15 Frankie Conley (USA), New Orleans. *Abe Attell forfeited GB/IBU recognition for failing to defend against Jim Driscoll*

22.02.12 Johnny Kilbane (USA) W PTS 20 Abe Attell (USA), Los Angeles – USA

21.05.12 Johnny Kilbane (USA) DREW 12 Jimmy Walsh (USA), Boston – USA

03.06.12 Jim Driscoll (GB) W CO 12 Jean Poesy (FR), NSC, London – GB/IBU

14.10.12 Johnny Kilbane (USA) W PTS 12 Eddie O'Keefe (USA), Cleveland – USA

03.12.12 Johnny Kilbane (USA) W RSC 8 Monte Attell (USA), Cleveland – USA

27.01.13 Jim Driscoll (GB) DREW 20 Owen Moran (FR), NSC, London – GB/IBU. *Jim Driscoll relinquished GB/IBU version of title*

29.04.13 Johnny Kilbane (USA) DREW 20 Johnny Dundee (USA), Los Angeles – USA

16.09.13 **Johnny Kilbane** (USA) W PTS 12 Jimmy Walsh (USA), Boston

04.09.16 **Johnny Kilbane** (USA) W CO 3 K. O. Chaney (USA), Cedar Point

26.03.17 **Johnny Kilbane** (USA) DREW 12 Eddie Wallace (USA), Bridgeport

21.04.20 **Johnny Kilbane** (USA) W CO 7 Alvie Miller (USA), Lorain

17.09.21 **Johnny Kilbane** (USA) W CO 7 Danny Frush (GB), Cleveland. *Johnny Kilbane forfeited NY recognition due to inactivity*

15.08.22 Johnny Dundee (USA) W CO 9 Danny Frush (GB), New York City – NY. *Johnny Dundee forfeited NY recognition when concentrating on his junior-lightweight title*

02.06.23 **Eugene Criqui** (FR) W CO 6 Johnny Kilbane (USA), New York City

26.07.23 **Johnny Dundee** (USA) W PTS 15 Eugene Criqui (FR), New York City. *Johnny Dundee relinquished title*

02.01.25 **Kid Kaplan** (USA) W RTD 9 Danny Kramer (USA), New York City

27.08.25 **Kid Kaplan** (USA) DREW 15 Babe Herman (USA), Waterbury

18.12.25 **Kid Kaplan** (USA) W PTS 15 Babe Herman (USA), New York City

28.06.26 **Kid Kaplan** (USA) W CO 10 Bobby Garcia (USA), Hartford. *Kid Kaplan relinquished title*

15.11.26 Honeyboy Finnegan (USA) W PTS 10 Chick Suggs (USA), Boston – MASS. *Honeyboy Finnegan forfeited Massachusetts recognition when unable to make the weight*

12.09.27 Benny Bass (USA) W PTS 10 Red Chapman (USA), Philadelphia – NBA

24.10.27 Tony Canzoneri (USA) W PTS 15 Johnny Dundee (USA), New York City – NY

10.02.28 **Tony Canzoneri** (USA) W PTS 15 Benny Bass (USA), New York City

28.09.28 **Andre Routis** (FR) W PTS 15 Tony Canzoneri (USA), New York City

27.05.29 **Andre Routis** (FR) W RSC 3 Buster Brown (USA), Baltimore

23.09.29 **Bat Battalino** (USA) W PTS 15 Andre Routis (FR), Hartford

15.07.30 **Bat Battalino** (USA) W CO 5 Ignacio Fernandez (PH), Hartford

12.12.30 **Bat Battalino** (USA) W PTS 15 Kid Chocolate (CUB), New York City

22.05.31 **Bat Battalino** (USA) W PTS 15 Fidel la Barba (USA), New York City

01.07.31 **Bat Battalino** (USA) W PTS 10 Bobby Brady (USA), Jersey City

23.07.31 **Bat Battalino** (USA) W PTS 10 Freddie Miller (USA), Cincinnati

04.11.31 **Bat Battalino** (USA) W PTS 10 Earl Mastro (USA), Chicago. *Bat Battalino forfeited title when overweight for a defence against Freddie Miller*

26.05.32 Tommy Paul (USA) W PTS 10 Johnny Pena (PR), Detroit – NBA

13.10.32 Kid Chocolate (CUB) W CO 12 Lew Feldman (USA), New York City – NY

09.12.32 Kid Chocolate (CUB) W PTS 15 Fidel la Barba (USA), New York City – NY

13.01.33 Freddie Miller (USA) W PTS 10 Tommy Paul (USA), Chicago – NBA

28.02.33 Freddie Miller (USA) W PTS 10 Baby Arizmendi (MEX), Los Angeles – NBA

21.03.33 Freddie Miller (USA) W PTS 10 Speedy Dado (PH), Los Angeles – NBA

19.05.33 Kid Chocolate (CUB) W PTS 15 Seaman Tommy Watson (GB), New York City – NY. *Kid Chocolate forfeited NY recognition for failing to defend against Frankie Klick*

01.01.34 Freddie Miller (USA) W PTS 10 Jackie Sharkey (USA), Cincinnati – NBA

30.08.34 Baby Arizmendi (MEX) W PTS 15 Mike Belloise (USA), New York City – NY. *Baby Arizmendi forfeited NY recognition when he contested the Californian version without NY authority*

21.09.34 Freddie Miller (USA) W PTS 15 Nel Tarleton (GB), Anfield Football Ground, Liverpool – NBA

01.01.35 Baby Arizmendi (MEX) W PTS 12 Henry Armstrong (USA), Mexico City – CALIF

181

17.02.35 Freddie Miller (USA) W CO 1 Jose Girones (SP), Barcelona – NBA

12.06.35 Freddie Miller (USA) W PTS 15 Nel Tarleton (GB), Stanley Racetrack, Liverpool – NBA

22.10.35 Freddie Miller (USA) W PTS 15 Vernon Cormier (USA), Boston – NBA

18.02.36 Freddie Miller (USA) W PTS 12 Johnny Pena (PR), Seattle – NBA

02.03.36 Freddie Miller (USA) W PTS 15 Petey Sarron (USA), Miami – NBA

11.05.36 Petey Sarron (USA) W PTS 15 Freddie Miller (USA), Washington – NBA

22.07.36 Petey Sarron (USA) W PTS 15 Baby Manuel (USA), Dallas – NBA

04.08.36 Henry Armstrong (USA) W PTS 10 Baby Arizmendi (MEX), Los Angeles – CALIF

03.09.36 Mike Belloise (USA) W CO 9 Dave Crowley (GB), New York City – NY

27.10.36 Henry Armstrong (USA) W PTS 10 Mike Belloise (USA), Los Angeles – CALIF/NY

04.09.37 Petey Sarron (USA) W PTS 12 Freddie Miller (USA), Johannesburg – NBA

05.10.37 Maurice Holtzer (FR) W PTS 15 Phil Dolhem (BEL), Algiers – IBU

29.10.37 Henry Arrnstrong (USA) W CO 6 Petey Sarron (USA), New York City – NY/NBA/CALIF. *Henry Armstrong relinquished NY/NBA/Californian version of title*

19.02.38 Maurice Holtzer (FR) DREW 15 Maurice Dubois (SWI), Geneva – IBU. *Maurice Holtzer relinquished IBU version of title*

17.06.38 Leo Rodak (USA) W PTS 15 Jackie Wilson (USA), Baltimore – NBA

17.10.38 Joey Archibald (USA) W PTS 15 Mike Belloise (USA), New York City – NY

24.10.38 Leo Rodak (USA) W PTS 15 Freddie Miller (USA), Washington – NBA

18.04.39 **Joey Archibald** (USA) W PTS 15 Leo Rodak (USA), Providence. *Joey Archibald forfeited NBA recognition when refusing to defend against Petey Scalzo*

28.09.39 Joey Archibald (USA) W PTS 15 Harry Jeffra (USA), Washington – NY

08.05.40 Jimmy Perrin (USA) W PTS 15 Bobby Ruffin (USA), New Orleans – LOUIS. *Jimmy Perrin forfeited Louisiana recognition following a defeat by Petey Scalzo in August, 1940*

15.05.40 Petey Scalzo (USA) W CO 6 Frankie Covelli (USA), Washington – NBA

20.05.40 Harry Jeffra (USA) W PTS 15 Joey Archibald (USA), Baltimore – NY

10.07.40 Petey Scalzo (USA) W RSC 15 Bobby Poison Ivy (USA), Hartford – NBA

29.07.40 Harry Jeffra (USA) W PTS 15 Spider Armstrong (C), Baltimore – NY

12.05.41 Joey Archibald (USA) W PTS 15 Harry Jeffra (USA), Washington – NY

19.05 41 Petey Scalzo (USA) W PTS 15 Phil Zwick (USA), Milwaukee – NBA

01.07.41 Richie Lemos (USA) W CO 5 Petey Scalzo (USA), Los Angeles – NBA

11.09.41 Chalky Wright (MEX) W CO 11 Joey Archibald (USA), Washington – NY

15.09.41 Harry Jeffra (USA) W PTS 12 Lou Transparenti (USA), Baltimore – MARY

18.11.41 Jackie Wilson (USA) W PTS 12 Richie Lemos (USA), Los Angeles – NBA

16.12.41 Jackie Wilson (USA) W PTS 12 Richie Lemos (USA), Los Angeles – NBA

19.06.42 Chalky Wright (MEX) W RSC 10 Harry Jeffra (USA), Baltimore – NY

25.09.42 Chalky Wright (MEX) W PTS 15 Lulu Constantino (USA), New York City – NY

20.11.42 Willie Pep (USA) W PTS 15 Chalky Wright (MEX), New York City – NY

18.01.43 Jackie Callura (C) W PTS 15 Jackie Wilson (USA), Providence – NBA

18.03.43 Jackie Callura (C) W PTS 15 Jackie Wilson (USA), Boston – NBA

08.06.43 Willie Pep (USA) W PTS 15 Sal Bartolo (USA), Boston – NY

16.08.43 Phil Terranova (USA) W CO 8 Jackie Callura (C), New Orleans – NBA

27.12.43 Phil Terranova (USA) W RSC 6 Jackie Callura (C), New Orleans – NBA

10.03.44 Sal Bartolo (USA) W PTS 15 Phil Terranova (USA), Boston – NBA

05.05.44 Sal Bartolo (USA) W PTS 15 Phil Terranova (USA), Boston – NBA

29.09.44 Willie Pep (USA) W PTS 15 Chalky Wright (MEX), New York City – NY

15.12.44 Sal Bartolo (USA) W PTS 15 Willie Roache (USA), Boston – NBA

19.02.45 Willie Pep (USA) W PTS 15 Phil Terranova (USA), New York City – NY

03.05.46 Sal Bartolo (USA) W CO 6 Spider Armstrong (C), Boston – NBA

07.06.46 **Willie Pep** (USA) W CO 12 Sal Bartolo (USA), New York City

22.08.47 **Willie Pep** (USA) W CO 12 Jock Leslie (USA), Flint

24.02.48 **Willie Pep** (USA) W RSC 10 Humberto Sierra (CUB), Miami

29.10.48 **Sandy Saddler** (USA) W CO 4 Willie Pep (USA), New York City

11.02.49 Willie Pep (USA) W PTS 15 Sandy Saddler (USA), New York City

20.09.49 Willie Pep (USA) W RSC 7 Eddie Compo (USA), Waterbury

16.01.50 Willie Pep (USA) W CO 5 Charley Riley (USA), St Louis

17.03.50 Willie Pep (USA) W PTS 15 Ray Famechon (FR), New York City

08.09.50 **Sandy Saddler** (USA) W RTD 8 Willie Pep (USA), New York City

26.09.51 Sandy Saddler (USA) W RTD 9 Willie Pep (USA), New York City

25.02.55 Sandy Saddler (USA) W PTS 15 Teddy Davis (USA), New York City

18.01.56 Sandy Saddler (USA) W RSC 13 Flash Elorde (PH), San Francisco. *Sandy Saddler relinquished title*

24.06.57 **Hogan Kid Bassey** (N) W RSC 10 Cherif Hamia (FR), Paris

01.04.58 Hogan Kid Bassey (N) W CO 3 Ricardo Moreno (MEX), Los Angeles

18.03.59 **Davey Moore** (USA) W RTD 13 Hogan Kid Bassey (N), Los Angeles

19.08.59 Davey Moore (USA) W RTD 10 Hogan Kid Bassey (N), Los Angeles

29.08.60 Davey Moore (USA) W PTS 15 Kazuo Takayama (JAP), Tokyo

08.04.61 Davey Moore (USA) W CO 1 Danny Valdez (USA), Los Angeles

13.11.61 Davey Moore (USA) W PTS 15 Kazuo Takayama (JAP), Tokyo

17.08.62 Davey Moore (USA) W RSC 2 Olli Maki (FIN), Helsinki

21.03.63 **Sugar Ramos** (CUB) W RTD 10 Davey Moore (USA), Los Angeles

13.07.63 Sugar Ramos (CUB) W PTS 15 Rafiu King (N), Mexico City

28.02.64 Sugar Ramos (CUB) W RTD 6 Mitsunori Seki (JAP), Tokyo

09.05.64 Sugar Ramos (CUB) W PTS 15 Floyd Robertson (GH), Accra

26.09.64 **Vicente Saldivar** (MEX) W RTD 11 Sugar Ramos (CUB), Mexico City

06.12.64 Vicente Saldivar (MEX) W RSC 11 Delfino Rosales (MEX), Guanajuato

07.05.65 Vicente Saldivar (MEX) W RSC 15 Raul Rojas (USA), Los Angeles

07.09.65 Vicente Saldivar (MEX) W PTS 15 Howard Winstone (GB), Earls Court, London

12.02.66 Vicente Saldivar (MEX) W CO 2 Floyd Robertson (GH), Mexico City

07.08.66 Vicente Saldivar (MEX) W PTS 15 Mitsunori Seki (JAP), Mexico City

29.01.67 Vicente Saldivar (MEX) W RSC 7 Mitsunori Seki (JAP), Mexico City

15.06.67 Vicente Saldivar (MEX) W PTS 15 Howard Winstone (GB), Ninian Park, Cardiff

14.10.67 Vicente Saldivar (MEX) W RTD 12 Howard Winstone (GB), Mexico City. *Vicente Saldivar relinquished title*

14.12.67 Raul Rojas (USA) W PTS 15 Antonio Herrera (COL), Los Angeles – WBA

23.01.68 Howard Winstone (GB) W RSC 9 Mitsunori Seki (JAP), Albert Hall, London – WBC

28.03.68 Raul Rojas (USA) W PTS 15 Enrique Higgins (COL), Los Angeles – WBA

24.07.68 Jose Legra (CUB) W RSC 5 Howard Winstone (GB), Coney Beach Arena, Porthcawl – WBC

28.09.68 Shozo Saijyo (JAP) W PTS 15 Raul Rojas (USA), Los Angeles – WBA

21.01.69 Johnny Famechon (A) W PTS 15 Jose Legra (CUB), Albert Hall, London – WBC

09.02.69 Shozo Saijyo (JAP) W PTS 15 Pedro Gomez (VEN), Tokyo – WBA

28.07.69 Johnny Famechon (A) W PTS 15 Fighting Harada (JAP), Sydney – WBC

07.09.69 Shozo Saijyo (JAP) W CO 2 Jose Pimental (MEX), Sapporo – WBA

06.01.70 Johnny Famechon (A) W CO 14 Fighting Harada (JAP), Tokyo – WBC

08.02.70 Shozo Saijyo (JAP) W PTS 15 Godfrey Stevens (CH), Tokyo – WBA

09.05.70 Vicente Saldivar (MEX) W PTS 15 Johnny Famechon (A), Rome – WBC

05.07.70 Shozo Saijyo (JAP) W PTS 15 Frankie Crawford (USA), Sendai – WBA

11.12.70 Kuniaki Shibata (JAP) W RSC 12 Vicente Saldivar (MEX), Tijuana – WBC

28.02.71 Shozo Saijyo (JAP) W PTS 15 Frankie Crawford (USA), Utsonomuja – WBA

03.06.71 Kuniaki Shibata (JAP) W CO 1 Raul Cruz (MEX), Tokyo – WBC

02.09.71 Antonio Gomez (VEN) W RSC 5 Shozo Saijyo (JAP), Tokyo – WBA

11.11.71 Kuniaki Shibata (JAP) DREW 15 Ernesto Marcel (PAN), Matsuyama – WBC

06.02.72 Antonio Gomez (VEN) W CO 7 Raul Martinez (MEX), Maracay – WBA

19.05.72 Clemente Sanchez (MEX) W CO 3 Kuniaki Shibata (JAP), Tokyo – WBC

19.08.72 Ernesto Marcel (PAN) W PTS 15 Antonio Gomez (VEN), Maracay – WBA

03.12.72 Ernesto Marcel (PAN) W RSC 6 Enrique Garcia (MEX), Panama City – WBA

16.12.72 Jose Legra (CUB) W RSC 10 Clemente Sanchez (MEX), Monterrey – WBC

05.05.73 Eder Jofre (BR) W PTS 15 Jose Legra (CUB), Brasilia – WBC

14.07.73 Ernesto Marcel (PAN) W RTD 11 Antonio Gomez (VEN), Panama City – WBA

08.09.73 Ernesto Marcel (PAN) W CO 9 Spider Nemoto (JAP), Panama City – WBA

21.10.73 Eder Jofre (BR) W CO 4 Vicente Saldivar (MEX), Salvador – WBC. *Eder Jofre forfeited WBC recognition for failing to defend against Alfredo Marcano*

16.02.74 Ernesto Marcel (PAN) W PTS 15 Alexis Arguello (NIC), Panama City – WBA. *Ernesto Marcel relinquished WBA version of title*

09.07.74 Ruben Olivares (MEX) W RSC 7 Zensuke Utagawa (JAP), Los Angeles – WBA

07.09.74 Bobby Chacon (USA) W RSC 9 Alfredo Marcano (VEN), Los Angeles – WBC

23.11.74 Alexis Arguello (NIC) W CO 13 Ruben Olivares (MEX), Los Angeles – WBA

01.03.75 Bobby Chacon (USA) W CO 2 Jesus Estrada (MEX), Los Angeles – WBC

15.03.75 Alexis Arguello (NIC) W RSC 8 Leonel Hernandez (VEN), Caracas – WBA

31.05.75 Alexis Arguello (NIC) W RSC 2 Rigoberto Riasco (PAN), Managua – WBA

20.06.75 Ruben Olivares (MEX) W RSC 2 Bobby Chacon (USA), Los Angeles – WBC

20.09.75 David Kotey (GH) W PTS 15 Ruben Olivares (MEX), Los Angeles – WBC

12.10.75 Alexis Arguello (NIC) W CO 5 Royal Kobayashi (JAP), Tokyo – WBA

06.03.76 David Kotey (GH) W RSC 12 Flipper Uehara (JAP), Accra – WBC

19.06.76 Alexis Arguello (NIC) W CO 3 Salvatore Torres (MEX), Los Angeles WBA. *Alexis Arguello relinquished WBA version of title*

16.07.76 David Kotey (GH) W RSC 3 Shig Fukuyama (JAP), Tokyo – WBC

05.11.76 Danny Lopez (USA) W PTS 15 David Kotey (GH), Accra – WBC

15.01.77 Rafael Ortega (PAN) W PTS 15 Francisco Coronado (NIC), Panama City – WBA

29.05.77 Rafael Ortega (PAN) W PTS 15 Flipper Uehara (JAP), Okinawa – WBA

13.09.77 Danny Lopez (USA) W RSC 7 Jose Torres (MEX), Los Angeles – WBC

17.12.77 Cecilio Lastra (SP) W PTS 15 Rafael Ortega (PAN), Torrelavega – WBA

15.02.78 Danny Lopez (USA) W RSC 6 David Kotey (GH), Las Vegas – WBC

15.04.78 Eusebio Pedroza (PAN) W CO 13 Cecilio Lastra (SP), Panama City – WBA

23.04.78 Danny Lopez (USA) W RSC 6 Jose de Paula (BR), Los Angeles – WBC

02.07.78 Eusebio Pedroza (PAN) W RSC 12 Ernesto Herrera (MEX), Panama City – WBA

15.09.78 Danny Lopez (USA) W CO 2 Juan Malvarez (ARG), New Orleans – WBC

21.10.78 Danny Lopez (USA) W DIS 4 Fel Clemente (PH), Pesaro – WBC
27.11.78 Eusebio Pedroza (PAN) W PTS 15 Enrique Solis (PR) San Juan – WBA
09.01.79 Eusebio Pedroza (PAN) W RTD 13 Royal Kobayashi (JAP), Tokyo – WBA
10.03.79 Danny Lopez (USA) W CO 2 Roberto Castanon (SP), Salt Lake City – WBC
08.04.79 Eusebio Pedroza (PAN) W RSC 11 Hector Carrasquilla (PAN), Panama City – WBA
17.06.79 Danny Lopez (USA) W CO 15 Mike Ayala (USA), San Antonio – WBC
21.07.79 Eusebio Pedroza (PAN) W RSC 12 Ruben Olivares (MEX), Houston – WBA
25.09.79 Danny Lopez (USA) W RSC 3 Jose Caba (DOM), Los Angeles – WBC
17.11.79 Eusebio Pedroza (PAN) W RSC 11 Johnny Aba (PNG), Port Moresby – WBA
22.01.80 Eusebio Pedroza (PAN) W PTS 15 Spider Nemoto (JAP), Tokyo – WBA
02.02.80 Salvador Sanchez (MEX) W RSC 13 Danny Lopez (USA), Phoenix – WBC
29.03.80 Eusebio Pedroza (PAN) W CO 9 Juan Malvarez (ARG), Panama City – WBA
12.04.80 Salvador Sanchez (MEX) W PTS 15 Ruben Castillo (USA), Tucson – WBC
21.06.80 Salvador Sanchez (MEX) W RSC 14 Danny Lopez (USA), Las Vegas – WBC
20.07.80 Eusebio Pedroza (PAN) W CO 9 Sa-Wang Kim (SK), Seoul – WBA
13.09.80 Salvador Sanchez (MEX) W PTS 15 Pat Ford (GU), San Antonio – WBC
04.10.80 Eusebio Pedroza (PAN) W PTS 15 Rocky Lockridge (USA), McAfee – WBA
13.12.80 Salvador Sanchez (MEX) W PTS 15 Juan Laporte (PR), El Paso – WBC
14.02.81 Eusebio Pedroza (PAN) W CO 13 Pat Ford (GU), Panama City – WBA
22.03.81 Salvador Sanchez (MEX) W RSC 10 Roberto Castanon (SP), Las Vegas – WBC
01.08.81 Eusebio Pedroza (PAN) W CO 7 Carlos Pinango (VEN), Caracas – WBA
21.08.81 Salvador Sanchez (MEX) W RSC 8 Wilfredo Gomez (PR), Las Vegas – WBC
05.12.81 Eusebio Pedroza (PAN) W CO 5 Bashew Sibaca (SA), Panama City – WBA
12.12.81 Salvador Sanchez (MEX) W PTS 15 Pat Cowdell (GB), Houston – WBC
24.01.82 Eusebio Pedroza (PAN) W PTS 15 Juan Laporte (PR), Atlantic City – WBA
08.05.82 Salvador Sanchez (MEX) W PTS 15 Rocky Garcia (USA), Dallas – WBC
21.07.82 Salvador Sanchez (MEX) W RSC 15 Azumah Nelson (GH), New York City – WBC. *Salvador Sanchez left WBC version of title vacant when he died in a road crash*
15.09.82 Juan Laporte (PR) W RTD 10 Mario Miranda (COL), New York City – WBC
16.10.82 Eusebio Pedroza (PAN) DREW 15 Bernard Taylor (USA), Charlotte – WBA
20.02.83 Juan Laporte (PR) W PTS 12 Ruben Castillo (USA), San Juan – WBC
24.04.83 Eusebio Pedroza (PAN) W PTS 15 Rocky Lockridge (USA), Liguma – WBA
25.06.83 Juan Laporte (PR) W PTS 12 Johnny de la Rosa (DOM), San Juan – WBC
22.10.83 Eusebio Pedroza (PAN) W PTS 15 Jose Caba (DOM), San Remo – WBA
04.03.84 Min-Keun Oh (SK) W CO 2 Joko Arter (PH), Seoul – IBF
31.03.84 Wilfredo Gomez (PR) W PTS 12 Juan Laporte (PR), San Juan – WBC
27.05.84 Eusebio Pedroza (PAN) W PTS 15 Angel Mayor (VEN), Maracaibo – WBA
10.06.84 Min-Keun Oh (SK) W PTS 15 Kelvin Lampkin (USA), Seoul – IBF
08.12.84 Azumah Nelson (GH) W RSC 11 Wilfredo Gomez (PR), San Juan – WBC
02.02.85 Eusebio Pedroza (PAN) W PTS 15 Jorge Lujan (PAN), Panama City – WBA
07.04.85 Min-Keun Oh (SK) W PTS 15 Irving Mitchell (USA), Pusan – IBF
08.06.85 Barry McGuigan (GB) W PTS 15 Eusebio Pedroza (PAN), Loftus Road, London – WBA

06.09.85 Azumah Nelson (GH) W CO 5 Juvenal Ordenes (CH), Miami – WBC
28.09.85 Barry McGuigan (GB) W RTD 8 Bernard Taylor (USA), King's Hall, Belfast – WBA
12.10.85 Azumah Nelson (GH) W CO 1 Pat Cowdell (GB), National Exhibition Centre, Birmingham – WBC
29.11.85 Ki-Yung Chung (SK) W RSC 15 Min-Keun Oh (SK), Chonju – IBF
15.02.86 Barry McGuigan (GB) W RSC 14 Danilo Cabrera (DOM), Dublin – WBA
16.02.86 Ki-Yung Chung (SK) W RTD 6 Tyrone Jackson (USA), Ulsan – IBF
25.02.86 Azumah Nelson (GH) W PTS 12 Marcos Villasana (MEX), Los Angeles – WBC
18.05.86 Ki-Yung Chung (SK) W PTS 15 Richard Savage (USA), Taegu – IBF
22.06.86 Azumah Nelson (GH) W RSC 10 Danilo Cabrera (DOM), San Juan – WBC
23.06.86 Steve Cruz (USA) W PTS 15 Barry McGuigan (GB), Las Vegas – WBA
30.08.86 Antonio Rivera (PR) W RTD 10 Ki-Yung Chung (SK), Osan – IBF
06.03.87 Antonio Esparragoza (VEN) W RSC 12 Steve Cruz (USA), Fort Worth – WBA
07.03.87 Azumah Nelson (GH) W CO 6 Mauro Gutierrez (MEX), Las Vegas – WBC
26.07.87 Antonio Esparragoza (VEN) W CO 10 Pascual Aranda (MEX), Houston – WBA
29.08.87 Azumah Nelson (GH) W PTS 12 Marcos Villasana (MEX), Los Angeles – WBC. *Azumah Nelson relinquished WBC version of title*
23.01.88 Calvin Grove (USA) W RSC 4 Antonio Rivera (PR), Gamaches, France – IBF
07.03.88 Jeff Fenech (A) W RSC 10 Victor Callejas (PR), Sydney – WBC
17.05.88 Calvin Grove (USA) W PTS 15 Myron Taylor (USA), Atlantic City – IBF
23.06.88 Antonio Esparragoza (VEN) DREW 12 Marcos Villasana (MEX), Los Angeles – WBA
04.08.88 Jorge Paez (MEX) W PTS 15 Calvin Grove (USA), Mexicali – IBF
12.08.88 Jeff Fenech (A) W RSC 5 Tyrone Downes (BAR), Melbourne – WBC
05.11.88 Antonio Esparragoza (VEN) W CO 8 Jose Marmolejo (PAN), Marsala – WBA
30.11.88 Jeff Fenech (A) W RSC 5 George Navarro (USA), Melbourne – WBC
28.01.89 Maurizio Stecca (ITA) W RSC 6 Pedro Nolasco (DOM), Milan – WBO
25.03.89 Antonio Esparragoza (VEN) W CO 10 Mitsuru Sugiya (JAP), Kawasaki – WBA
30.03.89 Jorge Paez (MEX) W CO 11 Calvin Grove (USA), Mexicali – IBF
08.04.89 Jeff Fenech (A) W PTS 12 Marcos Villasana (MEX), Melbourne – WBC. *Jeff Fenech relinquished WBC version of title*
21.05.89 Jorge Paez (MEX) DREW 12 Louie Espinosa (USA), Phoenix – IBF
02.06.89 Antonio Esparragoza (VEN) W CO 6 Jean-Marc Renard (BEL), Namur – WBA
16.06.89 Maurizio Stecca (ITA) W RSC 9 Angel Mayor (VEN), Milan – WBO
06.08.89 Jorge Paez (MEX) W PTS 12 Steve Cruz (USA), El Paso – IBF
16.09.89 Jorge Paez (MEX) W CO 2 Jose Mario Lopez (ARG), Mexico City – IBF
22.09.89 Antonio Esparragoza (VEN) W CO 5 Eduardo Montoya (MEX) Mexicali – WBA
11.11.89 Louie Espinosa (USA) W RSC 7 Maurizio Stecca (ITA), Rimini – WBO
09.12.89 Jorge Paez (MEX) W RSC 6 Lupe Gutierrez (USA), Reno – IBF
04.02.90 Jorge Paez (MEX) W PTS 12 Troy Dorsey (USA), Las Vegas – IBF
07.04.90 Jorge Paez (MEX) W PTS 12 Louie Espinosa (USA), Las Vegas – IBF/WBO
12.05.90 Antonio Esparragoza (VEN) W PTS 12 Chan-Mok Park (SK), Seoul – WBA
02.06.90 Marcos Villasana (MEX) W RSC 8 Paul Hodkinson (GB), G-Mex Centre, Manchester – WBC
08.07.90 Jorge Paez (MEX) DREW 12 Troy Dorsey (USA), Las Vegas – IBF/WBO. *Jorge Paez relinquished IBF/WBO versions of title*
30.09.90 Marcos Villasana (MEX) W RSC 8 Javier Marquez (MEX), Mexico City – WBC

26.01.91 Maurizio Stecca (ITA) W RSC 5 Armando Reyes (DOM), Sassari – WBO
30.03.91 Kyun-Yung Park (SK) W PTS 12 Antonio Esparragoza (VEN), Kwangju – WBA
11.04.91 Marcos Villasana (MEX) W RSC 6 Rafael Zuniga (COL), Mexico City – WBC
03.06.91 Troy Dorsey (USA) W CO 1 Alfred Rangel (USA), Las Vegas – IBF
15.06.91 Maurizio Stecca (ITA) W PTS 12 Fernando Ramos (MEX), Mantichiari – WBO
15.06.91 Kyun-Yung Park (SK) W RSC 6 Masuaki Takeda (JAP), Seoul – WBA
12.08.91 Manuel Medina (MEX) W PTS 12 Troy Dorsey (USA), Los Angeles – IBF
16.08.91 Marcos Villasana (MEX) W PTS 12 Ricardo Cepeda (PR), Marbella – WBC
14.09.91 Kyun-Yung Park (SK) W PTS 12 Eloy Rojas (VEN), Mokpo – WBA
09.11.91 Maurizio Stecca (ITA) W RTD 9 Tim Driscoll (GB), Campione d'Italia – WBO
13.11.91 Paul Hodkinson (GB) W PTS 12 Marcos Villasana (MEX), Maysfield Leisure Centre, Belfast – WBC
18.11.91 Manuel Medina (MEX) W TD 9 Tom Johnson (USA), Los Angeles – IBF
25.01.92 Kyun-Yung Park (SK) W CO 9 Seiji Asakawa (JAP), Seoul – WBA
14.03.92 Manuel Medina (MEX) W PTS 12 Fabrice Benichou (FR), Antibes – IBF
25.04.92 Paul Hodkinson (GB) W RSC 3 Steve Cruz (USA), Maysfield Leisure Centre, Belfast – WBC
25.04.92 Kyun-Yung Park (SK) W RSC 11 Koji Matsumoto (JAP), Ansan – WBA
16.05.92 Colin McMillan (GB) W PTS 12 Maurizio Stecca (ITA), Alexandra Palace, London – WBO

Super-Bantamweight
21.09.22 Jack Kid Wolfe (USA) W PTS 15 Joe Lynch (USA), New York City – NY. *Jack Kid Wolfe forfeited NY recognition when overweight for defence against Carl Duane and the title fell into disuse*
03.04.76 Rigoberto Riasco (PAN) W RTD 8 Waruinge Nakayama (K), Panama City – WBC
12.06.76 Rigoberto Riasco (PAN) W CO 10 Livio Nolasco (DOM), Panama City – WBC
01.08.76 Rigoberto Riasco (PAN) W PTS 15 Dong-Kyun Yum (SK), Pusan – WBC
10.10.76 Royal Kobayashi (JAP) W RSC 8 Rigoberto Riasco (PAN), Tokyo – WBC
24.11.76 Dong-Kyun Yum (SK) W PTS 15 Royal Kobayashi (JAP), Seoul – WBC
13.02.77 Dong-Kyun Yum (SK) W PTS 15 Jose Cervantes (COL), Seoul – WBC
21.05.77 Wilfredo Gomez (PR) W CO 12 Dong-Kyun Yum (SK), San Juan – WBC
11.07.77 Wilfredo Gomez (PR) W CO 5 Raul Tirado (MEX), San Juan – WBC
26.11.77 Soo-Hwan Hong (SK) W CO 3 Hector Carrasquilla (PAN), Panama City – WBA
19.01.78 Wilfredo Gomez (PR) W CO 3 Royal Kobayashi (JAP), Kitakyushu – WBC
01.02.78 Soo-Hwan Hong (SK) W PTS 15 Yu Kasahara (JAP), Tokyo – WBA
08.04.78 Wilfredo Gomez (PR) W RSC 7 Juan Antonio Lopez (MEX), Bayamon – WBC
06.05.78 Ricardo Cardona (COL) W RSC 12 Soo-Hwan Hong (SK), Seoul – WBA
02.06.78 Wilfredo Gomez (PR) W RSC 3 Sakad Petchyindee (TH), Korat – WBC
02.09.78 Ricardo Cardona (COL) W PTS 15 Ruben Valdez (COL) Cartagena – WBA
09.09.78 Wilfredo Gomez (PR) W RSC 13 Leonardo Cruz (DOM), San Juan – WBC
28.10.78 Wilfredo Gomez (PR) W RSC 5 Carlos Zarate (MEX), San Juan – WBC
12.11.78 Ricardo Cardona (COL) W PTS 15 Soon-Hyun Chung (SK), Seoul – WBA
09.03.79 Wilfredo Gomez (PR) W RSC 5 Nestor Jimenez (COL), New York City – WBC
16.06.79 Wilfredo Gomez (PR) W RSC 5 Jesus Hernandez (NIC), San Juan – WBC
23.06.79 Ricardo Cardona (COL) W PTS 15 Soon-Hyun Chung (SK), Seoul – WBA
06.09.79 Ricardo Cardona (COL) W PTS 15 Yukio Segawa (JAP), Hachinohe – WBA

28.09.79 Wilfredo Gomez (PR) W RSC 10 Carlos Mendoza (PAN), Las Vegas – WBC

26.10.79 Wilfredo Gomez (PR) W RSC 5 Nicky Perez (USA), New York City – WBC

15.12.79 Ricardo Cardona (COL) W PTS 15 Sergio Palma (ARG), Barranquilla – WBA

03.02.80 Wilfredo Gomez (PR) W RTD 6 Ruben Valdez (COL), Las Vegas – WBC

04.05.80 Leo Randolph (USA) W RSC 15 Ricardo Cardona (COL), Seattle – WBA

09.08.80 Sergio Palma (ARG) W CO 6 Leo Randolph (USA), Washington – WBA

22.08.80 Wilfredo Gomez (PR) W RSC 5 Derrick Holmes (USA), Las Vegas – WBC

08.11.80 Sergio Palma (ARG) W RSC 9 Ulisses Morales (PAN), Buenos Aires – WBA

13.12.80 Wilfredo Gomez (PR) W CO 3 Jose Cervantes (COL), Miami – WBC

04.04.81 Sergio Palma (ARG) W PTS 15 Leonardo Cruz (DOM), Buenos Aires – WBA

15.08.81 Sergio Palma (ARG) W RSC 12 Ricardo Cardona (COL), Buenos Aires – WBA

03.10.81 Sergio Palma (ARG) W PTS 15 Vichit Muangroi-et (TH), Buenos Aires – WBA

15.01.82 Sergio Palma (ARG) W PTS 15 Jorge Lujan (PAN), Cordoba – WBA

27.03.82 Wilfredo Gomez (PR) W RSC 6 Juan Meza (MEX), Atlantic City – WBC

11.06.82 Wilfredo Gomez (PR) W CO 10 Juan Antonio Lopez (MEX), Las Vegas – WBC

12.06.82 Leonardo Cruz (DOM) W PTS 15 Sergio Palma (ARG), Miami – WBA

18.08.82 Wilfredo Gomez (PR) W RTD 7 Roberto Rubaldino (MEX), San Juan – WBC

13.11.82 Leonardo Cruz (DOM) W CO 8 Benito Badilla (CH), San Juan – WBA

03.12.82 Wilfredo Gomez (PR) W RSC 14 Lupe Pintor (MEX), New Orleans – WBC. *Wilfredo Gomez relinquished WBC version of title*

16.03.83 Leonardo Cruz (DOM) W PTS 15 Soon-Hyun Chung (SK), San Juan – WBA

15.06.83 Jaime Garza (USA) W RSC 2 Bobby Berna (PH), Los Angeles – WBC

26.08.83 Leonardo Cruz (DOM) W PTS 15 Cleo Garcia (NIC), St Domingo – WBA

04.12.83 Bobby Berna (PH) W RTD 11 Seung-In Suh (SK), Seoul – IBF

22.02.84 Loris Stecca (ITA) W RSC 12 Leonardo Cruz (DOM), Milan – WBA

15.04.84 Seung-In Suh (SK) W CO 10 Bobby Berna (PH), Seoul – IBF

26.05.84 Jaime Garza (USA) W CO 3 Felipe Orozco (COL), Miami – WBC

26.05.84 Victor Callejas (PR) W RSC 8 Loris Stecca (ITA), Guaynabo – WBA

08.07.84 Seung-In Suh (SK) W CO 4 Cleo Garcia (NIC), Seoul – IBF

03.11.84 Juan Meza (MEX) W CO 1 Jaime Garza (USA), Kingston, NY – WBC

03.01.85 Ji-Won Kim (SK) W CO 10 Seung-In Suh (SK), Seoul – IBF

02.02.85 Victor Callejas (PR) W PTS 15 Seung-Hoon Lee (SK), San Juan – WBA

30.03.85 Ji-Won Kim (SK) W PTS 15 Ruben Palacios (COL), Suwon – IBF

19.04.85 Juan Meza (MEX) W RSC 6 Mike Ayala (USA), Los Angeles – WBC

28.06.85 Ji-Won Kim (SK) W CO 4 Bobby Berna (PH), Pusan – IBF

18.08.85 Lupe Pintor (MEX) W PTS 12 Juan Meza (MEX), Mexico City – WBC

09.10.85 Ji-Won Kim (SK) W CO 1 Seung-In Suh (SK), Seoul – IBF

08.11.85 Victor Callejas (PR) W RTD 6 Loris Stecca (ITA), Rimini – WBA. *Victor Callejas forfeited WBA recognition for failing to defend against Louie Espinosa*

18.01.86 Samart Pakayarun (TH) W CO 5 Lupe Pintor (MEX), Bangkok – WBC

01.06.86 Ji-Won Kim (SK) W CO 2 Rudy Casicas (PH), Inchon – IBF. *Ji-Won Kim relinquished IBF version of title*

10.12.86 Samart Payakarun (TH) W CO 12 Juan Meza (MEX), Bangkok – WBC

16.01.87 Louie Espinosa (USA) W RSC 4 Tommy Valoy (DOM), Phoenix – WBA

18.01.87 Seung-Hoon Lee (SK) W CO 9 Prayoonsak Muangsurin (TH), Pohang – IBF

05.04.87 Seung-Hoon Lee (SK) W CO 10 Jorge Urbina Diaz (MEX), Seoul – IBF

08.05.87 Jeff Fenech (A) W RSC 4 Samart Payakarun (TH), Sydney – WBC

10.07.87 Jeff Fenech (A) W RTD 5 Greg Richardson (USA), Sydney – WBC

15.07.87 Louie Espinosa (USA) W RSC 15 Manuel Vilchez (VEN), Phoenix – WBA

19.07.87 Seung-Hoon Lee (SK) W CO 5 Lion Collins (PH), Seoul – IBF

15.08.87 Louie Espinosa (USA) W CO 9 Mike Ayala (USA), San Antonio – WBA

16.10.87 Jeff Fenech (A) W TD 4 Carlos Zarate (MEX), Sydney – WBC. *Jeff Fenech relinquished WBC version of title*

28.11.87 Julio Gervacio (DOM) W PTS 12 Louie Espinosa (USA), San Juan – WBA

27.12.87 Seung-Hoon Lee (SK) W PTS 15 Jose Sanabria (VEN), Pohang – IBF. *Seung-Hoon Lee relinquished IBF version of title*

27.02.88 Bernardo Pinango (VEN) W PTS 12 Julio Gervacio (DOM), San Juan – WBA

29.02.88 Daniel Zaragoza (MEX) W RSC 10 Carlos Zarate (MEX), Los Angeles – WBC

21.05.88 Jose Sanabria (VEN) W CO 5 Moises Fuentes (COL), Bucaramanga – IBF

28.05.88 Juan J. Estrada (MEX) W PTS 12 Bernardo Pinango (VEN), Tijuana – WBA

29.05.88 Daniel Zaragoza (MEX) DREW 12 Seung-Hoon Lee (SK), Youchan – WBC

21.08.88 Jose Sanabria (VEN) W PTS 12 Vincenzo Belcastro (ITA), Capo d'Orlando – IBF

26.09.88 Jose Sanabria (VEN) W RSC 10 Fabrice Benichou (FR), Noget sur Marne – IBF

15.10.88 Juan J. Estrada (MEX) W RSC 11 Takuya Muguruma (JAP), Moriguchi – WBA

11.11.88 Jose Sanabria (VEN) W RSC 6 Thierry Jacob (FR), Gravelines – IBF

21.11.88 Daniel Zaragoza (MEX) W CO 5 Valerio Nati (ITA), Forli – WBC

10.03.89 Fabrice Benichou (FR) W PTS 12 Jose Sanabria (VEN), Limoges – IBF

04.04.89 Juan J. Estrada (MEX) W RSC 10 Jesus Poll (VEN), Los Angeles – WBA

29.04.89 Kenny Mitchell (USA) W PTS 12 Julio Gervacio (DOM), San Juan – WBO

11.06.89 Fabrice Benichou (FR) W CO 5 Franie Badenhorst (SA), Frasnone – IBF

22.06.89 Daniel Zaragoza (MEX) W PTS 12 Paul Banke (USA), Los Angeles – WBC

10.07.89 Juan J. Estrada (MEX) W PTS 12 Luis Mendoza (MEX), Tijuana – WBA

01.09.89 Daniel Zaragoza (MEX) W RSC 10 Frankie Duarte (USA), Los Angeles – WBC

09.09.89 Kenny Mitchell (USA) W PTS 12 Simon Skosana (SA), San Juan – WBO

07.10.89 Fabrice Benichou (FR) W PTS 12 Ramon Cruz (DOM), Bordeaux – IBF

03.12.89 Daniel Zaragoza (MEX) W PTS 12 Chan-Yung Park (SK), Seoul – WBC

09.12.89 Valerio Nati (ITA) W DIS 4 Kenny Mitchell (USA), Teramo – WBO

11.12.89 Jesus Salud (USA) W DIS 9 Juan J. Estrada (MEX), Los Angeles – WBA. *Jesus Salud forfeited WBA version of title for failing to defend against Luis Mendoza*

10.03.90 Welcome Ncita (SA) W PTS 12 Fabrice Benichou (FR), Tel Aviv – IBF

23.04.90 Paul Banke (USA) W RSC 9 Daniel Zaragoza (MEX), Los Angeles – WBC

12.05.90 Orlando Fernandez (PR) W RSC 10 Valerio Nati (ITA), Sassari – WBO

25.05.90 Luis Mendoza (COL) DREW 12 Reuben Palacios (COL), Cartagena – WBA

02.06.90 Welcome Ncita (SA) W RSC 7 Ramon Cruz (DOM), Rome – IBF

17.08.90 Paul Banke (USA) W RSC 12 Ki-Jun Lee (SK), Seoul – WBC

11.09.90 Luis Mendoza (COL) W RSC 3 Reuben Palacios (COL), Miami – WBA

29.09.90 Welcome Ncita (SA) W RSC 8 Gerardo Lopez (PAN), Aosta – IBF

18.10.90 Luis Mendoza (COL) W PTS 12 Fabrice Benichou (FR), Paris – WBA

05.11.90 Pedro Decima (ARG) W RSC 4 Paul Banke (USA), Los Angeles – WBC

19.01.91 Luis Mendoza (COL) W RSC 8 Noree Jockygym (TH), Bangkok – WBA

03.02.91 Kiyoshi Hatanaka (JAP) W RSC 8 Pedro Decima (ARG), Nagoya – WBC

27.02.91 Welcome Ncita (SA) W PTS 12 Jesus Rojas (COL), St Vincent – IBF

21.04.91 Luis Mendoza (COL) W PTS 12 Carlos Uribe (CH), Cartagena – WBA

24.05.91 Jesse Benavides (USA) W PTS 12 Orlando Fernandez (PR), Corpus Christi – WBO

30.05.91 Luis Mendoza (COL) W CO 7 Joao Cardosa de Oliveira (BR), Madrid – WBA

14.06.91 Daniel Zaragoza (MEX) W PTS 12 Kiyoshi Hatanaka (JAP), Tokyo – WBC

15.06.91 Welcome Ncita (SA) W PTS 12 Hurley Snead (USA), San Antonio – IBF

24.08.91 Daniel Zaragoza (MEX) W PTS 12 Huh Chun (SK) Seoul – WBC

31.08.91 Jesse Benavides (USA) W RSC 5 Fernando Ramos (MEX), Corpus Christi – WBO

28.09.91 Welcome Ncita (SA) W PTS 12 Jesus Rojas (COL), Sun City – IBF

07.10.91 Raul Perez (MEX) W PTS 12 Luis Mendoza (COL), Los Angeles – WBA

09.12.91 Daniel Zaragoza (MEX) W PTS 12 Paul Banke (USA), Los Angeles – WBC

20.03.92 Thierry Jacob (FR) W PTS 12 Daniel Zaragoza (MEX), Calais – WBC

27.03.92 Wilfredo Vasquez (PR) W RSC 3 Raul Perez (MEX), Mexico City – WBA

18.04.92 Welcome Ncita (SA) W PTS 12 Jesus Salud (USA), Treviola – IBF

23.06.92 Tracy Harris Patterson (USA) W RSC 2 Thierry Jacob (FR), Albany – WBC

27.06.92 Wilfredo Vasquez (PR) W PTS 12 Freddy Cruz (DOM), Gorle – WBA

Bantamweight

27.06.90 **George Dixon** (C) W RTD 18 Nunc Wallace (GB), The Pelican Club, London

23.10.90 **George Dixon** (C) W RSC 40 Johnny Murphy (USA), Providence. *George Dixon relinquished title*

09.05.92 **Billy Plimmer** (GB) W PTS 10 Tommy Kelly (USA), New York City

28.12.92 **Billy Plimmer** (GB) W 8 Joe McGrath (USA), New York City

24.09.94 **Billy Plimmer** (GB) DREW 25 Johnny Murphy (USA), New Orleans

26.11.94 **Billy Plimmer** (GB) W CO 3 Charley Kelly (USA), New York City

28.05.95 **Billy Plimmer** (GB) W CO 7 George Corfield (GB), NSC, London

25.11.95 **Pedlar Palmer** (GB) W DIS 14 Billy Plimmer (GB), NSC, London

12.10.96 **Pedlar Palmer** (GB) W PTS 20 Johnny Murphy (USA), NSC, London

25.01.97 **Pedar Palmer** (GB) W RSC 14 Ernie Stanton (USA), NSC, London

18.10.97 **Pedlar Palmer** (GB) W PTS 20 Dave Sullivan (USA), NSC, London

12.12.98 **Pedlar Palmer** (GB) W RSC 17 Billy Plimmer (GB), NSC, London

17.04.99 **Pedlar Palmer** (GB) W RSC 3 Billy Rotchford (USA), NSC, London

22.09.99 **Terry McGovern** (USA) W CO 1 Pedlar Palmer (GB), Tuckahoe

22.12.99 **Terry McGovern** (USA) W CO 2 Harry Forbes (USA), New York City. *Terry McGovern relinquished title*

26.05.00 **Dan Dougherty** (USA) W PTS 20 Tommy Feltz (USA), New York City

04.08.00 **Dan Dougherty** (USA) W PTS 25 Tommy Feltz (USA), New York City

11.11.01 **Harry Forbes** (USA) W CO 2 Dan Dougherty (USA), St Louis

23.01.02 **Harry Forbes** (USA) W CO 4 Dan Dougherty (USA), St Louis

27.02.02 **Harry Forbes** (USA) W PTS 15 Tommy Feltz (USA), St Louis

01.05.02 **Harry Forbes** (USA) DREW 20 Johnny Reagan (USA), St Louis

23.12.02 **Harry Forbes** (USA) W RSC 7 Frankie Neil (USA), Oakland

27.02.03 **Harry Forbes** (USA) W PTS 10 Andrew Tokell (GB), Detroit

13.08.03 **Frankie Neil** (USA) W CO 2 Harry Forbes (USA), San Francisco

04.09.03 **Frankie Neil** (USA) W CO 15 Billy de Coursey (USA), Los Angeles

16.10.03 **Frankie Neil** (USA) DREW 20 Johnny Reagan (USA), Los Angeles

17.06.04 **Frankie Neil** (USA) W CO 3 Harry Forbes (USA), Chicago

17.10.04 **Joe Bowker** (GB) W PTS 20 Frankie Neil (USA), NSC, London

29.05.05 **Joe Bowker** (GB) W PTS 20 Pinky Evans (USA), NSC, London. *Joe Bowker relinquished title*

20.10.05 **Jimmy Walsh** (USA) W PTS 15 Digger Stanley (GB), Chelsea, Mass. *Jimmy Walsh relinquished title*

22.04.07 Owen Moran (GB) W PTS 20 Al Delmont (USA), NSC, London – GB. *Owen Moran forfeited GB recognition when continuously campaigning as a featherweight*

08.01.08 Johnny Coulon (C) W PTS 10 Kid Murphy (USA), Peoria – USA

29.01.08 Johnny Coulon (C) W PTS 10 Kid Murphy (USA), Peoria – USA

10.02.08 Johnny Coulon (C) W CO 9 Cooney Kelly (USA), Peoria – USA

11.02.09 Johnny Coulon (C) W RTD 5 Kid Murphy (USA), New York City – USA

19.06.09 Monte Attell (USA) W CO 18 Frankie Neil (USA), San Francisco – CALIF

17.12.09 Monte Attell (USA) DREW 20 Danny Webster (USA), San Francisco – CALIF

30.01.10 Johnny Coulon (C) W CO 9 Earl Denning (USA), New Orleans – LOUIS

19.02.10 Johnny Coulon (C) W PTS 10 Jim Kendrick (GB), New Orleans – LOUIS

22.02.10 Frankie Conley (USA) W CO 42 Monte Attell (USA), Los Angeles – CALIF

06.03.10 Johnny Coulon (C) W CO 19 Jim Kendrick (GB), New Orleans – LOUIS

17.10.10 Digger Stanley (GB) W CO 8 Joe Bowker (GB), NSC, London – GB

05.12.10 Digger Stanley (GB) W PTS 20 Johnny Condon (GB), The Ring, London – GB

19.12.10 Johnny Coulon (C) NC 3 Earl Denning (USA), Memphis – LOUIS

26.02.11 Johnny Coulon (C) W PTS 20 Frankie Conley (USA), New Orleans – USA

14.09.11 Digger Stanley (GB) W PTS 20 Ike Bradley (GB), The Stadium, Liverpool – GB

03.02.12 Johnny Coulon (C) W PTS 20 Frankie Conley (USA), Los Angeles – USA

18.02.12 Johnny Coulon (C) W PTS 20 Frankie Burns (USA), New Orleans – USA

22.04.12 Digger Stanley (GB) W PTS 20 Charles Ledoux (FR), NSC, London – GB/IBU

23.06.12 Charles Ledoux (FR) W CO 7 Digger Stanley (GB), Dieppe – GB/IBU

24.06.13 Eddie Campi (USA) W PTS 20 Charles Ledoux (FR), Los Angeles – GB/IBU

31.01.14 Kid Williams (USA) W CO 12 Eddie Campi (USA), Los Angeles – GB/IBU

09.06.14 **Kid Williams** (USA) W CO 3 Johnny Coulon (C), Los Angeles

28.09.14 **Kid Williams** (USA) W CO 4 Kid Herman (USA), Philadelphia

06.12.15 **Kid Williams** (USA) DREW 20 Frankie Burns (USA), New Orleans

07.02.16 **Kid Williams** (USA) DREW 20 Pete Herman (USA), New Orleans

09.01.17 **Pete Herman** (USA) W PTS 20 Kid Williams (USA), New Orleans

05.11.17 **Pete Herman** (USA) W PTS 20 Frankie Burns (USA), New Orleans

22.12.20 **Joe Lynch** (USA) W PTS 15 Pete Herman (USA), New York City

25.07.21 **Pete Herman** (USA) W PTS 15 Joe Lynch (USA), New York City

23.09.21 **Johnny Buff** (USA) W PTS 15 Pete Herman (USA), New York City

10.11.21 **Johnny Buff** (USA) W PTS 15 Jackie Sharkey (USA), New York City

10.07.22 **Joe Lynch** (USA) W RTD 14 Johnny Buff (USA), New York City

22.12.22 **Joe Lynch** (USA) W PTS 15 Midget Smith (USA), New York City. *Joe Lynch forfeited NY recognition when he withdrew from a scheduled defence against Joe Burman*

10.10.23 Abe Goldstein (USA) W PTS 12 Joe Burman (USA), New York City – NY

21.03.24 **Abe Goldstein** (USA) W PTS 15 Joe Lynch (USA), New York City

16.07.24 **Abe Goldstein** (USA) W PTS 15 Charles Ledoux (FR), New York City

08.09.24 **Abe Goldstein** (USA) W PTS 15 Tommy Ryan (USA), New York City

19.12.24 **Eddie Martin** (USA) W PTS 15 Abe Goldstein (USA), New York City

20.03.25 **Charlie Rosenberg** (USA) W PTS 15 Eddie Martin (USA), New York City

23.07.25 **Charlie Rosenberg** (USA) W CO 4 Eddie Shea (USA), New York City

02.03.26 **Charlie Rosenberg** (USA) W PTS 10 George Butch (USA), St Louis. *Charlie Rosenberg forfeited title when overweight for defence against Bushy Graham*

26.03.27 Bud Taylor (USA) DREW 10 Tony Canzoneri (USA), Chicago – NBA

05.05.27 Teddy Baldock (GB) W PTS 15 Archie Bell (USA), Albert Hall, London – GB

24.06.27 Bud Taylor (USA) W PTS 10 Tony Canzoneri (USA), Chicago – NBA. *Bud Taylor relinquished NBA version of title*

06.10.27 Willie Smith (SA) W PTS 15 Teddy Baldock (GB), Albert Hall London – GB. *Willie Smith forfeited, GB recognition when he made no effort to defend title*

23.05.28 Bushy Graham (USA) W PTS 15 Izzy Schwartz (USA), New York City – NY. *Bushy Graham relinquished NY version of title*

18.06.29 Al Brown (PAN) W PTS 15 Vidal Gregorio (SP), New York City – NY

28.08.29 Al Brown (PAN) W PTS 10 Knud Larsen (DEN), Copenhagen – NY/IBU

08.02.30 Al Brown (PAN) W DIS 4 Johnny Erickson (USA), New York City – NY/IBU

04.10.30 Al Brown (PAN) W PTS 15 Eugene Huat (FR), Paris – NY/IBU

11.02.31 Al Brown (PAN) W PTS 10 Nick Bensa (FR), Paris – NY/IBU

20.05.31 Pete Sanstol (NOR) W PTS 10 Archie Bell (USA), Montreal – NBA

25.08.31 **Al Brown** (PAN) W PTS 15 Pete Sanstol (NOR), Montreal

27.10.31 **Al Brown** (PAN) W PTS 15 Eugene Huat (FR), Montreal

10.07.32 **Al Brown** (PAN) W PTS 15 Kid Francis (FR), Marseilles

19.09.32 **Al Brown** (PAN) W CO 1 Emile Pladner (FR), Toronto

18.03.33 **Al Brown** (PAN) W PTS 12 Dom Bernasconi (ITA), Milan

03.07.33 **Al Brown** (PAN) W PTS 15 Johnny King (GB), Belle Vue, Manchester

19.02.34 **Al Brown** (PAN) W PTS 15 Young Perez (FR), Paris. *Al Brown forfeited WBA recognition for failing to defend against Baby Casanova*

26.06.34 Sixto Escobar (PR) W CO 9 Baby Casanova (MEX), Montreal – NBA

08.08.34 Sixto Escobar (PR) W PTS 15 Eugene Huat (FR), Montreal – NBA

01.11.34 Al Brown (PAN) W CO 10 Young Perez (FR), Tunis – NY/IBU

01.06.35 Baltazar Sangchilli (SP) W PTS 15 Al Brown (PAN), Valencia, – NY/IBU

26.08.35 Lou Salica (USA) W PTS 15 Sixto Escobar (PR), New York City – NBA

15.11.35 Sixto Escobar (PR) W PTS 15 Lou Salica (USA), New York City – NBA

29.06.36 Tony Marino (USA) W CO 14 Baltazar Sangchilli (SP), New York City – NY/IBU

31.08.36 **Sixto Escobar** (PR) W RSC 13 Tony Marino (USA), New York City

13.10.36 **Sixto Escobar** (PR) W CO 1 Carlos Quintana (PAN), New York City

21.02.37 **Sixto Escobar** (PR) W PTS 15 Lou Salica (USA), San Juan

23.09.37 **Harry Jeffra** (USA) W PTS 15 Sixto Escobar (PR), New York City

20.02.38 **Sixto Escobar** (PR) W PTS 15 Harry Jeffra (USA), San Juan

02.04.39 **Sixto Escobar** (PR) W PTS 15 Kayo Morgan (USA), San Juan. *Sixto Escobar relinquished title*

04.03.40 Lou Salica (USA) DREW 15 George Pace (USA), Toronto – NBA

24.09.40 **Lou Salica** (USA) W PTS 15 George Pace (USA), New York City

13.01.41 **Lou Salica** (USA) W PTS 15 Tommy Forte (USA), Philadelphia

25.04.41 **Lou Salica** (USA) W PTS 15 Lou Transparenti (USA), Baltimore

16.06.41 **Lou Salica** (USA) W PTS 15 Tommy Forte (USA), Philadelphia

07.08.42 **Manuel Ortiz** (USA) W PTS 12 Lou Salica (USA), Los Angeles

01.01.43 **Manuel Ortiz** (USA) W PTS 10 Kenny Lindsay (C), Portland

27.01.43 **Manuel Ortiz** (USA) W RSC 10 George Freitas (USA), Oakland

10.03.43 **Manuel Ortiz** (USA) W RSC 11 Lou Salica (USA), Oakland

28.04.43 **Manuel Ortiz** (USA) W CO 6 Lupe Cordoza (USA), Fort Worth

26.05.43 **Manuel Ortiz** (USA) W PTS 15 Joe Robleto (USA), Los Angeles

12.07.43 **Manuel Ortiz** (USA) W CO 7 Joe Robleto (USA), Seattle

01.10.43 **Manuel Ortiz** (USA) W CO 4 Leonardo Lopez (USA), Los Angeles

23.11.43 **Manuel Ortiz** (USA) W PTS 15 Benny Goldberg (USA), Los Angeles

14.03.44 **Manuel Ortiz** (USA) W PTS 15 Ernesto Aguilar (MEX), Los Angeles

04.04.44 **Manuel Ortiz** (USA) W PTS 15 Tony Olivera (USA), Los Angeles

12.09.44 **Manuel Ortiz** (USA) W CO 4 Luis Castillo (MEX), Los Angeles

14.11.44 **Manuel Ortiz** (USA) W RSC 9 Luis Castillo (MEX), Los Angeles

25.02.46 **Manuel Ortiz** (USA) W CO 13 Luis Castillo (MEX), San Francisco

26.05.46 **Manuel Ortiz** (USA) W CO 5 Kenny Lindsay (C), Los Angeles

10.06.46 **Manuel Ortiz** (USA) W CO 11 Jackie Jurich (USA), San Francisco

06.01.47 **Harold Dade** (USA) W PTS 15 Manuel Ortiz (USA), San Francisco

11.03.47 **Manuel Ortiz** (USA) W PTS 15 Harold Dade (USA), Los Angeles

30.05.47 **Manuel Ortiz** (USA) W PTS 15 Kui Kong Young (USA), Honolulu

20.12.47 **Manuel Ortiz** (USA) W PTS 15 Tirso del Rosario (PH), Manila

04.07.48 **Manuel Ortiz** (USA) W RSC 8 Memo Valero (MEX), Mexicali

01.03.49 **Manuel Ortiz** (USA) W PTS 15 Dado Marino (USA), Honolulu

31.05.50 **Vic Toweel** (SA) W PTS 15 Manuel Ortiz (USA), Johannesburg

02.12.50 **Vic Toweel** (SA) W RTD 10 Danny O'Sullivan (GB), Johannesburg

17.11.51 **Vic Toweel** (SA) W PTS 15 Luis Romero (SP), Johannesburg

26.01.52 **Vic Toweel** (SA) W PTS 15 Peter Keenan (GB), Johannesburg

15.11.52 **Jimmy Carruthers** (A) W CO 1 Vic Toweel (SA), Johannesburg

21.03.53 **Jimmy Carruthers** (A) W CO 10 Vic Toweel (SA), Johannesburg

13.11.53 **Jimmy Carruthers** (A) W PTS 15 Pappy Gault (USA), Sydney

02.05.54 **Jimmy Carruthers** (A) W PTS 12 Chamrern Songkitrat (TH), Bangkok. *Jimmy Carruthers relinquished title*

19.09.54 Robert Cohen (FR) W PTS 15 Chamrern Songkitrat (TH), Bangkok – NY/EBU

09.03.55 Raton Macias (MEX) W RSC 11 Chamrern Songkitrat (TH), San Francisco – NBA

03.09.55 Robert Cohen (FR) DREW 15 Willie Toweel (SA), Johannesburg – NY/EBU

25.03.56 Raton Macias (MEX) W CO 10 Leo Espinosa (PH), Mexico City – NBA

29.06.56 Mario D'Agata (ITA) W RTD 6 Robert Cohen (FR), Rome – NY/EBU

01.04.57 Alphonse Halimi (FR) W PTS 15 Mario D'Agata (ITA), Paris – NY/EBU

15.06.57 Raton Macias (MEX) W RSC 11 Dommy Ursua (PH), San Francisco – NBA

06.11.57 **Alphonse Halimi** (FR) W PTS 15 Raton Macias (MEX), Los Angeles

08.07.59 **Joe Becerra** (MEX) W CO 8 Alphonse Halimi (FR), Los Angeles

04.02.60 **Joe Becerra** (MEX) W CO 9 Alphonse Halimi (FR), Los Angeles

23.05.60 **Joe Becerra** (MEX) W PTS 15 Kenji Yonekura (JAP), Tokyo. *Joe Becerra relinquished title*

25.10.60 Alphonse Halimi (FR) W PTS 15 Freddie Gilroy (GB), The Arena, Wembley – EBU

18.11.60 Eder Jofre (BR) W CO 6 Eloy Sanchez (MEX), Los Angeles – NBA

25.03.61 Eder Jofre (BR) W RTD 9 Piero Rollo (ITA), Rio de Janeiro – NBA

30.05.61 Johnny Caldwell (GB) W PTS 15 Alphonse Halimi (FR), The Arena, Wembley – EBU

19.08.61 Eder Jofre (BR) W RSC 7 Ramon Arias (VEN), Caracas – NBA

31.10.61 Johnny Caldwell (GB) W PTS 15 Alphonse Halimi (FR), The Arena, Wembley – EBU

18.01.62 **Eder Jofre** (BR) W RTD 10 Johnny Caldwell (GB), Sao Paulo

04.05.62 **Eder Jofre** (BR) W RSC 10 Herman Marquez (USA), San Francisco

11.09.62 **Eder Jofre** (BR) W CO 6 Joe Medel (MEX), Sao Paulo

04.04.63 **Eder Jofre** (BR) W CO 3 Katsutoshi Aoki (JAP), Tokyo

18.05.63 **Eder Jofre** (BR) W RTD 11 Johnny Jamito (PH), Quezon City

27.11.64 **Eder Jofre** (BR) W CO 7 Bernardo Caraballo (COL), Bogota

17.05.65 **Fighting Harada** (JAP) W PTS 15 Eder Jofre (BR), Nagoya

30.11.65 **Fighting Harada** (JAP) W PTS 15 Alan Rudkin (GB), Tokyo

01.06.66 **Fighting Harada** (JAP) W PTS 15 Eder Jofre (BR), Tokyo

03.01.67 **Fighting Harada** (JAP) W PTS 15 Joe Medel (MEX), Nagoya

04.07.67 **Fighting Harada** (JAP) W PTS 15 Bernardo Caraballo (COL), Tokyo

26.02.68 **Lionel Rose** (A) W PTS 15 Fighting Harada (JAP), Tokyo

02.07.68 **Lionel Rose** (A) W PTS 15 Takao Sakurai (JAP), Tokyo

06.12.68 **Lionel Rose** (A) W PTS 15 Chuchu Castillo (MEX), Los Angeles

08.03.69 **Lionel Rose** (A) W PTS 15 Alan Rudkin (GB), Melbourne

22.08.69 **Ruben Olivares** (MEX) W CO 5 Lionel Rose (A), Los Angeles

12.12.69 **Ruben Olivares** (MEX) W RSC 2 Alan Rudkin (GB), Los Angeles

18.04.70 **Ruben Olivares** (MEX) W PTS 15 Chuchu Castillo (MEX), Los Angeles

16.10.70 **Chuchu Castillo** (MEX) W RSC 14 Ruben Olivares (MEX), Los Angeles

03.04.71 **Ruben Olivares** (MEX) W PTS 15 Chucho Castillo (MEX), Los Angeles

25.10.71 **Ruben Olivares** (MEX) W RSC 14 Katsutoshi Kanazawa (JAP), Nagoya

14.12.71 **Ruben Olivares** (MEX) W RSC 11 Jesus Pimental (MEX), Los Angeles

19.03.72 **Rafel Herrera** (MEX) W CO 8 Ruben Olivares (MEX), Mexico City

30.07.72 **Enrique Pinder** (PAN) W PTS 15 Rafael Herrera (MEX), Panama City. *Enrique Pinder forfeited WBC recognition for failing to defend against the stipulated challenger*

20.01.73 Romeo Anaya (MEX) W CO 3 Enrique Pinder (PAN), Panama City – WBA

15.04.73 Rafael Herrera (MEX) W RSC 12 Rodolfo Martinez (MEX), Monterrey – WBC

28.04.73 Romeo Anaya (MEX) W PTS 15 Rogelio Lara (MEX), Los Angeles – WBA

18.08.73 Romeo Anaya (MEX) W CO 3 Enrique Pinder (PAN), Los Angeles – WBA

13.10.73 Rafael Herrera (MEX) W PTS 15 Venice Borkorsor (TH), Los Angeles – WBC

03.11.73 Arnold Taylor (SA) W CO 14 Romeo Anaya (MEX), Johannesburg – WBA

25.05.74 Rafael Herrera (MEX) W CO 6 Romeo Anaya (MEX), Mexico City – WBC

03.07.74 Soo-Hwan Hong (SK) W PTS 15 Arnold Taylor (SA), Durban – WBA

07.12.74 Rodolfo Martinez (MEX) W RSC 4 Rafael Herrera (MEX), Merida – WBC

28.12.74 Soo-Hwan Hong (SK) W PTS 15 Fernando Canabela (PH), Seoul – WBA

14.03.75 Alfonso Zamora (MEX) W CO 4 Soo-Hwan Hong (SK), Los Angeles – WBA

31.05.75 Rodolfo Martinez (MEX) W RSC 7 Nestor Jiminez (COL), Bogota – WBC

30.08.75 Alfonso Zamora (MEX) W CO 4 Thanomjit Sukhothai (TH), Los Angeles – WBA

08.10.75 Rodolfo Martinez (MEX) W PTS 15 Hisami Numata (JAP), Sendai – WBC

06.12.75 Alfonso Zamora (MEX) W CO 1 Socrates Batoto (PH), Mexico City – WBA

30.01.76 Rodolfo Martinez (MEX) W PTS 15 Venice Borkorsor (TH), Bangkok – WBC

03.04.76 Alfonso Zamora (MEX) W CO 2 Eusebio Pedroza (PAN), Mexicali – WBA

08.05.76 Carlos Zarate (MEX) W CO 9 Rodolfo Martinez (MEX), Los Angeles – WBC

10.07.76 Alfonso Zamora (MEX) W CO 3 Gilberto Illueca (PAN), Juarez – WBA

28.08.76 Carlos Zarate (MEX) W RSC 12 Paul Ferreri (A), Los Angeles – WBC

16.10.76 Alfonso Zamora (MEX) W RSC 12 Soo-Hwan Hong (SK), Inchon – WBA

13.11.76 Carlos Zarate (MEX) W CO 4 Waruinge Nakayama (K), Culiacan – WBC

05.02.77 Carlos Zarate (MEX) W RSC 3 Fernando Cabanela (PH), Mexico City – WBC

29.10.77 Carlos Zarate (MEX) W RSC 6 Danilio Batista (BR), Los Angeles – WBC

19.11.77 Jorge Lujan (PAN) W CO 10 Alfonso Zamora (MEX), Los Angeles – WBA

02.12.77 Carlos Zarate (MEX) W RSC 5 Juan Francisco Rodriguez (SP), Madrid – WBC

25.02.78 Carlos Zarate (MEX) W RSC 8 Albert Davila (USA), Los Angeles – WBC

18.03.78 Jorge Lujan (PAN) W RTD 11 Roberto Rubaldino (MEX), San Antonio – WBA

22.04.78 Carlos Zarate (MEX) W RSC 13 Andres Hernandez (PR), San Juan – WBC

09.06.78 Carlos Zarate (MEX) W CO 4 Emilio Hernandez (VEN), Las Vegas – WBC

15.09.78 Jorge Lujan (PAN) W PTS 15 Albert Davila (USA), New Orleans – WBA

10.03.79 Carlos Zarate (MEX) W CO 3 Mensah Kpalongo (TOGO), Los Angeles – WBC

08.04.79 Jorge Lujan (PAN) W RSC 15 Cleo Garcia (NIC), Las Vegas – WBA

02.06.79 Lupe Pintor (MEX) W PTS 15 Carlos Zarate (MEX), Las Vegas – WBC

06.10.79 Jorge Lujan (PAN) W CO 15 Roberto Rubaldino (MEX), McAllen – WBA

09.02.80 Lupe Pintor (MEX) W RSC 12 Alberto Sandoval (USA), Los Angeles – WBC

02.04.80 Jorge Lujan (PAN) W RSC 9 Shuichi Isogami (JAP), Tokyo – WBA

11.06.80 Lupe Pintor (MEX) DREW 15 Eijiro Murata (JAP), Tokyo – WBC

29.08.80 Julian Solis (PR) W PTS 15 Jorge Lujan (PAN), Miami – WBA

19.09.80 Lupe Pintor (MEX) W CO 12 Johnny Owen (GB), Los Angeles – WBC

14.11.80 Jeff Chandler (USA) W RSC 14 Julian Solis (PR), Miami – WBA

19.12.80 Lupe Pintor (MEX) W PTS 15 Albert Davila (USA), Las Vegas – WBC

31.01.81 Jeff Chandler (USA) W PTS 15 Jorge Lujan (PAN), Philadelphia – WBA

22.02.81 Lupe Pintor (MEX) W PTS 15 Jose Uziga (ARG), Houston – WBC

05.04.81 Jeff Chandler (USA) DREW 15 Eijiro Murata (JAP), Tokyo – WBA

25.07.81 Jeff Chandler (USA) W CO 7 Julian Solis (PR), Atlantic City – WBA

26.07.81 Lupe Pintor (MEX) W RSC 8 Jovito Rengifo (VEN), Las Vegas – WBC

22.09.81 Lupe Pintor (MEX) W CO 15 Hurricane Teru (JAP), Nagoya – WBC

10.12.81 Jeff Chandler (USA) W RSC 13 Eijiro Murata (JAP), Atlantic City – WBA

27.03.82 Jeff Chandler (USA) W RSC 6 Johnny Carter (USA), Philadelphia – WBA

03.06.82 Lupe Pintor (MEX) W RSC 11 Seung-Hoon Lee (SK) Los Angeles – WBC. *Lupe Pintor forfeited WBC recognition when unable to defend due to a motorcycle accident*

27.10.82 Jeff Chandler (USA) W RSC 9 Miguel Iriarle (PAN), Atlantic City – WBA

13.03.83 Jeff Chandler (USA) W PTS 15 Gaby Canizales (USA), Atlantic City – WBA

01.09.83 Albert Davila (USA) W CO 12 Kiko Bejines (MEX), Los Angeles – WBC

11.09.83 Jeff Chandler (USA) W RSC 10 Eijiro Murata (JAP), Tokyo – WBA

17.12.83 Jeff Chandler (USA) W RSC 7 Oscar Muniz (USA), Atlantic City – WBA

07.04.84 Richard Sandoval (USA) W RSC 15 Jeff Chandler (USA), Atlantic City – WBA

16.04.84 Satoshi Shingaki (JAP) W RSC 8 Elmer Magallano (PH), Kashiwara – IBF

26.05.84 Albert Davila (USA) W RSC 11 Enrique Sanchez (DOM), Miami – WBC. *Albert Davila relinquished WBC version of title*

04.08.84 Satoshi Shingaki (JAP) W PTS 15 Joves de la Puz (PH), Naha City – IBF

22.09.84 Richard Sandoval (USA) W PTS 15 Edgar Roman (VEN), Monaco – WBA

15.12.84 Richard Sandoval (USA) W RSC 8 Cardenio Ulloa (CH), Miami – WBA

26.04.85 Jeff Fenech (A) W RSC 9 Satoshi Shingaki (JAP), Sydney – IBF

04.05.85 Daniel Zaragoza (MEX) W DIS 7 Fred Jackson (USA), Aruba – WBC

09.08.85 Miguel Lora (COL) W PTS 12 Daniel Zaragoza (MEX), Miami – WBC

23.08.85 Jeff Fenech (A) W CO 3 Satoshi Shingaki (JAP), Sydney – IBF

02.12.85 Jeff Fenech (A) W PTS 15 Jerome Coffee (USA), Sydney – IBF

08.02.86 Miguel Lora (COL) W PTS 12 Wilfredo Vasquez (PR), Miami – WBC

10.03.86 Gaby Canizales (USA) W RSC 7 Richard Sandoval (USA), Las Vegas – WBA

04.06.86 Bernardo Pinango (VEN) W PTS 15 Gaby Canizales (USA), East Rutherford – WBA

18.07.86 Jeff Fenech (A) W RSC 14 Steve McCrory (USA), Sydney – IBF. *Jeff Fenech relinquished IBF version of title*

23.08.86 Miguel Lora (COL) W RSC 6 Enrique Sanchez (DOM), Miami – WBC

04.10.86 Bernardo Pinango (VEN) W RSC 10 Ciro de Leva (ITA), Turin – WBA

15.11.86 Miguel Lora (COL) W PTS 12 Albert Davila (USA), Barranquilla – WBC

22.11.86 Bernardo Pinango (VEN) W RSC 15 Simon Skosana (SA), Johannesburg – WBA

03.02.87 Bernardo Pinango (VEN) W PTS 15 Frankie Duarte (USA), Los Angeles – WBA. *Bernardo Pinango relinquished WBA version of title*

29.03.87 Takuya Muguruma (JAP) W CO 5 Azael Moran (PAN), Moriguchi – WBA

15.05.87 Kelvin Seabrooks (USA) W CO 5 Miguel Maturana (COL), Cartagena – IBF

24.05.87 Chan-Yung Park (SK) W RSC 11 Takuya Muguruma (JAP), Moriguchi – WBA

04.07.87 Kelvin Seabrooks (USA) NC 9 Thierry Jacob (FR), Calais – IBF

25.07.87 Miguel Lora (COL) W RSC 4 Antonio Avelar (MEX), Miami – WBC

04.10.87 Wilfredo Vasquez (PR) W RSC 10 Chan-Yung Park (SK), Seoul – WBA

18.11.87 Kelvin Seabrooks (USA) W RSC 4 Ernie Cataluna (PH), San Cataldo – IBF

27.11.87 Miguel Lora (COL) W PTS 12 Ray Minus (BAH), Miami – WBC

17.01.88 Wilfredo Vasquez (PR) DREW 12 Takuya Maguruma (JAP), Osaka – WBA

06.02.88 Kelvin Seabrooks (USA) W RSC 2 Fernando Beltran (MEX), Paris – IBF

30.04.88 Miguel Lora (COL) W PTS 12 Lucio Lopez (ARG), Cartagena – WBC

09.05.88 Kaokor Galaxy (TH) W PTS 12 Wilfredo Vasquez (PR), Bangkok – WBA

09.07.88 Orlando Canizales (USA) W RSC 15 Kelvin Seabrooks (USA), Atlantic City – IBF

01.08.88 Miguel Lora (COL) W PTS 12 Albert Davila (USA), Los Angeles – WBC

14.08.88 Sung-Il Moon (SK) W TD 6 Kaokor Galaxy (TH), Pusan – WBA

29.10.88 Raul Perez (MEX) W PTS 12 Miguel Lora (COL), Las Vegas – WBC

27.11.88 Sung-II Moon (SK) W CO 7 Edgar Monserrat (PAN), Seoul – WBA

29.11.88 Orlando Canizales (USA) W CO 1 Jimmy Navarro (USA), San Antonio – IBF

03.02.89 Israel Contrerras (VEN) W CO 1 Maurizio Lupino (ITA), Caracas – WBO

19.02.89 Sung-ll Moon (SK) W RSC 5 Chaiki Kobayashi (JAP), Taejon – WBA

09.03.89 Raul Perez (MEX) W PTS 12 Lucio Lopez (ARG), Los Angeles – WBC

24.06.89 Orlando Canizales (USA) W RSC 11 Kelvin Seabrooks (USA), Atlantic City – IBF

08.07.89 Kaokor Galaxy (TH) W PTS 12 Sung-ll Moon (SK), Bangkok – WBA

26.08.89 Raul Perez (MEX) W RTD 7 Cardenio Ulloa (CH), Santiago – WBC

18.10.89 Luisito Espinosa (PH) W RSC 1 Kaokor Galaxy (TH), Bangkok – WBA

23.10.89 Raul Perez (MEX) W PTS 12 Diego Avila (MEX), Los Angeles – WBC

22.01.90 Raul Perez (MEX) W PTS 12 Gaby Canizales (USA), Los Angeles – WBC

24.01.90 Orlando Canizales (USA) W PTS 12 Billy Hardy (GB), Crowtree Leisure Centre, Sunderland – IBF

07.05.90 Raul Perez (MEX) W RSC 9 Gerardo Martinez (USA), Los Angeles – WBC

30.05.90 Luisito Espinosa (PH) W RTD 8 Hurley Snead (USA), Bangkok – WBA

10.06.90 Orlando Canizales (USA) W PTS 12 Paul Gonzales (USA), El Paso – IBF

14.08.90 Orlando Canizales (USA) W RSC 5 Eddie Rangel (USA), Saratago Springs – IBF

02.09.90 Israel Contrerras (VEN) W RSC 9 Ray Minus (BAH), Nassau – WBO. *Israel Contrerras relinquished WBO version of title*

14.09.90 Raul Perez (MEX) DREW 12 Jose Valdez (MEX), Culican – WBC

12.10.90 Luisito Espinosa (PH) W CO 1 Yong-Man Chun (SK), Manila – WBA

29.11.90	Luisito Espinosa (PH) W PTS 12 Thalerngsak Sitbobay (TH), Bangkok – WBA
17.12.90	Raul Perez (MEX) W CO 8 Chanquito Carmona (MEX), Tijuana – WBC
25.02.91	Greg Richardson (USA) W PTS 12 Raul Perez (MEX), Los Angeles – WBC
12.03.91	Gaby Canizales (USA) W CO 2 Miguel Lora (COL), Detroit – WBO
04.05.91	Orlando Canizales (USA) W RSC 8 Billy Hardy (GB), Laredo – IBF
20.05.91	Greg Richardson (USA) W PTS 12 Victor Rabanales (MEX), Los Angeles – WBC
30.06.91	Duke McKenzie (GB) W PTS 12 Gaby Canizales (USA), Elephant and Castle Leisure Centre, London – WBO
12.09.91	Duke McKenzie (GB) W PTS 12 Cesar Soto (MEX), Latchmere Leisure Centre, London – WBO
19.09.91	Joichiro Tatsuyushi (JAP) W RTD 10 Greg Richardson (USA), Tokyo – WBC. *Joichiro Tatsuyushi relinquished title*
22.09.91	Orlando Canizales (USA) W PTS 12 Fernie Morales (USA), Indio – IBF
19.10.91	Israel Contrerras (VEN) W CO 5 Luisito Espinosa (PH) Manila – WBA
21.12.91	Orlando Canizales (USA) W RSC 11 Ray Minus (BAH), Laredo – IBF
15.03.92	Eddie Cook (USA) W CO 5 Israel Contrerras (VEN) Las Vegas – WBA
30.03.92	Victor Rabanales (MEX) W TD 9 Yong-Hoon Lee (SK), Los Angeles – WBC
23.04.92	Orlando Canizales (USA) W PTS 12 Francisco Alvarez (COL), Paris – IBF
13.05.92	Rafael del Valle (PR) W CO 1 Duke McKenzie (GB), Albert Hall, London – WBO
16.05.92	Victor Rabanales (MEX) W RSC 4 Luis Ocampo (ARG), Tuxtla – WBC

Super-Flyweight

02.02.80	Rafael Orono (VEN) W PTS 15 Seung-Hoon Lee (SK), Caracas – WBC
14.04.80	Rafael Orono (VEN) W PTS 15 Ramon Soria (ARG), Caracas – WBC
28.07.80	Rafael Orono (VEN) DREW 15 Willie Jensen (USA), Caracas – WBC
15.09.80	Rafael Orono (VEN) W RSC 3 Jovito Rengifo (VEN), Barquisimeto – WBC
24.01.81	Chul-Ho Kim (SK) W CO 9 Rafael Orono (VEN), San Christobal – WBC
22.04.81	Chul-Ho Kim (SK) W PTS 15 Jiro Watanabe (JAP), Seoul – WBC
29.07.81	Chul-Ho Kim (SK) W CO 13 Willie Jensen (USA), Pusan – WBC
12.09.81	Gustavo Ballas (ARG) W RSC 8 Sok-Chul Baek (SK), Buenos Aires – WBA
18.11.81	Chul-Ho Kim (SK) W RSC 9 Jackal Maruyama (JAP), Pusan – WBC
05.12.81	Rafael Pedroza (PAN) W PTS 15 Gustavo Ballas (ARG), Panama City – WBA
10.02.82	Chul-Ho Kim (SK) W CO 8 Koki Ishii. (JAP) Taegu – WBC
08.04.82	Jiro Watanabe (JAP) W PTS 15 Rafael Pedroza (PAN), Osaka – WBA
04.07.82	Chul-Ho Kim (SK) DREW 15 Raul Valdez (MEX), Daejon – WBC
29.07.82	Jiro Watanabe (JAP) W RSC 9 Gustavo Ballas (ARG), Osaka – WBA
11.11.82	Jiro Watanabe (JAP) W RTD 12 Shoji Oguma (JAP), Hamamatsu – WBA
28.11.82	Rafael Orono (VEN) W CO 6 Chul-Ho Kim (SK), Seoul – WBC
31.01.83	Rafael Orono (VEN) W CO 4 Pedro Romero (PAN), Caracas – WBC
24.02.83	Jiro Watanabe (JAP) W CO 8 Luis Ibanez (PERU), Tsu City – WBA
09.05.83	Rafael Orono (VEN) W PTS 12 Raul Valdez (MEX), Caracas – WBC
23.06.83	Jiro Watanabe (JAP) W PTS 15 Roberto Ramirez (MEX) Sendai – WBA
06.10.83	Jiro Watanabe (JAP) W RTD 11 Soon-Chun Kwon (SK), Osaka – WBA
29.10.83	Rafael Orono (VEN) W RSC 5 Orlando Maldonado (PR), Caracas – WBC
27.11.83	Payao Poontarat (TH) W PTS 12 Rafael Orono (VEN), Pattaya – WBC
10.12.83	Joo-Do Chun (SK) W CO 5 Ken Kasugai (JAP), Osaka – IBF
28.01.84	Joo-Do Chun (SK) W CO 12 Prayoonsak Muangsurin (TH), Seoul – IBF
15.03.84	Jiro Watanabe (JAP) W RSC 15 Celso Chavez (PAN), Osaka – WBA. *Jiro*

Watanabe forfeited WBA recognition for failing to defend against Kaosai Galaxy

17.03.84	Joo-Do Chun (SK) W CO 1 Diego de Villa (PH), Kwangju – IBF
28.03.84	Payao Poontarat (TH) W RSC 10 Guty Espadas (MEX), Bangkok – WBC
26.05.84	Joo-Do Chun (SK) W RSC 6 Felix Marques (PR), Wonju – IBF
05.07.84	Jiro Watanabe (JAP) W PTS 12 Payao Poontarat (TH), Osaka – WBC
20.07.84	Joo-Do Chun (SK) W CO 7 William Develos (PH), Pusan – IBF
21.11.84	Kaosai Galaxy (TH) W CO 6 Eusebio Espinal (DOM), Bangkok – WBA
29.11.84	Jiro Watanabe (JAP) W RSC 11 Payao Poontarat (TH), Kumamoto – WBC
06.01.85	Joo-Do Chun (SK) W CO 15 Kwang-Gu Park (SK), Ulsan – IBF
06.03.85	Kaosai Galaxy (TH) W CO 7 Dong-Chun Lee (SK), Bangkok – WBA
03.05.85	Elly Pical (INDON) W RSC 8 Joo-Do Chun (SK), Jakarta – IBF
09.05.85	Jiro Watanabe (JAP) W PTS 12 Julio Solano (DOM), Tokyo – WBC
17.07.85	Kaosai Galaxy (TH) W RSC 5 Rafael Orono (VEN), Bangkok – WBA
25.08.85	Elly Pical (INDON) W RSC 3 Wayne Mulholland (A), Jakarta – IBF
17.09.85	Jiro Watanabe (JAP) W RSC 7 Katsuo Katsuma (JAP), Osaka – WBC
13.12.85	Jiro Watanabe (JAP) W CO 5 Yun-Sok Hwang (SK), Taegu – WBC
23.12.85	Kaosai Galaxy (TH) W RSC 2 Edgar Monserrat (PAN), Bangkok – WBA
15.02.86	Cesar Polanco (DOM) W PTS 15 Elly Pical (INDON), Jakarta – IBF
30.03.86	Gilberto Roman (MEX) W PTS 12 Jiro Watanabe (JAP), Osaka – WBC
15.05.86	Gilberto Roman (MEX) W PTS 12 Edgar Monserrat (PAN), Paris – WBC
05.07.86	Elly Pical (INDON) W CO 3 Cesar Polanco (DOM), Jakarta – IBF
18.07.86	Gilberto Roman (MEX) W PTS 12 Ruben Condori (ARG), Salta – WBC
30.08.86	Gilberto Roman (MEX) DREW 12 Santos Laciar (ARG), Cordoba – WBC
01.11.86	Kaosai Galaxy (TH) W CO 5 Israel Contrerras (VEN), Curacao – WBA
03.12.86	Elly Pical (INDON) W CO 10 Dong-Chun Lee (SK), Jakarta – IBF. *Elly Pical forfeited IBF recognition when he challenged for the WBA S. flyweight title*
15.12.86	Gilberto Roman (MEX) W PTS 12 Kongtoranee Payakarun (TH), Bangkok – WBC
31.01.87	Gilberto Roman (MEX) W RSC 9 Antoine Montero (FR), Montpelier – WBC
28.02.87	Kaosai Galaxy (TH) W CO 14 Elly Pical (INDON), Jakarta – WBA
19.03.87	Gilberto Roman (MEX) W PTS 12 Frank Cedeno (PH), Mexicali – WBC
16.05.87	Santos Laciar (ARG) W RSC 11 Gilberto Roman (MEX), Reims – WBC
17.05.87	Tae-Il Chang (SK) W PTS 15 Soon-Chun Kwon (SK), Pusan – IBF
08.08.87	Jesus Rojas (COL) W PTS 12 Santos Laciar (ARG), Miami – WBC
12.10.87	Kaosai Galaxy (TH) W RSC 3 Byong-Kwan Chung (SK), Bangkok – WBA
17.10.87	Elly Pical (INDON) W PTS 15 Tae-Il Chang (SK), Jakarta – IBF
24.10.87	Jesus Rojas (COL) W RSC 4 Gustavo Ballas (ARG), Miami – WBC
26.01.88	Kaosai Galaxy (TH) W PTS 12 Kongtoranee Payakarun (TH), Bangkok – WBA
20.02.88	Elly Pical (INDON) W PTS 15 Raul Diaz (COL), Pontianak – IBF
08.04.88	Gilberto Roman (MEX) W PTS 12 Jesus Rojas (COL), Miami – WBC
09.07.88	Gilberto Roman (MEX) W RSC 5 Yoshiyuki Uchida (JAP), Kawagoe – WBC
03.09.88	Elly Pical (INDON) W PTS 12 Chang-Ki Kim (SK), Surabaya – IBF
03.09.88	Gilberto Roman (MEX) W PTS 12 Kiyoshi Hatanaka (JAP), Nagoya – WBC
09.10.88	Kaosai Galaxy (TH) W CO 8 Chang-Ho Choi (SK), Seoul – WBA
07.11.88	Gilberto Roman (MEX) W PTS 12 Jesus Rojas (COL), Las Vegas – WBC
15.01.89	Kaosai Galaxy (TH) W CO 2 Tae-Il Chang (SK), Bangkok – WBA
25.02.89	Elly Pical (INDON) W PTS 12 Mike Phelps (USA), Singapore – IBF
08.04.89	Kaosai Galaxy (TH) W PTS 12 Kenji Matsumura (JAP), Yokahama – WBA

29.04.89	Jose Ruiz (PR) W PTS 12 Jesus Rojas (COL), San Juan – WBO
05.06.89	Gilberto Roman (MEX) W PTS 12 Juan Carazo (PR), Los Angeles – WBC
29.07.89	Kaosai Galaxy (TH) W RSC 10 Alberto Castro (COL), Surin – WBA
09.09.89	Jose Ruiz (PR) W RSC 1 Juan Carazo (PR), San Juan – WBO
12.09.89	Gilberto Roman (MEX) W PTS 12 Santos Laciar (ARG), Los Angeles – WBC
14.10.89	Juan Polo Perez (COL) W PTS 12 Elly Pical (INDON), Roanoke – IBF
21.10.89	Jose Ruiz (PR) W RSC 12 Angel Rosario (PR), San Juan – WBO
31.10.89	Kaosai Galaxy (TH) W CO 12 Kenji Matsumura (JAP), Kobe – WBA
07.11.89	Nana Yaw Konadu (GH) W PTS 12 Gilberto Roman (MEX), Mexico City – WBC
20.01.90	Sung-Il Moon (SK) W PTS 12 Nana Yaw Konadu (GH), Seoul – WBC
29.03.90	Kaosai Galaxy (TH) W CO 5 Ari Blanca (PH), Bangkok – WBA
21.04.90	Robert Quiroga (USA) W PTS 12 Juan Polo Perez (COL), The Crowtree Leisure Centre, Sunderland – IBF
09.06.90	Sung-Il Moon (SK) W RTD 8 Gilberto Roman (MEX), Seoul – WBC
30.06.90	Kaosai Galaxy (TH) W RSC 8 Schunichi Nakajima (JAP), Chiang Mai – WBA
18.08.90	Jose Ruiz (PR) W RSC 8 Wilfredo Vargas (PR), Ponce – WBO
29.09.90	Kaosai Galaxy (TH) W CO 6 Yong-Kang Kim (SK), Suphan Buri – WBA
03.11.90	Jose Ruiz (PR) W PTS 12 Armando Velasco (MEX), Acapulco – WBO
06.10.90	Robert Quiroga (USA) W RTD 3 Vuyani Nene (SA), Benevento – IBF
20.10.90	Sung-Il Moon (SK) W TD 5 Kenji Matsumura (JAP), Seoul – WBC
09.12.90	Kaosai Galaxy (TH) W CO 6 Ernesto Ford (PAN), Petchabun – WBA
26.01.91	Robert Quiroga (USA) W PTS 12 Vincenzo Belcastro (ITA), Capo d'Orlando – IBF
16.03.91	Sung-Il Moon (SK) W RSC 4 Nana Yaw Konadu (GH), Zaragoza – WBC
06.04.91	Kaosai Galaxy (TH) W RSC 5 Jae-Suk Park (SK), Samut Songkram – WBA
15.06.91	Robert Quiroga (USA) W PTS 12 Akeem Anifowashe (N), San Antonio – IBF
20.07.91	Kaosai Galaxy (TH) W RSC 5 David Griman (VEN), Bangkok – WBA
20.07.91	Sung-Il Moon (SK) W CO 5 Ernesto Ford (PAN), Seoul – WBC
22.12.91	Kaosai Galaxy (TH) W PTS 12 Armando Castro*(MEX), Bangkok – WBA. *Kaosai Galaxy retired*
22.12.91	Sung-Il Moon (SK) W RSC 6 Torsak Pongsupa (TH), Inchon – WBC
15.02.92	Robert Quiroga (USA) W PTS 12 Carlos Mercado (COL), Salerno – IBF
22.02.92	Jose Quirino (MEX) W PTS 12 Jose Ruiz (PR), Las Vegas – WBO
10.04.92	Katsuya Onizuka (JAP) W PTS 12 Thalerngsak Sitbobay (TH), Tokyo – WBA

Flyweight

11.04.13	Sid Smith (GB) W PTS 20 Eugene Criqui (FR), Paris – GB/IBU
02.06.13	Bill Ladbury (GB) W RSC 11 Sid Smith (GB), The Ring, London – GB/IBU
26.01.14	Percy Jones (GB) W PTS 20 Bill Ladbury (GB), NSC, London – GB/IBU
26.03.14	Percy Jones (GB) W PTS 20 Eugene Criqui (FR), The Stadium, Liverpool – GB/IBU. *Percy Jones forfeited GB/IBU recognition for being overweight for scheduled defence against Joe Symonds*
25.01.15	Tancy Lee (GB) W RSC 17 Jimmy Wilde (GB), NSC, London – GB/IBU
18.10.15	Joe Symonds (GB) W RSC 16 Tancy Lee (GB), NSC, London – GB/IBU
14.02.16	Jimmy Wilde (GB) W RSC 12 Joe Symonds (GB), NSC, London – GB/IBU
24.04.16	Jimmy Wilde (GB) W RTD 11 Johnny Rosner (USA), The Stadium, Liverpool – GB/IBU
26.06.16	Jimmy Wilde (GB) W RSC 11 Tancy Lee (GB), NSC, London – GB/IBU
31.07.16	Jimmy Wilde (GB) W CO 10 Johnny Hughes (GB), Kensal Rise Athletic Ground, London – GB/IBU

187

18.12.16 **Jimmy Wilde** (GB) W CO 11 Young Zulu Kid (USA), Holborn Stadium, London

12.03.17 **Jimmy Wilde** (GB) W RTD 4 George Clark (GB), NSC, London

18.06.23 **Pancho Villa** (PH) W CO 7 Jimmy Wilde (GB), New York City

13.10.23 **Pancho Villa** (PH) W PTS 15 Benny Schwartz (USA), Baltimore

08.02.24 **Pancho Villa** (PH) W PTS 15 Georgie Marks (USA), New York City

30.05.24 **Pancho Villa** (PH) W PTS 15 Frankie Ash (GB), New York City

01.05.25 **Pancho Villa** (PH) W PTS 15 Clever Sencio (PH), Manila. *Pancho Villa died*

22.08.25 **Fidel la Barba** (USA) W PTS 10 Frankie Genaro (USA), Los Angeles

08.07.26 **Fidel la Barba** (USA) W PTS 10 Georgie Rivers (USA), Los Angeles

21.01.27 **Fidel la Barba** (USA) W PTS 12 Elky Clark (GB), New York City. *Fidel la Barba relinquished title*

28.10.27 Johnny McCoy (USA) W PTS 10 Tommy Hughes (USA), Los Angeles – CALIF

28.11.27 Frenchy Belanger (C) W PTS 10 Frankie Genaro (USA), Toronto – NBA

16.12.27 Izzy Schwartz (USA) W PTS 15 Newsboy Brown (USA), New York City – NY

19.12.27 Frenchy Belanger (C) W PTS 12 Ernie Jarvis (GB), Toronto – NBA

03.01.28 Newsboy Brown (USA) W PTS 10 Johnny McCoy (USA), Los Angeles – CALIF

06.02.28 Frankie Genaro (USA) W PTS 10 Frenchy Belanger (C), Toronto – NBA

09.04.28 Izzy Schwartz (USA) W PTS 15 Routier Parra (CH), New York City – NY

20.07.28 Izzy Schwartz (USA) W DIS 4 Frisco Grande (PH), New York City – NY

03.08.28 Izzy Schwartz (USA) W CO 4 Little Jeff Smith (USA), New York City – NY

29.08.28 Johnny Hill (GB) W PTS 15 Newsboy Brown (USA), Clapton Stadium, London – GB/CALIF. *Johnny Hill forfeited GB/Californian recognition following a defeat by Emile Pladner in a non-title bout*

02.03.29 Emile Pladner (FR) W CO 1 Frankie Genaro (USA), Paris – NBA/IBU

12.03.29 Izzy Schwartz (USA) W PTS 12 Frenchy Belanger (C), Toronto – NY

18.04.29 Frankie Genaro (USA) W DIS 5 Emile Pladner (FR), Paris – NBA/IBU

22.08.29 Willie la Morte (USA) W PTS 15 Izzy Schwartz (USA), Newark – NY

17.10.29 Frankie Genaro (USA) W PTS 15 Ernie Jarvis (GB), Albert Hall, London – NBA/IBU

21.11.29 Willie la Morte (USA) W CO 7 Frisco Grande (PH), Paterson – NY. *Willie la Morte forfeited NY recognition for failing to meet Midget Wolgast*

18.01.30 Frankie Genaro (USA) W RTD 12 Yvon Trevidic (FR), Paris – NBA/IBU

21.03.30 Midget Wolgast (USA) W PTS 15 Black Bill (CUB), New York City – NY

16.05.30 Midget Wolgast (USA) W CO 6 Willie la Morte (USA), New York City – NY

10.06.30 Frankie Genaro (USA) W PTS 10 Frenchy Belanger (C), Toronto – NBA/IBU

06.08.30 Frankie Genaro (USA) W PTS 10 Willie la Morte (USA), Newark – NBA/IBU

26.12.30 Frankie Genaro (USA) DREW 15 Midget Wolgast (USA), New York City

25.03.31 Frankie Genaro (USA) DREW 15 Victor Ferrand (SP), Madrid – NBA/IBU

13.07.31 Midget Wolgast (USA) W PTS 15 Ruby Bradley (USA), New York City – NY

16.07.31 Frankie Genaro (USA) W CO 4 Routier Parra (CH), North Adams – NBA/IBU

30.07.31 Frankie Genaro (USA) W CO 6 Jackie Harmon (USA), Waterbury – NBA/IBU

03.10.31 Frankie Genaro (USA) W PTS 15 Valentin Angelmann (FR), Paris – NBA/IBU

27.10.31 Young Perez (FR) W CO 2 Frankie Genaro (USA), Paris – NBA/IBU

31.10.32 Jackie Brown (GB) W RSC 13 Young Perez (FR), Belle Vue, Manchester – NBA/IBU

12.06.33 Jackie Brown (GB) W PTS 15 Valentin Angelmann (FR), Olympia, London – NBA/IBU

11.12.33 Jackie Brown (GB) W PTS 15 Ginger Foran (GB), Belle Vue, Manchester – NBA/IBU

18.06.34 Jackie Brown (GB) DREW 15 Valentin Angelmann (FR), Belle Vue, Manchester – NBA/IBU. *Jackie Brown forfeited IBU recognition for failing to meet Valentin Angelmann*

09.09.35 Benny Lynch (GB) W RTD 2 Jackie Brown (GB), Belle Vue, Manchester – NBA

16.09.35 Small Montana (PH) W PTS 10 Midget Wolgast (USA), Oakland – NY/CALIF

06.01.36 Valentin Angelmann (FR) W RTD 5 Kid David (BEL), Paris – IBU

16.09.36 Benny Lynch (GB) W CO 8 Pat Palmer (GB), Shawfield Park, Glasgow, – NBA

12.12.36 Valentin Angelmann (FR) W PTS 15 Ernst Weiss (AU), Paris – IBU. *Valentin Angelmann relinquished IBU version of title*

19.01.37 Benny Lynch (GB) W PTS 15 Small Montana (PH), The Arena, Wembley

13.10.37 Benny Lynch (GB) W CO 13 Peter Kane (GB), Shawfield Park, Glasgow. *Benny Lynch forfeited title when overweight for scheduled defence against Jackie Jurich*

22.09.38 Peter Kane (GB) W PTS 15 Jackie Jurich (USA), Anfield Football Ground, Liverpool – NY/IBU

30.11.38 Little Dado (PH) W PTS 10 Small Montana (PH), Oakland – CALIF/NBA. *Little Dado forfeited NBA/Californian recognition when failing to defend*

19.06.43 Jackie Paterson (GB) W CO 1 Peter Kane (GB), Hampden Park, Glasgow

10.07.46 Jackie Paterson (GB) W PTS 15 Joe Curran (GB), Glasgow. *Jackie Paterson forfeited NBA recognition when overweight for scheduled defence against Dado Marino*

20.10.47 Rinty Monaghan (GB) W PTS 15 Dado Marino (USA), Harringay Arena, London – NBA

23.03.48 Rinty Monaghan (GB) W CO 7 Jackie Paterson (GB), King's Hall, Belfast

05.04.49 Rinty Monaghan (GB) W PTS 15 Maurice Sandeyron (FR), King's Hall, Belfast

30.09.49 Rinty Monaghan (GB) DREW 15 Terry Allen (GB), King's Hall, Belfast. *Rinty Monaghan relinquished title*

25.04.50 Terry Allen (GB) W PTS 15 Honore Pratesi (FR), Harringay Arena, London

01.08.50 Dado Marino (USA) W PTS 15 Terry Allen (GB), Honolulu

01.11.51 Dado Marino (USA) W PTS 15 Terry Allen (GB), Honolulu

19.05.52 Yoshio Shirai (JAP) W PTS 15 Dado Marino (USA), Tokyo

15.11.52 Yoshio Shirai (JAP) W PTS 15 Dado Marino (USA), Tokyo

18.05.53 Yoshio Shirai (JAP) W PTS 15 Tanny Campo (PH), Tokyo

27.10.53 Yoshio Shirai (JAP) W PTS 15 Terry Allen (GB), Tokyo

23.05.54 Yoshio Shirai (JAP) W PTS 15 Leo Espinosa (PH), Tokyo

26.11.54 Pascual Perez (ARG) W PTS 15 Yoshio Shirai (JAP), Tokyo

30.05.55 Pascual Perez (ARG) W CO 5 Yoshio Shirai (JAP), Tokyo

11.01.56 Pascual Perez (ARG) W PTS 15 Leo Espinosa (PH), Buenos Aires

30.06.56 Pascual Perez (ARG) W RTD 11 Oscar Suarez (CUB), Montevideo

03.08.56 Pascual Perez (ARG) W RSC 5 Ricardo Valdez (ARG), Tandil

30.03.57 Pascual Perez (ARG) W CO 1 Dai Dower (GB), Buenos Aires

07.12.57 Pascual Perez (ARG) W CO 3 Young Martin (SP), Buenos Aires

19.04.58 Pascual Perez (ARG) W PTS 15 Ramon Arias (VEN), Caracas

15.12.58 Pascual Perez (ARG) W PTS 15 Dommy Ursua (PH) Manila

10.08.59 Pascual Perez (ARG) W PTS 15 Kenji Yonekura (JAP), Tokyo

05.11.59 Pascual Perez (ARG) W CO 13 Sadao Yaoita (JAP), Osaka

16.04.60 Pone Kingpetch (TH) W PTS 15 Pascual Perez (ARG), Bangkok

22.09.60 Pone Kingpetch (TH) W RSC 8 Pascual Perez (ARG), Los Angeles

27.06.61 Pone Kingpetch (TH) W PTS 15 Mitsunori Seki (JAP), Tokyo

30.05.62 Pone Kingpetch (TH) W PTS 15 Kyo Noguchi (JAP), Tokyo

10.10.62 **Fighting Harada** (JAP) W CO 11 Pone Kingpetch (TH), Tokyo

12.01.63 **Pone Kingpetch** (TH) W PTS 15 Fighting Harada (JAP), Tokyo

18.09.63 **Hiroyuki Ebihara** (JAP) W CO 1 Pone Kingpetch (TH), Tokyo

23.01.64 **Pone Kingpetch** (TH) W PTS 15 Hiroyuki Ebihara (JAP), Bangkok

23.04.65 **Salvatore Burruni** (ITA) W PTS 15 Pone Kingpetch (TH), Rome. *Salvatore Burruni forfeited WBA recognition for failing to defend against Horacio Accavallo*

02.12.65 Salvatore Burruni (ITA) W CO 13 Rocky Gattellari (A), Sydney – WBC

01.03.66 Horacio Accavallo (ARG) W PTS 15 Katsuyoshi Takayama (JAP), Tokyo – WBA

14.06.66 Walter McGowan (GB) W PTS 15 Salvatore Burruni (ITA), The Arena, Wembley – WBC

15.07.66 Horacio Accavallo (ARG) W PTS 15 Hiroyuki Ebihara (JAP), Buenos Aires – WBA

10.12.66 Horacio Accavallo (ARG) W PTS 15 Efren Torres (MEX), Buenos Aires – WBA

30.12.66 Chartchai Chionoi (TH) W RSC 9 Walter McGowan (GB), Bangkok – WBC

26.07.67 Chartchai Chionoi (TH) W CO 3 Puntip Keosuriya (TH), Bangkok – WBC

13.08.67 Horacio Accavallo (ARG) W PTS 15 Hiroyuki Ebihara (JAP), Buenos Aires – WBA. *Horacio Accavallo relinquished WBA version of title*

19.09.67 Chartchai Chionoi (TH) W RSC 7 Walter McGowan (GB), The Arena, Wembley – WBC

28.01.68 Chartchai Chionoi (TH) W RSC 13 Efren Torres (MEX), Mexico City – WBC

10.11.68 Chartchai Chionoi (TH) W PTS 15 Bernabe Villacampo (PH), Bangkok – WBC

23.02.69 Efren Torres (MEX) W RSC 8 Chartchai Chionoi (TH), Mexico City – WBC

30.03.69 Hiroyuki Ebihara (JAP) W PTS 15 Jose Severino (BR), Sapporo – WBA

19.10.69 Bernabe Villacampo (PH) W PTS 15 Hiroyuki Ebihara (JAP), Tokyo – WBA

28.11.69 Efren Torres (MEX) W PTS 15 Susumu Hanagata (JAP), Guadalajara – WBC

20.03.70 Chartchai Chionoi (TH) W PTS 15 Efren Torres (MEX), Bangkok – WBC

06.04.70 Berkrerk Chartvanchai (TH) W PTS 15 Bernabe Villacampo (PH), Bangkok – WBA

21.10.70 Masao Ohba (JAP) W RSC 13 Berkrerk Chartvanchai (TH), Tokyo – WBA

07.12.70 Erbito Salavarria (PH) W RSC 2 Chartchai Chionoi (TH), Bangkok – WBC

01.04.71 Masao Ohba (JAP) W PTS 15 Betulio Gonzalez (VEN), Tokyo – WBA

30.04.71 Erbito Salavarria (PH) W PTS 15 Susumu Hanagata (JAP), Manila – WBC

23.10.71 Masao Ohba (JAP) W PTS 15 Fernando Cabanela (PH), Tokyo – WBA

20.11.71 Erbito Salavarria (PH) DREW 15 Betulio Gonzalez (VEN), Caracas – WBC. *Erbito Salavarria forfeited WBC recognition for allegedly using an illegal stimulant*

04.03.72 Masao Ohba (JAP) W PTS 15 Susumu Hanagata (JAP), Tokyo – WBA

03.06.72 Betulio Gonzalez (VEN) W CO 4 Socrates Batoto (PH), Caracas – WBC

20.06.72 Masao Ohba (JAP) W CO 5 Orlando Amores (PAN), Tokyo – WBA

29.09.72 Venice Borkorsor (TH) W RTD 10 Betulio Gonzalez (VEN), Bangkok – WBC

02.01.73 Masao Ohba (JAP) W RSC 12 Chartchai Chionoi (TH), Tokyo – WBA. *Masao Ohba left WBA version of title vacant when he died in a road accident*

09.02.73 Venice Borkorsor (TH) W PTS 15 Erbito Salavarria (PH), Bangkok – WBC. *Venice Borkorsor relinquished WBC version of title*

17.05.73 Chartchai Chionoi (TH) W RSC 4 Fritz Chervet (SWI), Bangkok – WBA

04.08.73 Betulio Gonzalez (VEN) W PTS 15 Miguel Canto (MEX), Caracas – WBC

27.10.73 Chartchai Chionoi (TH) W PTS 15 Susumu Hanagata (JAP), Bangkok – WBA

189

01.06.91	Yong-Kang Kim (SK) W PTS 12 Elvis Alvarez (COL), Seoul – WBA
10.08.91	Isidro Perez (MEX) W PTS 12 Alli Galvez (CH), Santiago – WBO
07.09.91	Dave McAuley (GB) W CO 10 Jacob Matlala (SA), Maysfield Leisure Centre, Belfast – IBF
05.10.91	Yong-Kang Kim (SK) W PTS 12 Luis Gamez (VEN), Inchon – WBA
25.10.91	Muangchia Kitikasem (TH) W PTS 12 Alberto Jimenez (MEX), Bangkok – WBC
28.02.92	Muangchai Kitikasem (TH) W RSC 9 Sot Chitalada (TH), Samut Prakan – WBC
18.03.92	Pat Clinton (GB) W PTS 12 Isidoro Perez (MEX), Kelvin Hall, Glasgow – WBO
24.03.92	Yong-Kang Kim (SK) W CO 6 Jon Penalosa (PH), Inchon – WBA
11.06.92	Rodolfo Blanco (COL) W PTS 12 Dave McAuley (GB), Bilbao – IBF
23.06.92	Yuri Arbachakov (CIS) W CO 8 Maungchai Kitikasem (TH), Tokyo – WBC

L. Flyweight

04.04.75	Franco Udella (ITA) W DIS 12 Valentin Martinez (MEX), Milan – WBC. *Franco Udella forfeited WBC recognition for failing to defend against Rafael Lovera*
23.08.75	Jaime Rios (PAN) W PTS 15 Rigoberto Marcano (VEN), Panama City – WBA
13.09.75	Luis Estaba (VEN) W CO 4 Rafael Lovera (PAR), Caracas – WBC
17.12.75	Luis Estaba (VEN) W RSC 10 Takenobu Shimabakuro (JAP), Okinawa – WBC
03.01.76	Jaime Rios (PAN) W PTS 15 Kazunori Tenryu (JAP), Kagoshima – WBA
14.02.76	Luis Estaba (VEN) W PTS 15 Leo Palacios (MEX), Caracas – WBC
02.05.76	Luis Estaba (VEN) W PTS 15 Juan Alvarez (MEX), Caracas – WBC
01.07.76	Juan Guzman (DOM) W PTS 15 Jaime Rios (PAN), St Domingo – WBA
17.07.76	Luis Estaba (VEN) W CO 3 Franco Udella (ITA), Maracay – WBC
26.09.76	Luis Estaba (VEN) W RTD 10 Rodolfo Rodriguez (ARG), Caracas – WBC
10.10.76	Yoko Gushiken (JAP) W CO 7 Juan Guzman (DOM), Kofu – WBA
21.11.76	Luis Estaba (VEN) W RSC 10 Valentin Martinez (MEX), Caracas – WBC
30.01.77	Yoko Gushiken (JAP) W PTS 15 Jaime Rios (PAN), Tokyo – WBA
15.05.77	Luis Estaba (VEN) W PTS 15 Rafael Pedroza (PAN), Caracas – WBC
22.05.77	Yoko Gushiken (JAP) W PTS 15 Rigoberto Marcano (VEN), Sapporo – WBA
17.07.77	Luis Estaba (VEN) W PTS 15 Ricardo Estupinan (COL), Cruz – WBC
21.08.77	Luis Estaba (VEN) W RSC 11 Juan Alvarez (MEX), Cruz – WBC
18.09.77	Luis Estaba (VEN) W CO 15 Orlando Hernandez (CR), Caracas – WBC
09.10.77	Yoko Gushiken (JAP) W RSC 4 Montsayarm Mahachai (TH), Oita – WBA
30.10.77	Luis Estaba (VEN) W PTS 15 Sor Vorasingh (TH), Caracas – WBC
29.01.78	Yoko Gushiken (JAP) W RSC 14 Aniceto Vargas (PH), Nagoya – WBA
19.02.78	Freddie Castillo (MEX) W RSC 14 Luis Estaba (VEN), Caracas – WBC
06.05.78	Sor Vorasingh (TH) W PTS 15 Freddie Castillo (MEX), Bangkok – WBC
07.05.78	Yoko Gushiken (JAP) W RSC 13 Jaime Rios (PAN), Hiroshima – WBA
29.07.78	Sor Vorasingh (TH) W RTD 5 Luis Estaba (VEN), Caracas – WBC
30.09.78	Sung-Jun Kim (SK) W CO 3 Sor Vorasingh (TH), Seoul – WBC
15.10.78	Yoko Gushiken (JAP) W CO 4 Sang-Il Chung (SK), Tokyo – WBA
07.01.79	Yoko Gushiken (JAP) W CO 7 Rigoberto Marcano (VEN), Kawasaki – WBA
31.03.79	Sung-Jun Kim (SK) DREW 15 Hector Melendez (DOM), Seoul – WBC
08.04.79	Yoko Gushiken (JAP) W RSC 7 Alfonso Lopez (PAN), Tokyo – WBA
28.07.79	Sung-Jun Kim (SK) W PTS 15 Stony Carupo (PH), Seoul – WBC
29.07.79	Yoko Gushiken (JAP) W PTS 15 Rafael Pedroza (PAN), Kitakyushi – WBA
21.10.79	Sung-Jun Kim (SK) W PTS 15 Hector Melendez (DOM), Seoul – WBC

28.10.79	Yoko Gushiken (JAP) W RSC 7 Tito Abella (PH), Tokyo – WBA
03.01.80	Shigeo Nakajima (JAP) W PTS 15 Sung-Jun Kim (SK), Tokyo – WBC
27.01.80	Yoko Gushiken (JAP) W PTS 15 Yong-Hyun Kim (SK), Osaka – WBA
24.03.80	Hilario Zapata (PAN) W PTS 15 Shigeo Nakajima (JAP), Tokyo – WBC
01.06.80	Yoko Gushiken (JAP) W RSC 8 Martin Vargas (CH), Kochi City – WBA
07.06.80	Hilario Zapata (PAN) W PTS 15 Chi-Bok Kim (SK), Seoul – WBC
04.08.80	Hilario Zapata (PAN) W PTS 15 Hector Melendez (DOM), Caracas – WBC
17.09.80	Hilario Zapata (PAN) W RSC 11 Shigeo Nakajima (JAP), Gifu – WBC
12.10.80	Yoko Gushiken (JAP) W PTS 15 Pedro Flores (MEX), Kanazawa – WBA
01.12.80	Hilario Zapata (PAN) W PTS 15 Reynaldo Becerra (VEN), Caracas – WBC
08.02.81	Hilario Zapata (PAN) W RSC 13 Joey Olivo (USA), Panama City – WBC
08.03.81	Pedro Flores (MEX) W RTD 12 Yoko Gushiken (JAP), Gushikawa – WBA
24.04.81	Hilario Zapata (PAN) W PTS 15 Rudy Crawford (USA), San Francisco – WBC
19.07.81	Hwan-Jin Kim (SK) W RSC 13 Pedro Flores (MEX), Taegu – WBA
15.08.81	Hilario Zapata (PAN) W PTS 15 German Torres (MEX), Panama City – WBC
11.10.81	Hwan-Jin Kim (SK) W PTS 15 Alfonso Lopez (PAN), Daejon – WBA
06.11.81	Hilario Zapata (PAN) W RSC 10 Sor Vorasingh (TH), Korat – WBC
16.12.81	Katsuo Tokashiki (JAP) W PTS 15 Hwan-Jin Kim (SK), Sendai – WBA
06.02.82	Amado Ursua (MEX) W CO 2 Hilario Zapata (PAN), Panama City – WBC
04.04.82	Katsuo Tokashiki (JAP) W PTS 15 Lupe Madera (MEX), Sendai – WBA
13.04.82	Tadashi Tomori (JAP) W PTS 15 Amado Ursua (MEX), Tokyo – WBC
07.07.82	Katsuo Tokashiki (JAP) W CO 8 Masahara Inami (JAP), Tokyo – WBA
20.07.82	Hilario Zapata (PAN) W PTS 15 Tadashi Tomori (JAP), Kanazawa – WBC
18.09.82	Hilario Zapata (PAN) W PTS 15 Jung-Koo Chang (SK), Chonju – WBC
10.10.82	Katsuo Tokashiki (JAP) W PTS 15 Sung-Nam Kim (SK), Tokyo – WBA
30.11.82	Hilario Zapata (PAN) W RSC 8 Tadashi Tomori (JAP), Tokyo – WBC
09.01.83	Katsuo Tokashiki (JAP) W PTS 15 Hwan-Jin Kim (SK), Kyoto – WBA
26.03.83	Jung-Koo Chang (SK) W RSC 3 Hilario Zapata (PAN), Daejon – WBC
10.04.83	Katsuo Tokashiki (JAP) DREW 15 Lupe Madera (MEX), Tokyo – WBA
11.06.83	Jung-Koo Chang (SK) W RSC 2 Masaharu Iha (JAP), Taegu – WBC
10.07.83	Lupe Madera (MEX) W RSC 4 Katsuo Tokashiki (JAP), Tokyo – WBA
10.09.83	Jung-Koo Chang (SK) W PTS 12 German Torres (MEX), Daejon – WBC
23.10.83	Lupe Madera (MEX) W PTS 12 Katsuo Tokashiki (JAP), Sapporo – WBA
10.12.83	Dodie Penalosa (PH) W RSC 11 Satoshi Shingaki (JAP), Osaka – IBF
31.03.84	Jung-Koo Chang (SK) W PTS 12 Sot Chitalada (TH), Pusan – WBC
13.05.84	Dodie Penalosa (PH) W RSC 9 Jae-Hong Kim (SK), Seoul – IBF
19.05.84	Francisco Quiroz (DOM) W CO 9 Lupe Madera (MEX), Maracaibo – WBA
18.08.84	Jung-Koo Chang (SK) W RSC 9 Katsuo Tokashiki (JAP), Pohang – WBC
18.08.84	Francisco Quiroz (DOM) W CO 2 Victor Sierra (PAN), Panama City – WBA
16.11.84	Dodie Penalosa (PH) W PTS 15 Jum-Hwan Choi (SK), Manila – IBF
15.12.84	Jung-Koo Chang (SK) W PTS 12 Tadashi Kuramochi (JAP), Pusan – WBC
29.03.85	Joey Olivo (USA) W PTS 15 Francisco Quiroz (DOM), Miami – WBA
27.04.85	Jung-Koo Chang (SK) W PTS 12 German Torres (MEX), Ulsan – WBC
28.07.85	Joey Olivo (USA) W PTS 15 Moon-Jin Choi (SK), Seoul – WBA
03.08.85	Jung-Koo Chang (SK) W PTS 15 Francisco Montiel (MEX), Seoul – WBC
12.10.85	Dodie Penalosa (PH) W CO 3 Yani Hagler (INDON), Jakarta – IBF. *Dodie Penalosa forfeited IBF recognition when he challenged Hilario Zapata for the WBA flyweight title*

10.11.85	Jung-Koo Chang (SK) W PTS 12 Jorge Cano (MEX), Daejon – WBC
08.12.85	Myung-Woo Yuh (SK) W PTS 15 Joey Olivo (USA), Seoul – WBA
09.03.86	Myung-Woo Yuh (SK) W PTS 15 Jose de Jesus (PR), Suwon – WBA
13.04.86	Jung-Koo Chang (SK) W PTS 12 German Torres (MEX), Kwangju – WBC
14.06.86	Myung-Woo Yuh (SK) W RSC 12 Tomohiro Kiyuna (JAP), Inchon – WBA
13.09.86	Jung-Koo Chang (SK) W PTS 12 Francisco Montiel (MEX), Seoul – WBC
30.11.86	Myung-Woo Yuh (SK) W PTS 15 Mario de Marco (ARG), Seoul – WBA
07.12.86	Jum-Hwan Choi (SK) W PTS 15 Cho-Woon Park (SK), Pusan – IBF
14.12.86	Jung-Koo Chang (SK) W RSC 5 Hideyuki Ohashi (JAP), Inchon – WBC
01.03.87	Myung-Woo Yuh (SK) W RSC 1 Eduardo Tunon (PAN), Seoul – WBA
29.03.87	Jum-Hwan Choi (SK) W PTS 15 Tacy Macalos (PH), Seoul – IBF
19.04.87	Jung-Koo Chang (SK) W RSC 6 Efren Pinto (MEX), Seoul – WBC
07.06.87	Myung-Woo Yuh (SK) W RSC 15 Benedicto Murillo (PAN), Pusan – WBA
28.06.87	Jung-Koo Chang (SK) W RSC 10 Agustin Garcia (COL), Seoul – WBC
05.07.87	Jum-Hwan Choi (SK) W RSC 4 Toshihiko Matsuta (JAP), Seoul – IBF
09.08.87	Jum-Hwan Choi (SK) W RSC 3 Azadin Anhar (INDON), Jakarta – IBF
20.09.87	Myung-Woo Yuh (SK) W CO 8 Rodolfo Blanco (COL), Inchon – WBA
13.12.87	Jung-Koo Chang (SK) W PTS 12 Isidro Perez (MEX), Seoul – WBC
07.02.88	Myung-Woo Yuh (SK) W PTS 12 Wilibaldo Salazar (MEX), Seoul – WBA
12.06.88	Myung-Woo Yuh (SK) W PTS 12 Jose de Jesus (PR), Seoul – WBA
27.06.88	Jung-Koo Chang (SK) W RSC 8 Hideyuki Ohashi (JAP), Tokyo – WBC. *Jung-Koo Chang relinquished WBC version of title*
28.08.88	Myung-Woo Yuh (SK) W CO 6 Putt Ohyuthanakorn (TH), Pusan – WBA
05.11.88	Tacy Macalos (PH) W PTS 12 Jum-Hwan Choi (SK), Manila – IBF
06.11.88	Myung-Woo Yuh (SK) W CO 7 Bahar Udin (INDON), Seoul – WBA
11.12.88	German Torres (MEX) W PTS 12 Soon-Jung Kang (SK), Seoul – WBC
12.02.89	Myung-Woo Yuh (SK) W RSC 10 Katsumi Komiyama (JAP), Chungju – WBA
19.03.89	Yul-Woo Lee (SK) W CO 9 German Torres (MEX) Taejon – WBC
02.05.89	Muangchai Kitikasem (TH) W PTS 12 Tacy Macalos (PH), Bangkok – IBF
19.05.89	Jose de Jesus (PR) W RSC 9 Fernando Martinez (MEX), San Juan – WBO
11.06.89	Myung-Woo Yuh (SK) W PTS 12 Mario de Marco (ARG), Seoul – WBA
25.06.89	Humberto Gonzalez (MEX) W PTS 12 Yul-Woo Lee (SK), Seoul – WBC
24.09.89	Myung-Woo Yuh (SK) W CO 11 Kenbun Taiho (JAP), Suanbo – WBA
06.10.89	Muangchai Kitikasem (TH) W RSC 7 Tacy Macalos (PH), Bangkok – IBF
21.10.89	Jose de Jesus (PR) W PTS 12 Isidro Perez (MEX), San Juan – WBO
09.12.89	Humberto Gonzalez (MEX) W PTS 12 Jung-Koo Chang (SK), Seoul – WBC
14.01.90	Myung-Woo Yuh (SK) W RSC 7 Hitashi Takashima (JAP), Seoul – WBA
19.01.90	Muangchai Kitikasem (TH) W RSC 3 Chung-Jae Lee (SK), Bangkok – IBF
24.03.90	Humberto Gonzalez (MEX) W CO 3 Francisco Tejedor (COL), Mexico City – WBC
10.04.90	Muangchai Kitikasem (TH) W PTS 12 Abdy Pohan (INDON), Bangkok – IBF
29.04.90	Myung-Woo Yuh (SK) W PTS 12 Luis Gamez (VEN), Seoul – WBA
06.05.90	Jose de Jesus (PR) W CO 5 Alli Galvez (CH), Talcahuano – WBO
04.06.90	Humberto Gonzalez (MEX) W RSC 3 Luis Monzote (CUB), Los Angeles – WBC
24.07.90	Humberto Gonzalez (MEX) W RSC 5 Jung-Keun Lim (SK), Los Angeles – WBC
29.07.90	Michael Carbajal (USA) W RSC 7 Muangchai Kitikasem (TH), Phoenix – IBF

26.08.90 Humberto Gonzalez (MEX) W CO 8 Jorge Rivera (MEX), Cancun – WBC

10.11.90 Jose de Jesus (PR) W RSC 7 Abdy Pohan (INDON), Medan – WBO

10.11.90 Myung-Woo Yuh (SK) W PTS 12 Luis Gamez (VEN), Seoul – WBA

08.12.90 Michael Carbajal (USA) W CO 4 Leon Salazar (PAN), Scottsdale – IBF

19.12.90 Rolando Pascua (PH) W CO 6 Humberto Gonzalez (MEX), Los Angeles – WBC

17.02.91 Michael Carbajal (USA) W CO 2 Macario Santos (MEX), Las Vegas – IBF

17.03.91 Michael Carbajal (USA) W PTS 12 Javier Varquez (MEX), Las Vegas – IBF

25.03.91 Melchor Cob Castro (MEX) W RTD 10 Rolando Pascua (PH), Los Angeles – WBC

28.04.91 Myung-Woo Yuh (SK) W RSC 10 Kajkong Danphoothai (TH), Masan – WBA

10.05.91 Michael Carbajal (USA) W PTS 12 Hector Patri (ARG), Davenport – IBF

03.06.91 Humberto Gonzalez (MEX) W PTS 12 Melchor Cob Castro (MEX), Las Vegas – WBC

17.12.91 Hiroi Ioka (JAP) W PTS 12 Myung-Woo Yuh (SK), Osaka – WBA

27.01.92 Humberto Gonzalez (MEX) W PTS 12 Domingo Sosa (DOM), Los Angeles – WBC

15.02.92 Michael Carbajal (USA) W PTS 12 Marcos Pancheco (MEX), Phoenix – IBF

31.03.92 Hiroki Ioka (JAP) W PTS 12 Noel Tunacao (PH), Osaka – WBA

07.06.92 Humberto Gonzalez (MEX) W RSC 12 Kwang-Sun Kim (SK), Seoul – WBC

15.06.92 Hiroki Ioka (JAP) W PTS 12 Bong-Jun Kim (SK), Osaka – WBA

Mini-Flyweight

14.06.87 Kyung-Yung Lee (SK) W CO 2 Masaharu Kawakami (JAP), Bujok –

IBF. *Kyung-Yung Lee relinquished IBF version of title*

18.10.87 Hiroki Ioka (JAP) W PTS 12 Mai Thornburifarm (TH), Osaka – WBC

10.01.88 Luis Gamez (VEN) W PTS 12 Bong-Jun Kim (SK), Pusan – WBA

31.01.88 Hiroki Ioka (JAP) W RSC 12 Kyung-Yung Lee (SK), Osaka – WBC

24.03.88 Samuth Sithnaruepol (TH) W RSC 11 Domingo Lucas (PH), Bangkok – IBF

24.04.88 Luis Gamez (VEN) W RSC 3 Kenji Yokozawa (JAP), Tokyo – WBA. *Luis Gamez relinquished WBA version of title*

05.06.88 Hiroki Ioka (JAP) DREW 12 Napa Kiatwanchai (TH), Osaka – WBC

29.08.88 Samuth Sithnaruepol (TH) W PTS 15 In-Kyu Hwang (SK), Bangkok – IBF

13.11.88 Napa Kiatwanchai (TH) W PTS 12 Hiroki Ioka (JAP), Osaka – WBC

11.02.89 Napa Kiatwanchai (TH) W PTS 12 John Arief (INDON), Bangkok – WBC

23.03.89 Samuth Sithnaruepol (TH) DREW 12 Nico Thomas (INDON), Jakarta – IBF

16.04.89 Bong-Jun Kim (SK) W RSC 7 Agustin Garcia (COL), Seoul – WBA

10.06.89 Napa Kiatwanchai (TH) W RSC 11 Hiroki Ioka (JAP), Osaka – WBC

17.06.89 Nico Thomas (INDON) W PTS 12 Samuth Sithnaruepol (TH), Jakarta – IBF

06.08.89 Bong-Jun Kim (SK) W PTS 12 Sam-Jung Lee (SK), Seoul – WBA

31.08.89 Rafael Torres (DOM) W PTS 12 Yamil Caraballo (COL), Santa Domingo – WBO

21.09.89 Eric Chavez (PH) W CO 5 Nico Thomas (INDON), Jakarta – IBF

22.10.89 Bong-Jun Kim (SK) W RSC 9 John Arief (INDON), Pohang – WBA

12.11.89 Jum-Hwan Choi (SK) W RSC 12 Napa Kiatwanchai (TH), Seoul – WBC

07.02.90 Hideyuki Ohashi (JAP) W CO 9 Jum-Hwan Choi (SK), Tokyo – WBC

10.02.90 Bong-Jun Kim (SK) W RSC 3 Petchai Chuwatana (TH), Seoul – WBA

22.02.90 Fahlan Lukmingkwan (TH) W RSC 7 Eric Chavez (PH), Bangkok – IBF

13.05.90 Bong-Jun Kim (SK) W TD 5 Silverio Barcenas (PAN), Seoul – WBA

08.06.90 Hideyuki Ohashi (JAP) W PTS 12 Napa Kiatwanchai (TH), Tokyo – WBC

14.06.90 Fahlan Lukmingkwan (TH) W PTS 12 Joe Constantino (PH), Bangkok – IBF

31.07.90 Rafael Torres (DOM) W PTS 12 Husni Ray (INDON), Jakarta – WBO

15.08.90 Fahlan Lukmingkwan (TH) W PTS 12 Eric Chavez (PH), Bangkok – IBF

25.10.90 Ricardo Lopez (MEX) W RSC 5 Hideyuki Ohashi (JAP), Tokyo – WBC

03.11.90 Bong-Jun Kim (SK) W PTS 12 Silverio Barcenas (PAN), Seoul – WBA

20.12.90 Fahlan Lukmingkwan (TH) DREW 12 Domingo Lucas (PH), Bangkok – IBF

02.02.91 Hi-Yon Choi (SK) W PTS 12 Bong-Jun Kim (SK), Pujan – WBA

19.05.91 Ricardo Lopez (MEX) W RSC 8 Kimio Hirano (JAP), Shizuoka – WBC

15.06.91 Hi-Yon Choi (SK) W PTS 12 Sugar Ray Mike (PH), Seoul – WBA

02.07.91 Fahlan Lukmingkwan (TH) W PTS 12 Abdy Pohan (INDON), Bangkok – IBF

21.10.91 Fahlan Lukmingkwan (TH) W PTS 12 Andy Tabanas (PH), Bangkok – IBF

26.10.91 Hi-Yon Choi (SK) W PTS 12 Bong-Jun Kim (SK), Seoul – WBA

22.12.91 Ricardo Lopez (MEX) W PTS 12 Kyung-Yun Lee (SK), Inchon – WBC

22.02.92 Hi-Yon Choi (SK) W RSC 10 Ryuichi Hosono (JAP), Seoul – WBA

23.02.92 Fahlan Lukmingkwan (TH) W CO 2 Felix Naranjo (COL), Bangkok – IBF

16.03.92 Ricardo Lopez (MEX) W PTS 12 Domingo Lucas (PH), Mexico City – WBC

14.06.92 Fahlan Lukmingkwan (TH) W RSC 8 Said Iskander (INDON), Bangkok – IBF

13.06.92 Hi-Yon Choi (SK) W CO 3 Rommel Lawas (PH), Inchon – WBA